Xiong Shili's *Treatise on Reality and Function*

OXFORD CHINESE THOUGHT

Series Editors
Eric L. Hutton and Justin Tiwald

Zhu Xi: Selected Writings
Edited and translated by Philip J. Ivanhoe

Treatise on Awakening Mahāyāna Faith
Translated by John Jorgensen, Dan Lusthaus, John Makeham, Mark Strange

The Daode jing Commentary of Cheng Xuanying
Translated by Friederike Assandri

Xiong Shili's *Treatise on Reality and Function*
Edited and translated by John Makeham

Xiong Shili's *Treatise on Reality and Function*

An Annotated Translation

Edited and Translated by
JOHN MAKEHAM

OXFORD
UNIVERSITY PRESS

Oxford University Press is a department of the University of Oxford. It furthers the University's objective of excellence in research, scholarship, and education by publishing worldwide. Oxford is a registered trade mark of Oxford University Press in the UK and certain other countries.

Published in the United States of America by Oxford University Press
198 Madison Avenue, New York, NY 10016, United States of America.

© Oxford University Press 2023

All rights reserved. No part of this publication may be reproduced, stored in a retrieval system, or transmitted, in any form or by any means, without the prior permission in writing of Oxford University Press, or as expressly permitted by law, by license, or under terms agreed with the appropriate reproduction rights organization. Inquiries concerning reproduction outside the scope of the above should be sent to the Rights Department, Oxford University Press, at the address above.

You must not circulate this work in any other form
and you must impose this same condition on any acquirer.

CIP data is on file at the Library of Congress
ISBN 978-0-19-768869-4 (pbk.)
ISBN 978-0-19-768868-7 (hbk.)

DOI: 10.1093/oso/9780197688687.001.0001

Paperback printed by Marquis Book Printing, Canada
Hardback printed by Bridgeport National Bindery, Inc., United States of America

Contents

Series Editors' Foreword   vii
Acknowledgments   ix
Abbreviation   xi
Translator's Introduction   xiii

Treatise on Reality and Function (體用論)

Foreword by Han Yuankai   1

Superfluous Words   5

1 Explaining Transformation   15

2 Buddhist Teachings, A   55

3 Buddhist Teachings, B   104

4 Forming Material Things   178

5 Explaining Mind (Forthcoming)[1]   238

Works Cited   239
Index   249

---

[1] This chapter title appears in the original table of contents. It was never published as a chapter in the *Treatise*. For details, see the Translator's Introduction.

Series Editors' Foreword
Eric L. Hutton and Justin Tiwald

Chinese writings from pre-modern times constitute a vast body of texts stretching back over 2,500 years. This corpus is one of the richest in human history, measured in terms of the variety and depth of the philosophical and religious views it contains. While Western studies of China have been growing, however, many riches from the Chinese tradition have remained untranslated or have been given only partial translations, sometimes scattered across multiple publication venues. This situation obviously poses a problem for those who want to learn about Chinese thought but lack the ability to read Chinese. Moreover, it also poses a problem even for scholars who specialize in Chinese thought and can read Chinese because it is not easy to read across all the time periods and genres in the Chinese corpus. Not only did the Chinese language change over time, but in some genres particular vocabularies are developed and familiarity with certain earlier texts—sometimes quite a large number of texts—is presumed. For this reason, scholars who focus on one tradition of Chinese thought from a given era cannot simply pick up and immediately understand texts from a different tradition of thought in another era. The lack of translations is thus an impediment even to specialists who can read Chinese but wish to learn about aspects of Chinese thought outside their normal purview. Furthermore, scholars are often hampered in their teaching by the lack of translations that they can assign to students, which then becomes a barrier to promoting greater understanding of Chinese history and culture among the general public.

By offering English translations of Chinese texts with philosophical and religious significance, Oxford Chinese Thought aims to remedy these problems and make available to the general public, university students, and scholars a treasure trove of materials that has previously been largely inaccessible. The series focuses on works that are historically important or stand to make significant contributions to contemporary discussions, and the translations seek to strike a reasonable balance between the interests of specialists and the needs of general readers and students with no skills in Chinese. Translators for the series are leading scholars and experts in the traditions and texts that they render, and the volumes are meant to be suitable for classroom use while meeting the highest standards of scholarship.

We are pleased to add the present volume to the list of titles in our series and hope that it will help foster in readers a heightened appreciation for the wealth of insights to be found among Chinese texts, as well as inspire them with a desire to explore Chinese thought further. We look forward to presenting readers with more gems from the Chinese tradition, such as this one.

Acknowledgments

I wish to acknowledge and thank Peter Wong for assisting with the preparation of the Chinese text that appears on the companion website.

Abbreviation

T: *Taishō shinshū Daizōkyō* 大正新修大藏經 (*Taishō* Revised *Tripiṭaka*), edited by Takakusu Junjirō 高楠順次郎 and Watanabe Kaigyoku 渡邊海旭 et al. (Tokyo: Taishō issaikyō Kankōkai, 1924–1934).

Translator's Introduction

Xiong Shili 熊十力 (1885–1968) is widely recognized as a founding figure of the modern New Confucian school of philosophy and as one of most important and creative Chinese philosophers of the twentieth century. Xiong's "ultimate concern" throughout his long intellectual career was to show that "Reality and function are non-dual" (體用不二). Reality (*ti* 體; also variously *benti* 本體, *shiti* 實體) is the source of the phenomenal (function; *yong* 用) yet is not different from the phenomenal. Xiong drew syncretically on a diverse range of resources in the Chinese philosophical tradition to construct his own overarching metaphysical vision. He was particularly inspired by the view found in *Yijing* 易經 (Book of Change) that the cosmos is perpetually and vigorously changing.

Xiong's philosophical training began with Buddhist philosophy—in particular, Yogācāra Buddhism. Over the thirty-year period from the early 1920s he moved from a largely uncritical belief in Yogācāra philosophy to a position where it served as a foil for his own syncretic metaphysics, although his major criticisms were already prosecuted in his 1932 publication, *Xin weishi lun* 新唯識論 (New Treatise on Nothing but Consciousness), in which he targets examples of what he identifies as Yogācāra's ontological dualism and pluralism. These critiques are grounded in the Mahāyāna doctrine of conditioned origination or conditioned arising (also known as dependent arising) (緣起, 緣生; *pratītyasamutpāda*), that everything arises from causes and conditions and has no self-nature, no intrinsic nature (自性; **svabhāva*). In turn, Madhyamaka—the other main system of Mahāyāna Buddhist philosophy—provided a deconstructive method, a radical apophasis, central to which is the concept of emptiness (空; *śūnyatā*). Even if phenomena are experienced as temporally extended continua, they "exist" only interdependently and conventionally. There can be no arising, ceasing, change, or movement for that which is devoid of inherent nature. To be a conventional phenomenon is to be empty.

Despite the fact that neither *ti* nor *yong* has exclusive precedence in Xiong's "non-duality of *ti* and *yong*" thesis, his writings during the 1930s and 1940s evidence a recurrent bias toward *ti*, in which *yong* is subordinated to *ti*, reinforced by the persistent claim that phenomena lack self-nature, and the portrayal of *yong*'s ontological dependence on *ti*, just as an image depends on the brightness of the mirror to exist. Over the course of the 1950s, Xiong's ontological views changed radically. He not only came to insist on the ontological parity between *ti* and *yong*, but also on their ontological identity. *Ti yong lun* 體用論 (Treatise on Reality and Function) represents the mature expression of Xiong's signature metaphysical doctrine of the "non-duality of *ti* and *yong*," articulated within the broader context of advancing a systematic critique of both Madhyamaka and Yogācāra Buddhist thought, the culmination of nearly four decades of critical engagement.

Ti yong lun can be regarded as the third and final iteration of Xiong's *Xin weishi lun*, the first and second versions published in 1932 and 1944, respectively.[2] As Xiong himself states:

> The book is actually a revision of my old work, *New Treatise on the Uniqueness of Consciousness*. (The abbreviated title is *New Treatise*.) There are two editions of the *New Treatise*. The first, a literary edition, was written when I was ill, and is very brief. The second, a vernacular edition, was written at a time of national calamity when I was in exile [in Sichuan]. Now that this new book has been completed, both versions of the *New Treatise* can be destroyed and discarded, as there is no need to preserve them.[3]

Xiong commenced writing *Ti yong lun* in the autumn of 1956,[4] and, with the assistance of the President of the Chinese Academy of Sciences, Guo Moruo 郭沫若 (1892–1978), he submitted the manuscript of *Ti yong lun*[5] to Kexue chubanshe 科學出版社 (China Science Publishing) for publication on November 24, 1957.[6] The stitch-bound volume was duly published in

---

[2] An abridged version of the 1944 edition was published in 1953.

[3] *Ti yong lun, Xiong Shili quanji* 熊十力全集 (The Complete Writings of Xiong Shili), 10 vols. (Wuhan: Hubei jiaoyu chubanshe, 2001), vol. 7, p. 7. Elsewhere in *Ti yong lun*, he refers to these earlier editions variously as "the old draft" and "the first draft." *Ti yong lun*, pp. 34, and pp. 42, 123, respectively.

[4] Idem, p. 7.

[5] Xiong submitted the manuscript under the title *Lun ti yong* 論體用 (On Reality and Function), but, in January 1958, he requested that the title be changed to *Ti yong lun*.

[6] This information is based on the following correspondence: (1) Xiong's letter to editors at Kexue chubanshe, January 7, 1958; original correspondence available at https://auction.artron.net/paimai-art00573311604/. (2) The editors' reply to Xiong, January 21, 1958; original correspondence also

April 1958, by Longmen lianhe shuju 龍門聯合書局, an imprint then owned by the Kexue chubanshe. The photolithographically reproduced text was transcribed by Xiong's secretary, Feng Yongzhuo 封用拙.[7]

It is important to point out that Xiong had originally planned to include "Ming xin pian" 明心篇 (Explaining Mind) as a two-part chapter in *Ti yong lun* but because of illness he was unable to do so and so decided to publish *Ti yong lun* without that final chapter. (The table of contents of the original 1958 edition lists "Ming xin pian" as the fifth chapter, "forthcoming.") The following year, however, he published *Ming xin pian* as a separate book. The 2001 Hebei jiaoyu chubanshe edition of the complete works of Xiong Shili published *Ti yong lun* and *Ming xin pian* as two separate books.[8] Over two years, 2018 and 2019, Shanghai guji chubanshe published a new collection of Xiong Shili writings in 14 volumes.[9] One of these volumes, published in 2019, combines *Ti yong lun* and *Ming xin pian* under a single title, as originally intended by Xiong.[10]

I have used the original 1958 edition (courtesy of Shi Wei 施薇) as the base text for my translation but have closely consulted both the 2001 and 2019 editions. The page numbers interspersed in the translated text (marked in square brackets) refer to the 2001 edition, as it is the most widely accessible edition and also faithfully retains the original full-form Chinese characters. (The same pagination as the 2001 edition is used in the Chinese text on the companion website <https://global.oup.com/us/companion.websites/9780197688694/>. I have edited the Chinese text so that paragraph divisions and textual revisions correspond with the translated text.) I have made my own editorial decisions about paragraph divisions and have also introduced subheadings that do not appear in any of the Chinese editions.

---

available at https://auction.artron.net/paimai-art00573311604/. (3) Xiong's letter to the editors at Kexue chubanshe, February 9, 1958; original correspondence available at https://auction.artron.net/paimai-art0062720286/.

[7] Guo Qiyong 郭齊勇, "Editor's Postface," *Xiong Shili quanji* 熊十力全集 (The Complete Writings of Xiong Shili) (Wuhan: Hubei jiaoyu chubanshe, 2001), vol. 7, p. 900.

[8] *Xiong Shili quanji*, vol. 7.

[9] *Shili congshu* 十力叢書 (Collection of Xiong Shili's Writings) (Shanghai: Shanghai guji chubanshe, 2018, 2019).

[10] *Ti yong lun: wai yi zhong* 體用論:外一種 (Treatise on Reality and Function; Supplementary Correspondence and Additional Notes).

Key concepts and topics in the *Treatise*

Bentilun and onto-cosmology

At the very opening of the author's preface, "Superfluous Words," Xiong states:

> This work was written specifically to solve the cosmological problem of the non-duality of Reality and function. (The Reality of the cosmos [宇宙實體] is abbreviated at *ti* 體. When Reality transforms and moves to then become the myriad images [萬象] of the cosmos, this is the functioning [功用] of Reality, abbreviated as *yong* 用. "The myriad images of the cosmos" is a generic term for all kinds of material [物質] and "pure and spirit-like" [精神] phenomena.)[11]

There is much to unpack in this passage. *Ti* and *yong* are here used as abbreviations for "the Reality of the cosmos" and "the functioning of Reality," respectively, where the latter refers to Reality's transforming into material phenomena and "pure and spirit-like" phenomena. Elsewhere in the *Treatise*, Xiong reiterates that his discussion of Reality and function is undertaken in the context of cosmology and that "'Reality' (體) is an abbreviation of 'the intrinsic Reality of the cosmos' (宇宙本體). (*Benti* 本體 is also called *shiti* 實體.) and 'function' (用) is Reality's transforming into function (功用)."[12]

Before interrogating what Xiong means by "the cosmological problem of the non-duality of Reality and function" and "the Reality of the cosmos," the term *benti* 本體 needs to be explained. Above and elsewhere, Xiong glosses *benti* as *shiti*. As he explains, "Although *shiti* 實體 and *benti* 本體 differ in one character, their meaning is the same. *Ben* 本: because it has always existed it is also the 'itself' [自身] of the myriad things. *Shi* 實 refers to its being true and real."[13] In other words, *benti* refers to the intrinsic Reality of cosmos, the

---

[11] *Ti yong lun*, p. 5. As in his earlier and later works, Xiong's provides extensive auto-commentary. In this translation, Xiong's auto-commentary is marked by the use of smaller font text within parentheses (round brackets). Xiong justifies his extensive use of auto-commentary as follows (*Ti yong lun*, pp. 8, 9): "Although the auto-comments in this book may seem to be prolix, it is better to err on the side of being prolix than it is to be elliptic.... There are some who have said that long comments should be moved out of the main text; that the flow of the text should not be interrupted. The reason I have not adopted their suggestions is that if one does not search for the meaning when reading, but merely savors the style of writing, then this is just the same as not reading."

[12] Idem, p. 35.
[13] Idem, p. 14.

intrinsic Reality of the myriad things that constitute the phenomenal world. Xiong identifies four characteristics of this "intrinsic Reality":

> In general terms, there are four characteristics. First, intrinsic Reality is the origin of the myriad principles; the point of emergence for the myriad defining attributes; and the beginning (始) of the myriad transformations. (*Shi* 始: like root/basis [本].) Second, it is precisely in its being without that to which it stands in contrast (無對) that intrinsic Reality has that to which it stands in contrast (有對); and it is precisely in its having that to which it stands in contrast that it is without that to which it stands in contrast. Third, intrinsic Reality has no beginning and no end. Fourth, intrinsic Reality is manifest as inexhaustible, endless great function, and, as such, should be said to be changing. And yet, when all is said and done, because the flow of great function never alters intrinsic Reality's inherent productivity and re-productivity, vigor, and all kinds of other defining attributes, then it should be said to be unchanging.[14]

Although intrinsic Reality is characterized in terms of being an origin, point of emergence, and beginning, elsewhere Xiong makes it plain that the relationship between intrinsic Reality and its phenomenal manifestation is not like that of mother and offspring or creator and created.[15]

As to the enigmatic second characteristic, Xiong provides the following explanation by invoking his most widely deployed analogy, that of the ocean and waves:

> That which has something to which it stands in contrast is precisely that which has nothing to which it stands in contrast. (Analogous to seeing an undifferentiated body of water in the myriad waves, that which has something to which it stands in contrast is precisely that which has nothing to which it stands in contrast.) That which has nothing to which it stands in contrast is precisely that which has something to which it stands in contrast. (That which has nothing to which it stands in contrast cannot be sought for apart from that which has something to which it stands in contrast.)[16]

---

[14] Ibid.
[15] Idem, pp. 4, 96, 107, 110, 141.
[16] Idem, p. 87.

Abstracted as a whole from the myriad individuated waves, the ocean is without that to which it stands in contrast, yet this very abstraction simultaneously places it in contrast to the waves. Conversely, there is no ocean apart from the numerous waves. This second characteristic is discussed in more detail below.

The third characteristic needs no explanation. As for the fourth characteristic, Xiong makes the same point about Reality's being neither exclusively "changing" nor exclusively "non-changing" using the terms "constant" and "severed":

> It should be understood that Reality is neither constant (常) nor severed (斷) (*Duan* 斷 means "severed" [斷絕].), hence I also name it "constantly turning over" (恆轉). *Chang* 常 means not severed. *Hengzhuan* 恆轉 means not constant. Neither constant nor severed, [there is only] instant after instant of arising and ceasing, ceasing and arising, hence I name it "constantly turning over." I use this term to make Reality explicit through its functioning (即用顯體). (The term *xian* 顯 here means "making explicit with words." This is a different sense from [how *xian* is used in the word] *xianxian* 顯現 [to manifest].)[17]

Reality is neither exclusively constant nor exclusively changing—rather it is constantly turning over, constantly transforming into function.

In fact, already in his 1926 publication, *Weishixue gailun* 唯識學概論 (A General Account of Yogācāra Learning), Xiong had introduced the concept of constantly turning over (恆轉) to explain the operation of consciousness: "'Constantly' means 'not severed,' 'turning over' conveys the sense of 'not constant.' Not severed and not constant—that is, moment by moment shedding the past and ceaselessly creating the new. This is what is called 'the power of generation,' which the scripture compares to a great torrent."[18] The scripture referred to here is famous pilgrim-monk Xuanzang's 玄奘 (602–664) translation of Yogācāra master Vasubandhu's (世親; fourth century) *Triṃśikā* (*Weishi sanshi lun song* 唯識三十論頌; Thirty verses), in which the *ālaya* (store) consciousness[19] is described as "constantly turning over, like a

---

[17] Idem, p. 15.
[18] Xiong, *Weishixue gailun*, *Xiong Shili quanji*, vol. 1, p. 448. Note that an earlier version of *Weishixue gailun* was published in 1923 and is also included in *Xiong Shili quanji*, vol. 1.
[19] Also known as the eighth consciousness, this consciousness is one of eight or nine identified by Buddhists.

torrent" (恆轉如瀑流).²⁰ In *Cheng weishi lun* 成唯識論 (Demonstration of Nothing but Consciousness) Xuanzang provides the following description of the operation of the *ālaya* consciousness:

> Is the *ālaya* consciousness severed or constant? It is neither severed nor constant because it is constantly turning over.... "Turning over" means that since beginningless time, thought-moment by thought-moment this consciousness arises and ceases, transforming from one thought-moment to the next.... It is said to be "constant" so as to refute [the view] that it is severed; "turning over" to convey [the sense] that it is not constant. Just like a torrent, [the ceasing of] cause and [the arising of] effect is so-of-itself.²¹

Although clearly inspired by this passage's account of the constantly turning over, Xiong made the concept his own by applying it to his thesis that Reality (the intrinsic Reality of the cosmos) and function (the dynamic process of intrinsic Reality's transformation into phenomena, the myriad existents) are non-dual (體用不二):

> It should be understood that Reality completely and utterly transforms into the great function that is the disparate myriad existents; that outside the flow of great function there is no Reality. It is like the way the ocean completely becomes the myriad waves—that is, beyond the myriad waves there is no ocean. The non-duality of Reality and function is also like this.²²

> Even though all dharmas are profusely and multifariously differentiated, actually it is undifferentiated Reality in its entirety that is transforming and moving without interruption, flowing incessantly; as the old passes away, completely relinquished, the new arises ever anew; vastly producing, capaciously producing—the undifferentiated whole of limitless great existents (大有).²³

We can now return to the question of what Xiong means by "the cosmological problem of the non-duality of Reality and function" and "the Reality

---

[20] T1586.31, 60b8.
[21] T1585.31, 12b28–12c5. I am grateful to Sang Yu 桑雨 for drawing my attention to this passage. I also note that the terms *duan* 斷 and *chang* 常 are irrevocably linked to the Buddhist doctrine of the "two views" (二見): the view of eternalism (常見) and the view of nihilism (斷見), which are also known as the "two extremes" (二邊): either that things endure over time or that things cease to exist.
[22] *Ti yong lun*, pp. 14–15.
[23] Idem, p. 93.

of the cosmos." Xiong maintains that it was "in the context of cosmology that I came to realize that Reality and function are non-dual."[24] He defines "cosmos" as "the generic term for all mental and material dharmas,"[25] but distinguishes between a narrow and broad sense of "cosmology." The narrow sense refers "specifically to dharma characteristics or phenomena,"[26] whereas the broad sense refers "both to intrinsic Reality and phenomena."[27]

As with a number of other scholars, Guo Qiyong 郭齊勇 maintains that Xiong's discussion of "*benti/shiti*" and its connection with what Xiong refers to as the "cosmos," is best described as "onto-cosmology" (*yuzhou benti lun* 宇宙本體論):

> "Onto-cosmology" is cosmology that fathoms the source, root, and inherent character of the cosmos; it is also ontology that explores the genesis, development, and transformation of the cosmos. One of the characteristics of Xiong Shili's philosophy is that *benti* is not discussed separated from the cosmos and cosmos is not discussed separated from *benti*. "*Benti*" is the *ti* of the cosmos' arising, ceasing, and transformation; "cosmos" is the *yong* that depends on *benti* to appear, that is, it is the flow of *benti*'s great transformation.[28]

The identification of Xiong's metaphysics as a kind of onto-cosmology is most likely inspired by Mou Zongsan's 牟宗三 (1909–1995) use of the term, which features widely in the first volume of Mou's *Xinti yu xingti* 心體與性體 (Intrinsic Reality of the Mind and Intrinsic Reality of the Nature; 1968). For example, in distinguishing between his own notion of a Chinese "moral metaphysics" (道德的形上學) and a Kantian "metaphysics of morality" (道德之（底）形上學), Mou writes:

> Whereas the latter places an emphasis on explaining the a priori inherent nature of morality, the former places an emphasis on metaphysics and encompasses all of existence, and so it is appropriate that it should contain some "ontological statements" and some "cosmological statements," or collectively "onto-cosmological statements."

[24] Idem, p. 95.
[25] Idem, p. 68.
[26] Idem, p. 62.
[27] Idem, p. 72.
[28] Guo Qiyong, *Xiong Shili zhexue yanjiu* 熊十力哲學研究 (A Study of Xiong Shili's Philosophy) (Beijing: Renmin daxue chubanshe, 2011) (originally published 1993), p. 39.

此後者重點在道德，即重在說明道德之先驗本性;而前者重點則在形上學，乃涉及一切存在而為言者，故應含有一些「本體論的陳述」與「宇宙論的陳述」，或綜曰「本體宇宙論的陳述」 (onto-cosmological statements）。[29]

More recently, Chen Lai 陳來 also refers to the later-period Xiong Shili's *bentilun* variously as a "cosmo-ontology" (宇宙本體論) and "onto-cosmology" (本體宇宙論).[30] Commenting more generally on the term *bentilun*, he states[31]: "China does not have [the concept of] '*onto*,' that is, 'being,' but Chinese philosophy itself does have discussion of *benti* 本體 and *shiti* 實體, hence it has its own *bentilun*."[32] Given these comments, it seems likely that Chen would not oppose translating *bentilun* as "ontology" but would insist on highlighting that this sense of ontology is culturally particular.

Yang Guorong 楊國榮 similarly elaborates:

After the category of "*bentilun*" was introduced into modern Chinese philosophy it was not solely used as the corresponding concept for ontology; rather, to a considerable degree, it included both the sense of *cunzai* 存在 (being) that is covered in "ontology" and also integrated related concepts from traditional Chinese philosophy, thus acquiring quite a unique meaning. . . . As a concept in modern Chinese philosophy, *bentilun* can neither simplistically be equated with ontology, nor can it easily be merely summed up as doctrines concerning *benti* in traditional Chinese philosophy. . . . *Bentilun* would seem to be closer to *xingershangxue* 形而上學 (metaphysics) in the broad sense.[33]

---

[29] Mou Zongsan, *Xinti yu xingti*, vol. 5 of *Mou Zongsan quanji* 牟宗三全集 (The Complete Works of Mou Zongsan) (Taipei: Lianjing, 2003), p. 11. The English translation "onto-cosmological statements" is in Mou's text.

[30] Chen Lai, *Renxue bentilun* 仁學本體論 (Ontology of Humaneness-Centered Learning) (Beijing: Sanlian shudian, 2014), pp. 2–3, 53.

[31] *Bentilun* is one of the terms used in modern Chinese to translate the term "ontology." Other translations that have been or that continue to be used are *cunyoulun* 存有論, *cunzailun* 存在論, and *shilun* 是論.

[32] Chen, *Renxue bentilun*, p. 13. Chen also acknowledges (p. 14) that great changes have taken place in the use and understanding of *onto* and ontology since the time of the ancient Greeks. He maintains (somewhat more contentiously) that if we take Descartes's and Spinoza's respective accounts of substance (實體) in their ontologies as representative of such a change, then it can be seen that Chinese accounts of *shiti* 實體 are not so fundamentally different from those of Descartes and Spinoza.

[33] Yang Guorong, "Xingershangxue yu zhexue de neizai shiyu" 形而上學與哲學的內在視域 (Metaphysics and the Inner Horizon of Philosophy), *Xueshu yuekan* (2004.12): 21, 22. The idea that Chinese conceptions of "ontology" differ from those of Western conceptions is also illustrated in the

xxii   TRANSLATOR'S INTRODUCTION

Did Xiong Shili use the term *bentilun* to mean ontology or is it more appropriate to render his understanding of *bentilun* as "theory of intrinsic Reality"? And if he did use it to mean ontology, how did he understand ontology? In the appendix to his 1950 publication, *Cui huo xian zong ji* 摧惑顯宗記 (Record to Destroy Confusion and Make My Tenets Explicit), Xiong makes his view clear.

Philosophy consists of the following divisions:

1. Ontology (本體論); also called metaphysics. It is the field of learning that thoroughly investigates the Reality of the cosmos (宇宙實體).
2. Cosmology (宇宙論). It is the field of learning that explains the cosmos' myriad images. (The phenomenal world.)
3. Theory of human life (人生論).[34] It examines the intrinsic nature of life and investigates the content of human life.... (It is also popularly known as *shenghuo zhexue* 生活哲學.)
4. Epistemology (知識論); also called *renshilun* 認識論.

Whereas in Western philosophy these four divisions have perhaps been separated a little too severely, in Chinese philosophy [historically] we never had these categories of division. In terms of their usefulness to philosophers, however, it is indeed the case that [philosophical] investigation should be undertaken on the basis of these four categories of division. Nowadays, we explore Chinese philosophy on the basis of these four divisions, and so

---

case of *cunyoulun* 存有論. Consider, for example, Mou Zongsan's following statement in *Yuan shan lun* 圓善論 (On the *Summum Bonum*, 1985, vol. 22 of *Mou Zongsan quanji*, p. 327):

> The Western [conception of] ontology starts with the verb "to be" (是、在); discussion of principles concerning this verb is called ontology (存有論).... I call this type of ontology "internal ontology" (內在的存有論), that is, [it is concerned with] analyzing the being (存有性) internal to a thing's existence. In the Chinese tradition, however, the emphasis is not on internal ontology. China's tradition of wisdom also has its ontology, but its ontology is not concerned with internally (inwardly) analyzing the being of things that exist, analyzing the conditions of their possibility, but rather is concerned with transcendentally (externally) explaining the principles whereby they exist. The interest lies solely in explaining how a thing comes to have its existence rather than how existing things are constituted.... Contained within this type of ontology is also a cosmology concerning the source of the cosmos's unceasing production and reproduction, and that is why I often refer to them in combination as "onto-cosmology."

[34] *Lebensphilosophie*.

we see that Chinese philosophy includes these four divisions, with none omitted. Among these four divisions, however, it is ontology alone [that exhaustively traces] where the myriad principles originate, that is the locus all scholarship returns to, and that is the source of all knowledge.... I maintain that although there is no harm in distinguishing the terms "cosmology" and the "theory of human life," actually the principles [each is concerned with] are consistent and cannot be split apart.... In discussing cosmology and the theory of human life, however, unless one has achieved a thorough realization of intrinsic Reality, then no matter which direction one pursues one will become mired in conceptual elaboration (戲論 [*prapañca]).... In exhaustively tracing principles, the profoundly wise invariably trace them to their root; in engaging in learning, those of expansive mind invariably fathom that learning to its source. It is for this reason that ever since antiquity the wise have persistently investigated ontology without interruption.[35]

Three years later, in responding to a claim made by an interlocuter that ontology (本體論) and cosmology (宇宙論) are distinctions drawn only by Western scholars and are not found in Indian Buddhism, Xiong insists that the terms *bentilun* and *yuzhoulun* also apply to Indian Buddhist philosophy, just as they apply to Chinese philosophy and Western philosophy:

Let me ask you the following. Is not the aim of the vast Buddhist canon to bear witness to the consummate nature (圓成實性)?[36] How can you casually claim that Buddhism has no ontology? From the Āgama sutras to the [scriptures of] Hīnayāna and Mahāyāna, Buddhist accounts of the five aggregates (五蘊)[37] have listed the "aggregate of form" (色蘊) as the first of the five. From within, the characteristics of the sense faculties, and from without, the characteristics of the material cosmos, are broken down and distinguished; described side by side, they are collectively classed as form aggregates. Does this not capture what cosmology means?[38]

---

[35] Appendix to *Cui huo xian zong ji*, *Xiong Shili quanji*, vol. 5, p. 537.
[36] A term for suchness: reality as it truly is without any conceptual overlay.
[37] The five *skandha*s (aggregates, heaps)—form, sensation, perception, volition, and consciousness—are used to explain the contingent, compositional nature of human existence and to highlight its lack of intrinsic self-entity. The form aggregate refers to material existence.
[38] Appendix, *Xin weishilun (shanding ben)* 新唯識論(刪定本) (New Treatise on the Uniqueness of Consciousness; Abridged Edition), *Xiong Shili quanji*, vol. 6, p. 281.

The non-duality of Reality and function

Having now teased out some key terminological issues, how does the non-duality of Reality and function thesis relate to the cosmos? Fundamentally, it amounts to the view that "the myriad images of the cosmos have always been nothing other than Reality's producing and reproducing, transforming and changing."[39] Here, as elsewhere in the *Treatise*, "the myriad images" refers to the phenomena that constitute the cosmos.[40] Crucially, it is Reality itself that transforms into such phenomena:

> How should Reality be explained? Great function has always been the general term for the myriad mental and material images. The myriad mental and material images are not manifest based on nothing—they definitely have Reality. But this Reality neither towers above the myriad mental and material images nor lies concealed behind the myriad mental and material images—rather, it must be understood that Reality is precisely "the itself" (自身) of the myriad mental and material images.[41]

What does it mean to say that Reality is "the itself" of the myriad phenomena? It means that Reality *is* the myriad phenomena:

> Hitherto, scholars who have discussed Reality and phenomena all say that whereas phenomena transform and change, Reality is what is real. As such, phenomena and Reality constitute a two-tier world. If, however, [the matter is considered] on the basis of my account that Reality and function are non-dual, then **it is Reality that is phenomena** (This is analogous to the ocean's being the waves.) and that **it is phenomena that are Reality**. [JM emphasis] (This is analogous to there being no ocean that is apart from the numerous waves.) The arising and ceasing in impermanence of phenomena is precisely the arising and ceasing in impermanence of Reality. . . . Although phenomena and Reality are differentiated, ultimately, they cannot be split in two—this doctrine is definitive. It should be said that **Reality and phenomena have always been one** [JM emphasis], that it is precisely that which transforms

---

[39] *Ti yong lun*, p. 4.
[40] "'The myriad images of the cosmos' is a generic term for all kinds of material [物質] and 'pure and spirit-like' [精神] phenomena" (Idem, p. 5); "'Cosmos': the generic term for all mental and material dharmas." (Idem, p. 69.)
[41] Idem, p. 98.

and changes that is real, and that it is precisely that which is real that transforms and changes.[42]

In other words, there is a kind of identity between Reality and phenomena.

There is a strong isomorphism between the Tiantai Three Truths doctrine and Xiong's understanding of this identity relation between Reality and function. According to the Three Truths doctrine, any dharma (any entity or phenomenon, mental or physical) is empty (空) because it is causally determined through multiple networks of causes and conditions and has no self-nature. At the same time, because *this* dharma can be referred to—even negatively, in the sense of its not being *that* dharma—it can also be said to be provisionally posited (假). Thus, any dharma is both empty and provisionally posited, with neither emptiness nor provisional positing being privileged over the other. The realization that emptiness is provisional positing (emptiness can be provisionally posited) and that provisional positing is emptiness (the provisional posited is empty of self-nature) is the third of the Three Truths and is known as the Middle/Center (中). In the hands of Tiantai theorists such as Zhiyi 智顗 (538–597),[43] however, the relationship between these Three Truths becomes one of mutual identity such that the Middle is both Emptiness and Provisional, just as Emptiness is both Provisional and the Middle, and Provisional is both Emptiness and the Middle.[44] Xiong Shili's thesis that *ti* and *yong* are non-dual can also be seen to reflect Zhiyi's understanding of the Three Truths.

As a whole,[45] *ti* is absolute and does not have anything to which it stands in contrast (無對):[46]

"Subsuming function into Reality" (攝用歸體) is for there to be a complete absence [of any function to which Reality] stands in contrast, such that neither mental nor material phenomena can be named. (*She* 攝 means

---

[42] Idem, p. 126.

[43] Zhiyi is recognized as the de facto founder of the Tiantai School of Buddhism.

[44] On this point, see comments by Andō Toshio 安藤俊雄, cited in Brook Ziporyn, *Evil and/or/as the Good: Omnicentrism, Intersubjectivity, and Value Paradox in Tiantai Buddhist Thought* (Cambridge MA: Harvard University Asia Center, 2000), p. 119 and the broader analysis by Ziporyn, pp. 118–122.

[45] *Ti yong lun*, p. 98: "*Quanti* 全體 is also a name for Reality. It is named as such because Reality is a whole"; p. 121: "*Quanti* 全體: Because Reality is a great whole and there is nothing to which it stands in contrast, it is also called 'Reality qua whole.'"

[46] Elsewhere, Xiong refers to *ti* as absolute, *yiyuan* 一元; see *Ming xin pian* 明心篇 (Explaining Mind), *Xiong Shili quanji*, vol. 7, pp. 267, 315.

"to subsume." Take the analogy of when looking at ice one does not preserve the characteristic of ice but directly realizes water, that it is nothing but water. Now, in the context of cosmology, to say that function is subsumed into Reality is to observe various mental and material phenomena and directly realize their intrinsic Reality. If we refer exclusively to intrinsic Reality, it is without form or conscious deliberation; hence neither mental nor material phenomena can be named.)[47]

In terms of the Three Truths, *ti* is the functional equivalent of Emptiness. Subsuming *yong* into *ti* (攝用歸體) amounts to privileging *ti* and focusing on *ti*'s lack of any characteristics. If the experiential subject were to stop at this point, however, then this would amount to abandoning *yong* in order to perceive *ti*, and thus fundamentally undermine the non-duality thesis. Yet precisely because *ti* is deemed to be absolute, it thereby stands in contrast to the non-absolute, to the relative, which is the provisionally posited. As cited earlier, "It is precisely in its being without that to which it stands in contrast that intrinsic Reality has that to which it stands in contrast; and it is precisely in its having that to which it stands in contrast that it is without that to which it stands in contrast." In other words, abstracted from the myriad individuated waves, the ocean is without that to which it stands in contrast, yet this very abstraction simultaneously places it in contrast to the waves. Moreover, the ocean cannot be sought apart from the waves: "That which has nothing to which it stands in contrast cannot be sought for apart from that which has something to which it stands in contrast." In other words, the absolute cannot be sought apart from the relative. To be relative in this sense is functionally equivalent to the Provisional, and that which is provisionally posited is *yong*, the analogy for which is the myriad waves.

The non-duality of *ti* and *yong* is the perspective of the Middle:

Reality's transformation into the countless functions of unceasing production and reproduction is analogous to the ocean's transforming into the unabating numerous waves. (The principle of "with regard to Reality, *it* is function [即體即用]" can be realized from this.) The countless functions all take Reality as their self (自身).... Take the example of the numerous waves—each takes the ocean as itself. (The itself of wave A is the ocean, the itself of wave B is also the ocean, and this is the case right through to all of the countless waves. From this we can realize the principle of "with regard to function, *it* is Reality" [即

---

[47] *Treatise*, p. 19.

用即體]. "With regard to function, *it* is Reality" means that it is function that is Reality [功用即是實體], just as that it is the numerous waves themselves that are the ocean.) Hence, [in explaining] the meaning of the non-duality of Reality and function, only the metaphor of the ocean and the myriad waves comes quite close to the mark.[48]

It should be understood that although Reality and function can be differentiated, actually they cannot be differentiated. Where they can be differentiated is that Reality is without distinctions (Like the ocean, it has always been a complete whole.) and function is a myriad particulars. (Like the way the numerous waves appear as individuated.) Where they cannot be differentiated is that with regard to Reality, *it* is function (即體即用) (Like the way the ocean completely becomes the numerous waves.), and with regard to function, *it* is Reality (即用即體). (Like the way there is no ocean apart from the numerous waves.) Accordingly, none of the profusion of the myriad existents is fixed and this should be called function. That which is undifferentiated and all-pervading (渾然充塞) and is without deliberate action yet there is nothing it does not do is intrinsic Reality qua the flow of great function. (*Hunran* 渾然 refers to its being an indivisible great whole; *chongsai* 充塞 refers to its being all pervading and omnipresent.) Function is constituted of Reality (This is analogous to all the countless wave forms' [漚相] being constituted of the ocean.), and Reality depends on being function to exist. (This is analogous to how the ocean does not transcend the countless wave forms to exist independently.)[49]

The ocean is the myriad waves and the myriad waves are the ocean; the Empty is the Provisional and the Provisional is the Empty. *Ti* and *yong* are non-dual and this is the perspective of the Middle.

"The pure and spirit-like" and "matter and energy"; expansion and contraction

The claim that Reality depends on function to exist means that Reality can be experienced only as function: "With regard to Reality's transforming

---

[48] Idem, pp. 96, 97.
[49] Idem, p. 53.

and moving to become function, it is only in function that the properties of Reality can be grasped."[50]

What are these properties? In the *Treatise*, Xiong focuses in particular on "the pure and spirit-like" (精神) and "matter and energy" (質力): "I hold that Reality's transformation into function has always been the great flow of the pure and spirit-like and matter and energy, undifferentiated as one."[51] He further notes that matter (物質) includes energy within it, and within humans he identifies the pure and spirit-like variously with the mind and the nature. The pure and spirit-like and matter and energy have always existed. By virtue of matter's submitting to the pure and spirit-like, material things are set in motion:

> The Grand Primordium stage of the cosmos was desolate and devoid of things; although matter and energy were hidden and not immediately manifest, it cannot be said that originally there was no matter. Before organisms had appeared, although the pure and spirit-like was hidden and not immediately manifest, it cannot be said that originally the pure and spirit-like did not exist. The pure and spirit-like does not exist alone separated from matter. . . . From the desolation [that characterized the Grand Primordium], the cosmos began to develop ceaselessly, and it was precisely the pure and spirit-like within matter that eliminated its closure, striving to be active so as to transform and modify matter, ceaselessly advancing without constraint.[52]

The pure and spirit-like and matter and energy are respectively identified with Qian and Kun in the *Book of Change*, and also with expansion (*pi* 闢) and contraction (*xi* 翕). When Reality transforms into function, within function there lie concealed two opposing incipient tendencies, *yin* and *yang*, which manifest as the two impetuses (勢) of expansion and contraction. "Expansion refers to the pure and spirit-like. It is called expansion because it has qualities such as vigor, opening up, and ascending. Contraction refers to matter."[53]

These two impetuses exemplify the principle that enables transformation to occur: "mutually opposing and mutually completing" (相反相成). In

---

[50] Idem, p. 6.
[51] Idem, p. 138.
[52] Idem, pp. 134, 137.
[53] Idem, p. 120.

order to explain this principle, Xiong draws on the numbers one, two, and three, as formulated in *Laozi* 老子 (*zhang* 42):

> The dictum in *Laozi* that "one generates two and two generates three" is elaborating on the purport of three lines constituting a trigram in the *Great Change*. *Laozi* uses this to express the principle of "mutually opposing and mutually completing." There being one, then there is two. This two is in opposition to one. At the same time, there is also a three, which is based on the one. (Three is not identical to one but only based on one.) Although in opposition to two, three can transform two such that they revert to harmony. This is what the *Book of Change* means by "Great Harmony is preserved through union."[54] Only by virtue of the two opposites becoming harmonized is the development of the whole thus brought to completion.[55]

One is able to generate two because the idea of "one" is inseparable from the idea of "not-one" and the combination of "one" and "not one" is two. This move from one to its opposite, "not-one," plays a strikingly similar role to Hegel's notion of sublation or suspension (*Aufheben*): the idea of a finite determination transitioning to its opposite, as described in Part I of his *Encyclopaedia of Philosophical Sciences*, which is often called *The Encyclopaedia Logic*. As described by Julie E. Maybee, for Hegel, every logical concept has three parts or moments. For our immediate purposes, it is the transition of the first to second moment that is relevant:

> The first moment—the moment of the understanding—is the moment of fixity, in which concepts or forms have a seemingly stable definition or determination (EL §80). The second moment—the "*dialectical*" (EL §§79, 81) or "*negatively rational*" (EL §79) moment—is the moment of instability. In this moment, a one-sidedness or restrictedness (EL Remark to §81) in the determination from the moment of understanding comes to the fore, and the determination that was fixed in the first moment passes into its opposite (EL §81). Hegel describes this process as a process of "self-sublation" (EL §81).... The moment of understanding sublates *itself* because its own

---

[54] "Tuan" 彖 (Judgment), Qian hexagram, *Zhou yi* 周易 (Book of Change), Kong Yingda 孔穎達 (574–648) et al., comp., *Zhou yi zhengyi* 周易正義 (Correct Interpretation of the *Book of Change*), 1.7b, in Ruan Yuan 阮元 (1764–1849) comp., *Shisan jing zhushu* 十三經注疏 (The Thirteen Classics with Annotations and Sub-Commentaries) (Taipei: Yiwen yinshuguan, 1985).
[55] *Ti yong lun*, pp. 15–16.

character or nature—its one-sidedness or restrictedness—destabilizes its definition and leads it to pass into its opposite. The dialectical moment thus involves a process of *self*-sublation, or a process in which the determination from the moment of understanding sublates *itself*, or both cancels and preserves *itself*, as it pushes on to or passes into its opposite.[56]

In turn, three is generated by grasping the unity of the opposites—this is what Xiong means by stating that three is based on one but is not identical to one. It is not identical because two is also integrated with three. Again, the similarity with the third moment in Hegel's dialectical method is striking: the unity of the opposition between the first two determinations.[57] As for the principle of "mutually opposing and mutually completing," this can be understood to refer to the opposition of one and two, and the harmonious union or synthesis of one and two in the unity that is three.

How, then, does Xiong relate these ideas to the concepts of *xi* and *pi*?

The constantly turning over almost began to become things that offer material resistance and lose its self-nature. Hence the contraction impetus can be said to be an opposing function (反作用). Just as the contraction impetus arises, however, a different impetus arises in opposition to, yet simultaneously with, contraction. (The two impetuses are not different entities; much less do they have temporal sequence. Hence it is said that they arise simultaneously.) This other impetus has always been an expression of the self-nature of the constantly turning over, yet it is not identical to the constantly turning over. For example, ice is made up of water, but ice is not identical to water. This other impetus is robust, vigorous, and self-conquering and so is not willing to become materialized—just the opposite of contraction. . . . Furthermore, this impetus that is unwilling to become materialized is able to operate within contraction, such that it becomes in charge. . . . This robust and vigorous impetus that does not become materialized is named "expansion."[58]

---

[56] Julie E. Maybee, "Hegel's Dialectics," in *Stanford Encyclopedia of Philosophy*. Available via https://plato.stanford.edu/entries/hegel-dialectics/, 2016, cited August 5, 2022. "EL" refers to *The Encyclopedia Logic [Enzyklopädie der philosophischen Wissenschaften I]*.

[57] In the 1944 vernacular edition of the *Xin weishi lun*, *Xiong Shili quanji*, vol. 3, p. 10, when Xiong cited this same passage from *Laozi* to explain the principle of "mutually opposing and mutually completing" he explicitly denied that he had drawn on Hegel.

[58] *Ti yong lun*, p. 17.

"The constantly turning over" is another name for intrinsic Reality. The reason that *pi* is not identical to the constantly turning over, to intrinsic Reality, is because *pi* (expansion) exercises a controlling role over *xi* (contraction); intrinsic Reality itself does not play such a role.

The constantly turning over is *ti*, and *xi* and *pi* are *yong*. In terms of Xiong's one, two, three dialectical method, the constantly turning over corresponds to one, *xi* corresponds to two, and *pi* corresponds to three:

> The constantly turning over is one. In being expressed as contraction, it almost does not preserve its self-nature, and this is two—this is what is meant by "one generates two" [in *Laozi*]. However, the constantly turning over is, after all, constantly just as its nature is, and would never become materialized. Hence, just as the contraction impetus arises, simultaneously the expansion impetus arises, and this expansion is three. This is what is meant by "two generates three."[59]

I again note that this characterization of *xi* as the tendency not to preserve its self-nature (the constantly turning over, which is synonymous with Reality), has distinct resonances with Hegel's account of self-sublation. As for *pi* (three), it represents the harmonious merging or synthesis of the constantly turning over (one) and *xi* (two).

Criticisms of Buddhist thought

Xiong's criticisms of Buddhism focus on two major traditions of Mahāyāna Buddhist doctrine, which, following Buddhist doxographers in the Tang period, he refers to as the Emptiness school (空宗) and the Existence school (有宗). For Xiong, the Emptiness school consists of teachings on emptiness (*kong* 空) as expounded in the *Da boreboluomiduo jing* 大般若波羅蜜多經 (*Mahāprajñāpāramitā-sūtra*; Perfection of Wisdom Sutra) and texts associated specifically with the Madhyamaka school. The Existence School refers to Yogācāra.

Xiong's account the "non-duality of *ti* and *yong*," as set out in the *Treatise*, is developed against a detailed and systematic critique of both schools. Despite his critique, Xiong also acknowledges a profound intellectual debt

---

[59] Idem, p. 17.

to both schools: "My thought has certainly benefited from the inspiration I have received from both the Emptiness and the Existence schools. If I had not started with these two schools, I would certainly not have come to understand how to think for myself, and so what could I have followed in order to awaken and enter [true cognition of] (悟入) the *Book of Transformation*?"[60] He further relates: "It is, moreover, not the case that I am someone opposed to Buddhist teachings. Not only was I fond of the learning of the Mahāyāna Emptiness school in my youth, to this day I have never stopped being fond of it."[61]

One of his points of agreement with the Buddhists is the idea of impermanence: "It is my belief that particular things, even the largest such as the cosmos, ultimately must perish. In talking about emptiness with respect to particular things, the Buddhists are not at all talking nonsense."[62] "The axiom that 'all phenomena are impermanent' is plain, clear, and undeniable."[63] Indeed, this idea is fundamental to Xiong's doctrine of transformation: "My discussions of transformation serve to show that all phenomena are without self-entity (自體)"[64] and "that nothing abides even for a moment."[65] Despite agreement on this point, however, Xiong's understanding of the significance of impermanence differs diametrically from that of the Buddhists:

> When the Buddhists claim that all phenomena are impermanent, their aim is to censure. In this book, however, [my claim] is that instant by instant, all phenomena are just arising and ceasing, ceasing and arising, in a dynamic succession of uninterrupted transformation.... When the Buddhists explain the doctrine that [all things] cease in an instant, they highlight only impermanence. In this treatise, I explain that transformation's agency is incessant, vibrant, and dynamic. This is a fundamental point of difference between the Buddhists and me.[66]

---

[60] Idem, p. 7.
[61] Idem, p. 103.
[62] Idem, p. 8.
[63] Idem, p. 25.
[64] Idem, p. 11.
[65] Idem, p. 31.
[66] Idem, pp. 12, 27.

1. Key criticisms of the Emptiness school

Xiong regards the Buddhist distinction between dharma nature (法性) and dharma characteristics (法相) as the conceptual equivalent of his own Reality and function distinction. He argues that the Emptiness School's doctrine of *po xiang xian xing* 破相顯性 (refuting dharma characteristics in order to reveal the dharma nature) was logically incoherent because "if characteristics are completely refuted, then the nature also will be non-existent. Why is this so? The nature is 'the itself' of the characteristics; if the characteristics are completely refuted, then how could 'the itself' of the characteristics exist? [In other words, the nature will be non-existent because] the nature will have already been annihilated."[67]

He was also critical of the Emptiness School masters for being obsessed with emptiness and mired in quiescence: "Being mired in quiescence, they did not awaken to the exuberance of production and reproduction, and, being obsessed with emptiness, they did not recognize the wondrousness of transformation and retransformation. What I do not agree with is the Buddhists' doing away with function in the pursuit of Reality."[68] "Although the school does not say that Reality also ceases, the sort of Reality it had in mind is merely one that is quiescent and devoid of production and transformation—how different is that from extinction?"[69]

Much of Xiong's discussion of the doctrine of emptiness focusses on the views of Indian philosopher, Nāgārjuna (龍樹; ca. 150–250 CE), who is celebrated for his philosophy of the "middle way" (*madhyamaka*) based on the concept of "emptiness." In his discussion of Nāgārjuna's *Zhongguan lun* 中觀論 (Treatise on the Middle Way), Xiong maintains that Nāgārjuna's fundamental thesis is that "by investigating conditioned origination one will thoroughly understand the true nature (實性) of dharmas (*Shixing* 實性 is like saying "Reality" [實體])."[70] He criticizes this thesis on the following grounds:

> [Nāgārjuna also insisted that] causally conditioned dharmas are dharmas that arise and cease whereas Reality is a non-arising and non-ceasing dharma. . . . He says that a dharma that neither arises nor ceases is the Reality of dharmas that arise and cease—this is a case of name and actuality

---

[67] Idem, p. 43.
[68] Idem, p. 55.
[69] Idem, p. 73.
[70] Idem, p. 85.

failing to correspond with one another.... Hence, we can understand that, in the end, Nāgārjuna's account of conditioned origination did not investigate the true source of the myriad dharmas, and his error cannot be concealed.[71]

Xiong disapproves of the distinction drawn between conditioned (有為) and unconditioned (無為) dharmas in Buddhist thought.[72] On a Buddhist reckoning, as an unconditioned dharma, Reality (dharma nature) neither arises nor ceases and is also unable to be causal. For Xiong, this would thus not only imply that some other ontological support undergirds or gives rise to the phenomenal world of conditioned dharmas but would also sunder the non-duality of *ti* and *yong*.

2. Key criticisms of the Existence school

Xiong's main criticisms of the Existence school focuses on the doctrine of seeds (種子; *bīja*). In standard Yogācāra doctrine, the *ālayavijñāna* (store consciousness) is understood to store both pure and impure seeds—a metaphor—just as the memory stores good and bad memories. These seeds retain the impressions of past experiences and "perfume" new experiences on the basis of that previous conditioning.[73] According to Xuanzang's *Cheng weishi lun*, both pure seeds and impure seeds are of two kinds: innate (本有)

---

[71] Idem, p. 92.

[72] This distinction had been strenuously reiterated by Ouyang Jingwu 歐陽竟無 (1871–1943), Xiong's former teacher, in his 1922 publication, *Weishi jueze tan* 唯識抉擇談 (Talks on the Resolutions of Nothing but Consciousness), where he discussed it in terms of *ti* and *yong*. For more details, see John Jorgensen, "Setting the Scene: The Different Perspectives of Yang Wenhui and Ouyang Jingwu on the *Treatise on Awakening Mahāyāna Faith* as an Authoritative Statement of Mahāyāna Doctrine," in John Makeham, ed., *The Awakening of Faith and New Confucian Philosophy* (Boston: Brill, 2021), pp. 79–80.

[73] As John Powers explains, seeds "are the latent residua of a person's actions. Every volitional action deposits a predisposition within one's mental continuum, which represents a propensity to perpetuate that sort of action and also guarantees the karmic repercussions of one's moral choices. As the metaphor of seeds implies, they lie dormant until the proper conditions for their manifestation are present and then give rise to mental states that resemble the original impulses that led to their creation. A popular metaphor associated with this process is often referred to as 'perfuming' in contemporary discussions of Yogācāra. This translates the Sanskrit term *vāsanā*, which designates predispositions or habituations. In this context, perfuming refers to the idea that these tendencies condition the seeds that constitute the mental stream, similarly to the way in which perfume pervades a cloth. The general disposition of any given mental continuum is a reflection and function of these accumulated tendencies." See his "Yogācāra: Indian Buddhist Origins," in John Makeham, ed., *Transforming Consciousness: Yogācāra Thought in Modern China* (New York: Oxford University Press, 2014), p. 46.

seeds that have existed since beginningless time and newly arisen (始起) or newly perfumed (新熏) seeds.[74]

In chapter 3, "Buddhist Teachings, B," Xiong identifies five doctrinal deficiencies of the Existence school.

1. By positing seeds stored in the store consciousness to be the initial condition to effect arising, the doctrine is really no different from the non-Buddhist doctrine of a spirit-cum-*ātman* (神我).
2. The teaching that innate seeds served as the initial cause of all dharmas was originally established so as to oppose the non-Buddhist doctrine that the transformations of the deity Maheśvara are the cause of everything. In then positing a store consciousness in which to store seeds this effectively amounted to refusing to allow a heavenly deity entrance through the front door, while ushering in a spirit-cum-*ātman* (the store consciousness) through the back door.
3. Dividing seeds into innate seeds and newly perfumed seeds simply serves to cause confusion.
4. The Mahāyāna Existence school maintains that each of the eight consciousnesses is actually a cluster of mind and mental associates (心所), and names each cluster as "manifest activity" (現行).[75] "The term 'manifest' (現) means 'to be evident.' The term 'activity' (行) means 'passing flow.' Each of the eight consciousness clusters has an image (象) that is evident, but it is not fixed; rather, it is a ceaseless passing flow, and so each cluster is collectively named as 'manifest activity.'"[76] Because each of the eight clusters of manifest activity has seeds, which are all concealed within the store consciousness, this amounts to separating the cosmos into a two-tier world of the concealed and the manifest.
5. "Asaṅga[77] clearly took seeds to be the origin of the myriad dharmas, yet he also taught that suchness (真如)[78] is the Reality of the myriad

---

[74] T1585, 31.8b23–28. Newly perfumed seeds are formed by the imprint of the karmic impressions derived from the other seven consciousnesses on the store consciousness.

[75] The appearance of things in their manifest aspect in the seven consciousnesses as they merge from seeds in the eighth consciousness; the activity of consciousness.

[76] *Ti yong lun*, p. 71.

[77] Yogācāra ostensibly begins with the fourth-century Indian thinkers, brothers Asaṅga (無著) and Vasubandhu (世親).

[78] Suchness (*tathatā*): reality as it truly is without any conceptual overlay.

dharmas. As such, how was he able to avoid the error of two tiers of intrinsic Reality?"[79]

Ultimately, however, "Buddhist teachings (*fofa* 佛法) have always been teachings about transcending the mundane world (出世法)."[80] Even though Xiong acknowledges that the Emptiness school regarded dharma nature to be merely empty quiescence, whereas the Existence school opposed this view, hoping to lead people to recognize that dharma nature is real, "I maintain that, when all is said and done, the two schools share an unshakable fundamental belief: The Reality of the myriad dharmas (Dharma nature.) is devoid of production and reproduction, devoid of flow and movement, devoid of change and transformation... and this is why dharma nature is said neither to arise nor to cease. The Existence school was unwilling to change this fundamental belief."[81] Being unable to arise and cease, cease and arise, unconditioned dharma nature is also unable to be causal, thereby cleaving the nature and characteristics in two and jettisoning any basis for the non-duality of *ti* and *yong*.

Despite these strong criticisms, Xiong nevertheless affirms the bodhisattva ideal:

> Although [Nāgārjuna's] teachings are problematic as models, crucially, no matter how indescribably long-lasting, complicated, dangerous, and polluted the mighty environment in which humans live might be, [his teachings are proof] that there is also a remarkable wisdom that arises of its own accord, transcending the mundane world. [Nāgārjuna] observed that nothing has a fixed nature, which he called emptiness, and so he had the courage to defy creative transformation, to extinguish the cosmos, and [to undertake] the great vow [to save and convey all sentient beings to deliverance].[82]

> The Buddha felt compassion for sentient beings for being deluded and so wanted to block the great flow of production and reproduction to transform the mundane world into the village where there is nothing, or the wilderness of quiescent extinction. Although this is a different path from that of we Confucians, nevertheless just as water and fire destroy one another, they also generate one another. Would it not be wonderful if the Mahāyāna bodhisattvas'

---

[79] Idem, p. 72.
[80] Idem, p. 45.
[81] Idem, p. 60.
[82] Idem, pp. 100–101.

great vow to liberate sentient beings, and their strength in resisting creative transformation, were able to be used in fashioning and bringing to completion [the way of] Heaven and Earth and assisting the myriad things!?[83]

This reference to fire and water is consistent with Xiong's notion of mutually opposing and mutually completing, an interpretation reinforced by his related comment that "I firmly believe that the discernment of emptiness must yield to 'reflecting on authenticity' and 'establishing authenticity,'"[84] just as contraction must yield to expansion.

The legacy of Xiong's Reality-function onto-cosmology

Prominent contemporary Chinese philosopher, Chen Lai, maintains that of the metaphysical systems developed by Xiong Shili, Liang Shuming 梁漱溟 (1893–1988), Feng Youlan 馮友蘭 (1895–1990), and Ma Yifu 馬一浮 (1883–1967), it is Xiong's mature ontology developed in the 1950s and early 1960s that provides the greatest prospect for further development.[85] For Chen, that prospect lies in the establishment of an ontology that posits humaneness qua Reality (仁體) as the inherent source of the cosmos.

In 2014, Chen Lai published *Ontology of Humaneness-Centered Learning*, a work that has recently been praised as a model for the development of contemporary Chinese philosophy.[86] According to Chen:

> The theoretical crux of the ontology of humaneness-centered learning is that humaneness is taken as intrinsic Reality (本體), just as principle is taken as intrinsic Reality in the ontology of principle-centered learning (理學). Humaneness' serving as intrinsic Reality is also called humaneness qua intrinsic Reality (仁體). The theory in which humaneness serves as

---

[83] Idem, p. 102.
[84] Idem, p. 103.
[85] Idem, pp. 8, 12.
[86] Yang Lihua 楊立華, "Wei Zhongguo zhexue xin shidai dianji: Chen Lai xiansheng rentilun shulun" 為中國哲學新時代奠基：陳來先生仁體論述論 (Laying the Foundations for a New Era of Chinese Philosophy: A Discussion of Mr Chen Lai's Theory of Humaneness as Reality), *Zhongguo zhexueshi* (2022.2): 5–10. Ding Yun 丁耘, "Zhexue yu ti yong: Ping Chen Lai jiaoshou *Renxue bentilun*" 哲學與體用：評陳來教授《仁學本體論》(Philosophy and *Ti-Yong*: A Review of Professor Chen Lai's *Ontology of Humaneness-Centered Learning*), *Zhexuemen*, 31(2015): 279, similarly praised Chen's volume as "the first [Chinese] work of pure philosophy to appear in China this century."

intrinsic Reality is the ontology of humaneness-centered learning, which is also called the theory of humaneness as Reality (仁體論), and which can also be called the ontology of humaneness (仁本體論).[87]

As for Chen's understanding of *benti*, it explicitly draws on Xiong's understanding:

By the time he wrote *Treatise on Reality and Function* in his late years, Xiong formally declared that the crux of his philosophy was his theory of Reality and function. . . . His mature theory of Reality and function maintains that both Reality and function really exist, that Reality is not outside function, that Reality is "the itself" of function, that Reality itself completely transforms into great function, that with regard to function, *it* is Reality, that with regard to Reality, *it* is function, and that Reality itself is productive, reproductive and transforming. I maintain that it is these statements that are true contribution of his ontology.[88]

The establishment of intrinsic Reality (本體) in my doctrine of humaneness as Reality (仁體) serves to put in place a source for the existence of the world, its interconnectedness, its productivity and reproductivity, and its movement. This source does not refer to the genesis of the cosmos, hence intrinsic Reality is not the First Mover. Rather, it is the inner source for the cosmos' inexhaustible, constant existence. This intrinsic Reality is neither the same as nor is it apart from the world; with regard to Reality, *it* is function; intrinsic Reality is itself ceaselessly productive and reproductive and the great function that is phenomena is also ceaselessly productive and reproductive. The meaning of this "with regard to Reality, *it* is function" is explained most clearly Xiong Shili's late work, *Treatise on Reality and Function*.[89]

Generally speaking, in Xiong Shili's philosophy, "with regard to Reality, *it* is function" is referring to Reality's transforming into function (and in this sense it is said that Reality is function). "With regard to function, *it* is Reality" is referring to function itself being Reality (and in this sense it is said that function is Reality). The former emphasizes Reality, and the latter emphasizes function. . . . The originality of Xiong's understanding of the

---

[87] *Renxue benti lun*, p. 30.
[88] Idem, pp. 48–49.
[89] Idem, p. 12.

ti-yong relational model has an important theoretical significance and that is why I also affirm and incorporate it.[90]

In addition to prescribing that humaneness is one body, a whole[91]—just as Xiong related that Reality is also called "Reality qua whole [全體] because it is perfectly complete and has no boundaries"[92]—Chen further prescribes that humaneness is the ceaseless flow of production and reproduction and also draws on the concepts of expansion and contraction:

> Now, in establishing my ontology of humaneness-centered learning, these two aspects must be combined, that is, the combination of humaneness as production and reproduction and humaneness as one body. With reference to cosmology, production and reproduction is expansion (闢) and one body is contraction (翕); both are the Reality and function of humaneness.[93]

Summary of main contents of the *Treatise*

The author of the brief Foreword is ostensibly Han Yuankai 韓元愷 (Xiangsheng 庠生), one of Xiong's former students when Xiong first taught at Peking University between 1922 and 1924. According to Guo Qiyong, Han had moved from Shaoyang 邵陽 in Hunan to Shanghai in 1956, to serve as Xiong Shili's assistant. Han had been classified as a landlord and consequently lost his livelihood. Guo also notes: "From the style of writing, however, this Foreword was written by Mr Xiong himself, and simply presented under the name of Han Yuankai."[94] The Foreword briefly introduces the Buddhist

---

[90] Idem, p. 53.
[91] Idem, p. 30.
[92] *Ti yong lun*, p. 104.
[93] *Renxue bentilun*, p. 39. It should be noted that, in his own ontology, Chen attaches greater importance to contraction than to expansion.
[94] Guo Qiyong, *Tiandi jian yige dushuren: Xiong Shili zhuan* 天地間一個讀書人:熊十力傳 (A Scholar Poised between Heaven and Earth: A Biography of Xiong Shili) (Taipei: Yeqiang chubanshe, 1994), pp. 125, 128. This is not the only example of Xiong's employing such a literary device. In 1950 he published *Cui huo xian zong ji*, which is a book-length rejoinder to a lengthy 1948 review of his magnum opus, *New Treatise on the Uniqueness Consciousness* (vernacular edition, 1944) by the cleric Yinshun 印順 (1906–2005), "Ping Xiong Shili de *Xin weishi lun*" 評熊十力的新唯識論 (Review of Xiong Shili's *New Treatise on the Uniqueness of Consciousness*), reproduced in *Xiong Shili quanji*, supplementary volume A. Xiong's rejoinder is published in vol. 5 of *Xiong Shili quanji*, where he describes the work as having been "narrated" by his student and amanuensis, Huang Genyong 黃艮庸, but still "faithful to my intended meaning" (p. 395). A shorter, earlier version of Xiong's rejoinder was published in 1949, in the journal *Xueyuan* 學原 (vol. 2, issues 11/12), under the name of Huang Genyong and titled "*Xin lun* pingzhang Ru-Fo zhu da wenti zhi shenshu" 新論平章儒佛諸大問題

concepts of dharma nature and dharma characteristics as well as Xiong's own pair of key concepts, the pure and spirit-like and matter, and highlights that the *Treatise* was written to elucidate the tenet of the non-duality of Reality and function.

This author's preface, "Superfluous Words," sets out the aim of the *Treatise* and its relation to early editions of *New Treatise on the Uniqueness of Consciousness*. It highlights the non-duality of Reality and function thesis and its connection with the *Book of Change*, and recounts the major influences on, and directions of, Xiong's learning over his lifetime, including his intellectual debt to Buddhist learning. It also criticizes the Emptiness and Existence schools of Buddhism as well as Daoist thinkers, Laozi and Zhuangzi; provides an apologetic for Xiong's extensive use of auto-commentary; and recounts the physical ailments he suffered while writing the *Treatise*.

The first main section of Chapter 1, "Explaining Transformation," introduces the principle of transformation and includes discussion of Reality's characteristics, how transformation is accomplished, and the principle in *Laozi* that "one generates two and two generates three." The second section provides a detailed account of the two impetuses of contraction and expansion, their role in transformation and in the appearance of living entities, and their connection with the principle of mutually opposing and mutually completing. The following section on arising and ceasing introduces and defends in detail the Buddhist doctrine that all things cease in an instant (*chana* 剎那; *kṣaṇa*). In the next section Xiong explains that he defends the idea that all things arise and cease instant by instant and do not abide even for a moment, "in order to show that the two impetuses of one contraction and one expansion constantly create and do not grow exhausted; that they are ever renewing and do not hold onto the old."[95] The chapter concludes with a presentation of the five characteristics of transformation.

Chapter 2, "Buddhist Teachings, A," begins with a comparison of the Buddhist concepts of dharma nature and dharma characteristics and Reality and function. The first main section of this chapter then introduces the doctrines of the Emptiness school and includes discussions on such topics as the Buddhist concept of the five aggregates, the purport of the *Heart Sutra*, and the apophatic method of "refuting characteristics in order to reveal

---

之申述 (A Detailed Account of the *New Treatise*'s Deliberations on Major Issues in Buddhism and Confucianism). See the Editor's Postface to vol. 5 of *Xiong Shili quanji*, p. 777.

[95] *Ti yong lun*, p. 31.

the nature." This is followed by Xiong's detailed criticisms of the Emptiness school. The chapter's second main section (albeit much shorter than the first main section) introduces the doctrines of the Existence school and includes discussions on such topics as the three periods of the Buddha's teachings, suchness, seeds, and comparisons with the Emptiness school.

Xiong relates that in "Buddhist Teachings, B," he will "continue to discuss the Existence school in general terms, but I will also elaborate my account of the Emptiness school with respect to matters I have more to talk about."[96] Chapter 3 is the longest chapter in the *Treatise*. It opens with a discussion of the Existence school's development of the doctrine of conditioned origination, in particular the role of seeds as the causal condition of mental and material dharmas, followed by Xiong's account of the five doctrinal deficiencies of the Existence school (see above). Next, he discusses the Emptiness school's three proofs for the doctrine of emptiness: by breaking material things down into atoms, the appearance of things is emptied; by breaking time down into instants, material appearances and mental appearances are both emptied; and by observing that it is because numerous conditions come together that dharmas arise (i.e., conditioned arising/origination) shows that dharmas have always been empty. This is followed by his critical assessment of the three proofs. Next is Xiong's commentary on verse 18 of Nāgārjuna's *Treatise on the Middle Way*, followed by an extended discussion of the following passage from the same text: "If one sees that all dharmas are produced from numerous conditions, then one will be able to see the Buddha's dharma body." The focus on the Emptiness school continues with a discussion of three teachings of the doctrine of emptiness—emptiness is non-existence; emptiness does not obstruct existents; and that dharma nature is empty—followed by Xiong's evaluation of the school's doctrine of emptiness, in which he concludes: "Even if it were to be said that the school's aim was to refute attachments, in its relentless and exhaustive refuting, it was still attached to the view of emptiness."[97] The chapter concludes with a reiteration of Xiong's non-duality of Reality and function thesis, followed by an evaluation of the Emptiness school's and the *Book of Change*'s respective views on the myriad phenomena and human life.

At the conclusion to Chapter 3, Xiong writes: "Next, I should elaborate on dharma characteristics. (The mental and the material are collectively called "dharma

---

[96] Idem, p. 62.
[97] Idem, p. 94.

characteristics.") This elaboration is roughly divided into two chapters: 'Forming Material Things' (成物) and 'Explaining Mind' (明心), and related in that order."[98] As already noted, "Explaining Mind" was not included in the 1958 edition of the *Treatise* but was subsequently published as a separate book in 1959. (It is actually longer than the entire *Treatise*.) The opening section of Chapter 4, "Forming Material Things," emphasizes the idea that "the myriad images of the cosmos are not the clustering of many, many atoms, but rather are an absolute and all-encompassing power's . . . differentiating to form the myriad particular entities" and that "Reality [實體] is also called Reality qua whole [全體] because it is perfectly complete and has no boundaries."[99] Next, the concepts of contraction and expansion and their mutual opposition and mutual completion are again taken up and discussed, as is their connection with Qian and Kun in the *Book of Change*. In the ensuing discussion of matter and energy, Xiong emphasizes that the *Book of Change* took Kun to be matter and energy (and Qian to be the pure and spirit-like), and that in ancient times "primal *qi*" (元氣) was also a name for matter and energy. We also learn that what *Zhongyong* 中庸 (Balance as the Norm) explains as being "so small that they cannot be broken apart" (小莫能破), and what Hui Shi 惠施 (fourth century BCE) called "the smallest ones" correspond with the theory of atoms. Xiong then distinguishes two referents for "the smallest ones": (1) things that unceasingly transform and change such that none abides even temporarily, and (2) when several of the "smallest ones" cluster together in a given locale such that they form a homogeneous, harmonious system, then this is called a "grouping of the smallest ones." Each of these "groupings of the smallest ones," in turn, independently clusters, and this is how all things come to be formed. He then turns to identify three major fallacies in "cosmological accounts of Reality" (宇宙論中談本體者): (1) seeking the absolute outside of the relative; (2) discussions of ontology in Western learning simply amount to the doctrine that there is no Reality (無體之論), as exemplified by the two antagonistic traditions of idealistic monism and material monism; and (3) material monism takes matter to be the sole origin of the myriad existents, with the pure and spirit-like becoming a biproduct. Turning next to the pure and spirit-like, Xiong proceeds to identify two of its unique features: (1) whereas matter has boundaries, the pure and spirit-like has no boundaries; and (2) the speed at which the pure and spirit-like operates cannot be measured. In a

---

[98] Idem, p. 104.
[99] Idem, pp. 106, 107.

conclusion directed at both idealistic monism and material monism, Xiong states: "Having outlined these two features, it is evident that the pure and spirit-like and matter absolutely lack similar features and so cannot be said to be in a cause-and-effect relationship."[100] This is followed by Xiong's account of the three major modifications undergone by living entities that enabled the pure and spirit-like to attain the means for it manifestly to express its own power: (1) transitioning from being fixed to moving (inorganic things to animals), (2) from moving in a crouched manner to standing erect, and (3) the structures of the nervous system and the brain increasingly became more compact and keener. The chapter concludes with some general remarks on the development of the cosmos and the role played by the principle of "manifesting that which was originally concealed."

---

[100] Idem, p. 132.

Foreword
Han Yuankai

When I was young, I moved away to Peking University to study, where I became a student of Mr Xiong from Huanggang 黃岡.[1] After two years, I returned to the south, tilling fields by myself in the Zi River (資江) region of Hunan. When not working, my sole enjoyments were the sound of springs and the beauty of mountains. Time has slipped away and suddenly I am now older than sixty. Having remained ignorant throughout my life I have never glimpsed the Great Way—bringing shame to my teacher. Recently, I learned that he has been frail and ill, living in Shanghai, away from his hometown. Having made the long trip to Shanghai to serve him, he presented me with a copy of his esteemed volume, *Treatise on Reality and Function*. Having pondered its contents repeatedly, I now make so bold as to declare: "He reaches to the vast and the great and fully reveals the fine and subtle."[2]

Mr Xiong's learning began with the two wheels of Mahāyāna Buddhism. (The Emptiness (空) school and the Existence (有) school[3] are like the two wheels on a chariot.[4]) The cosmologies of both schools distinguish "nature" and "characteristics."[5] The first is the dharma that neither arises nor ceases; what is called "suchness" (真如). It is dharma nature (法性).[6] (This like "Reality" [實體].) The second is dharmas that arise and cease, which are also called conditionally arisen dharmas (因緣法). These are dharma characteristics (法相). (This is like "phenomena.") Nature and characteristics are divided into the two realms of arising and ceasing and non-arising and non-ceasing. Ever since Buddhist teachings came East more than a thousand years ago, all venerable teachers

---

[1] Xiong first taught at Peking University between 1922 and 1924. As the following sentences makes clear, it must have been in that period that Han studied under Xiong.
[2] "Zhongyong" 中庸 (Balance as the Norm), *Liji* 禮記 (Book of Rites), Kong Yingda et al., comp., *Liji zhushu* 禮記註疏 (*Liji* with Annotations and Sub-commentary), 53.8b, *Shisan jing zhushu*: "Therefore by esteeming his virtuous nature the gentleman follows the path of enquiry and learning, reaching to the vast and the great and exhausting the fine and the subtle."
[3] See "Translator's Introduction."
[4] Mahāyāna (大乘) literally means "great vehicle/chariot."
[5] Short for dharma nature (法性) and dharma characteristics (法相): the true nature of things (suchness) and dependently arisen dharmas.
[6] The true nature of things; synonymous with suchness (真如; *tathatā*).

and mature persons of virtue have respectfully upheld this distinction. At first, Mr Xiong also did so but, in the end, he had doubts, and only then did he investigate freely. Looking upward and downward he observed and investigated Heaven and Earth; near at hand, he drew from his own person, further away, he drew from other things. Eventually, he spontaneously achieved comprehensive understanding. Having suddenly attained awakening through *Bian jing* 變經 (Book of Transformation), his inspirations grew increasingly grander and he began to admire just how long ago it has already been since these principles [in the *Book of Transformation*] were first elaborated by the sage [Confucius] (The *Yi jing* 易經 [Book of Change] is also called the *Book of Transformation*.) and so, returning to the fold of Confucius, he created and elucidated the tenet of "the non-duality of Reality (體) and function (用)." From then on, [it became clear that] there is nowhere that this tenet does not apply, be it in any of the six directions or any of the four seasons,[7] no matter how small or great, fine or coarse. This is why this treatise was written.

One matter I have tried to ponder is the following. In transforming into the myriad images of the cosmos, if it were not for Reality's (實體) having [two] opposing incipient tendencies (相反之幾), then by what means might transformation be accomplished? If it did not have a complex nature, how could it develop? Hence it can be understood that neither the philosophical monism of the idealists who speculate that the origin of the cosmos is purely
[p. 4]
the pure and spirit-like in nature (精神性) nor that of the materialists who speculate that the origin of the cosmos is purely matter in nature, is a doctrine that has deeply penetrated the root of principles (理根). (The origin of all existents, the root of the myriad principles, is what is called the "root of principles." See Guo Xiang's 郭象 [c. 252–312] *Zhuangzi zhu* 莊子注 [Notes to *Zhuangzi*].[8]) As such, it is hardly the case that this treatise by Mr Xiong merely serves to remedy the errors of the Buddhists! Every single word in this book speaks of Mr Xiong's experience. And just as there are Buddhist scriptures that encompass

---

[7] The six directions are the four cardinal directions and above and below. The six directions and four seasons can be understood as metaphors for space and time, respectively.

[8] In commenting on Zhuangzi's 莊子 (fl. fourth century BCE) statement about Lao Dao 老聃 (Laozi 老子; trad. sixth century BCE) in the "Tianxia" 天下 (All Under Heaven) chapter of *Zhuangzi*, "He takes the profound as his root," Guo Xiang comments: "The root of principles lies in the extremities of the Grand Primordium, which cannot be deemed shallow." Guo Qingfan 郭慶藩 (1844–1896), *Zhuangzi jishi* 莊子集釋 (Collected Commentaries on *Zhuangzi*) (Taipei: Muduo chubanshe, 1982), p. 1097. Hereafter, *Zhuangzi*.

immeasurable meanings in just a few words, so too this book is in that category.

Long separated from my teacher, I never thought that a dull-witted old man such as I would still be able personally to receive a copy of this sublime treatise. Now it is cold in Shanghai. "All through spring, the misty rain constantly caresses the tiles/For the whole day, the ethereal wind is unable to make the flag fly fully."[9] [So too,] the charm of this book lingers. With respect, this is my foreword. I also note that this book was transcribed by Mr Feng Yongzhuo 封用拙.[10] [Mr. Xiong] requested that two hundred copies be printed for preservation.[11] The Jiayin month of the Wuxu year of the Chinese calendar; Spring 1958 of the Common Era. Disciple Han Yuankai, old peasant from Nanyue 南嶽.

Addendum. I asked: "In this treatise, why do you term the myriad images[12] of the cosmos as 'function' (功用)?" Mr Xiong replied: " 'Function' refers to ceaseless production and reproduction; to incessant transformation and movement. The myriad images of the cosmos have always been nothing other than Reality's producing and reproducing without interruption, transforming and moving ceaselessly. It is not the case that Reality is like a mother and the myriad images are like her offspring, which become individuated. Accordingly, the myriad images are also termed function."[13]

---

[9] Li Shangyin 李商隱 (813–858), "Chong guo shengnü ci" 重過聖女祠 (Once More Passing the Shrine of a Goddess), in *Quan Tang shi* 全唐詩 (Complete Works of Tang Poetry) (Beijing: Zhonghua shuju, 1979), p. 6184.
[10] Feng Yongzhuo was Xiong's secretary from 1956 to 1966.
[11] See Xiong's letter to the editors at Kexue chubanshe 科學出版社 (China Science Publishing), dated January 7, 1958, available at https://auction.artron.net/paimai-art00573311604/.
[12] The myriad things.
[13] They are the functioning of Reality itself.

Superfluous Words

This work[1] was written specifically to solve the cosmological problem of the non-duality of Reality and function. (The Reality of the cosmos [宇宙實體] is abbreviated at *ti* 體. When Reality transforms and moves to then become the myriad images [萬象] of the cosmos, this is the functioning [功用] of Reality, abbreviated as *yong* 用. "The myriad images of the cosmos" is a generic term for all kinds of material [物質] and 'pure and spirit-like' [精神] phenomena.[2]) The meaning of Reality and function was first expounded in the *Book of Transformation*. (See the "Yuan nei sheng" 原內聖 [To the Origin of Inner Sageliness] chapter of my *Yuan Ru* 原儒 [To the Origin of the Ru].[3] In antiquity, the *Book of Change* was called the *Book of Transformation* because it elucidates the way of transformation.) All of the late Zhou period [1046–256 BCE] Confucians and masters (諸子) inherited *Da yi* 大易 [Great Change] and probed deeply into Reality and function. (The *Book of Change* is also called the *Great Change*.) In the main, the Confucians did not depart greatly from Confucius' original purport. (It was not, however, a case that they were unable to depart; this a matter I am unable to elaborate here.) The writings of the masters and the hundred schools must have been extremely abundant, but today there is no way to examine whether any dealt specifically with the topic of Reality and function. (Sima Tan 司馬談 [c. 165–110 BCE] said: "[The] scriptures and [attached] traditions of the six disciplines number to the thousands and ten-thousands."[4] On the basis of this, we can infer that a large school was associated with each of the masters, that their writings were definitely numerous, but those writings have [virtually] all disappeared. Wang Chuanshan 王船山 [1619–1692] despised the Qin for destroying learning.[5])

---

[1] This is Xiong Shili's author's preface.
[2] On p. 114, Xiong notes that "cosmos" is "the generic term for all mental and material dharmas."
[3] *Yuan Ru*, *Xiong Shili quanji*, vol. 6, pp. 599–600; 609–610.
[4] Cited by Sima Qian 司馬遷 (born c. 145 BCE), "Taishi gong zixu" 太史公自序 (Sequence of His Honor, the Grand Scribe's Own [History]), *Shiji* 史記 (Records of the Grand Scribe) (Beijing: Zhonghua shuju, 1983), 130.3290. Following Hans van Ess's translation in William Nienhauser Jr., ed., *The Grand Scribe's Records, Volume XI: The Memoirs of Han China, Part IV* (Bloomington and Nanjing: Indiana University Press and Nanjing University Press, 2019), p. 319. For van Ess's explanation of the title of this memoir, see p. 363. The six disciplines/six arts (六藝): *Rites, Music, Documents, Odes, Change,* and *Spring and Autumn Annals*.
[5] Xiong seems to be referencing Wang Chuanshan's (Fuzhi 夫之) comment about the collapse of "lineage models" (家法) in the Qin dynasty (although that notion properly applies to the Han dynasty rather than the Qin). See *Huang shu* 黃書 (Yellow Book), in Zeng Guofan 曾國藩 (1811–1872)

All that can be made use of are fragments of the Daoist writings of Laozi and Zhuangzi. Yet what they call the "Way" (A term for Reality.) still lacks true insight. I will cite a few examples of their errors. Laozi talked [of the Way] as "being formed of a composite," and they took nothingness as fundamental[6]—this is their first great error. (See the "Yuan nei sheng" chapter of my *To the Origin of the Ru*.[7]) Laozi and Zhuangzi both maintained that the Way transcends the ten thousand things. ("The ten thousand things" includes Heaven and Earth and humans. The "Tianxia" 天下 [All under Heaven] chapter of *Zhuangzi* states that Laozi and Guan Yin 關尹 [trad. sixth century BCE] both made *Taiyi* 太一 the main principle.[8] *Taiyi* means absolute, and is a term used to refer to the Way. Although Laozi opposed the notion of an Emperor of Heaven, he nevertheless took the Way to be the absolute, to be the ruler of the myriad things, which is tantamount to an Emperor of Heaven in a different guise. Zhuangzi said: "Although it seems as if there is a true ruler, there is a singular lack of any sign of its presence."[9] Although the phrase "Although it seems as if there is" deliberately raises doubt, the intent is no different from that of Laozi.) If one truly understands that Reality and function are non-dual, then it will be understood that the Way is "the itself" (自身) of the ten thousand things. It is surely not the case that there is a *Taiyi* or a True Ruler

[p. 6]

above the myriad things. This is their second error. (If it is understood that Reality and function are non-dual, then it is patently evident that "the itself" of a grain of sand is the great Way. If even a grain of sand is so large that there is nothing outside it, then all the more so is this the case for humans! In exclaiming how small humans are, Zhuangzi certainly did not understand that Reality and function are non-dual.) The Daoists had a preponderant bias to look within emptiness and stillness (虛靜)[10] to grasp the Way. This is the diametrical opposite of the *Great Change*, which guides people by means of the functions of robustness and vigor, and transformation and movement, enabling them thereby to awaken to Reality. Thus, in

---

and Zeng Guoquan 曾國荃 (1824–1890), comps., *Chuanshan yishu* 船山遺書 (Surviving Writings of Wang Fuzhi) (Jinling: 1865), 35.4b.

[6] Paraphrasing Sima Tan, in *Shiji*, 130.3292.

[7] See *Yuan Ru*, pp. 590–591. My translation of *hun cheng* 混成 in *Dao de jing* 道德經 (The Classic of the Way and Its Power), *zhang* 25, is based on Xiong's gloss in *Yuan Ru*.

[8] "Taking the root as essence, and things as dross; regarding accumulation as deficiency; and dwelling with the numinous in indifferent solitude—such were the techniques of the Way in antiquity. When Guan Yin and Lao Dan heard of these techniques they delighted in them, establishing them to maintain [the idea of] constant nothingness and making Taiyi (太一) the main principle." *Zhuangzi*, p. 1093.

[9] "Qi wu lun" 齊物論 (Discourse on Making All Things Equal), *Zhuangzi*, p. 55.

[10] Here "stillness" is being used in a disparaging sense. As the "Buddhist Teachings, A" chapter makes clear, for Xiong "stillness" can have a positive sense.

employing submissive weakness to serve as function, even though Laozi was outraged by the ruling class, he did not dare to put "the whole world" (天下) first and was unwilling to mount a revolution. This is their third great error. It is indeed the case that Daoist cosmology failed to be thoroughgoing [in its investigation] of Reality and function. Although there are many of Zhuangzi's subtle phrases scattered [in various writings], the theses he holds are, on the whole, untenable. Zhuangzi was gifted, but with respect to the Way, he was still at some remove.

Of the late Zhou masters, it is only the Daoists who can be investigated to some degree. Although Mozi's 墨子 [fifth to fourth centuries BCE] writings are mostly no longer extant, nevertheless from the essays in the "Tian zhi" 天志 (Heaven's Will) [triad of chapters in the book *Mozi* (Master Mo)] we are able to know that Mozi's writings had nothing to do with cosmology. None of Hui Shi's 惠施 [fourth century BCE] writings are extant, which is most regrettable.

Someone inquired about the following: "Sir, in your writings you posit the tenet that Reality and function are non-dual. Nevertheless, you talk only about Reality's transforming and moving to become function, and do not explain what Reality's properties are."

I replied: "With regard to Reality's transforming and moving to become function, it is only in function that the properties of Reality can be grasped. You should understand that function has such properties as the pure and spirit-like, matter and energy—these are the properties of Reality. What is the reason? It is because Reality is the itself of function. Take the analogy of how the numerous waves have such properties as wetness and motility. These are precisely the properties of the ocean, because the ocean is the itself of the numerous waves. If, separated from function, you wanted to look for the properties of Reality (This sort of error is like wanting to look for the properties of the ocean separated from the numerous waves.), you would certainly find nothing. (There is no Reality separated from function. Where would you go to look for the properties of Reality? This is analogous to there being no ocean that is apart from the numerous waves. Where else [other than the waves] would you look for the properties of the ocean?) Having not found anything, you give rein to the imagination. This is almost like the Prajñā (般若; [Perfection of] Wisdom) scholars who say that Reality (實相)[11] is quiescent extinction, or the Mahāyāna Existence school masters who say that suchness is without arising, without creating, constant,

---

[11] This technical term is synonymous with suchness, dharma nature, *nirvāṇa*, the unconditioned, and so forth.

and unmoving. If you were to understand fully that Reality and function are non-dual then you would certainly believe that separated from function there is no Reality that can be spoken of. If you were still in doubt, I would certainly give you thirty blows!" (In order to motivate people, Chan masters used a staff to strike them.)

[p. 7]

The book is actually a revision of my old work, *Xin weishi lun* 新唯識論 (New Treatise on the Uniqueness of Consciousness). (The abbreviated title is *New Treatise*.) There are two editions of the *New Treatise*. The first, a literary edition, was written when I was ill, and is very brief. The second, a vernacular edition, was written at a time of national calamity when I was in exile [in Sichuan]. Now that this new book has been completed, both versions of the *New Treatise* can be destroyed and discarded, as there is no need to preserve them. (When I was about to reach [the age of still] being disliked, I began to turn to learning. <*Lunyu* 論語 (Analects) says: "The Master said, 'If by the age of forty a man is still disliked there is no hope for him.'"[12]> Reading, thinking, and sitting for long periods without getting up became normal. I slept little at night, and then had acute neurasthenia, and severe spermatorrhea. For an extended period from when I was forty to fifty-two, everyday [there was a period in which] I refused to speak. If I spoke up to about ten sentences, then I would spontaneously emit semen. Later, I discarded my books and reflected on my thoughts. By the time I was fifty-three or fifty-four, the suffering from spermatorrhea gradually eased, until at sixty-five I began to be free of this suffering completely. During my life, I have not dared to write books. Occasionally, I have casually drafted some small pamphlets. The vernacular edition of the *New Treatise* was written when in exile[13] and is excessively careless. The reason it was previously published is because it contains the fundamental teaching of "the non-duality of Reality and function." Now that this small pamphlet [*Ti yong lun*] has been completed, the *New Treatise* should be discarded. The *Book of Change* is the main authority for my learning, and I have posited "the non-duality of Reality and function" as the tenet of that learning. In regard to function, the mind actively "opens up the development of things" [開物].[14] This is the great

---

[12] *Lunyu* 17.26, D. C. Lau, trans., *The Analects* (Harmondsworth: Penguin, 1979), p. 148. On the angle brackets < >, see the note on p. 12.

[13] Xiong was based in Sichuan from early 1938 to early 1946.

[14] "Xici, shang" 繫辭上 (Attached Statements, A), *Zhou yi*, 7.26b. Here, "the mind" is a reference to "the pure and spirit-like" (精神), both of which are associated with expansion (闢): "Expansion perpetually unfolds yet does not lose the vigor of Reality, and so expansion is simply referred to as the mind.... Expansion is the great mind of the cosmos—it is also called the great generative vitality of the cosmos." See Chapter 1, pp. 28, 31. On contraction and expansion, see "Translators' Introduction."

significance of [the operations of] Qian 乾 and Kun 坤.[15] There are absolutely no points of similarity with the Buddhist doctrine of "nothing but consciousness" [唯識 (*vijñaptimātra*)].[16] There is no need to preserve the *New Treatise*.)

The chapters "Buddhist Teachings, A" and "Buddhist Teachings, B" in this book evaluate Mahāyāna learning, in particular paying detailed attention to the Emptiness school. My life of learning began with Mahāyāna. In the late Qing dynasty, after the Boxer Uprising [1899–1901], portents of the collapse of Chinese culture had already arrived. I felt very deeply about this. In my youth I took part in revolution,[17] but realizing that I had no talent for such practical undertakings I then wanted to focus solely on studying Chinese philosophical thought. Finding no affinity for the paths of either Han Learning or Song Learning,[18] I turned to the Six Classics in pursuit of this thought but, at the time, I was unable to discern that the Six Classics were in disarray [having been corrupted, and their true meaning] obscured by commentaries and annotations. I even went so far as to slander the Six Classics as books that served to protect the imperial system. I then became inclined to the path of Buddhist learning, beginning directly with the Mahāyāna Existence school's doctrine of nothing but consciousness (唯識論). Before long I set aside the Existence school to study the Mahāyāna Emptiness school, for which I formed a deep affinity. After some time, however, I no longer dared to regard observing emptiness (觀空)[19] to be [a doctrinal tenet] I could commit myself to. Later, after seeking within myself, I suddenly became awakened through [reading] the *Great Change*. As for the meaning of "Reality and function," when I examined it in the light of the *Book of Transformation*, I became even more free of doubts. From this point on, I knew where to return to. (Returning to the fold of Confucius.) Nevertheless, my thought has certainly benefited from the inspiration I have received from both the Emptiness and the Existence

---

[15] Chapter 4, pp. 226, 234: "The significance of Qian and Kun in the *Great Change* is that Qian is the pure and spirit-like, Kun is matter, but it is Qian that is active.... The pure and spirit-like is active in opening-up the development of things.... The *Great Change* takes Qian to be the pure and spirit-like and Kun to be matter and energy."

[16] For explanations of this technical term, see the "Introduction" to Makeham, ed., *Transforming Consciousness*, p. 22.

[17] Xiong participated in the 1911 Revolution but his participation in the anti-Qing revolutionary movements started in the early years of the new century; see Yu Sang, *Xiong Shili's Understanding of Reality and Function, 1920–1937* (Boston: Brill, 2020), pp. 13–16.

[18] On the Han Learning and Song Learning distinction, see my *Transmitters and Creators: Chinese Commentators and Commentaries on the Analects* (Cambridge, MA: Harvard University Asia Center, 2008), pp. 277–280.

[19] In Chapter 2, p. 89, Xiong writes: "What does 'observing emptiness' mean? It means that there should be no deluded attachment to any dharma. 'Emptiness' simply means the emptying of deluded attachments."

schools. If I had not started with these two schools, I would certainly not have come to understand how to think for myself, and so what could I have followed in order to awaken and enter (悟入) [true cognition of] the *Book of Transformation*? Because this book [the *Treatise*] is quite detailed about Buddhist doctrines, I have explained my background. ("Background" here refers to the origins of my learning and to my experiences.)

[p. 8]

The observation of emptiness in *Da bore* 大般若 (*Da bore jing* 大般若經 [Perfection of Wisdom Sutra][20] is revered by the Emptiness school as its most fundamental sutra.) is profound, extremely profound, "emptying" all the way down. The observation of existents in the *Great Change* is profound, extremely profound, exhausting the marvels of existents. (*Change* has the Guan 觀 [Observing] hexagram and the Dayou 大有 [Great Existents] hexagram. The Guan hexagram talks about observing life, ceaseless production and reproduction, about how the great existents come to be.[21]) The observation of emptiness and the observation of existents represent human wisdom's highest level of development. It is only by having comprehensively and deeply observed the cosmos and human life that the understanding of either the Emptiness school or the Existence school was made possible. Sacrificing human life to the various self-centered desires of the small self is like a cicada making a cocoon to tie itself up or a spider making a web to restrain itself. How difficult it is for people to understand that the cosmos and human life are inherently empty. There are some people of little knowledge, who, upon hearing about emptiness, slander Buddhism—I have often seen them show no awareness of their own limitations. (They are unaware of their limited capabilities.) Emptiness is certainly not a product of subjective illusion. As Tao Yuanming 陶淵明 [c. 365–427] said in one of his poems: "Human life is inherently illusory and ultimately returns to emptiness."[22] It is my belief that particular things, even the largest such as the cosmos, ultimately must perish. In talking about emptiness with respect to particular things, the Buddhists are not at all talking nonsense.

---

[20] *Da bore boluomiduo jing* 大般若波羅蜜多經 (*Mahāprajñāpāramitā-sūtra*; T220), a collection of sixteen sutras.

[21] In "Buddhist Teachings, B," p. 156, Xiong writes that the Dayou hexagram "acclaims the abundance of the cosmos' myriad images (萬象)." In *Ming xin pian*, p. 278, Xiong explicitly confirms that the term *you* in "Dayou" refers to the myriad things (and not to the more abstract notion of "existence").

[22] A modified version of a line in the fourth of six poems listed under the title "Gui yuan tian ju" 歸園田居 (Returning to Live in the Countryside) in Wang Yao 王瑤 ed., *Tao Yuanming ji* 陶淵明集 (*Tao Yuanming's Collected Writings*) (Beijing: Zuojia chubanshe, 1956), p. 37.

Someone asked: "Acknowledging that the cosmos and human life truly exist is common knowledge shared by everyone. The cosmological views of philosophers are also all based on common knowledge. As such, surely the observation of existents in the *Great Change* is certainly not different from the cosmological views of philosophers?"

I replied: "No, no, that is not the case. If you do not make a clear distinction here, not only will you have insulted the words of the sage [Confucius], I am really afraid that this would also show that you have severed your eye of wisdom (慧眼).[23] The existents observed by the sage are the True Realm (真際) that is naturally inherent in the cosmos and human life. The sage directly merged with the-whole-that-is-Reality and its great function (全體大用) ("The-whole-that-is-Reality" refers to the Reality of the cosmos. "Great function" refers to Reality's transforming into great function. The myriad things have always been the same Reality and the same function as the cosmos; only the sage was able personally to merge with Reality and function.); he regarded the myriad things in Heaven and Earth as one with himself, and the worries and troubles [of others] as being the same as his own; and he had none of the deluded attachments of the small self. Calm and at ease, he flowed everywhere with Great Transformation. ("Calm and at ease": see the *Analects*.[24]) Rare indeed is it for the existents explained by philosophy not to be the existents to which the inversions of ordinary people (世間顛倒) are attached. How could philosophy and the learning of the sage be talked about in the same breath!?"

Although the auto-comments in this book may seem to be prolix, it is better to err on the side of being prolix than it is to be elliptic. In *Yaojiang xue'an* 姚江學案 (Case Studies of Wang Yangming) there is the phrase, "As for Reality, *it* is function; as for function, *it* is Reality (即體即用、即用即體).[25] In the past I have met intelligent people who all maintain that these

---

[23] Here the term is being used in a non-technical sense to mean capacity for correct discernment.

[24] *Lunyu* 7.36: "The true gentleman is calm and at ease; the Small Man is fretful and ill at ease." Translation by Arthur Waley, *The Analects of Confucius* (London: Allen and Unwin, 1938), p. 131.

[25] Paraphrase of a passage by Wang Yangming 王陽明 (1442–1529), *Chuan xi lu* 傳習錄 (Record of Practicing What Has Been Transmitted), *Wang Yangming quanji* 王陽明全集 (Complete Works of Wang Yangming), 2 vols. (Shanghai: Shanghai guji chubanshe, 1992), vol. 1, p. 31. "As for Reality, function is determined by Reality; as for function, Reality is [manifest] as function. This is what is meant by, 'Reality and function are a single source.'" (即體而言，用在體；即用而言，體在用。是謂體用一源。) (Xiong cites the original version of the passage in Chapter 2, p. 85. My translation is informed by Xiong's comments at *Xin weishi lun* [vernacular edition; 1944], pp. 239–240 and *Xin weishi lun* [abridged edition; 1952], p. 120). A related passage is found in Wang Yangming, "Da Wang Shitan Neihan" 答汪石潭內翰 (Reply to Wang Shitan, Drafter in the Office of the Grand Secretariat), *Wang Yangming quanji*, vol. 1, p. 146: "'Reality and function are a single source': knowing that whereby Reality is function then one will know that whereby function is Reality." (夫體用一源也。知體之所以爲用則知用之所以爲體者也。)

phrases are easy to understand, but I knew that they most certainly did not. I would interrogate them: "The two terms Reality and function

[p. 9]

in both phrases are interchangeable. In talking about Reality and function in these phrases, what is it that is termed Reality and what is it that is termed function? As for the two *ji* 即 terms in each phrase, is their meaning reduplicated in each phrase or do they each have their own distinct meaning in each phrase?" Dumbstruck, they would be unable to answer.

In the past, there was a highly talented student at Peking University who came to see me to discuss the Chan notion that it is in [everyday] functions that the nature is seen (作用見性).[26] In the course of discussion, he cited a large number of Chan sayings. I interrogated him: "What does 'functions' mean? What does 'the nature' mean? What does it mean to say that 'it is in functions that the nature is seen'?" He became alarmed. I have taught for many years and am deeply familiar with the habits of students. Having undertaken to carry on and further develop the work of the former sages, I dare not fail to devote myself fully to the task. There is no shortage of people who are fond of learning and who ponder matters deeply—as such, one should not blame an old man for being finicky.

There are some who have said that long comments should be moved out of the main text; that the flow of the text should not be interrupted. The reason I have not adopted their suggestions is that if one does not search for the meaning when reading, but merely savors the style of writing, then this is just the same as not reading.

The auto-commentary inserted within the main text is marked by square brackets [].[27] Sub-comments in the auto-commentary are marked by these symbols 「 」.[28] This is the same as in *To the Origin of the Ru*, but in that work I did not provide an explanation, and I received a lot of letters asking about the symbols. I note this here.

Early winter, Dingyou year of the Xia calendar; 20 November, 1957, Xiong Shili, recorded at the Guanhai 觀海 Pavilion, Shenjiang 申江.

---

[26] The idea that performing routine mundane activities is itself to perceive the nature—our inherent buddha nature.
[27] These have been substituted with parentheses (round brackets) ().
[28] These have been substituted with angle brackets < >.

I began writing the draft of *Treatise on Reality and Function* in the autumn of 1956, which triggered both the vascular sclerosis and heart disease I have long suffered, leaving me feeling that my brain was empty. The doctor of traditional Chinese medicine said that this was due to anemia. In gratitude to the friends who urged me to stop writing, I wrote the following poem, titled "Ten Thousand Things":

The ten thousand things all pass away,
How can my life abide for long?
I have not achieved half the tasks I set my mind to,
Leaving a deficiency in Heaven and Earth.
What can be done to remedy this deficiency?
Surely it will have to await those who will come after me.
Looking back on the past, it too is hazy and obscure.
Alas, I am only hurting myself.
I must deal with this by having nothing that I need rely on,
Leisurely abandoning myself to Heaven's constancy.
Alas! I am still riding on the wind;
It is deluded, and so too am I.

Notes. I have not achieved half the tasks I set my mind to (In my youth it was my ambition to take humaneness as my burden,[29] but I quickly became debilitated. I was not even able to hold a pen to write down any of the thoughts and feelings I wanted to express.), leaving a deficiency in heaven-and-earth. (An old treatise states: "Heaven is deficient in the North-West; Earth is deficient in the South-East."[30] In the North-West of China there are many tall mountains that obscure Heaven and when Heaven loses its lofty
[p. 10]
brilliance then it is deficient. The South-East is near to the sea and suffers from bogginess. This is where the Earth is deficient.) **Heaven's constancy.** (Heaven means "self-so" [自然]. Constancy refers to its being a norm.) **Alas! I am still riding the wind.** (Zhuangzi

---

[29] Allusion to *Lunyu* 8.7.
[30] "Dili zhi" 地理志 (Treatise on Geography), Fang Xuanling 房玄齡 et al., comps., *Jinshu* 晉書 (Book of Jin) (Beijing: Zhonghua shu ju, 1974), p. 409. For related passages in other early texts, see Yao Zhihua 姚治華, "*Taiyi sheng shui* yu Taiyi Jiugong zhan 《太乙生水》與太乙九宮占 (*The Great Unity Generates Water* and the Divination [Method] of "The [Circulation of the] Great Unity in the Nine Palaces"), in Pang Pu 龐樸 ed., *Gumu xinzhi* 古墓新知 (New Knowledge from Ancient Tombs) (Taipei: Taiwan guji chubanshe, 2002), pp. 51, 54–57.

said that Liezi soared around riding the wind.[31] In saying that he depended on the wind is to say that he was not yet able to be without that which he depended on. Zhuangzi said: "Has human life always been so deluded?"[32] *Mang* 芒 [=茫] means confusion [惑]. Being in decline, I have not been able to elaborate on the *Book of Change*, and so must look to talented persons in the future to do so. Just as Liezi's riding the wind is a case of his having been deluded, so too I am deluded. Is human life inherently unable to resist succumbing to delusion?)

---

[31] "Xiao yao you" 逍遙遊 (Free and Easy Wandering), *Zhuangzi*, p. 17; Burton Watson, trans., *The Complete Works of Chuang-tzu* (New York: Columbia University Press, 1968), p. 32. "Lieh Tzu could ride the wind and go soaring around with cool and breezy skill, but after fifteen days he came back to earth. As far as the search for good fortune went, he didn't fret and worry. He escaped the trouble of walking, but he still had to depend on something to get around. If he had only mounted on the truth of Heaven and Earth, ridden the changes of the six breaths, and thus wandered through the boundless, then what would he have had to depend on? Therefore, I say, the Perfect Man has no self; the Holy Man has no merit; the Sage has no fame."

[32] "Qi wu lun," *Zhuangzi*, p. 56.

1
Explaining Transformation

In ancient times, Indian Buddhists called all mental and material phenomena "*xing* 行." The word *xing* 行 has two senses: passing flow and appearance.[1] They held that moment by moment, mental and material phenomena are on the long path of transformation and flow. (Just as the old ceases, the new arises—this is called transformation. The passing of the old and the arising of the new is continuous and uninterrupted, and, accordingly, they are said to flow.) They are not immutable, firmly abiding things—thus accounting for the sense of passing flow. Even though mental and material phenomena pass and flow unceasingly, they also have appearances that deceptively manifest. For example, in flashing lightning there is the deceptive appearance of images of redness—thus accounting for the sense of appearance. The appearances of material phenomena can be sensed. The appearances of mental phenomena cannot be sensed by the sense faculties but internally one can be aware of them. Because mental and material phenomena have the above two senses, they are both named *xing*. Because this term [conveys these two senses] with great veracity I will also use it.

The Buddhists' attitude to all phenomena is undoubtedly based on their attitude to human life being that of transcending birth [and death] (超生). *Chaosheng* 超生 means to transcend birth and death; it corresponds to "transcending the mundane world" (出世). (See *Ci'en zhuan* 慈恩傳 [Biography of Xuanzang].[2]) The Buddhists discern impermanence (無常) in all phenomena. "Discern" (觀) has the senses of "to illuminate" and "to examine intensely." The term *wu* 無 in *wuchang* 無常 means "does not have." The term *chang* 常 means "permanence." [The Buddhists] discern that all phenomena are impermanent. That is to say, that which is discerned in all material phenomena is impermanence and that which is discerned in all mental phenomena is

---

[1] Inter alia, the term *xing* translates the Sanskrit terms *saṃskāra*, *ākāra*, *carya*, and *pratipad*. *Saṃskāra* refers to conditioned phenomena; and *ākāra* can refer to both appearance and defining activity. *Carya* and *pratipad* have senses associated with movement, travel, carrying out.

[2] "Jing Da Ci'en Si Shi Xuanzang zhuan" 京大慈恩寺釋玄奘傳 (Biography of Master Xuanzang of the Da ci'en Temple in the Capital), Daoxuan 道宣 (596–667), comp., *Xu Gaoseng zhuan* 續高僧傳 (Biographies of Eminent Monks, Continued), T2060.50, 455c7.

impermanence. Accordingly, it is said that all phenomena are impermanent. Only by undertaking this method of discernment can one be free of defiled attachment to any phenomenon and thereby transcend the ocean of birth and death. This is the fundamental tenet of Buddhism. (The Buddhists say that the mundane world is the ocean of birth and death, and that human life is pitiful because it is drowning in that ocean.[3]) Therefore, when the Buddhists talk about impermanence, the attitude toward phenomena is one of censure. In this book, my discussions of transformation serve to show that all phenomena are without self-entity (自體). While the purport may seemingly be compatible with the Buddhist claim that phenomena are impermanent,

[p. 12]

in fact, there is a world of difference. When the Buddhists claim that all phenomena are impermanent, their aim is to censure. In this book, however, [my claim] is that instant by instant, all phenomena are just arising and ceasing, ceasing and arising, in a dynamic succession (綿綿) of uninterrupted transformation. (*Mianmian* 綿綿 means "succession." This is because, instant by instant, the prior extinguishes and the succeeding arises, uninterrupted.) Based on this view of the cosmos, human life can only advance and ascend; and with regard to phenomena, there is nothing to censor nor is there that to which there can be defiled attachment. These are the fundamentals [of this book], which in no way resemble [the Buddhists'] teaching of transcending the mundane world. ("Arising and ceasing, ceasing and arising" means that all phenomena, at every instant, cease as soon as they arise, and arise as soon as they cease.)

The principle of transformation

As stated above, all mental and material phenomena lack self-entity, and the cosmos is nothing other than transformation (變化) and secret movement. (*Bianhua* 變化 is henceforth abbreviated as *bian* 變.) The new arises ever anew, the old passes away and does not remain. Is it not a marvel!? Now, there are two major questions that await to be answered. First, is there that which is able to transform? Second, how is this transformation accomplished? Let me start with the first question. I maintain that there is no harm in provisionally positing that the Reality of the cosmos is able to transform. How do we

---

[3] See, for example, *Shou lengyan jing* 首楞嚴經 (*Śūraṃgama-sūtra*; Sutra on Heroic Progress), T945.19, 111b10–12.

know that there is such a Reality? Because the myriad transformations are not generated from nothing. It is like the numerous waves (漚)[4]—if there were no ocean then they could not arise. ("The numerous waves" is employed as an analogy for the myriad transformations. "The ocean" is employed as an analogy for Reality.) Logically, it certainly could not be established that non-existence gives rise to existents. (A crucial point.)

Conventional presumptions about non-existence (無) can broadly be divided into two kinds: specific and general. An example of a general presumption about non-existence would be the presumption that the Supreme Void (太虛)[5] is utterly empty, and that this is what is called non-existence. Those who make such a presumption are greatly deluded and misled, and their presumption does not constitute a reliable basis of evidence. The Supreme Void includes the myriad existents, hence the characteristic of existents is not different from [the Supreme] void, and the characteristic of [the Supreme] void is not different from existents. It has never been the case that these are two characteristics (相) that can be separated (*Xiang* 相 means characteristic. The "two characteristics" are [the Supreme] Void and existents.) and yet convention makes the false presumption that there is a great, empty, non-existent realm, which is called the Supreme Void. Apart from the profoundly deluded, who would believe this? Hence, a general presumption about non-existence is completely in error.

Those who make specific presumptions about non-existence say that for each and every phenomenon (事) and principle (理) there are times when a presumption can be made that they are non-existent. For example, when I fled the [Japanese] bandits and entered Sichuan,[6] I did not take a single book

---

[4] The standard meaning of *ou* 漚 is foam or bubbles. Xiong, however, employed the term to refer to waves, as is evident from descriptions such as "the numerous incessantly leaping waves" (騰躍不住的眾漚) at *Ti yong lun*, p. 161—neither froth nor bubbles "leap." Also, Xiong's erstwhile disciple, Mou Zongsan 牟宗三 (1909–1995), explicitly confirms that by *hai ou* 海漚 Xiong meant waves (海漚就是小波浪). See Mou Zongsan, *Zhuangzi* "Qi wu lun" *jiangyan lu (5)* 莊子〈齊物論〉講演錄（五）(Lectures on *Zhuangzi*, "Discourse on Making All Things Equal" [5]), *Ehu yuekan* 鵝湖月刊 323 (2002.5): 4.

[5] At *Ming xin pian*, p. 286, Xiong describes Supreme Void as follows: "The Supreme Void is still and vacant, hence it is said to be empty." See also *Dao de jing* (=*Laozi*), *zhang* 25: "There is something inchoately formed, born before Heaven and Earth. Still and vacant, depending on nothing and unchanging. Circulating, it does not tire. One may take it as the mother of all under Heaven." Wang Bi's 王弼 (226–249) annotation states: " 'Still and vacant' means having no form." See Wang Bi, *Laozi Dao de jing zhu* 老子道德經注 (*Laozi's Classic of the Way and Its Power* Annotated) in Lou Yulie 樓宇烈, ed., *Wang Bi ji jiaoshi* 王弼集校釋 (Wang Bi's Collected Writings Collated and Annotated) (Beijing: Zhonghua shuju, 1980), vol. 1, p. 63.

[6] After the Marco Polo Bridge Incident in July 1937, Xiong fled Peking, eventually arriving in Sichuan in Spring 1938.

that previously had been regularly available to me. Every time I wanted read a particular book I was unable to do so. At times such as these one could say that a particular book is non-existent. Let's take another example: the many principles discussed by scholars, whether in ancient times or today. If, after having applied myself to ponder it, there is a particular principle that I am unable to accept, then it can be said that such a principle is non-existent. All these kinds of presumption belong to the category of specific presumptions about non-existence.

Quite a few people have remarked that it is certainly not the case that specific presumptions about non-existence [mean that the object of the presumption]
[p. 13]
is actually non-existent. For example, if a particular book is not by my side one may not yet say that it is non-existent because perhaps the book does exist in some other location. Or take the other example of a certain principle that someone is unable to believe—this might be because that person was of limited intelligence and unable to grasp the principle. As such, this does not mean that the principle is certainly non-existent. I think that this kind of explanation is one-sided. Even if a particular book exists in some other location, with reference to its specifically being by my side, it is certainly non-existent. As for the principle example, there is no doubt that many people will make the false presumption that a certain principle is non-existent because they do not understand the principle. Indeed, there are also many principles in ancient and modern times that, when all is said and done, are foolish nonsense, and which actually do not exist. For example, in the past, poor people took it as a matter of course that they should serve their exploiters, whereas these days it is universally acknowledged that such a principle does not exist. There are countless such examples. Therefore, there does exist that which specific presumptions about non-existence refer to as non-existent,[7] and this should not be rejected as baseless.

As for a general presumption about non-existence [such as the example cited above], which holds that Supreme Void exists but that it has always been empty, devoid of content, it is nearly always this [thesis] that is the source of the illusion that existents are generated from non-existence. This fabrication by false discrimination must be critiqued. Hitherto, those who have upheld the nothingness (虛無) thesis can broadly be divided into two groups: the

---

[7] That is, there is a sense in which non-existence does exist.

extremists and the non-extremists. On the one hand, on the basis of common knowledge, the non-extremists did not deny that the myriad things in the cosmos truly exist, yet, on the other hand, being unable fully to realize intrinsic Reality, they made the false presumption that existents are generated from non-existence. Most of the figures associated with Dark Learning (玄學) in the Wei-Jin period[8] belong to this group. Their doctrines probably began with [those of] Laozi. (Zhang Hengqu 張橫渠 [1020–1077] named Heaven as the Supreme Void and [held that] the transformation of *qi* 氣 relies upon the Supreme Void to arise—this is also [an example of] the doctrine that existents are generated from non-existence.[9])

As for the extremists, not only did they contravene true principle (正理), but they also contravened common knowledge. In not acknowledging that the myriad images of the cosmos actually exist they contravened common knowledge—moreover, they did so brazenly. In also not acknowledging the existence of intrinsic Reality they contravened true principle. Since their doctrine has no Reality, therefore there is no function. Although their perspective was muddled and in error the doctrine they upheld is consistent. In China, no one has ever advocated this kind of thinking. In ancient India, there were non-Buddhist nihilists who maintained that everything is empty (空). Buddhist scriptural texts strenuously refuted them, showing no leniency, even going so far as to claim that it would be preferable to embrace the [extreme] view of the existence of inherent selfhood (我見) [with a conviction]

---

[8] *Xuanxue*: dark/obscure/mysterious/abstruse/profound learning. As I have noted elsewhere: "Wang Bi 王弼 (226–49), He Yan [何晏 (ca. 190–249)], and Guo Xiang 郭象 (d. 312) are typically identified as *xuanxue* thinkers by modern scholars. *Xuanxue* thought might loosely be described as discussions of, and writings on, such abstract philosophical concepts as 'to initiate no action' (*wu wei* 無為), 'emptiness' (*xu* 虛), 'one and the many' (*yiduo* 一多), 'root and branches' (*benmo* 本末), and the 'emotional responses' (*qing* 情) and 'pattern' (*li* 理). The trouble with such a description is that thinkers less readily identifiable as *xuanxue* thinkers also addressed many of these themes and concepts." See my *Transmitters and Creators*, p. 25, n. 6.

[9] Zhang Hengqu is Zhang Zai 張載. These assertions are problematic. Xiong is probably referring to Zhang's statement in the "Taihe" 太和 (Great Harmony) chapter of his *Zhengmeng* 正蒙 (Correcting Youthful Ignorance): "From the Supreme Void, there is the name 'Heaven'; from the transformation of *qi*, there is the name 'the Way.'" (由太虛，有天之名；由氣化，有道之名。) See Lin Lechang 林樂昌 comp., *Zhengmeng hejiao jishi, shang* 正蒙合校集釋，上 (*Correcting Youthful Ignorance* with Combined Collations and Collected Interpretations, Part A) (Beijing: Zhonghua shuju, 2012), p. 60. This does not, however, seem to be a statement of identity between the Supreme Void and Heaven, nor is it consistent with the claim that the transformation of *qi* relies upon the Supreme Void. As for Xiong's implication that Zhang Zai maintained that *qi* is a product of the Supreme Void, this is inconsistent with Zhang's view that the Supreme Void is simply a mode of *qi*: "The condensation and dispersion of *qi* in the Supreme Void is analogous to the solidification of ice in water. When one knows that the Supreme Void is simply *qi* itself, one sees that there cannot be nothingness (*wu*)." (This last passage is the translation of JeeLoo Liu in *Neo-Confucianism: Metaphysics, Mind, and Morality* [Hoboken: Wiley-Blackwell, 2017], pp. 70, 72, slightly mod. This passage is also from the "Great Harmony" chapter, *Zhengming hejiao jishi, shang*, p. 50.)

as immense as Mt Sumeru[10] rather than self-conceitedly uphold the view that everything is empty (空見).[11] As everyone knows, the Buddhists talk non-stop about refuting the view of the existence of inherent selfhood, and so for them [to go so far as] to talk like this about the non-Buddhist view of emptiness it is evident that they deemed it to be ultimate delusion. In sum, the cosmos is real and replete, everlasting and ceaseless. Scholars must not descend into nothingness, fostering frivolous conceptual elaboration (戲論). [p. 14]

There are also many philosophers who acknowledge that the myriad images of the cosmos objectively exist yet are unwilling to acknowledge that there is Reality (實體), with some even detesting any mention of ontology (本體論). (Although *shiti* 實體 and *benti* 本體 differ in one character, their meaning is the same. *Ben* 本: because it has always existed it is also the "itself" [自身] of the myriad things. *Shi* 實 refers to its being true and real.) This view and the view of those in ancient India who upheld the doctrine of non-causality are both superficial views. I maintain that of course the cosmos has a true source and that the myriad existents do not suddenly arise. It is analogous to being at the edge of the ocean, carefully observing the multitude of waves—the old passes away and does not remain; the new arises ever anew. It should be understood that each and every wave-image has the ocean as its true source. Confucius' exclamation when standing by a river[12] [was on account of] his discerning the true and the constant (真常) as he watched the passing water. Only the most exalted sages can achieve such wondrous and heavenly-inspired awakening. If one acknowledges only that the myriad things of the cosmos really exist but does not acknowledge that there is intrinsic Reality, then this is like a child standing on shore of the ocean acknowledging only that the multitude of waves really exist but not understanding that each and every wave is due to the transformation of the ocean. Now, while the case of the child is unsurprising, is it not the height of stupidity for an adult to have the same

---

[10] Mt Sumeru is the massive mountain at the center of the world in Buddhist cosmology.

[11] These two views are also known as reification/eternalism (常見) and nihilism (斷見). As two extreme views (二邊), both are to be avoided and a middle path pursued instead. The passage that Xiong paraphrases can be traced to *Da baoji jing* 大寶積經 (*Mahāratnakūṭa-sūtra*; Great Treasures Collection Sutra), T310.11, 634a14–16: "It would be preferable to embrace the [extreme] view of the existence of inherent selfhood [with a conviction as immense] as Mt Sumeru rather than self-conceitedly uphold the view that everything is empty. What is the reason for this? [It is because] release from all [extreme] views relies on emptiness. If one were to give rise to the view that everything is empty, then one would be unable to avoid [being attached to that extreme view]."

[12] *Analects* 9.17: "Standing by a river, the Master said: 'Passing is as such—not ceasing, day and night.'"

understanding as that of the child? The wise trace the wonder of things to their source and so come to understand transformation, drawing analogies from what is near at hand; the foolish remain long lost yet do not realize it—is it not lamentable!?

Someone asked: "What kinds of characteristics does intrinsic Reality (本體) have?

I replied: "In general terms, there are four characteristics. First, intrinsic Reality is the origin of the myriad principles; the point of emergence for the myriad defining attributes; and the beginning (始) of the myriad transformations. (*Shi* 始: like root/basis [本].) Second, it is precisely in its being without that to which it stands in contrast (無對) that intrinsic Reality has that to which it stands in contrast (有對); and it is precisely in its having that to which it stands in contrast that it is without that to which it stands in contrast.[13] Third, intrinsic Reality has no beginning and no end. Fourth, intrinsic Reality is manifest (顯) as inexhaustible, endless great function, and, as such, should be said to be changing. And yet, when all is said and done, because the flow of great function never alters intrinsic Reality's inherent productivity and reproductivity, vigor, and all kinds of other defining attributes, then it should be said to be unchanging. In the foregoing, in general terms, I have cited four characteristics. If students diligently fathom this with an open mind, then they should not worry that there will not come a time when they are liberated and fully awakened." (The word *xian* 顯 in "intrinsic Reality is manifest as" means *xianxian* 顯現 [manifest].)

Above, I already stated that "there is no harm in provisionally positing that the intrinsic Reality of the cosmos is able to transform." Here I need to add a few words. The word *neng* 能 (able) in "able to transform" (能變) is only a descriptive term, and does not mean that there is that which is transformed to stand in contrast with it [as that which has been transformed by the transformer].[14] If it were the case that it is a "transformer" that gives rise to "that which is transformed," then necessarily this would be to take the transformer to transcend that which is transformed, and to exist by itself.[15] Not only would this be the same as the anthropomorphic deities of religion, moreover it would commit the grave error of having subject (能) and object (所)

---

[13] Abstracted from the myriad individuated waves, the ocean is without that to which it stands in contrast, yet this very abstraction simultaneously places it in contrast to the waves. Conversely, there is no ocean apart from the numerous waves. See also the discussion in the "Translator's Introduction."

[14] Here Xiong is trying to disambiguate this usage from the Yogācāra technical term *nengbian* 能變 "transformer."

[15] Again, the issue at play here is the sundering of *ti* and *yong*.

confronting one another and unable to be perfectly inter-melded. It should be understood that Reality completely and utterly transforms into
[p. 15]
the great function that is the disparate myriad existents; that outside the flow of great function there is no Reality. It is like the way the ocean completely becomes the myriad waves—that is, beyond the myriad wavs there is no ocean. The non-duality of Reality and function is also like this. Reality is undifferentiated and has no image, yet in becoming function it is a proliferation of a myriad particulars. Hence, it is from the perspective of Reality's becoming function that it is lauded as "able." Herein lies the significance of why Reality is termed "able to transform."

I have now explained that Reality is able to transform. It should be understood that Reality is neither constant (常) nor severed (斷) (Duan 斷 means "severed" [斷絕].), hence I also name it "constantly turning over" (恆轉). *Chang* 常 means not severed. *Hengzhuan* 恆轉 means not constant. Neither constant nor severed, [there is only] instant after instant of arising and ceasing, ceasing and arising, hence I name it "constantly turning over." I use this term to make Reality explicit through its functioning (即用顯體). (The term *xian* 顯 here means "making explicit with words." This is a different sense from [how *xian* is used in the word] *xianxian* 顯現 [to manifest]. The meaning of "manifest" is [made clear in the analogy of] the ocean manifesting as the myriad waves. The meaning of the term *xian* 顯 will depend on the context of its use.)

Having provided a summary answer to the first question, I now turn to the second: How is this transformation accomplished? In order to answer this question, it is of course necessary to seek out the most general principle among the inexhaustible myriad transformations. I maintain that this is nothing other than the great principle of "mutually opposing and mutually completing" (相反相成). This is because when we speak of transformation there must be a standing in contrast. In other words, it is only because there are two opposing incipient tendencies internal to the Reality of the cosmos that transformation can be accomplished and continue its development. Transformation is certainly not a matter of singularity (單純). (*Dan* 單 means "solitary" and "not having that to which it stands in contrast." *Chun* 純 means "pure" [純一] and "without contradiction.") How could singularity possibly attain transformation? If, however, the two facets confront one another, exclusively opposing one another with no reconciliation, then even though one extends (伸) and the other contracts (屈), if the one that extends were only to extend, this would result in depletion through excess, and so creative transformation would cease. Therefore, I say that transformation must follow the principle of mutually opposing and mutually completing.

Of China's most ancient philosophical books, none is like the *Great Change*. In the beginning, Emperor Fu Xi 伏羲 drew the lines of the hexagrams (卦爻) in order to explain the principles of the cosmos' transformation. His book consists of sixty-four hexagrams, each of which is made up of two trigrams. When divided, each trigram is made up of three lines. (The word "lines" [爻] is very broad in meaning, but in general terms it simply expresses transformation and movement.[16]) Hitherto, it has been rare for interpreters of the *Change* to pay attention to this. I have often sought for the meaning of the *Great Change* in *Laozi*. The dictum in *Laozi* that "one generates two and two generates three" [p. 16] is elaborating on the purport of three lines constituting a trigram in the *Great Change*. *Laozi* uses this to express the principle of "mutually opposing and mutually completing." There being one, then there is two. This two is in opposition to one. At the same time, there is also a three, which is based on the one. (Three is not identical to one but only based on one.) Although in opposition to two, three can transform two such that they revert to harmony. This is what the *Book of Change* means by "Great Harmony is preserved through union."[17] Only by virtue of the two opposites becoming harmonized is the development of the whole thus brought to completion. If there was only singularity then there would certainly be no transformation, and if there were only contradiction and no reconciliation then there would be much harm. If one aspect is superior, this will lead to excess and depletion. How could transformation lead to this?

Contraction and expansion

Above, I already explained the principle of transformation. Next, I should discuss contraction (翕) and expansion (闢), and arising (生) and ceasing (滅), for then I will be able to make clear that all transformations are accomplished by virtue of the principle of transformation. (*Bianhua* 變化 is also abbreviated as *bian* 變.) I will begin with contraction and expansion. Above, I already explained that intrinsic Reality must become function qua the

---

[16] "Xici, xia," *Zhou yi*, 8.8b: "The lines are that which imitate the movement of all under Heaven."
[17] "Tuan" 彖 (Judgment), Qian hexagram, *Zhou yi*, 1.7b.

myriad particulars. Accordingly, it can be provisionally posited that intrinsic Reality is capable of transformation, which I also call "constantly turning over." "Constantly turning over": absolutely formless (無) yet excels (善) at moving. (*Wu* 無: without form, not non-existent [空無]. *Shan* 善: a term of acclamation.) Its movement is continuous and unending. "Continuous" means that just as the prior movement ceases, the subsequent movement immediately arises; just like the uninterrupted flash after flash of lightning is said to be continuous. What is termed "continuous" is not that of a prior movement's extending to a subsequent moment of time. "Unending": it is said to be unending because it continues perpetually. If it were granted that it has an end, then it would cease. Is that how things really are? This unending movement is, of course, not a singular impetus (單純的勢用).[18] (On the two words, *dan* 單 and *chun* 純, see above.) For every movement there is a coalescence (攝聚). (*She* 攝 means "to draw in"; *ju* 聚 means "to gather together.") If there were no coalescence, there [would be only] floating with nothing to hold on to; an endless expanse devoid of things. Therefore, as soon as the impetus that is movement arises there is a kind of coalescence. The extreme ferocity of coalescence's might is such that, quite unexpectedly, it becomes countless tiny particles. These are what *Zhongyong* 中庸 (Balance as the Norm) explains as being "so small that they cannot be broken apart" (小莫能破),[19] and what Master Hui [Hui Shi 惠施 (fourth century BCE)] called "the smallest ones" (小一).[20] (Each single particle can be said to be a small unit in the constitution of a large object hence they are called smallest ones.) This is how the material cosmos began. Having reached this point, then the constantly turning over almost began to become things that offer material resistance and lose its self-nature. Hence the contraction impetus can be said to be an opposing function (反作用).[21]

Just as the contraction impetus arises, however, a different impetus arises in opposition to, yet

[p. 17]

simultaneously with, contraction. (The two impetuses are not different entities; much less do they have temporal sequence. Hence it is said that they arise simultaneously.)

---

[18] *Shiyong* 勢用: more literally, "impetus function." The two impetuses of expansion and contraction are both the "function" or "functioning" of Reality.

[19] Paraphrase of "Zhongyong," 52.7b. For Xiong's more detailed explanation of this passage, see Chapter 4, p. 195. *Zhongyong* was originally a chapter in *Liji* but began to be treated as a separate book during the Song dynasty. In the notes, my references to it are as a chapter in *Liji*, hence "Zhongyong."

[20] "Tianxia" 天下 (All Under Heaven), *Zhuangzi*, p. 1102.

[21] Because it operates in a way that tends toward opposing or being contrary to its self-nature, that is, Reality.

This other impetus has always been the manifest expression of the self-nature of the constantly turning over, yet it is not identical to the constantly turning over. For example, ice is made up of water, but ice is not identical to water. This other impetus is robust, vigorous, and self-conquering and so is not willing to become materialized—just the opposite of contraction. ("Not to become materialized" means not to transform into something that offers material resistance. Subsequent uses of the phrase "become materialized" have this same sense.) Furthermore, this impetus that is unwilling to become materialized is able to operate within contraction, such that it becomes in charge, and by doing so it reveals its supreme vigor, eventually being able to transform contraction, ultimately causing contraction to accord with and to ascend together with itself. ("Itself" is posited as expansion's [闢] self-reference. "Ascend" means to move upward.) The *Book of Change* states: "Great Harmony is preserved through union, and only then can there be the benefit of steadfastness through uprightness."[22] This robust and vigorous impetus that does not become materialized is named "expansion."

As stated above, the constantly turning over moves to become contraction, and as soon as there is contraction then there is expansion. Only by virtue of there being a standing in contrast (有對) is transformation accomplished. The constantly turning over is one. In being expressed as contraction, it almost does not preserve its self-nature, and this is two—this is what is meant by "one generates two" [in *Laozi*]. However, the constantly turning over is, after all, constantly just as its nature is, and would never become materialized. Hence, just as the contraction impetus arises, simultaneously the expansion impetus arises, and this expansion is three. This is what is meant by "two generates three" [in *Laozi*].[23] Above, I already explained that transformation simply follows the great principle of mutually opposing and mutually completing. From this [passage in *Laozi*], this [principle] is already in evidence. Summarizing the above, the contraction impetus coalesces to become material things. That is, on the basis of contraction, material phenomena (物行) are provisionally posited. (For the word *xing* 行, see above. Material things [物] are phenomena, hence the term material phenomena. References to mental phenomena [心行] below follow this same pattern.) The expansion impetus operates within

---

[22] "Tuan," Qian hexagram, *Zhou yi*, 1.7b. This interpretation is based on Xiong's gloss in *Ming xin pian*, p. 279: "*Zhen* 貞 means steadfastness through uprightness. This says that the benefit of the way of Great Harmony lies in steadfastness through uprightness."

[23] *Dao de jing*, *zhang* 42: "The Way generates one, one generates two, two generates three, and three generates the ten thousand things."

contraction and is able to make contraction change direction and follow itself. ("Itself" is posited as expansion's self-reference.) That is, on the basis of expansion, mental phenomena are provisionally posited. Contraction and expansion are the two aspects of the flow of great function, and because they cannot be broken down [into two separate entities] it is said that the material and the mental are not two entities.

In the past, many Chinese specialists of the *Book of Change* stated that material things descend, and mental things ascend. For example, Han Confucians said that "When *yang* 陽 advances, *yin* 陰 retreats."[24] They identified *yin* with the material and *yang* with the mental. What they meant by "advance" was "to ascend"; and what they meant by "retreat" was "to descend."

[p. 18]

Accordingly, many people think that what I mean by contraction is "to descend," and that what I mean by expansion is "to ascend." This kind of far-fetched association is wrong. If it were said that expansion has the nature of ascent, then that would be correct. As for saying that contraction is to descend, the reasoning is flawed. It should be understood that contraction is simply the impetus to coalesce and not that it must descend. When viewed solely from the perspective of the contraction impetus' traces ("Traces" refers to its becoming material phenomena.), it certainly seems to be descending—this is why material things have a sinking impetus. Despite this, contraction ultimately accords with expansion and then ascends together with it. One must not make the false presumption that contraction and expansion are perpetually in mutual opposition, trading places with one another in gaining the upper hand.

As soon as the flow of intrinsic Reality becomes contraction, expansion is already present. What is the reason? When contraction is about to become a material thing it seems to be hastening toward descent—this can be called "opposing" (反).[25] And yet, because intrinsic Reality does not, after all, change its self-nature, as soon as the contraction impetus is formed, the expansion impetus occurs together with it. Expansion [alters its own natural course] and returns to contraction in its sinking impetus, embracing it so as to ascend (升) together with it (*Sheng* 升 means "to ascend" [向上].), and in doing so is able manifestly to express intrinsic Reality's inherent defining

---

[24] *Yi wei: Qian zuodu* 易緯 : 乾鑿度 (Apocryphon to the *Book of Change*: Opening the Laws of the Hexagram Qian), A.6b, *Qinding Siku quanshu*.

[25] Opposing its true nature.

characteristics such as vigor and purity. This is what makes expansion unique. (I wrote "inherent defining characteristics such as" because there is no way to list all of them.)

Expansion gives rise to function in accord with intrinsic Reality. "In accord" means that expansion does not lose the defining characteristics of intrinsic Reality. (For example, ice appears out of water, and, after all, never loses water's wet nature.) This [is what is meant by] "as for function, *it* is Reality" and so I spoke of "in accord." Although contraction becomes material things [actually] there are no fixed material things. The material things we see in the world are traces of the contraction impetus, so-called traces of transformation.

Someone asked about the following: "Your thesis, sir, is that the flow of intrinsic Reality accomplishes transformation by means of expansion and contraction; that it is on the basis of expansion that we talk about there being mental phenomena, and on the basis of contraction that we talk about there being material phenomena. Although the thesis is attractive, if we seek truth from facts, then given that mental phenomena only begin to be seen in animals, and the development of animals definitely began only after the cosmos had condensed, it is thus beyond doubt that material phenomena existed before mental phenomena arose. If it were as you have claimed—that it is by means of contraction and expansion that transformation is accomplished, that is, the Reality of mental and material phenomena is the same and only their functions are different; and that mental and material phenomena cannot be divided into a sequence of one preceding the other—then your thesis verges on being unavoidably abstruse (玄) and baseless."

I replied: "So, you detest the abstruse! How is fathoming principles to their ultimate point not abstruse!? (The origin of the myriad transformations, the root of the myriad things, that where the myriad principles return to—this is called "the ultimate.") 'Abstruse' is what the *Book of Change* refers to as: 'It embraces all the ways under Heaven. It is as such, and nothing more can be said about it.'[26] ("Embrace" means to include, and here is saying that

---

[26] "Xi ci, shang," 7.26b: "The Master said: 'As for the *Change*, what does it do? The *Change* deals with the way things start up and how matters reach completion; and embraces all the ways under Heaven. It is as such, and nothing more can be said about it.'" Translation by Richard John Lynn, *The Classic of Changes: A New Translation of the I Ching as Interpreted by Wang Pi* (New York: Columbia University Press, 2004), p. 63, mod.

[p. 19]
there is nothing that it does not include.) 'Subsuming function into Reality' (攝用歸體)[27] is for there to be a complete absence [of any function to which Reality] stands in contrast, such that neither mental nor material phenomena can be named. (*She* 攝 means "to subsume." Take the analogy of when looking at ice one does not preserve the characteristic of ice but directly realizes water, that it is nothing but water. Now, in the context of cosmology, to say that function is subsumed into Reality is to observe various mental and material phenomena and directly realize their intrinsic Reality. If we refer exclusively to intrinsic Reality, it is without form or conscious deliberation [作意],[28] hence neither mental nor material phenomena can be named.) By 'tracing Reality to reveal function' (原體顯用) ("Tracing" means to trace the principle from its source. Tracing Reality's being revealed as function should [be understood] as described below.) then function [will be revealed to be] one contraction and one expansion, and that it is through their mutual opposition that transformation is accomplished. Hence, contraction and expansion perpetually turn over together, and do not have a sequential order in which one precedes the other. (Function does not proceed by itself; it must have one contraction and one expansion perpetually turning over together, opposing, and then becoming harmonized—this is why it is called function.) Contraction coalesces to become material things; hence contraction is simply referred to as things. Expansion perpetually unfolds yet does not lose the vigor of its intrinsic Reality, and so expansion is simply referred to as the mind. The mind's discrimination of things without being obscured; penetration of things without being impeded; and control of things with unrelenting effort (For example, the *Book of Change* says: "Fashions and brings to completion the [Way of] Heaven and Earth," "Assists the myriad things"[29]— these are the efforts it makes in controlling things. The superior power of this control

---

[27] "Subsuming function into Reality" is originally a Buddhist phrase. See, for example, Fazang 法藏 (643–712), *Xiu Huayan ao zhi wang jin huanyuan guan* 修華嚴奧旨妄盡還源觀 (Practicing the Discernment of Exhausting Delusion and Returning to the Source through the Profound Purport of Huayan), T1867.45, 639a29. The Sanlun School master, Jizang 吉藏 (549–623), had already employed the phrase as part of his scheme of doctrinal classification; see Jizang, *Fahua yishu* 法華義疏 (Elucidation of the Meaning of the *Lotus Sutra*), T1721.34, 506a22–6b1, and Li Tongxuan 李通玄 (635–730 or 646–740), *Xin Huayan jing lun* 新華嚴經論 (Treatise on the New Translation of the *Flower Ornament Sutra*), T1739.36, 734c26–29.

[28] This is a technical term in Yogācāra, and would usually refer to "attentiveness," one of the five omnipresent mental associates (五遍行), but, based on Xiong's gloss of the term in *Ming xing pian*, p. 284, here it has the sense of conscious deliberation. For Xiong's early discussion of this term in Yogācāra (where he includes it in his own grouping of six omnipresent mental associates), see my annotated translation of Xiong's 1932 literary edition of *Xin weishi lun*, *New Treatise on the Uniqueness of Consciousness* (New Haven: Yale University Press, 2015), pp. 236–237.

[29] Loose paraphrase of a passage in the "Xiang" 象 (Images) commentary to the Tai 泰 (Greatness) hexagram, *Zhou yi*, 2.21a: "By fashioning and bringing to completion the Way of Heaven and Earth the ruler assists Heaven and Earth [in realizing] what is appropriate, so that the people are supported."

is especially evident in [the mind's] not becoming mired in material desires.) are precisely [expressions of] the impetus that unfolds with vigor, hence we know that the mind is none other than expansion. ("None other than" is used only when the referent is the same, but the names are different, such as when it is said that "Zhongni is none other than Confucius.") The mind and things have the same Reality and there is no sequential order into which they can be separated. The truth is indeed as such—what point is there to doubt it? You think that at its point of genesis (本際) the cosmos was exclusively material and not mental. (*Benji* 本際 corresponds to "beginning point"; here I have borrowed a Buddhist term.) This is a shallow view. If originally there were no mental phenomena, and later suddenly mental phenomena appeared, then this would be a case of nonexistence's generating existents—an impossibility."

A shared conventional presumption is that at the Grand Primordium (泰初)[30] stage of the cosmos, vast undifferentiated *qi* gradually divided and condensed to form countless heavenly [bodies] or the container world (器界). (What the Buddhist call the "container world" refers to heavenly bodies or the material cosmos.) After the passage of a very long period of time, gradually there were organisms on earth. And from when there were animals and right through to humans, mental phenomena began to appear but before this there certainly were no mental phenomena that can be verified. The conventional view amounts merely to this. What is particularly not understood is that before there were organisms on earth, and before animal perception and advanced human mentation had been discovered, the great mind of the cosmos—the expansion impetus—had to flow throughout the Six Voids; it had no fixed location yet there is no location where it was not. (The Six Voids are the four cardinal directions and above and below; in other words, the Supreme Void.) At that time in the development of the material cosmos, living entities had not yet formed, or they had had only just appeared (Such as plants.) and their [structural] organization was still very crude. At that time, even though expansion's impetus was latently operating in the material world, ultimately it was

[p. 20]

unable to be manifestly expressed, and so it might have seemed that there was no mind. In the Kan 坎 trigram of the *Book of Change*, the *yang* [line] is trapped between [two] *yin* [lines] and cannot get out, hence this image.[31] (*Yang* represents the mind; *yin* represents things. *Yang* is trapped in *yin*; that is, the image

---

[30] See Chapter 4, pp. 188, 199. Xiong variously uses both *taichu* 泰初 and *taichu* 太初.

[31] Kan trigram: ☵ Broken lines are *yin* lines and the unbroken lines are *yang* lines.

of the mind's being blocked by things.) The flow of intrinsic Reality is nothing but the brilliant, vigorous, uninterrupted unfolding of expansion. Its contracting to become things is the means by which contraction serves as the tool of expansion. Expansion's reliance on contraction in order to accomplish transformation is a case of the principle perforce being "so of itself" (自然) and is not done purposefully; creative transformation is inherently without purpose. ("Creative transformation" refers to intrinsic Reality's flow. "Without purpose": this is because Reality is without form or image; it is not like we humans who deliberately want to create.) Expansion has no fixed location yet there is no location where it is not; and because its impetus is entirely without focus, it cannot help but to drift and disperse. In contrast, contraction undergoes differentiation and condenses to form the myriad things. Having been formed, then things have [structural] organization and are not diffuse. Hence, through contraction, expansion has a tool enabling it to express its impetus manifestly.

The evolution of the material world can be roughly divided into two levels. The first is the level of material obstruction (質礙). (Matter is obstructive, hence "material obstruction.") From undifferentiated primal vastness to the countless heavenly bodies, right through to all the "dusts" (塵)—all are forms of material obstruction. (The word "dust" is from Buddhist texts and is another way of saying "matter" [物質].) [They are said to be] forms of material obstruction because [no signs of] vital functions have been discovered in them. This is why people in the past described material things as "stagnant" and "sinking." Because they have such characteristics they are collectively termed "the level of material obstruction."

The second is the level of living entities (生機體). This level innovatively evolved on the basis of the level of material obstruction. That is, because of their unique [structural] organization they formed into individual entities with vital functions, and so this level is called the level of living entities. This level is further divided into four sub-levels: the level of biological entities (Here and below, "living entities" [生機體] is abbreviated as *jiti* 機體.); the level of lower-order zoological entities; the level of higher-order zoological entities; and the level of human entities. The second, third, and fourth of these levels are all based on the immediately preceding level. The biggest contrast between the second, third, and fourth levels and their immediately preceding level is actually that each of these three later levels is suddenly created and is of a different kind. Both in ancient times and today, understanding of transformation has been superficial, with attention being paid only to the material world. Consequently, material things have been taken as the origin, as having existed first, all the while there being a failure to understand that material things are made by the contracting impetus in the flow of intrinsic Reality.

The flow of intrinsic Reality has always been the brilliant, vigorous, uninterrupted unfolding of the expansion impetus. (The *Great Change* says the following about the defining characteristics of Qian 乾. First, that it is brilliant because it is not obscured. Second, that it is robust and vigorous, advancing relentlessly because it never alters its intrinsic nature.[32] These two defining characteristics are the root of the myriad defining characteristics. What I refer to as expansion is just like Qian in the *Book of Change*.) The reason that intrinsic Reality contracts to become things is because expansion must have a tool that serves to focus its powerful function, as already explained above. When contraction begins to be things, necessarily it increasingly hastens toward solidification—this is the how the level of material resistance comes to be formed. Expansion is the

[p. 21]

great mind of the cosmos—it is also called the great generative vitality (生命) of the cosmos. (The word *shengming* 生命 in this treatise has a different purport from the way the word is conventionally used.) Secretly operating at the level of material resistance, it is certainly utterly vigorous and unrelenting. This is what is meant in the *Book of Change* when it says: 'The origin of Qian (乾元) controls Heaven.'[33] (*Qian yuan* 乾元 refers to intrinsic Reality. "Heaven" refers to the countless heavenly bodies. In elaborating on Wang Fusi's 王輔嗣 learning, Kangbo 康伯 said that of all things, the heavenly bodies are the largest and that they are all controlled by the origin of Qian.[34] Heavenly bodies are things [that offer] material resistance, and

---

[32] "Wenyan" 文言 (Words of the Text) commentary on the Qian hexagram, 1.18b, describes Qian as "robust and vigorous." Although there is no passage that describes Qian as "brilliant" (陽明), "Xici, xia," 8.15a does describe Qian as something that is *yang* 陽.

[33] Xiong explains how he understands *Qian yuan* 乾元 in the following passage in Chapter 4, p. 185: "The *Book of Change* explains (明) that the origin of Qian (乾元) differentiates to become Qian and Kun. (*Ming* 明 means "to explain" [闡明]. *Qian yuan* 乾元 means "the origin of Qian." It is not the case that Qian itself is the origin. The origin of Kun is the origin of Qian. It is not the case that Kun has a separate origin. The origin of Qian is also called Taiji [Supreme Pivot]; it is the Reality of Qian and Kun.)" Based on Xiong's gloss of *Qian yuan*, the original passage in the *Book of Change* ("Commentary on the Judgement" to the Qian hexagram, 1.18b) can be translated as follows: "Great, indeed, is the origin of Qian. The myriad things rely on it for their beginning, and so it controls Heaven."

[34] Wang Fusi is Wang Bi 王弼; Kangbo is Han Kangbo 韓康伯 (332–380). This is an interpretive paraphrase of Wang Bi's commentary on the Judgment (Tuan 彖) rather than a commentary by Han. The following translation of Wang's commentary is made on the basis of Xiong's comments: "Heaven is the name for [things that have] form; Qian* uses forms. Form [is manifest] in the accumulation of things. To have the [limited] form of Heaven and yet still be able to be preserved forever without loss as the head of things. As for the one that controls Heaven, how could this be anything but supreme vigor?!" *Zhou yi zhengyi*, 1.6a. *Richard John Lynn, trans., *The Classic of Changes*, p. 141, notes: "It is likely that Wang has used *jian* (strength) as a pun on *Qian* (both characters seem to have had the same pronunciation in the archaic Chinese of his day: *g'ian), implying that as the two sound alike, so their meanings are similar if not identical." I have also consulted Rudolph Wagner's translation of this

the origin of Qian actually secretly moves them, hence Han says "control." This is different from Zheng's 鄭 note.[35]) Things [that offer] material resistance, however, have already realized a propensity for being densely turbid. (In the past, when people said that things were densely turbid, they were referring specifically to the level of material resistance. "Densely turbid" has such senses as closure [錮閉] and descent [退墜]—just the opposite of expansion's unfolding nature and ascending nature. If scholars have not had personal experience of generative vitality [生命] then it is very difficult to discuss such matters with them.) It is certainly difficult for expansion's powerful function suddenly to be displayed at the level of material resistance and so destroy that closure. Rather, expansion needs to be deeply concealed and to accumulate over an extended period of time, then, eventually it will suddenly break through. Like a remote subterranean river that eventually overflows, becoming marshes and rivers. Accordingly, it is certainly no random occurrence that via the level of material resistance the level of living entities suddenly appeared in the material world. Indeed, from its concealed configuration within the level of material resistance, expansion secretively commanded, eventually causing the organization of the material world to move from being coarse and large to being one of increasing differentiation. (At the level of material resistance, the Buddhists call things such as heavenly bodies "large" because their form is coarse and large. Later, living entities emerged—that is, various small things. For example, the bodies of human entities are no taller than seven *chi* 尺 ["feet"]—this is an example of increasing fineness in differentiation.) From simple to increasingly complex (At the level of material obstruction, if we infer [that things can be] broken down to a small cosmos of atoms and electrons, it can also be seen that they have organization and are not drifting and scattered. If this were not the case, then they would not be able to form heavenly bodies and the various large creatures on earth. However, it remains the case that the organization of large things was simple. Later, as living entities emerged, it started to be apparent that the organization of living entities is unusually complex.); and from stagnant to increasingly subtle. (The organization of living entities is extremely fine and wondrous, and so expansion's powerful function

---

passage in his chapter, "A Building Block of Argumentation: Initial Fu 夫 as a Phrase Status Marker," in Joachim Gentz and Dirk Meyer, eds., *Literary Forms of Argument in Early China* (Leiden, Brill, 2015), p. 51.

[35] Zheng refers to Zheng Xuan 鄭玄 (127–200). In Zheng's fragmentary comment preserved in Wang Yinglin 王應麟 (1223–1296), comp., *Zhou yi Zheng Kangcheng zhu* 周易鄭康成注 (Zheng Xuan's Commentary on the *Book of Change*), in Zhang Yuanji 張元濟 (1867–1959) comp., *Sibu congkan, sanbian* 四部叢刊三編 (Collectanea of the Four Categories, Third Series) (Shanghai: Shangwu yinshuguan, 1935–1936), 1.1b, Zheng says that the genesis of the myriad things was based on Heaven.

has something to rely on in order to be expressed. Given that the level of material obstruction is stagnant, the expansion impetus remains hidden and not expressed [at that level].) The reason that organization at the level of living entities is vastly different from that at the level of material obstruction is no doubt due to that brilliant and vigorous great power's ceaseless control and commanding operation (斡運). ("Great power" refers to expansion. *Yun* 運 means "to move"; "to operate"; *wo* 斡 has the sense of "to command.") Those who are skilled at discerning transformation would understand this line of reasoning (趣). (*Qu* 趣: "line of reasoning" [理趣].) As for expansion's operating within things, from the level of material resistance through to generating the level of living entities, it gradually transformed things and in doing so manifested its superior function by itself. From indiscernible to distinct, from hidden to manifest—like a deluge, nothing was able to constrain its impetus! When it came to the level of human entities, then expansion's impetus became abundantly developed—

[p. 22]

almost to its ultimate extent. The natural endowments and powers of humans can indeed be said to be like one who governs Heaven and Earth and stores up the myriad things such that none is his equal. This is precisely because we human entities represent a high point in the development of the expansion impetus. (Examination into living entities by people today is still shallow.) Accordingly, when viewed from the perspective of the development of the cosmos as a whole, step by step, brilliant and vigorous expansion destroys material closure (物質之閉錮), recovering the cosmos' radiant and active constant nature. Clearly, this is no random occurrence. The thesis that the material came first, and the mental came after, is, of course, a shallow view and not worth disputing in depth.

Summarizing the foregoing, the constantly turning over becomes great function, that is, there is no Reality that exists by itself, separated from function. Like the ocean that becomes the numerous waves, there is no ocean that exists by itself separated from the numerous waves. Function does not proceed by itself; there must be one contraction and one expansion. As the contraction impetus coalesces, it gives rise to the manifestation of the material cosmos, replete with a myriad images. As the expansion impetus unfolds, it is whole and without boundaries (Expansion is whole and cannot be divided, hence it has no boundaries.); it is utterly vigorous and does not descend (The expansion impetus continuously ascends and does not descend.); indeed, it has no fixed location yet there is no location where it is not. Containing what is beyond contraction or all things, and pervading contraction or all things, expansion is able to cause contraction to accompany itself in turning over, preserving Great Harmony through union. ("Itself" is posited as expansion's self-reference.) The expansion impetus does not alter the *de* 德 of its Reality (*De* 德 contains two senses: defining characteristics [德性][36] and potent functioning [德用].) and so, in it, intrinsic Reality can be cognized. This is the meaning of what in the past I called "understanding Reality in function" (即用明體).

Someone asked: "Expansion is inherently a perfect unity (一) (*Yi* 一 means "unity," and not the number "one.") and is a name for the great mind of the cosmos. As for humans and the myriad things each having a mind, is this the same mind as the great mind of the cosmos?"

I replied: "Did not Mencius say: 'There is only one Way'?[37] The great mind of the cosmos is the immeasurable mind that pervades all humans and all things. This is what is meant by 'unity is immeasurable' (一爲無量). The immeasurable mind of all humans and all things is the great mind of the cosmos. This is what is meant by 'The immeasurable is unity' (無量爲一).[38] This is what Laozi meant when he said: 'Mystery upon mystery.'"[39]

He further asked: "With the movement of the constantly turning over, contraction then becomes things. Is it then the case that Reality is inherently imbued with a material character?" ("The constantly turning over" is a name for intrinsic Reality; see above.)

I replied: "Reality has always had the two natures of the pure and spirit-like and the material. (Because they are inherently endowed therefore it is said "has always had.".). The reason that 'contraction' is spoken of, rather than
[p. 23]
directly speaking of the material, is because it is named according to its function. (Moving such that there is contraction—this is intrinsic Reality's function. In fact, contraction is the material.) The material is not something that is fixed, it has always been Reality's flow; rather, it is the aspect that manifests as if it were condensing. The reason that 'expansion' is spoken of, rather than directly speaking of the pure and spirit-like, is also because it is named according to its function. (Moving such that there is expansion—this is precisely Reality's function.

---

[36] Xiong's gloss of the phrase *xin zhi dexing* 心之德性 in *Ming xin pian*, p. 153, sheds further light on how he understands *dexing*: "'*De* 德' is like 'to get.' [*Xin zhi dexing* 心之德性] refers to that which enables the mind to get to be the mind, differentiating it from material things. '*Xing* 性' is like 'characteristic.' For example, it is commonly said that the characteristic of fire is to blaze upward, and the characteristics of water are motility and wetness. There is surely nothing that does not have its own unique characteristics."

[37] *Mencius* 3A.1.

[38] See, for example, *Shou lengyan jing*, T945.19, 121a4–5.

[39] *Dao de jing, zhang* 1.

In fact, expansion is the pure and spirit-like, and it is also called the mind.) It refers to the aspect that is brilliant, robust, ascending, unfolding, and unwilling to be transformed into material things. The two natures of the pure and spirit-like and the material are the two mutually opposing extremes. It is by mutually opposing that they mutually complete, and it is through this process that Reality transforms into great function."

Arising and ceasing

Above I have elucidated how it is by means of contraction and expansion that transformation is accomplished because neither contraction nor expansion holds on to any former constancy (不守故常). Next I should discuss arising and ceasing (生滅). Before doing so, it is first necessary to explain what *chana* 剎那 [kṣaṇa] means. *Chana* is the absolutely smallest unit of measurement into which Indian Hīnayāna Buddhists divided time. For example, *juan* 136 of the [*Apidamo*] *da piposha lun* [阿毘達磨]大毘婆沙論 ([*Abhidharma-*]*mahā-vibhāṣā-śāstra*; Treatise of the Great Commentary on the Abhidharma) states: "The interval of time it takes for a strong man to snap his fingers is sixty-four *chana*."[40] I do not know how the number of sixty-four was calculated. In ancient times there were no implements to measure time; even today clocks still cannot determine the measurement for a *chana*. How then could it be claimed that the time it takes for a strong man to snap his fingers is sixty-four *chana*? There are some who say that the speed with which a strong man snaps his fingers is just like the passage of sixty-four *chana* and is used to describe a *chana*'s measurement as being extremely small, and that a *chana* cannot be calculated numerically. *Juan* 18 of Kuiji's 窺基 [632–682] [*Cheng*] *weishi* [*lun*] *shuji* [成]唯識[論]述記 (Commentary on *Demonstration of Nothing but Consciousness*)[41] states: "*Nian* 念 is another name for *chana*."[42] Based on this, then the interval of time of the sudden movement of a thought-moment (念) in one's mind is what is called a *chana*. As one turns within to discern a thought-moment as it suddenly arises,

---

[40] T1545.27, 701b14.
[41] Xuanzang's disciple, Kuiji, is regarded by Chinese Buddhist tradition as the first patriarch of the Weishi 唯識 (Nothing but Consciousness) or Faxiang school (法相宗), which is based on Xuanzang's work. Kuiji's *Cheng weishi lun shuji* is important for providing crucial glosses on Xuanzang's *Cheng weishi lun* 成唯識論 (Demonstration of Nothing but Consciousness), the foundational text of the East Asian Yogācāra tradition.
[42] T1830.43, 340b12.

immediately it is extinguished. Since thought-moment here is another name for *chana*, it can be understood that *chana* cannot be said to be time. Rather, it is only because of the ceaseless arising and ceasing of thought-moment after thought-moment in one's own mind that [the notion of] *chana* is provisionally posited. I am very much in favor of Master Kuiji's account. What is conventionally called time is merely space's altered characteristic. Space has divisions, such as the directions east and west. Time also has divisions, such as past, present, and future. In sum, time and space are both forms (形式) in which actual things exist. If we explain *chana* by mixing in the conventional concept of time, then this amounts to extrapolating that unfathomable transformation is an actual entity.

[p. 24]

Zhuangzi said: "Footprints are produced by treading. Those who hold on to the footprints will be unable to discern the treading. Things are formed by transformation. Is it likely that those who are mired in form will be able to catch a glimpse of transformation?"[43] Although my references to *chana* in this book consistently present it as the smallest, briefest unit of time that cannot be broken down any further, crucially, such a presumption is provisionally posited merely for discursive expedience. Scholars must transcend the conventional concept of time in the hope of avoiding having words interfere with the true meaning [of transformation], and so be able to comprehend the wonders of transformation.

Having now explained *chana*,[44] I should discuss arising and ceasing. All dharmas have always been inherently non-existent. Now, as they suddenly emerge, this is called arising (生). ("Dharmas" is the generic term for the myriad existents. Here, whether talking about contraction and expansion or the mental and the material, I refer to them all as dharmas. Below, this is the same.) In all cases, after dharmas have arisen they definitely do not abide but rather return to become nothing—this is called "ceasing" (滅). Arising and ceasing have always been matters that ordinary people have all understood, and as such, there should be no doubts. Yet ordinary people all mistakenly believe that once having arisen, all dharmas must abide, and only a long time after do they cease. To elaborate, [according to this view,] all things arise and must either abide for a long period or abide for a temporary period—it is certainly not the case

---

[43] The reference is to the "Tian yun" 天運 (The Turning of Heaven) chapter in *Zhuangzi*, p. 536: "Footprints are produced by treading. Is it likely that footprints are the treading?" Xiong's "quotation" is really an extended gloss.

[44] In what follows, I translate *chana* as "instant" unless context requires a more technical treatment.

that in the interval of an instant (*chana*) they suddenly cease to exist. Even if they cease rapidly, the arising and ceasing definitely do not occur at the same instant. The views of ordinary people are all like this, but this is where problems begin.

If we examine the Buddhist teachings, [they teach that] all things cease in an instant (刹那滅). This means that in all cases, just as a dharma arises, then at this same interval of an instant it ceases, and most definitely will not abide for a moment. ("A moment" describes an extremely brief period of time and amounts to there being no temporal period that can be spoken of.) Arising and ceasing are both located in the same interval of an instant, just like two ends of a steelyard are high and low at the same time. This Buddhist analogy is superb! From Śākyamuni through to the followers of Hīnayāna and Mahāyāna later on, there was no differing thesis. Nevertheless, non-Buddhist scholars were particularly unable to believe and to understand this doctrine. Their many criticisms can still be examined in Mahāyāna writings. Even today, when people like me talk to others about the doctrine that all things cease in an instant, we still regularly encounter objections. As for those philosophers in ancient and modern times well versed in the investigation of change, with regard to the myriad images of the cosmos, although they discuss how there is a constant dispatching of the old and advancing to the new, crucially, by and large their accounts are very general. Using a few very lively and piercing phrases, they merely describe how things do not hold on to any former constancy. It is rare for them to affirm fully and clearly, and to state bluntly, that [all things] cease in an instant. According to the doctrine that [all things] cease in an instant, just as they arise, all dharmas immediately cease, and in between [these two occurrences]
[p. 25]
they do not abide for an instant. Stated as such, this is to fall into [the extreme] view of emptiness (空見): that nothing exists at all. Even the existence of one's body and one's mind are denied. Because of this, those who hear about it refuse to accept it. I once encountered a fierce objector who said: "According to what you have said, all dharmas cease in an instant. Before us there is a rock. If this rock ceased in an instant, then it would never have existed. If I were to pick up this rock and hit you on the head, would you not feel pain?" I laughed but did not say anything. People like that focus only on the traces of the great flow of transformation, and so are incapable of grasping the wonders of transformation. In other words, they see only things and so are incapable of understanding that which is intrinsic to things. The

Buddhist doctrine that all things cease in an instant truly illuminates the principles of things in the finest detail. In what follows, one by one, I will respond to and resolve the doubts of ordinary people, based on Mahāyāna doctrine and also incorporating my own thoughts.[45]

All dharmas cease in an instant

The first is your presumption that no dharma instantaneously ceases as soon as it arises. If it were indeed as you presume, then the myriad images of the cosmos should all abide permanently—yet, having been formed (成), the myriad things must also perish (毀). (*Cheng* 成 refers to the condensing [凝成] of the myriad things. *Hui* 毀 means "perish" [壞滅].) Where there is birth, there must be death. Where there is fullness, there must be emptiness. ("Fullness": just when something is filled to capacity, this is fullness. "Emptiness": when something gradually becomes depleted and destroyed, this is emptiness.) Where there is accumulation there must be dispersal. (Whenever things are formed through the mutual attraction and combination of elements, this is called accumulation. Whenever things are destroyed, this is dispersal.) The axiom that "all phenomena are impermanent" is plain, clear, and undeniable. ("All phenomena" [諸行] is the same as saying "the myriad things." The word *xing* 行 is explained in detail at the beginning of this chapter.) Why are you so afraid of the word "perish"?

Second, you say: "It is not that I do not believe that after phenomena have arisen then they must cease; it is just that I don't believe that as soon as phenomena arise they immediately cease. Even though phenomena do not abide permanently, at the very least they abide temporarily and only later do they cease." This is what you think. Now, let me ask you the following. If phenomena were able to abide temporarily when they arise, would it be due to phenomena's own power that enables them to abide, or would it be due to having relied upon some other power that they abide? Both of these presumptions are mistaken. Why? If it were said that it is due to phenomena's own power that enables them to abide, then they should abide permanently and not cease. Why then would it be that they abide only temporarily and not

---

[45] The following series of arguments used to prosecute the thesis that all dharmas cease in an instant, principally draws on Asaṅga's *Mahāyāna-sūtrālaṃkāra* (*Dasheng zhuangyan jing lun* 大乘莊嚴經論; Ornament for Great Vehicle Discourses), T1604.31, 646b6–c22. Xiong already rehearsed many of these arguments in the 1932 literary edition of the *Xin weishi lun, Xiong Shili quanji*, vol. 2, pp. 43–46; see my translation, *New Treatise*, pp. 101–106.

permanently? If it is agreed that it is due to having relied upon some other power that they are able to abide, and that the cosmos never had a creator, then how could some other power cause phenomena to abide?[46] Neither of your presumptions can be established. Hence, we know that as soon as phenomena arise, they cease, and do not abide temporarily.

[p. 26]

Third, you say: "Once phenomena have arisen, if they do not encounter destructive causes (毀壞因) then they will be able to abide. (*Huihuai yin* 毀壞因 is henceforth abbreviated to *huai yin* 壞因.) Phenomena cease only when they encounter destructive causes. Take, for example, black iron. Because it has fire as its destructive cause, it ceases, and only then does the scorching red iron newly arise. So long as the time of the destructive cause has not yet arrived, the black iron is able to continue to abide." ("Destructive cause" refers to the fire.)

The reason you maintain this explanation is simply because you have not thoroughly investigated the truth of the matter. You should understand that, in all cases, things cannot arise without a cause. (Even the case of things themselves having the power to appear is provisionally said to be a cause.[47]) Whenever things cease, they certainly do not wait for a destructive cause and only then begin to cease. Rather, this is just the way it is, so of itself (法爾自然) (*Faer* 法爾 is like saying "self-so" [自然].)—it cannot be said that cessation also waits for a cause. The flow of great function is utterly robust and utterly vigorous, utterly wondrous, and utterly strange. Each and every instant suddenly arises and suddenly ceases, and not an iota of a former thing remains—this flow is always bursting forth in renewal. And so, I say that whenever things cease, actually they do not need to wait for a cause. Ordinary people mistakenly believe that the cessation of the black iron is due to the fire's serving as the destructive cause. Little do they realize that when the black iron and the fire are combined, this is precisely when the black iron ceases and it is also precisely when the red iron arises. (In the interval of one instant, the black iron ceases and it is precisely this instant that the red iron arises. Because the time at which the arising occurs and the ceasing occurs is so tightly interconnected, it is not a different [moment of] time.) Actually, the power of the fire merely suffices to serve as the inductive cause (牽引因) of the red iron, enabling it to arise ("It" refers to the red iron. "Inductive

---

[46] Xiong's point is that if everything depended on an external cause or causes to exist, then given that there is no creator, this would lead to the problem of infinite regress.

[47] This comment is clearer when read in the light of a later comment in this same paragraph: "Because the fire is unable to create the red iron, the red iron's arising is actually due to its own inherent power of production; it is just that it is able to arise only when it encounters the fire qua inductive cause. If there were no fire qua inductive cause, the red iron would still not arise."

cause": Because the fire is unable to create the red iron, the red iron's arising is actually due to its own inherent power of production; it is just that it is able to arise only when it encounters the fire qua inductive cause. If there were no fire qua inductive cause, the red iron would still not arise.) and it cannot be said that the fire is the destructive cause of the black iron. The cessation of the black iron is so-of-itself, and actually it does not need to wait for a cause. In other words, its cessation is not due to its having been destroyed by the fire. Because the fire arises, the red iron and the fire arise together. If there were no fire, then, necessarily, the red iron would not arise. Accordingly, it should be said that fire has the power to induce the red iron to arise. Ordinary people do not understand that this fire is the inductive cause of the red iron, and mistakenly presume that the fire is the destructive cause of the black iron. This is an inverted view (倒見).

This person raised another objection: "Ordinary people all see that before the black iron is brought together with the fire, it abides and does not cease. Only when it is brought together with the fire does the black iron cease. This proves that the cessation of the black iron is due to fire qua destructive cause."

I replied: "Do you really believe that before the black iron has encountered the fire that it actually does not cease? In fact, the black iron completely ceases in an instant—it is just that you did not perceive it. As the black iron of the previous instant ceases, the black iron of the following instant newly arises. However, because the newly arisen black iron and the previous

[p. 27]

black iron are extremely similar, [leading you to think that] what you saw before and after are not different, therefore you say that it is just as if the previous black iron continued to abide until later."

This person further enquired about the following: "When before us we see the black iron and fire together, only the red iron arises, and the black iron does not arise again. Clearly, it remains the case that the fire is the destructive cause of the black iron."

I replied: "At the time when the former black iron ceased, the red iron encountered the fire and suddenly arose, and the black iron did not arise again. In the myriad transformations of the cosmos, sometimes when a new category (類型) is created the former category is discarded. Such is the wonder of sudden transformation. How is it that your understanding is so impeded?"

In sum, when things cease, in all cases they do not wait for a cause. This principle must be profoundly realized through personal experience—only then will the significance of the awakening be deep and far-reaching. In the flow of great transformation, instant by instant, the old is removed and the new is created. Therefore, when things cease, in all cases, it is so-of-itself; it is not the case that they wait for a cause and only then cease. Because cessation does not wait for a cause, the doctrine that [all things] cease in an instant is able to be established. (If they had to wait for a cause and only then begin to cease, then until such time as the destructive cause was present, things would firmly abide, in which case the doctrine that [all things] cease in an instant would not be able to be established.)

Fourth, as for your claim that "All things are able to abide temporarily but eventually they must cease," my reply would be to ask you: "If a dharma has ceased, is it able to continue to arise?" If you say that is has ceased and does not continue to arise, then you would have fallen [in the error] of nihilism (斷見). If you say that as soon as it ceases, it immediately continues to arise, then you should not say that all things are able to abide temporarily. How so? If something were to abide temporarily, this would be [a state in which] the agency of great transformation's removal of the old and creation of the new has already been suspended, so how could new things continue to arise? You should understand, in all cases, as soon as things arise, they cease. Instant by instant, the things that came before completely cease, and those that come after newly arise. Transformation's agency never stops for a moment. Hence, the myriad things perpetually arise in succession, never ceasing. You also need to understand that when the Buddhists explain the doctrine that [all things] cease in an instant, they highlight only impermanence. In this treatise, I explain that transformation's agency is incessant, vibrant, and dynamic. This is a fundamental point of difference between the Buddhists and me.

Fifth, you maintain: "All who say that all things cease as soon as they arise, focus one-sidedly on the ceasing aspect, and fail to avoid engaging in empty abstraction." Little do you realize that although the error of engaging in empty abstraction can be attributed to the Buddhists, it cannot be attributed to me. As I have said, instant by instant, [all things] continuously cease and do not abide is precisely [the same in its purport as] instant by instant, [all things] continuously arise without interruption. Arising and ceasing are inherently intersubsumptive: when arising is mentioned, ceasing is already present; when ceasing is mentioned, arising is already present. As I have stated above, transformation follows the law of mutually opposing and
[p. 28]
mutually completing. I will continue to use "one, two, and three" to demonstrate this. As a prior instant newly arose, this is "one." And yet, at precisely this interval of an instant, the newly arisen dharma suddenly

ceases—this ceasing is "two."[48] Two is certainly in opposition to one (One is arising, two is ceasing—hence, in opposition.), but as a subsequent instant (剎) quickly continues on from the prior instant, there is another new arising, and this is "three." (*Chana* 剎那 is also abbreviated as *cha* 剎. Other places where *cha* is used follow this abbreviation.) The three looks to the prior [instant] as an end, and to a subsequent [instant] as a beginning—this is what is meant by "each end is succeeded by a new beginning" (終則有始).[49] All things arise and cease, cease and arise, instant by instant; and from beginning to end, they conform to the rule of one, two, and three, constantly creating anew and not holding on to the old. This is what the *Book of Change* refers to as "utterly profuse yet they cannot be thrown into disarray."[50]

Sixth, you ask: "If all things arise and cease instant by instant, what is it that ordinary people all perceive to be old things?" ("Instant by instant" [剎那剎那] is abbreviated as *cha cha* 剎剎. Hereafter, this abbreviation is used.) It should be understood that instant by instant all things arise as soon as they cease, and that if they do not encounter external conditions then that which arises in the subsequent instant will perpetually seem to be like it was in the past. For example, if the black iron that had just ceased in the prior instant did not have fire as its external condition, then as it continued to arise in the subsequent instant, it would still seem to be like the black iron of the prior instant. This is called a "semblance that accompanies arising" (相似隨轉). (*Zhuan* 轉 means "to arise" [起]. To arise resembling what was prior is called a "semblance that accompanies arising." Glossing *zhuan* 轉 as *qi* 起 is based on Chinese translations of Buddhist texts.) Because of the semblance that accompanies arising, we perceive the new object before us still to be the former object. In fact, for all things, those that came before completely cease, and all those that come after newly arise. However, because a new thing resembles a previous thing, it is looked upon as it were the old thing.

This person further asked: "If it is the case that all things arise and cease, instant by instant, why are we not able to perceive this?"

I replied: "Instant by instant, arising and ceasing, ceasing and arising. Because the passing flow is so tightly integrated, how could you possibly

---

[48] Note that the arising and ceasing occur in same instant: "at precisely this interval of an instant."
[49] See, for example, "Tuan," Qian hexagram, 3.4b; "Qiu shui" 秋水 (Autumn Floods) chapter, *Zhuangzi*, p. 585.
[50] This is a paraphrase, and creative appropriation, of a passage in "Xici zhuan, shang," *Zhou yi*, 7.16b: "[The line statements] speak of the most mysterious things under heaven, yet one should not be repulsed by them. They speak of the most active things under heaven, yet one should not be confused by them."

perceive it? If, because you cannot perceive this instantaneous arising and ceasing, you choose not to believe in it, then let me ask you the following. With every passing breath, your body replaces the old with the new, and yet you still regard yourself to be the same self as the old one. Simply because you cannot perceive it, does this mean that you are going to deny that your body replaces the old with the new?"

Seventh, you maintain: "It is most certainly not the case that when all things first arise they are changing—it is indeed mistaken." If it is indeed as you presume (計) (*Ji* 計 is like saying "to guess"; other places where *ji* 計 is used have this same sense.), then when all things first arise, they would abide and not cease. Such things would have already kept to a fixed form and so be unable to change. However, people have all seen how everything constantly changes (轉) from one state to another. (Here *zhuan* 轉 means "change.")
[p. 29]
For example, milk can change into curd—the milk clearly has no fixed form. [We know that] the milk has no fixed form because from when it first arose it was changing. You should understand that instant by instant the process from milk to curd passes through countless semblances that accompany arising. Over the course of this process, however, the points of similarity necessarily gradually decrease. In broad outline, because of variations in temperature and other conditions that are encountered, as subsequent instants continue on from prior instants, the milk that arises gradually becomes dissimilar to the former milk, such that by the time it becomes curd, it is then of an entirely different state. You presume that when the milk first arises, it is devoid of change and has to pass through a long period of time before it changes into curd. How ignorant you are when it comes to observing things—you will never awaken!

Eighth, you criticize me, saying, "If all things cease as soon as they arise, then in this instant they would change suddenly rather than change gradually. In fact, all things gradually undergo [a process of] accumulation before they attain full flourishing. At the very beginning of the cosmos, primal *qi* (元氣) had not yet differentiated. It is particularly difficult to calculate when the countless heavens coalesced. The explanation that this was the result of sudden transformation seems hardly likely. As for the organs of animals or the structures of human societies, all were simple in the beginning, but in the end tended to become complex. This suffices to show that all things arose by way of gradual transformation."

My response is as follows. "Having examined your thesis, I find that it suffices to prove my own point. If all things abided when they first arose, they would have certainly kept to a fixed form, so how could they gradually attain full flourishing? Because instant by instant everything suddenly transforms, a thing at the subsequent moment newly arises to carry on from [the thing at] the prior [instant], and so necessarily flourishes much more than [the thing at] the prior [instant]. This can be compared to the flow of a river current. Just as a prior [moment of] flow ceases, a subsequent [moment of] flow arises to continue on from the prior [moment of flow], becoming ever more immense. This principle can be grasped everywhere—what point is there in hindering yourself? Sudden transformation and gradual transformation require one another in order to be realized. At each single instant, everything is suddenly transforming. Gradual transformation can be explained in terms of countless instants of arising and ceasing, ceasing and arising, flowing on in continuous succession. Zhu Xi 朱熹 [1130–1200] said: 'Heaven, Earth, the mountains, and the rivers—they do not accumulate the small to become large.' (See *Zhongyong zhangju* 中庸章句 [Section and Sentence Commentaries on *Zhongyong* (Balance as the Norm).].[51]) Was this statement made because of his belief in numinous powers? We cannot know. If, however, we use [the idea of] sudden transformation in an instant to explain why he said this, then this statement tallies wonderfully with the truth—truly sublime. Zhuangzi was very skilled at talking about transformation, and talked of 'moving yet leaving no sediment.'[52] (The flow of great transformation is "moving" [運]. Instant by instant, suddenly transforming, with no past thing remaining is "leaving no sediment.") This is precisely what "sudden transformation in an instant" means. ("Sudden transformation in an instant" means that every single instant is nothing other than sudden transformation. In other places where I have not provided a note to explain it, this is how it should be understood.) The myriad things all suddenly transform in an instant and do not temporarily abide, do not keep to a fixed form, and so gradually attain full flourishing. If, when things first arose, they abided and did not cease, then they would perpetually keep to

---

[51] Paraphrase of Zhu Xi's following annotation: "However, Heaven, Earth, the mountains, and the rivers—it is actually not through a process of accumulation that they become large." See *Zhongyong zhangju*, zhang 25, *Sishu zhangju jizhu* 四書章句集注 (Section and Sentence Comments and Collected Annotations on the Four Books) (Beijing: Zhonghua shuju, 1983), p. 35.

[52] "Tian dao" 天道 (The Way of Heaven), *Zhuangzi*, p. 457: "It is the way of Heaven to move leaving no sediment and so the myriad things are brought to completion. It is the way of the emperor to move leaving no sediment and so the whole realm rallies to him. It is the way of the sage to move leaving no sediment and so all within the seas submit to him."

[p. 30]
their already formed state—how could they then gradually flourish?"

Someone asked: "If at a prior instant [a thing] ceases as soon as it arises, and never extends to a subsequent instant, how can it become gradual?"

I replied: "If a thing is able to extend from a prior instant to a subsequent instant, then that thing does not cease, so what new arising is there to speak of? In fact, the interstice between the prior ceasing and the subsequent arising is very tightly interconnected. As the subsequent arises to succeed the prior it is simply so of itself (自然) that its flourishing is enhanced. Thus, the doctrine of gradual transformation is demonstrated."

Ninth, with regard to things, sometimes you people give rise to the view of eternalism (常見) and sometimes you give rise to the view of nihilism (斷見). (*Duan* 斷: "to sever.") Take the example of a tree. Now, just as in the past, one always sees it and so mistakenly assumes that it constantly exists—this to give rise to the view of eternalism. Suddenly you see that it has burned away and so you mistakenly assume that it has ceased to exist—this is to give rise to the view of nihilism. Both views are mistaken. If you hold that when things first arise, they constantly abide, then no subsequent things should ever arise again. If you hold that as soon as things cease then they are severed, this would also entail that no subsequent things should ever arise again. You should understand that for all things, instant by instant the old passes away (故故), ceasing entirely. This explains why there are no things that endure permanently. (*Gu* 故 is the same as "the old" [舊]. *Gu gu* 故故: layer upon layer of relegation to the past—that is, nothing that has passed away remains until later. This is "the old passes away, ceasing entirely." In other places where I have not provided a note to explain *gu gu*, this is how it should be understood.) Instant by instant, all things cease and pass away, giving rise to the new. This explains why there are no things that are severed.

Tenth, you criticize me, saying: "The Buddha taught that all things have the two principles of norms and their maintenance (軌持), hence they are named dharmas (法).[53] *Chi* 持 means 'to uphold'; 'not to abandon itself' (自體). (*Ziti* 自體 is like saying "itself" [自身]. Take the example of a writing brush, which is a thing. This brush is able to maintain itself and not reject and lose itself, and so it is able to

---

[53] In the entry under *fa* 法 in the *Digital Dictionary of Buddhism*, Charles Muller notes: "The word dharma is originally derived from the Indic root *dhṛ*, with the meaning of 'that which preserves or maintains,' especially that which preserves or maintains human activity." See http://www.buddhism-dict.net/cgi-bin/xpr-ddb.pl?q=%E6%B3%95; A. Charles Muller, ed., *Digital Dictionary of Buddhism*. http://buddhism-dict.net/ddb, edition of April 30, 2020. The sense of "norm" was subsequently derived from this primary sense.

constitute a brush. If "the itself" of the brush were to undergo a hundred transformations in an instant, then it would not be able to maintain itself and so would not constitute a brush. The case for other things can be extrapolated on the basis of the brush example.) *Gui* 軌 means 'norm' (規範). Norms are able to lead people (物) to form understanding (*Wu* 物 is like "people." *Guifan* 規範 is like "rule." This is saying that all things have rules, which can lead people to form understanding.), and so the significance of norms is especially important. The *Shi jing* 詩經 (Book of Odes) says: 'Where there is a thing, there is a rule.'[54] All things have rules—they are not in disarray, devoid of order. For this reason, we are able to form an understanding of things. The Buddhists' use of the two principles of norms and their maintenance to explain things is in implicit agreement with the *Book of Odes*. Actually, it is because all of the myriad things have the two principles of norms and their maintenance that makes our knowledge possible and the means for science to be established. Now, you claim that all things cease as soon as they arise and do not abide for a moment, and hence nothing has ever maintained self-entity (任持自體). In other words, there has never been anything that exists. Since things do not exist, of course there are no norms that can be sought. If this were truly the case, then knowledge would not be possible, and science

[p. 31]

would also have no basis. How could such a thesis make sense?"

I reply to you as follows. "This criticism you raise is intriguing; unfortunately, it is unpersuasive. On the one hand, the Buddha taught that all things cease in an instant, yet, on the other hand, he used norms and their maintenance to explain things—is that not a self-contradiction? Explaining things in terms of the two principles of norms and their maintenance [actually] means the following. Just as something at the prior instant ceases, in the subsequent instant a new thing arises; and this succession of semblances to prior things is incessant, therefore only by postulating that all things really exist can one then proceed to seek for the principles of things (物則). (The rules that pertain to things are called "the principles of things.") This account is based on conventional truth, and serves to affirm mundane teachings (世間法)—it does not contravene the truth."

Addendum. The Buddhists have the doctrine of the "two truths": ultimate truth and conventional truth. For example, ordinary people all agree

---

[54] "Zheng min" 烝民 (The Multitudes) (Mao 260), *Shisan jing zhushu*, 18/3.11b.

that the physical world exists, and the Buddhists teach in accord with this conventional view; this is called conventional truth. As for that which transcends conventional knowledge, and proceeds to seek the truth, that is ultimate truth.

Eleventh, you enquire about the following: "Instant by instant, all things suddenly transform—this seems to be like a great cyclone drifting about with no foundation."

My reply: "No, no. Transformation does not suddenly occur with no basis; as already explained, there must be a true source. ("True source": a term to describe Reality.) The true source contains the myriad existents and is inexhaustible. *Zhongyong* describes its wondrousness as 'a constantly flowing deep spring'[55]—an excellent analogy. ("Deep spring": that which is inexhaustible; a metaphor for the true source. "Constantly flowing" refers to Reality's transforming into great function; endlessly productive and reproductive, like a deep spring that always flows and has no end. This is a metaphor for great function.) **Because their inherent nature is replete** (Reality is the inherent nature of great function; it is like the way that the ocean is the inherent nature of the myriad waves. There is nothing in which the inherent nature is deficient.) **the myriad transformations are ever renewing.**"

Above I have discussed [how things] arise and cease instant [by instant], and explained that nothing abides even for a moment, in order to show that the two impetuses of one contraction and one expansion constantly create and do not grow exhausted; that they are ever renewing and do not hold onto the old. In other words, the flow of intrinsic Reality is without end, without stagnation—nothing more, nothing less. This is what the *Book of Change* means when it says: "this refers to revealing the subtle [principles] of the myriad things" (妙萬物而為言者).[56]

---

[55] "Zhongyong," 53.12a. Based on Xiong's interpretation, the original passage can be translated as follows: "Vast and all pervading, like a deep spring that constantly flows."

[56] "Shuo gua" 說卦 (Explaining the Trigrams) commentary, *Zhou yi*, 9.6a. This translation is based on Xiong's gloss of the phrase from the "Shuo guo commentary" in correspondence with Ren Hongxiu 任鴻雋 (1886–1961), "Da Ren Shuyong xiansheng" 答任叔永先生 (Reply to Mr Ren Shuyong). This undated correspondence (possibly written late in 1958 or in 1959) is appended to *Ming xin pian*, p. 310. There Xiong uses the phrase to refer to philosophy; here he uses it to refer to the flow of Reality. The relevant passage reads: "Han Confucians said 'principles that are subtle are said to be sublime.'* By comprehensively observing the myriad things, philosophy grasps their profoundly subtle principles. Its words directly gather together the extremely subtle (直湊單微).** There is nothing it does not include yet it does not get fixated on images, hence the expression 'revealing the subtle [principles] of the myriad things.'" *The reference here is to Xun Yue 荀悅 (148–209 CE), "Zayan, xia" 雜言下 (Miscellaneous Words, B), *Shenjian* 申鑒 (Extended Reflections), Huang Xingzeng 黃省曾 (1496–1546) annot., *Shenjian zhu* 申鑒注 (Annotated *Extended Reflections*), 5.3b, *Sibu congkan chubian* 四部叢刊初編 (Collectanea of the Four Categories, First Series) (Shanghai: Shangwu yinshuguan, 1919–1922). **The 2001 edition of *Ti yong lun* mistakenly gives the

The principle that all things cease as soon as they arise is beyond doubt. The *Book of Change* specialist Yao Peizhong 姚配中 [1792–1844] said that everything has only a temporary existence. (See his chapter, "*Yi* 'zhuan,' Qian gua" 易傳乾卦 [The Qian Hexagram in the "Attached Statements" of the *Book of Change*]. Here, although I have changed his words, it is based on his intended meaning.)[57]

[p. 32]

I still find Yao's account to be insufficiently penetrating. The "Attached Statements Commentary" to the *Book of Change* says: "Swift yet not hasty; far reaching yet not moving."[58] This reveals the meaning of ceasing in an instant—[as such,] what thing can abide momentarily? Instant by instant, the power of great transformation ceases as soon as it arises and arises as soon as it ceases. Such is the rapidity with which the old is discarded and the new is created; and in doing so, great transformation certainly does not adopt a posture of ferocious haste, hence it is said "swift yet not hasty." Further, because [things] cease in an instant, a prior thing never proceeds to a subsequent moment; however, because of the semblances that, instant by instant, accompany arising it appears as if the prior thing reaches a subsequent moment. Hence it is said, "far reaching yet not moving." (On the meaning of "semblances that accompany arising," see above.) The purport behind the subtle words of the Exalted Sage (宣聖)[59] and of Śākyamuni tallied with one another remotely across different lands—is this not remarkable?!

Zhuangzi was skilled at expounding the meaning of the *Book of Change*. The "Da zong shi" 大宗師 (Great Ancestral Teacher) chapter says: "There was a person who, fearing that he might lose his boat, hid it in a remote and secure hidden ravine. Fearing that a particular mountain would disappear, he hid the mountain in a deep marsh. This can indeed be said to have hidden them very securely, yet in the middle of the night (A metaphor for being in the midst of the unseeable.), quite unexpectedly, a powerful monster (A metaphor for transformation.) put both the boat and the mountain on his back and scurried

---

character *chong* 沖 instead of *dan* 單. In his 1949 book, *Han Feizi pinglun* 韓非子評論 (Evaluation of Han Feizi), *Xiong Shili quanji*, vol. 5, p. 341, Xiong glosses this phrase (where it is correctly given as 直湊單微). The translation of the phrase is based on Xiong's gloss.

[57] Xiong seems to be referring to the following passage in Yao Peizhong, *Zhou yi Yao shi xue* 周易姚氏學 (Mr Yao's Studies on the *Book of Change*) (Hubei [n.p.]: Chongwen shuju, 1877), 14.6b: "Change is within things, from their beginning to the end. When they reach their end then they alter; when they alter they transform. When this one ends that one begins; when this one dies that one is born."

[58] "Xici zhuan, shang," 7.25b. Translated so as to reflect Xiong's sentiments.

[59] Confucius; traditionally regarded as the author of the "Shi yi" 十翼 (Ten Wings) commentaries to the *Book of Change*, which includes the "Appended Statements" commentary.

away, disappearing without a trace. (A metaphor for the wondrous swiftness of transformation, such that no clue can be apprehended.) Incredibly, the whereabouts of both the boat and the mountain were unknown."[60] (Here I have translated this passage using vernacular Chinese.) The [purport of] this passage is immense and profound. In his annotation, Guo Zixuan 郭子玄 [c. 252–312] wrote:

> No power that comes from lacking power is greater than transformation. Hence, Heaven and Earth are lifted up [and carried away] in order to advance to the new; the mountain ranges are carried [and taken way], so as to discard the old. The past does not stand still for a moment and suddenly the new has already been entered into; and so, there has never been a time when the myriad things in Heaven and Earth were not shifting. Everything in the world is new but it is looked upon as old. The boat changes daily yet it is regarded as if it were as before. The mountain changes daily yet it is seen to be as previously. All that I now closely encounter, I lose—it has all gone into Darkness. Thus, the "I" of the past is no longer the "I" of the present. "I" and "the present" pass together. Is it likely that previously I was able to preserve the past? Yet no one in the world is aware of this. Instead, they say that what is encountered now can be bound and so be present. Is this not ignorance!?[61]

Zixuan's explanation is inherited directly from Zhuangzi who had used it to explore the *Great Change*—it is particularly worth savoring.

Both the Buddhists and our Confucian *Book of Change* perceived the principle that all things cease in an instant. Although Laozi and Zhuangzi had deep insight into the purport of the *Book of Change*, I exclusively take the *Book of Change* as my authority, as my concerns are actually quite different from those of the two "schools." (Laozi and Zhuangzi are both Daoists; and the Daoists and the Buddhists are referred to as the "two schools" [二氏].) "Ceasing in an instant" is actually "removing the old and generating the new, instant by instant." The Confucians use this to show that the human way and administration of the masses should give expression to the vigor of Heaven's movement, constantly removing the old and taking up the new,

---

[60] "Da zong shi," *Zhuangzi*, p. 243. In the light of Xiong's interpretation, the original passage can be translated: "People say it is safe to hide a boat in a ravine or a mountain in a marsh. Yet in the middle of the night a strong man carries them off on his back, and in the darkness, you do not know where they are."

[61] Guo Zixuan is Guo Xiang 郭象. See *Zhuangzi*, p. 244.

[p. 33]

tirelessly self-strengthening. (From "The Confucians" up to here is one sentence. The Qian hexagram takes its image from the vigor of Heaven's movement so as to show that the defining characteristic associated with the flow of intrinsic Reality is utmost vigor.[62] The "Shuo gua" 說卦 [Explaining the Trigrams] commentary says: "Ge 革 [Overturning] removes the old; Ding 鼎 [Cauldron] takes up the new."[63] "Tirelessly self-strengthening" is also an image of Qian.) The Buddhists take "ceasing in an instant" to be impermanence, and deem it be observing emptiness (空觀),[64] and so end up becoming opposed to human life. Although Laozi and Zhuangzi also perceived that [all things] arise and cease in an instant, in the end they returned to the self-so as their foundation (歸本自然), preserving quietude and following transformation (任化) (In both the way of self-cultivation and the way of providing order for the masses, Laozi and Zhuangzi took preserving quietude as the foundation. "Following transformation" is to follow the transformation of the self-so.), while abandoning human ability (人能). (Neither Laozi nor Zhuangzi earned the distinction of fashioning and bringing to completion [the Way of] Heaven and Earth and assisting the myriad things.[65] This is because they failed to understand the purport of "the sage realizes his capacities by himself" (成能), as stated in the *Book of Change*.[66]) All in all, the two schools are one-sided and so lost the proper way. There is no need to discuss this in depth here.

Five characteristics of transformation

How magnificent transformation is! Yet, it is so subtle that it is difficult to describe. Here I will briefly highlight five of its characteristics. The first is the characteristic of illusory existents (幻有). It is by means of contraction and expansion that transformation is accomplished—instant by instant, bursting forth. Like illusory appearances of a mountain peak in the clouds, rapidly (率爾) changing shape [illusory existents] suddenly cease and suddenly arise. (All of the myriad existents are nothing other than the transformation of one

---

[62] The "Tuan" commentary to the Qian hexagram, *Zhou yi*, 1.16b, states: "The movement of Heaven is vigorous. The gentleman tirelessly strengthens himself."
[63] The reference should actually be to the "Za gua" 雜卦 (Assorted Hexagrams) commentary (*Zhou yi*, 9.15b) and not the "Shuo gua" commentary.
[64] In Chapter 2, p. 96, Xiong glosses *kong guan* 空觀 as follows: "*Guan* 觀 is 'to observe' [觀察]. To observe that all things have always been empty is called observing emptiness."
[65] See note 29 in this chapter.
[66] "Xici, xia," 8.24a. Translation based on Xiong's gloss of *cheng neng* 成能, *Ming xin pian*, p. 263.

contraction and one expansion. Although they "exist" they are not fixed and so are said to be "illusory existents." *Shuaier* 率爾 has the sense of "arising suddenly.") Like the sudden turning of a wind wheel (風輪),[67] toppling mountains and convulsing oceans, transformation has awesome power. The strangeness of the myriad transformations is indeed like this, hence they are called "illusory existents." "Illusory existents": the abundant great existents (大有) have no fixed form (相) (*Xiang* 相: form/characteristic [相狀]. The [purport of the] Great Existents hexagram in the *Book of Change* is worth savoring.[68]), hence they are said to be illusory. (Here the word "illusory" is an adjective and has no negative sense.)

The second is Reality (真實). The myriad transformations are all the flow of Reality. (*Zhenshi* 真實 refers to intrinsic Reality [本體].) One flower, one dharma realm (法界); one leaf, one *rulai* 如來. (*Fajie* 法界 refers to Reality [實體]. *Rulai* 如來: no place whence it came [無所從來], hence the term.[69] Here I use it as an alternative term for Reality.)[70] It is hardly the case that the true characteristic/mark (實相)[71] can be sought apart from illusory characteristics/marks (幻相). Which intelligent person would be misled about the treasure they harbor within? ("Treasure": a metaphor for Reality [真實]. This is saying that people should not mislead themselves about what is real.)

The third is perfection (圓滿). As great transformation circulates, there is nowhere it is not perfect. Take the example of written words. The single character *ren* 人 necessarily includes all people, and distinguishes all that is not human, otherwise the word would not be able to stand for what it represents. Hence the single character *ren* 人 includes all existents, bar none.[72] Just

---

[67] Xiong may be drawing on the following passage in the *Daban niepan jing* 大般涅槃經 (*Mahāparinirvāṇa-sūtra*; Great Nirvana Sutra), T7.1, 191c22–26: "Earthquakes have eight causal conditions. The first is that the earth is lodged in water. In turn, this great body of water is lodged in a wind wheel. In turn, this wind wheel is lodged in space. Sometimes ferocious winds blow up with great force and blast the wind wheel. Once the wind wheel moves then the water also moves, and once the water moves then the earth moves." Traditionally, the translation of T7 has been attributed to Faxian 法顯 (d. c. 420). Recently, Michael Radich has shown that "the *Mahāparinirvāṇa-sūtra T* no. 7 is much closer to the style of certain texts ascribed to 'Guṇabhadra' than it is to 'Faxian.'" See "Was the *Mahāparinirvāṇa-sūtra* 大般涅槃經 T7 Translated by 'Faxian'?: An Exercise in the Computer-Assisted Assessment of Attributions in the Chinese Buddhist Canon," *Hualin International Journal of Buddhist Studies*, 2.1 (2019): p. 266.

[68] In the "Buddhist teachings, B" chapter, p. 156, Xiong writes that the Dayou hexagram (hexagram 14) "acclaims the abundance of the cosmos' myriad images (萬象)."

[69] See, for example, *Jin'gang bore boluomi jing* 金剛般若波羅蜜經 (*Vajracchedikā-prajñāpāramitā-sūtra*; Diamond Sutra), T235.8, 752b4.

[70] Dharma realm (*dharmadhātu*) has several meanings; here Xiong employs it in the sense of Reality realm; the manifestation of suchness. *Rulai* or "thus come one" is typically a rendering of *tathāgata*, a buddha or the Buddha. "No place whence it came" implies that Reality is uncaused, or in Buddhist terms, is unconditioned.

[71] This Buddhist term is synonymous with suchness.

[72] The logic here is that although the term *ren* refers to all people, in making this distinction it simultaneously makes implicit reference to all that is not *ren*.

as with the character *ren* 人, so too it is the same with all the countless characters. Zhuangzi said: "Mt Tai is not large, and an autumn hair is not small."[73] This is not a deliberate attempt to make strange remarks. From the perspective of the non-uniformity of the myriad existents, large and small are distinguished. From the perspective that the myriad things co-exist, none stands alone, and they are of one taste and uniform (一味平等)—so what distinctions of large and small are there? There is also a saying: "To subsume one hundred million eons (億劫)[74] into an instant; to contain infinity in a single mote." (Even though a trillion [億萬] years is very long, it is subsumed into an instant;

[p. 34]

although immeasurable worlds are vast, they are contained in a single mote.) As great transformation circulates, it assumes a myriad intersubsumptive shapes and appearances, and there is nowhere it is deficient. Its wondrousness is difficult to ponder.

The fourth is inter-pervasion (交遍). Because of the profuse flourishing of the myriad transformations, it is said that there are infinite worlds (界). These infinite worlds (世界) (*Shijie* 世界 is abbreviated as *jie* 界.), at the same location, pervade each other. (Infinite worlds in one locus, each and every one inter-pervading fully.) It is not like many horses being unable to occupy the same location (For example, in the eastern corner there is one horse, but it would certainly be impossible to place numerous horses there by piling them on top of one another. With respect to this kind of situation, the sense of inter-pervasion cannot be established, and that is why at the sentence begins "It is not like."), but rather is like the light from a myriad lamps mutually enmeshing.[75] (A thousand lamps arranged in a room, the light from each lamp fully pervading the room. In other words, a thousand lamps in one room, layer upon layer, enmeshing and layering one another, not obscuring one another, hence "light [from a myriad lamps] mutually enmeshing." Infinite worlds each inter-penetrating—principle [理] is also like this.)

---

[73] "Qi wu lun," *Zhuangzi*, p. 79: "Nothing in the world is larger than the tip of an autumn hair, and Mt Tai is small."

[74] Based on his comment, it would thus seem that Xiong deems an "eon" (劫; *kalpa) to be 10,000 years.

[75] The mutually enmeshing lamp lights analogy is almost certainly based on Huayan master Chengguan's 澄觀 (738–839) description of the third of the *Shi xuan* 十玄 (Ten mysterious [gateways]); see Chengguan, *Da Huayan jing lüece* 大華嚴經略策 (Outline of [Chengguan's] [Commentary on] the *Flower Garland Sutra* [大方廣佛華嚴經疏; T1735]), T1737.36, 707b15–16: the gateway of the intersubsumption of one and many, in which their differences are maintained (一多相容不同門).

For example, ordinary people maintain that the Beijing many other people and I are all located in is the one and the same Beijing. In fact, however many people there are in Beijing is however many Beijings there are. For example, in person Zhang's life, his affective interactions (交感) with Beijing change daily (日化), and these affective interactions are certainly quite different from those experienced by person Li. (*Hua* 化 is like "change" [變異]. Subsequent uses follow this.) In person Li's life, his affective interactions with Beijing change daily, and these affective interactions are also different from those experienced by person Zhang. Hence, Zhang and Li each have their own Beijing. Ordinary people, however, maintain that it is not the case that Beijing is not one and the same, rather, it is simply because what Zhang and Li each takes in (攝受) about Beijing is different, and so it seems to be that Beijing is not one and the same. Little do they realize that what Zhang and Li each takes in about Beijing differs precisely because Beijing has never been one and the same. If Beijing were one and the same, how could it be that what Zhang and Li each takes in is different? These conventional accounts treat result as cause and cannot be relied upon. In sum, "Beijing" is extremely complex and cannot be said to be one. As such, the multiple Beijings at one location, each pervading fully, are like one thousand lamps in a room, their many lights (光光) mutually enmeshing—is it not a marvel?! (*Guang* 光 is reduplicated because the lights are numerous.)

The fifth is "inexhaustible" (無盡). Taiji 太極 (Supreme Pivot) is a boundless and inexhaustible great treasure store (*Taiji* is [another] name for Reality.) and so of course its flow is inexhaustible. ("Flow" is function. In the old draft I wrote, "The flow of intrinsic Reality is called function."[76]) As its myriad currents surge forth, the past has already ceased, the present does not abide, and the future will arise in constant renewal; instant by instant the old ceases and the new arises. This is what specialists of the *Book of Change* acclaimed as "the myriad things exist in rich abundance"[77] and what *Balance as the Norm* praised as "perfect genuineness that is unceasing."[78] These five characteristics

---

[76] By "old draft" here Xiong is referring the 1932 edition of the *New Treatise*, p. 39, where he writes: "As a word, 'function' refers to the flow of intrinsic Reality."

[77] Alluding to the following passage in "Xici, xia" commentary, 7.12b–13b (translated on the basis of how I understand Xiong to have interpreted the passage): "[The Way] arouses the myriad things but does not share in the worries of the sage [ruler]. Its consummate potency and its great achievements are supreme. The rich abundance [of the myriad things] is referred to as 'great achievements'; the daily renewal [of the myriad things] is referred to as 'consummate potency.' Production and reproduction is referred to as 'change.'"

[78] "Zhongyong," 53.5b.

elucidate transformation, and although it is extremely difficult to exhaust its profundities, they come close.
[p. 35]

When I was young, I was fond of exploring cosmology. At the time when the rapid changes occurred, I took part in revolution and was forced to stop my studies.[79] Later, when I tried to pick up my former studies, I became profoundly distressed that my intelligence was limited, so I reflected extensively, seeking verification in books. Although the old books from the late Zhou period had perished, the odd fragments occasionally preserved by people in the Han [206 BCE–220 CE] period provided much to ponder. And yet, this was really only like a small fire—how could it inspire great understanding? As for post-Han corpora of writings, trying to find something in them that would help me to probe deeply into what I was seeking proved to be even more futile. Left with no choice, I widely searched Buddhist teachings. I inquired into the Nothing but Consciousness (唯識)[80] treatises with the Venerable Master from Yihuang 宜黃 [Ouyang Jingwu 歐陽竟無 (1871–1943)], but, before long, I grew tired of its analysis for being too divorced from reality, and then returned to the period before [the advent of Yogācāra] to explore Nāgārjuna's (龍樹 [ca. 150–250]) learning.[81] In pursuing Buddhist teachings, I applied my energies to the Emptiness and Existence schools of Mahāyāna. I did not, however, pay much attention to Buddhist debates about mental [phenomena] and material [phenomena]. (This topic should be dealt with separately.) Rather, it was exclusively Buddhist discourse on the nature and characteristics (性相) that I strenuously explored. (What the Buddhists call the nature and characteristics, I call Reality and function.) The reason I advocate the non-duality of Reality and function in my cosmology is because I could not agree with Buddhist teachings, and so, turning back, from further away I drew from other things, and near at hand I drew from my own person, gradually becoming awakened, and so returned to the *Great Change*. In what follows, I will discuss Buddhist teachings. All this really amounts to is to summarize the main purport of the Mahāyāna Emptiness and Existence schools' [respective accounts of] the nature and characteristics, so as to differentiate them clearly.

---

[79] See "Superfluous Words," p. 9.
[80] The Yogācāra school.
[81] The Madhyamaka school.

2
Buddhist Teachings, A

I wish to rectify the Mahāyāna Emptiness and Existence schools' theses about the nature and characteristics. [In order to do so,] it is necessary that I provide separate, brief explanations of the two terms, Reality and function, as used in this treatise, and the two Mahāyāna terms, dharma nature and dharma characteristics.

Reality and function, dharma nature and dharma characteristics

I will first explain Reality and function. (Hitherto, scholars have been unrestrained in their use of the two characters, *ti* 體 and *yong* 用. In this treatise I discuss Reality and function in the context of cosmology—they have a particular meaning. Readers must seek their meaning on the basis of this treatise's system.) "Reality" (體) is an abbreviation of "the intrinsic Reality of the cosmos" (宇宙本體) (*Benti* 本體 is also called *shiti* 實體.) and "function" (用) is Reality's transforming into function (功用).
[p. 36]
(Reality transforms and moves without stopping; produces and reproduces without exhaustion. It is with respect to its transforming and moving, producing and reproducing that it is said to be the function of Reality.) Function has the two aspects of contraction and expansion, transforming endlessly yet always following the principle of mutually opposing and mutually completing. This is what is called function (功用). (Also abbreviated as *yong* 用.)

How magnificent are the myriad images of the cosmos! Of the profound and mysterious nothing is more subtle than the pure and spirit-like (精神); of the manifest and bright nothing is more exuberant than matter (物質). Supreme, the pure and spirit-like (至精) sets matter in motion (運物) and is the initiator (始) of movement. (*Jing* 精 is the abbreviation of *jingshen* 精神. *Zhi* 至 is a term of acclamation. *Shi* 始 means "to activate" [主動]; it does not refer to temporal beginning. "Sets matter in motion": from within, the pure and spirit-like commands and sets in motion [幹運]¹ all material things, actively guiding things.) Supreme, matter (至物) contains the pure and spirit-like and submits to transformation (承化). (*Wu* 物 is the abbreviation of *wuzhi* 物質. *Zhi* 至 has the same meaning as above. "Submits to transformation": The movement of matter [is due to] its submitting to the pure and spirit-like, advancing together with it and not descending. [Concerning] this sentence and the previous sentence [in the main text], readers should consult the third section of second folio of *To the Origin of the Ru*, where there is a general discussion of *Great Change*.²) The pure and spirit-like and the material are intersubsumptive and interactive. Their transformation as the non-uniformity of the myriad existents (萬有不齊) is the great functioning of intrinsic Reality. ("Great" is a term of acclamation.)

This treatise posits the tenet that Reality and function are non-dual. You students must not seek for Reality outside of the flow of great function. I am confident that my judgment on this matter cannot be shaken, as it is the fruit gained after a lifetime of painstaking enquiry—I would not dare to talk nonsense.

Someone asked: "Why do you say that Reality and function are non-dual?"

I replied: "Reality itself gives rise to transformation and movement and so becomes function. Would you say that Reality and function are two? It is like the ocean, which itself gives rise to transformation and movement and so becomes the numerous waves. ("Numerous waves" is an analogy for function. "Ocean" is an analogy for Reality.) Would you say that the ocean and the numerous waves are two [distinct entities]?"

Having thus explained Reality and function, now I will explain the two terms *faxing* 法性 and *faxiang* 法相.

The character *fa* 法 [dharma] is the most common generic term in Buddhist studies. The myriad existents are collectively called "dharmas."

The character *xiang* 相 (To be read on the fourth tone.) has two explanations in Buddhist texts. 1. *Xiang* means "characteristic/form" [相狀]. (Each dharma has a type of characteristic. For example, material dharmas have the characteristic of material obstruction and can be seen. Mental dharmas do not have the characteristic of obstruction, and, although they cannot be seen, nevertheless one can perceive them within oneself. They have the characteristic of having no [physical] characteristic [無相之相], and they have a formless form [無狀之狀].) 2. *Xiang* is like *ti* 體 (Reality). (In glossing

---

¹ Translated on the basis of Xiong's gloss of this term in "Explaining Transformation," p. 31: "*Yun* 運 means 'to move'; 'to set in motion'; *wo* 斡 has the sense of 'to command.'"

² The division Xiong refers to is no longer used in later editions of *Yuan Ru*. He is probably referring to an extended note on p. 730 of the 2001 edition.

the character *xiang* with the character *ti*, this sense of *xiang* is different from that of characteristic/form.)

The character *xing* 性 also has more than one sense. There are examples in Buddhist texts where it is glossed as "nature" in the sense of "moral nature" (德性), such as good nature,
[p. 37]
bad nature, and so forth. Where it is glossed with the character *ti* 體 (Reality), this sense of *xing* is the same as that sense of *xiang* when it is glossed as *ti*.[3]

Faxiang 法相 is the collective term for mental and material dharmas. Because mental and material dharmas are not permanent (恆常) (Mental and material dharmas are not things that never change.) they are not fixed. (This can be understood on the basis of the previous comment.) As they transform, change, and secretly move, there are characteristics that deceptively appear ("Deceptive": although they appear as characteristics, they are not fixed, hence the text says, "deceptively appear.") and so they are called "dharma characteristics." (Dharma characteristics are like what is commonly called "phenomena.")

Faxing 法性 refers to the Reality of the myriad dharmas, which is called *zhenru* 真如 (suchness). (The character *xing* 性 in *faxing* 法性 should be interpreted as having the sense of the character *ti* 體; see the note above. "Myriad dharmas" refers to mental and material dharmas. The Reality of mental and material dharmas is called *zhenru* 真如. *Zhen* 真: real; *ru* 如: unchanging. For details, see the Tang work, *[Dasheng] baifa [ming men lun] shu* [大乘]百法[明門論]疏 [Commentary on the *Mahāyāna śatadharma-prakāśamukha-śāstra* (Lucid Introduction to the One Hundred Dharmas)].[4])
The term "dharma nature" (法性) in Mahāyāna and the term "Reality" (實體) in this treatise are equivalent. The term "dharma characteristics" (法相) in Mahāyāna and the term "function" (功用) in this treatise are equivalent. However, Buddhist discussions of nature and characteristics ("Dharma nature" is abbreviated as "nature" and "dharma characteristics" is abbreviated as "characteristics." See master Kui[ji]'s Commentary on *Demonstration of Nothing but Consciousness* and so

---

[3] Historically, *xiang* 相, *xing* 性, and *ti* 體 had been variously used to translate the Sanskrit term *sva-bhāva*.

[4] Puguang 普光 (d. c. 664 CE), *Dasheng baifa ming men lun shu*, T1837.44, 60c15, 21–22: "In general terms, there are six kinds of unconditioned dharmas.... The sixth is *zhenru*.... Dharma nature has always been inherently quiescent and extinguished. It has the characteristic of not moving and is called *zhenru*." Unconditioned dharmas neither arise nor cease. In classical Indian Buddhism, "They lack a generative cause or dependence upon a collocation of causes and conditions, as well any activity that generates its own effect." In contrast, "Conditioned dharmas arise through the cooperative efficacy of a specific generative cause and a collocation of other requisite causes and conditions; and once arisen, they themselves act as generative causes." Collett Cox, "From Category to Ontology: The Changing Role of Dharma in Sarvāstivāda Abhidharma," *Journal of Indian Philosophy*, 32.5/6 (December 2004): 556–558.

forth.⁵) and the purport of this treatise's "Reality and function are non-dual" are extremely antithetical and cannot be reconciled.

Mahāyāna learning is divided into the two wheels of Emptiness (空) and Existence (有). (These two schools are like the two wheels on a chariot.) The Emptiness school established the two truths (諦) of ultimate and conventional. (*Di* 諦 means "true/real" [實].) [According to the Emptiness school,] because ordinary people maintain that the actual principles of things are in accord with how they have been explained, conventional truth is thus established. [According to the Emptiness school,] because ultimate truth truly exists, and is not something that conventional truth can grasp, ultimate truth is thus established. In the domain of conventional truth, the Emptiness school does not refute dharma characteristics. When it comes to expounding ultimate truth, however, the Emptiness school strenuously refutes characteristics in order to reveal the nature (破相以顯性). (*Xian* 顯 is like "clearly show." This is saying that dharma characteristics are refuted so as to reveal the dharma nature and awaken people.) In consequence of this, however, neither dharma characteristics nor dharma nature is established. In other words, both Reality and function are empty. (In what follows, when using the terms "nature" and "characteristics," sometimes I will replace them directly with "Reality" and "function," respectively.)

The Existence school arose so as to correct the errors of the Emptiness school—an extremely laudable aim. It is particularly regrettable that [the teachings of this school] were fragmented and broken and it never reached the origin (本原).⁶ (Xuanzang was a venerable master of the Existence school. His promulgation of the learning of Asaṅga [無著] and Vasubandhu [世親]⁷ can indeed be said to be supreme! For more than a millennium, the intelligentsia has only ever revered and has never cast doubt upon this school. When I began to discover the fallacies of the Vasubandhu line [of Yogācāra], I had wanted to write a detailed treatise on the matter, but I feared that I did not have the energy to sustain me. A detailed treatment would have been tediously lengthy.) Now I should rectify [the errors of the] two schools. I will begin with Nāgārjuna's learning. (Because Nāgārjuna was the progenitor of the Emptiness school, it is called "Nāgārjuna's learning.")

---

⁵ There are multiple examples of these abbreviations in *Cheng weishi lun shuji*.
⁶ The origin of the cosmos; Reality.
⁷ The fourth-century CE progenitors of Yogācāra.

1. Doctrines of the Emptiness school

What do I mean by saying that the Emptiness school refutes characteristics in order to reveal the nature? Here I will adduce evidence from the *Bore xin jing* 般若心經 (Heart Sutra),[8] and so [my arguments] will be beyond
[p. 38]
doubt. The *Heart Sutra* is a small book that selects and summarizes the profound and subtle [teachings] of the *Da bore[boluomiduo] jing* 大般若[波羅蜜多]經 (*Mahāprajñāpāramitā-sūtra*; Perfection of Wisdom Sutra),[9] compiled as an outline of the essential ones. The *Perfection of Wisdom Sutra* (Hereafter abbreviated as *Da jing* 大經.) is the fundamental canon of the Emptiness school, variously referred to as the king of the sutras, the mother of the buddhas. It makes clear its main tenet at the very beginning of the sutra: "[Avalokiteśvara Bodhisattva,] perceiving that the five aggregates (蘊) are all empty...."[10] This phrase comprehensively encompasses the purport of the entire *Perfection of Wisdom Sutra*. The "five aggregates" is another term for dharma characteristics. When all dharma characteristics are broken down and separately placed in clusters, then these are said to be "aggregates." (*Yun* 蘊 means "cluster" [聚].)

1.1 The five aggregates

In total there are said to be five aggregates. The first is form (色) and it includes all [material] things. (In Buddhist texts, the word *se* 色 has both a broad and a narrow sense. In its narrow sense, it refers to blue-green, yellow, red, white, and other colors. In its broad sense, it refers to all material things. Here the term is employed in its broad sense.) Everything from our bodies all the way through to large things in Heaven and Earth is included in form.

The next four aggregates are sensation (受), perception (想), mental formation (行), and consciousness (識). These include all mental dharmas,

---

[8] A short sutra that articulates the doctrine of emptiness.
[9] A collection of sutras that articulate the doctrine of the perfection of wisdom.
[10] The five aggregates (*yun* 蘊; *skandha*) are used to explain the contingent, compositional nature of human existence and to highlight its lack of intrinsic essence or selfness. There are six Chinese translations of the *Heart Sutra*. Based on the wording of the passages he cites, Xiong could have been using either *Mohe bore boluomiduo xin jing* 摩訶般若波羅蜜多心經, translated by Xuanzang (T251) or *Bore boluomiduo xin jing* 般若波羅蜜多心經, translated by Prajñā 般若 and Liyan 利言 (eighth century) (T253). I will refer to the T251 translation. This particular passage is at T251.8, 848c6.

broken down into these four [aggregates]. The sensation aggregate is so called because it refers to receiving (受) pain, pleasure, and so forth from cognitive objects (境). (*Shou* 受 means "to receive.") This is to establish the sensation aggregate on the basis of the function of sensations.

The perception aggregate is so called because it refers to apprehending images in cognitive objects. For example, when a blue-green color is "taken as cognitive object" (緣), it is presumed that it is blue-green and not red, white, and so forth—this is to apprehend an image. (The character *yuan* 緣 has the senses of "to climb up," "to think about," and so forth.) In this way, knowledge is developed by discriminating things and analyzing principles. This is to establish the perception aggregate on the basis of the function of knowledge.

The mental formation aggregate is so called because it refers to giving rise to constructs when a cognitive object that is taken as the cause of consciousness is mentally grasped. (*Xing* 行 means "to construct." For example, upon seeing a flower that is attractive I think about snapping its stem—this is a construct. If we extend this to all actions or open it up [to include] even the grandest enterprises, they are all constructs.) This is to establish the mental formation aggregate on the basis of the function of intention.

Further, it should be understood that the sensation, perception, and mental formation aggregates are all called "mental associates" (心所 [*caitta*]). "Mental associates" is just like saying "all the various functions of the mind." The reason they are called mental associates is that although they are not identical to the mind, nevertheless they belong to the mind. Within the mental formation aggregate, however, there is not just one mental associate, but many. You students should understand that no separate aggregate is established for any of them, but they are all included within the mental formation aggregate.

Having now explained that three of the aggregates are mental associates, I turn finally to the consciousness aggregate, which includes the eight consciousnesses. (Note: *Cheng* [*weishi*] *lun* 成[唯識]論 [Demonstration of Nothing but Consciousness Treatise] states: "Whenever 'consciousness' is referred to [in this treatise], this also includes each of the mental associates."[11] Since I have distinguished [the categories] of the five aggregates and mental associates, therefore the consciousness aggregate [refers] only to the mind and does not include mental associates. In the past, I noticed that readers of Buddhist texts often find it difficult to understand the distinction

---

[11] Xuanzang, *Cheng weishi lun*, T1585.31, 1a28–29: "In this treatise, the word 'consciousness' also includes mental associates."

between the mind and mental associates. I would say to them, "Buddhists like to use the analytical method to dissect the mind into fragments. In seeking understanding, all you need to focus on are their theories.") In the beginning, the Hīnayānists taught that there are six

[p. 39]

consciousnesses: the visual consciousness, the auditory consciousness, the olfactory consciousness, the gustatory consciousness, the tactile consciousness, and the thinking consciousness. The Mahāyāna Existence school was the first to add the seventh consciousness, the *manas*, and the eighth consciousness, the *ālaya*. Although the Hīnayānists lacked the names, "seventh consciousness" and "eighth consciousness," they nevertheless already had that which corresponds to the sense of those consciousnesses, as has been detailed in various treatises. In sum, the sensation aggregate refers specifically to [material] things, and the other four aggregates all refer to the mental [dharmas.] Accordingly, the five aggregates are collectively divided into the two aspects of mental and material.

1.2 The purport of the *Heart Sutra*

Above I have explained the meaning of the names of the five aggregates. Now I turn to explain the purport of the *Heart Sutra*. What is meant by "the five aggregates are all empty"? *Kong* 空 means non-existent (空無). This is saying that because no dharma has real self-entity (自性) all dharmas should be said to be empty. (As noted above, in Chinese translations of Buddhist texts, the character *xing* 性 is sometimes glossed as *ti* 體. Here, *zixing* 自性 is the same as saying "self-entity" [自體]. In what follows, other places where *zixing* 自性 is used, the sense is the same. Readers must remember this. "Has no real . . . ": ordinary people believe that all things have real self-entity. Here, "has no real . . . " serves to refute their confusion.) Taking the case of the form aggregate, form dharmas do not have real self-entity; that is, form dharmas have always been empty. (Buddhists break down material things into atoms [極微] so as to show that material things do not have real self-entity. For this reason, it is said that form dharmas are empty.) Taking the case of the sensation aggregate, as a mental associate sensation has no real self-entity—that is, it has always been empty. Taking the case of the [other] mental associates[12] and all

---

[12] Three of the aggregates are mental associates: sensation, perception, and mental formation. Here the reference is to the latter two.

the way through to the consciousness aggregate, none has real self-entity—that is, they have always been empty. ("All the way through to": those in between are omitted because their case can be extrapolated. The Buddhist use the doctrine of conditioned arising [緣生][13] to explain that because no dharma has real self-entity, they are all empty.)

The *Perfection of Wisdom Sutra*, *juan* 556, states: "As [the Buddha] taught, we absolutely do not arise. We have only nominal labels (假名) and none has self-nature. (All people are attached to the existence of a self. Little do they realize that what is referred to as "I" is merely a self that is falsely presumed on the basis of form, sensation, and the rest of the five aggregates. If I am separated from the five aggregates, just where am I? It is thus understood that "I" is a nominal label and has always been without self-nature.) Dharmas are the same. They have only nominal labels, and none has self-nature. What is form? It can neither be apprehended (Form dharmas do not have real self-entity, so how could they be apprehended?) nor can it arise. (Form dharmas do not have real self-entity and have never arisen.) What are the sensation, perception, mental formation, and consciousness aggregates? They can neither be apprehended nor can they arise . . . "[14] and so forth. There are countless examples of statements like this in the *Perfection of Wisdom Sutra*. The *Heart Sutra* provides a summary account of their essential meaning.

The *Heart Sutra* states: "Form is not different from emptiness; emptiness is not different from form. Form is emptiness; emptiness is form. Feeling, cognition, formation, and consciousness are also like this."[15] Ordinary people say that form is different from emptiness because form really exists and is not non-existent. They say that emptiness is different from form because emptiness

[p. 40]

does not have that which exists (無所有) and form dharmas do exist. Now, if we apply the principle of ultimate truth, and break form dharmas down to atoms and then further break them down to *linxu* 鄰虛) (When atoms are further broken down then there are no existent things; this is called *linxu*.)[16] then form

---

[13] The doctrine that everything arises from causes and conditions and has no inherent self-nature. Xiong also uses the term *yuanqi* 緣起 (conditioned origination).
[14] T220.7, 869a28–b2.
[15] T251.8, 848c7–8.
[16] *Linxu* 鄰虛 is Paramārtha's (真諦; 499–569) translation of *paramāṇu* (atom); *jiwei* 極微 is Xuanzang's translation of *paramāṇu*. In Chapter 3, p. 127, in discussing the Mahāyāna Emptiness school's three proofs for the doctrine of emptiness, Xiong further clarifies what he means by the distinction between *jiwei* and *linxu*: "Take, for example, the first doctrinal proof, which infers that atoms have no substance, and names this *linxu*. . . . When the bodhisattvas broke things down to atoms, they additionally stated that atoms have no substance. Thereupon, the fixed nature of the myriad things was completely stripped away, with nothing remaining."

dharmas are ultimately non-existent. Because form is emptiness, form and emptiness are not different from one another. That is why the sutra states, "Form is not different from emptiness; emptiness is not different from form."

Since form and emptiness are not different from one another, the sutra further explains: "Form is emptiness; emptiness is form (色即是空、空即是色。)." These two *ji* 即 characters clearly indicate that form and emptiness are one, not two, because form dharmas do not have real self-entity.

"Feeling, cognition, formation, and consciousness are also like this." These four aggregates and emptiness are not different from one another, but rather are identical with one another. Because the explanation for each of these is the same as for form, there is no need to cite the relevant passages. ([For details of the thesis that] none of these four aggregates has real self-entity, it is necessary to examine *Yuan sheng lun* 緣生論 [**Pratītyasamutpāda-śāstra*; Treatise on Conditioned Arising],[17] but I am afraid that the text is too prolix and so will not cite it.)

The *Heart Sutra* further states: "This emptiness characteristic of all dharmas (諸法空相) does not arise and does not cease; is not defiled and is not pure; and does not increase and does not decrease. Accordingly, in emptiness there is no form, feeling, cognition, mental formation, or consciousness."[18] This takes up from and expands upon the previous passage. "All dharmas" refers collectively to mental and material dharmas. "Empty": non-existent. "Emptiness characteristic": given that emptiness is not the same as existence, "emptiness characteristic" is spoken of nominally. (*Xiang* 相: characteristic [相狀]. "Emptiness characteristic" is simply the characteristic of having no characteristic [無相之相].) In all cases, where a dharma previously did not exist but now does exist, this is called arising; and when arising has thoroughly disintegrated, this is called ceasing. Because the emptiness characteristic has always been without arising (無生) the sutra says it "does not arise." To be without arising is to be without ceasing, hence the sutra says it "does not cease." The contamination of delusion is called "defilement" and the opposite is called "purity." The emptiness characteristic does not have contamination and so the sutra says it "is not defiled." Since it has always been without defilement, the term "pure" cannot be established either, so the sutra says it "is not pure." If something is augmented because of a concern that it is deficient, this is called "to increase." If something is reduced because it is overfull, this is called "to decrease." The emptiness characteristic is patently devoid of

---

[17] A work by Ullaṅgha (爵楞迦; d.u.), translated by Dharmagupta (達摩笈多; d. 619) (T1652).
[18] T251.8, 848c9–10.

things, so what would there be to increase? Hence the sutra says it "does not increase." To be without increase is to be without decrease, hence the sutra says it "does not decrease." The foregoing has briefly explained the emptiness characteristic of all dharmas, and that they are far removed from such differentiating characteristics as arising and ceasing, purity and impurity, increase and decrease.

"In emptiness there is no form, feeling, cognition, mental formation, or consciousness." According to this, the five aggregates are all empty, and dharma characteristics are thoroughly refuted. In the past, I once met a person who said that the *Heart Sutra* [expounds] the doctrine that everything is empty. I rebuked him, asking him, "Why are you being so flippant? Those skilled at the zither excel at hearing the sound beyond the chords. Those accomplished in

[p. 41]

the Way are able to grasp the meaning beyond the sage's words. The very first thing you say is 'everything is empty,' and without further ado you have passed judgment on the *Heart Sutra*. Yet do you really understand the *Heart Sutra* and the *Perfection of Wisdom Sutra*? On his death bed, Xuanzang recited the *Heart Sutra*, and Kuiji composed the [*Bore boluomiduo xin jing*] *you zan* [般若波羅蜜多心經]幽贊 (Profound Explanation of the *Heart Sutra*)[19]—how can you pass judgment on it so frivolously?"

In stating that the five aggregates are all empty, the *Heart Sutra* truly refuted all dharma characteristics, however, its purpose in refuting characteristics was so as to reveal the nature (顯性). (*Xian* 顯 is like "to make manifest." [This was done out of] a concern that ordinary people are mistakenly attached to dharma characteristics and so are unable to realize the dharma nature fully. This is like a dull-witted person who, when looking at the clouds and mist pervading the sky [has his vision] blocked by the clouds and mist, and surprisingly fails to realize that the sun has been there all the time. Thus, in order to point out dharma nature it is first necessary to refute dharma characteristics.) The sutra passage cited above, from "This emptiness characteristic of all dharmas" to "Accordingly, in emptiness there is no form, feeling, cognition, mental formation, or consciousness," is profound and vast (淵廣) in its purport. (*Yuan* 淵 means "profound"; *guang* 廣 means "vast.") Those who do not understand it, search merely on the surface. Only with the complete refutation of dharma characteristics is that the emptiness characteristic. Is it then

---

[19] T1710. In the 2001 edition of *Ti yong lun*, the abbreviated title is mistakenly given as *You zan* 幽讚. This is corrected in the 2019 edition.

not the case that everything is empty? From the revelation that "the emptiness characteristic of all dharmas does not arise and does not cease; is not defiled and is not pure; and does not increase and does not decrease," those who are skilled at understanding, having pondered deeply, will suddenly empty all existents (空諸所有), and unencumbered, realize the Reality (實相) of all dharmas. (Here the character *xiang* 相 is glossed as *ti* 體, and corresponds to Reality [實體].) This is being able to grasp the meaning that lies beyond the sage's words. With this passage, the sutra subtly reveals wondrous agency (神機). (*Shen* 神 is like "wondrous.") It is a great pity that dull-witted people have never been able to apprehend [the real significance of the passage].

The great agency and great function (大機大用) of the Prajñā school resides exclusively in refuting characteristics so as to reveal the nature [viz. Reality]. (The Emptiness school, which is also called the Prajñā school, took the *Perfection of Wisdom Sutra* as its main authority.) The *Da zhidu lun* 大智度論 (*Mahāprajñāpāramitā-śāstra*; Treatise on the Great Perfection of Wisdom)[20] states: "The Mahāyāna sutras have only one Dharma seal (法印), 'the Reality of all dharmas' (諸法實相), and [that is why] they are called sutras that fully reveal the meaning (了義經). If a [scripture] does not have the Reality seal, then it is an aberrant teaching."[21] (The term "Dharma" in "Dharma seal" refers to Buddhist doctrinal teachings or principles of learning. "Seal" is like that which is used on official documents, where it is relied upon to certify the authenticity of a document. Mahāyāna sutras take the explication of Reality [實相] to be their main concern, and so Reality is the Dharma seal of Mahāyāna learning. A sutra that has the seal of Reality is a sutra that fully reveals the meaning [of Reality]; otherwise, it is merely an aberrant teaching. "Fully reveal the meaning" is the term for exhausting the source and penetrating to the very bottom. The character *xiang* 相 in *shixiang* 實相 is glossed as Reality [體]. "The Reality of all dharmas" is another term for "dharma nature" or what in the secular world is called "the Reality of the cosmos.") The *[Miaofa] lianhua jing* [妙法]蓮華經 (*Saddharmapuṇḍarīka-sūtra*; Lotus Sutra) states: "I have distinguishing characteristics adorning my body (The sutras explain that there were thirty-two excellent distinguishing characteristics[22] and that they were extremely decorative.)

---

[20] This commentary on the *Mahāprajñāpāramitā-sūtra* is traditionally attributed to Nāgārjuna (T1509).

[21] The passage is actually a paraphrase of a passage cited in Tiantai master Zhiyi's 智顗 (538–597) *Miaofa lianhua jing xuanyi* 妙法蓮華經玄義 (The Profound Doctrine of the *Lotus Sutra*), T1716.33, 779c12–14. Zhiyi identifies the text he cites as *Shilun* 釋論, which could be a reference to *Da zhidu lun*; see Sengrui's 僧叡 (fl. 400) preface at T1509.25, 57a1.

[22] See, for example, *Yuqie shidi lun* 瑜伽師地論 (*Yogācārabhūmi-śāstra*; Discourse on Stages of Concentration Practice), T1579.30, 566c11–567a4.

and the light [emanating from my body] illuminates the mundane realm. Revered by the countless sentient beings, I will explain the seal of Reality for them."[23] (The Buddha is revered by countless sentient beings and so he explains the seal of Reality for them.) From this it can be seen that Mahāyāna's refutation of characteristics is a method of apophatic exegesis (遮詮) that reveals the dharma nature/the Reality of dharmas in a concealed (密) manner. (*Mi* 密: the intention behind it is deep and subtle. Apophatic: When Buddhists explain the Dharma, they use the methods of both apophatic

[p. 42]

and kataphatic exegesis [表詮]. Kataphatic exegesis is like explicitly saying to a poor person who has never seen a gold vessel before, that [the vessel in front of them] is a gold vessel. The method of apophatic exegesis is like when there is a person who has a superstitious belief in ghosts enters a large, dark room, looks toward a low table but cannot see it clearly, and then suspects it is a ghost, at which point you use all sorts of reasoning to explain that it is not a ghost, but avoid explicitly saying that it is low table, until finally you enable the deluded person to understand that it is a table.) The [Dharma] seal of Reality ratifies all the Mahāyāna sutras and not just the *Heart Sutra*. Dharmas are refuted so as to reveal the nature—who said that everything is empty!? To conduct a balanced discussion of an ancient learning it is first necessary to discern its origins and subsequently to examine its flow of transformations. One cannot cavalierly misrepresent wise people of ancient times. I have used the phrase, "refute characteristics so as to reveal the nature," to reveal the profundity of the Emptiness school. Above, the *Heart Sutra* can be used to comprehend the *Perfection of Wisdom Sutra*, and, below, it can be used to verify the four treatises, and so grasp that which interconnects them all. (The four treatises are: *Treatise on the Great Perfection of Wisdom*; *Zhong lun* 中論 [*Mūlamadhyamaka-kārikā*; Treatise on the Middle Way]; *Bai lun* 百論 [*Śata-śāstra*; One Hundred Verses Treatise]; and *Shi'er men lun* 十二門論 [*Dvādaśanikāya-śāstra*; Twelve Gateways Treatise].) Students, if you still doubt what I say, then all you need to do is please search deeply in the sutras and treatises for that interconnection.

Addendum. In the first draft of the *New Treatise*, I feel that the section where I interpreted the *Heart Sutra* deviates from the correct glossing.[24] In the 1953 abridged edition of the *New Treatise*, I still did not get around to correcting this. It is only here that I have commenced that revision.

---

[23] T262.9, 8b2–3.
[24] Xiong is referring to the 1944 vernacular edition, pp. 156–165. He does not discuss the *Heart Sutra* in the 1932 literary edition.

Although my glosses of the passages from the *Heart Sutra* are certainly different from those in the old drafts,[25] the purport [of my comments on] "refuting characteristics in order to reveal the nature" has not changed.

1.3 Criticisms of the Mahāyāna Emptiness school

As stated above, the first masters of the Mahāyāna Emptiness school (大空) had in fact taken [the teaching of] "refuting characteristics in order to reveal the nature" as the central authority for their doctrines. (*Da kong* 大空 is an abbreviation of *Dasheng kong zong* 大乘空宗 [Mahāyāna Emptiness school]; hereafter, the same abbreviation is used. The learning of the Emptiness school takes the *Perfection of Wisdom Sutra* as its foundation. This sutra is voluminous, and its content is extremely heterogeneous. No doubt this is because it was formed by selecting and assembling the teachings of many masters from earlier and later periods. In our country, people have always recognized Nāgārjuna as the progenitor of the Mahāyāna Emptiness school, but I conjecture that there ought to have been many before him who discussed emptiness, and that it is only because by his time that the Emptiness school had started to become large that later students of the school treated Nāgārjuna as its progenitor. "Central authority": this is like the office of a country's governing body. All great schools of learning have an abundance of aims, and even though there is great complexity [among the doctrines], there must be a ruling purpose that is the basis of the multitude of doctrines. Here "central authority" is deployed as an analogy for this.) "Refuting characteristics is in order to reveal the nature." Dharma nature/ the Reality of dharmas is inherently unable to be emptied and the many sutras all have the imprint of the [Dharma] seal of Reality—so how could one possibly say that everything is empty!? (Here "the many sutras" refers to the Mahāyāna canon.) This [teaching] is the original source of the Mahāyāna Emptiness school, and its true identity should be returned to it and the ancient wise masters should no longer be wronged. It must, however, also be understood that if we follow the [logic of] the "refuting characteristics to reveal the nature" thesis, fully drawing out its implications, then characteristics will all have been emptied, so how can the nature continue to exist? This is where the various Mahāyāna Emptiness school masters had launched a counterattack on themselves

---

[25] Here Xiong is retrospectively treating the 1944 and 1953 editions of the *New Treatise* as preliminary drafts of *Ti yong lun*.

[p. 43]
without ever having become aware of their having done so.

Someone asked: "How could the Mahāyāna Emptiness school masters have possibly been like that?"

I replied: "Do you doubt me? You have simply yet to understand that Reality and function are non-dual. What the Buddhists call dharma nature corresponds with what I call Reality. What the Buddhists call dharma characteristics corresponds with what I call function. I have already addressed this above. 'Characteristics' refers to Reality's deceptively manifesting as characteristics/forms as it produces and reproduces, flows and moves, which is what I call 'function.' This is analogous to an ocean's transforming into numerous waves. (The numerous waves are analogous to dharma characteristics and the ocean is analogous to dharma nature. In what follows, this is the same.) The nature is 'the itself' of the myriad dharmas. ("Myriad dharmas" is another term for dharma characteristics.) This is analogous to the ocean's being 'the itself' of the numerous waves. Hence, I say that Reality and function are non-dual. If you fully understand the meaning of this ("Meaning of this" refers to "Reality and function are non-dual.") then you ought to understand that if characteristics are completely refuted, then the nature also will be non-existent. Why is this so? The nature is 'the itself' of the characteristics; if the characteristics are completely refuted, then how could 'the itself' of the characteristics exist? [In other words, the nature will be non-existent because] the nature will already have been annihilated. (Take note of this.) Characteristics are the nature's producing and reproducing, flowing and moving. (Producing and reproducing, flowing and moving, hence this is termed "function.") If characteristics are completely refuted, then the nature would be a nature that is lifeless, inactive, quiescent, and extinguished—how is this different from nothingness? (Take note of this.) Accordingly, although the original intention of the Mahāyāna Emptiness school masters was to refute characteristics to reveal the nature, they ended up emptying characteristics such that the nature was also emptied with the characteristics. In other words, function was emptied and Reality was also emptied. Thus, I was not being harsh when I said that the [Mahāyāna Emptiness school] masters had launched a counterattack on themselves. Indeed, their scholarship is not without fault." (The reason I did not agree with the person who said that the *Heart Sutra* [expounds the doctrine] that everything is empty, is because he had never truly sought for the meaning of the sutra. Having merely observed the passage in the sutra that says, 'the five aggregates are all empty,' he then proceeded to criticize it irresponsibly, and that is why I severely reprimanded him. Buddhist teachings are, after all, profound and far-reaching. Even though I say that they are not without error, with respect to exhausting the loftiest [realms], and going into the finest detail [of analysis], these are areas where it is fully deserving of affirmation. I have never flippantly criticized Buddhism.)

Someone asked: "With respect to conventional truth, the Emptiness school does not refute dharma characteristics, but you, sir, call it to account for emptying characteristics such that the nature is also emptied. Is this not somewhat excessive?"

I replied: "Nāgārjuna's *Treatise on the Middle Way* states: 'The nature of all dharmas is empty ("All dharmas" here refers to the five aggregates, which are also collectively called "dharma characteristics." "The nature" is to be explained as *ti* 體. This is saying that all dharmas are without true self-entity [自體], they are inherently empty.) but because the inversions of ordinary people give rise to (生) false dharmas, from their perspective they are real.' (*Sheng* 生 is like *qi* 起 [to give rise to]. This is saying that dharma characteristics are inherently empty but [because of] the inversions of ordinary people, in their own minds they create false dharmas, and they all take these false dharmas to be real existents. See the "Guan si di pin" 觀四諦品 [Contemplation of the Four Noble Truths Section] of the *Treatise on the Middle Way*.[26]) Carefully pondering this passage [p. 44] it is patently evident that dharma characteristics are false dharmas created by the inversions of ordinary people, but which they mistakenly take to be real existents. Buddhist teachings have never granted that dharma characteristics are real existents. The very opening [of the *Heart Sutra*] states that all dharmas are without self-entity, which is to say that dharma characteristics are inherently empty. As for conventional truth's not emptying dharma characteristics, this is said simply to accord with [the views of] ordinary people. Conventionally speaking, dharma characteristics are real. Water is said to be real; grain is said to be real; and cloth is said to be real. The Buddhists also simply go along with this. Do you think you can use Buddhist teachings to refute this? If you do, then you do not understand the purport of conventional truth and it would be a challenge for me to analyze and explain to you what conventional truth is."

Someone enquired about the following: "Sir, your use of the 'non-duality of Reality and function' doctrine to rectify the Emptiness school's discourse on the nature and characteristics can indeed be said to be meticulous and rigorous. One doubtful issue, however, is the following. [You maintain that]

---

[26] *Zhong lun*, T1564.30, 32c20–21. The cited passage is actually Piṅgala's (青目; fourth century) commentary, which is appended to Kumārajīva's (鳩摩羅什; 344–413) Chinese translation.

the term 'dharma nature' in Buddhist teachings corresponds with 'the Reality of the cosmos' (The term "dharma nature" is an abbreviation of "the true nature of the myriad dharmas." The character *xing* 性 is to be interpreted as the character *ti* 體. This gloss first appeared in the various texts that Kumārajīva was in charge of translating and Xuanzang also continued this practice.[27]) and that term 'dharma characteristics' in Buddhist teachings is the collective term for the myriad mental and material images. And because the myriad mental and material images are all endlessly producing and reproducing, continuously transforming and moving, you call them function rather than dharma characteristics. Although the two names differ, actually they are the same [referent.] ("The two names" refers to dharma characteristics and function.) Only your learning promulgates [the doctrine] that Reality and function are non-dual. In the discourse of the Mahāyāna Emptiness school, however, the nature is an unconditioned dharma that neither arises nor ceases (The Buddhists teach that the true nature of the myriad dharmas is a dharma that neither arises nor ceases; it is also called an unconditioned dharma. An unconditioned [無為] dharma is so called because it does not create.) and characteristics are conditioned (有為) dharmas that arise and cease. (The Buddhists teach that, instant by instant, the myriad mental and material images all cease as soon as they arise and arise as soon as they cease, in an uninterrupted succession of arising and ceasing. It is for this reason that the mental and material phenomena are collectively termed dharmas that arise and cease. Only the Buddhists pay particular attention to observing cessation, and so the Buddhist sutras often state that [all things] cease in an instant [剎那滅]. There are clear accounts in both the sutras and the treatises that are worth noting. *Youwei* 有為 means "create" [造作]. It goes without saying that the mind also creates. Things also create. The wind moves, the clouds fly, water flows, and flowers bloom—these are all are creations. How much more so is this case for the largest of things, [that is, Heaven and Earth].) Given this, then the two aspects of the nature and characteristics are each separated by a huge chasm—a distinctly two-tier world (One tier neither arises nor ceases, is unconditioned; the other tier arises and ceases, is conditioned. No interconnection is possible between the two.), yet you still say that dharma nature is the Reality of dharma characteristics. Surely this is an odd thesis!? I do not know what sort of relationship there is between the two aspects of the nature and characteristics in the Mahāyāna Emptiness school's cosmology. I have long harbored this nagging puzzlement and am frustrated at being unable to resolve it. Sir, I hope you will

---

[27] The closest examples I could find are in Kuiji's *Cheng weishi lun shuji*, such as T1830.43, 291b8–9; 555b9.

[p. 45] instruct me clearly."

I replied: "An excellent query! If one were to use the doctrine of the non-duality of Reality and function to assess and make a determination about the Buddhist's [doctrine of] the nature and characteristics, then it should be said that dharma nature is 'the itself' of the myriad dharmas. (Here, "myriad dharmas" refers to dharma characteristics.) There should be no doubt about what sort of relationship there is between them. The Buddhists, however, cleave the nature and characteristics in two, and so, of course, you must have this query. I checked the *Fo di jing lun* 佛地經論 (*Buddha-bhūmi-sūtra-śāstra* [Treatise on the *Buddha-bhūmi-sūtra*]), which states: 'The pure Reality of dharmas (法界) (In Chinese translations of Buddhist texts, broadly speaking, the character *jie* 界 has three meanings: category [類], cause [因], and Reality [體].[28] Here the character *jie* should be interpreted as Reality. *Fajie* 法界 corresponds to "the Reality of the myriad dharmas," and it is another term for *faxing* 法性 [dharma nature/the Reality of dharmas]. "Pure" is saying that Reality has no defilements.) is analogous to space (虛空)[29]: even though it pervades all sorts of things (諸色) and all kinds of images (相), Reality is but of a single taste (體惟一味).'[30] (*Zhu se* 諸色 is like saying "all manner of things." *Xiang* 相 is like "manifest images" [現象]. This is saying that space is so large that there is nothing beyond it; that it thoroughly pervades all sorts of things and all kinds of manifest images. In other words, space universally pervades and contains all kinds of manifest images. Despite this, it cannot be said that space has all sorts of manifest images. Why is this? Space itself has always been space and has never transformed to become these manifest images. This is because space neither arises nor ceases and does not create, and so it says, "Reality is but of a single taste.") Accordingly, the various manifest images are only what space contains, includes—they certainly cannot be said to be space itself transforming to become these various manifest images. Dharma nature/the Reality of dharmas is just like space; although it includes the myriad dharmas it cannot be said that Dharma nature/the Reality of dharmas itself transforms to become the myriad dharmas. ("Myriad dharmas" refers to dharma characteristics.) Having carefully pondered the Buddhist's account of the relationship between the nature and characteristics

---

[28] These meanings can be discerned among the ten attributed to the term in *Apidamo da piposha lun*, T1545.27, 367c21–368a16.

[29] As Jorgensen et al. note: "The equivalent Sanskrit term, *ākāśa* [虛空], does not refer to simple physical 'space' in which objects cannot share the same space at the same time. Rather *ākāśa* neither displaces nor is displaced by any object; it permeates rather than obstructs." See *Treatise on Awakening Mahāyāna Faith* (New York: Oxford University Press, 2019), p. 72, n. 47.

[30] T1530.26, 304b25–27 (where *wei* 唯 rather than *wei* 惟 is used).

on the basis of the above few lines from the *Treatise on the Buddha-bhūmi-sūtra*, it is really eye-opening." (Someone asked: "Did not the Buddhists effectively treat space as dharma nature/the Reality of dharmas?" I replied: "You cannot baselessly say something like that. The *Treatise on the Buddha-bhūmi-sūtra* clearly states 'it can be compared to space'; where did it ever state that space is dharma nature/the Reality of dharmas? Space neither arises nor ceases, does not create, and does not transform and move; this description simply has points of similarity with what the Emptiness school calls dharma nature, and that is why they used it as an analogy.")

There must be a reason that the Buddhists cleaved the nature and characteristics in two. Buddhist teachings (佛法) are fundamentally teachings about transcending the mundane world (出世法) that oppose human life. (Here, the two *fa* 法 characters refer to Buddhist doctrines or teachings.) Even if the great flow of the cosmos' "vast productivity" (大生) and "capacious productivity" (廣生) were obstructed (For "vast productivity" and "capacious productivity," see the "Great Commentary" to the *Book of Change*.[31]), and even if the earth disappeared and space were obliterated, they would have absolutely no lingering affections. This is why they are known for having great compassion [for the suffering of sentient beings] and great awakening, and for being heroic and fearless. (In Buddhist texts, the term "transcend the mundane world" is just like saying "transcends the ocean of cyclic existence." This is why Śākyamuni aroused the aspiration to cultivate the Way. Later, although the development of the various schools of Hīnayāna and Mahāyāna flourished, crucially none altered

[p. 46]

the original intention to transcend the mundane world. Those later students of Buddhism, however, did not seek for the correct understanding of the meaning of "transcend the mundane world," [with some] going so far as to think that being undefiled in the mundane world amounted to transcending the mundane world, and consequently were unable to understand the truth about Buddhist teachings. Such was their utter confusion.) That which Buddhists hold in esteem is, of course, dharma nature, which neither arises nor ceases, is constant (如如) and unmoving, quiescent and extinguished (寂滅), and without acting (無為). (*Ruru* 如如 is a term describing how dharma nature does not change. Buddhist texts translated before the Tang dynasty used *ruru* 如如 as an alternative term for dharma nature.[32] Xuanzang changed to

---

[31] "Xici, shang," 7.14b–15a: "When Qian is still, it is focused and when it moves it is direct. By this means, vast productivity is brought about. When Kun is still, it is contraction and when it moves it is expansion. By this means, capacious productivity is brought about." Translated to reflect Xiong's understanding of contraction and expansion.

[32] For example, *Da zhidu lun*, T1509.25, 334a12.

using *zhenru* 真如. The character *ji* 寂 in *jimie* 寂滅 refers to the complete cessation of afflictions; it does not refer to the annihilation of dharma nature. *Wuwei* 無為: devoid of production and transformation, and devoid of generation, hence dharma nature is compared to space.) The Buddhists maintain that dharma characteristics arise due to the inversions of ordinary people and are not formed from the transformation of suchness. (The passage from the *Treatise on the Middle Way* about conventional truth cited above is worth pondering again.[33]) This is, of course, mixing sentiment and logic, something that Xunzi 荀子 [third century BCE] faulted in his essay, "Jie bi" 解蔽 (Dispelling Fixations). In the past, sometimes the more intelligent a wise person was, the stranger their fixations would be. On the one hand, their learning would be uniquely innovative; on the other hand, they would tendentiously reason by analogy. This is why Zhang Hengqu [Zhang Zai] warned about baseless [attempts] to exhaust [principle] to the greatest extent. ("Baseless": deficient in what can be relied upon. In seeking to exhaust principle to the broadest and greatest extent, one must take "seeking truth from facts" as one's foundation, otherwise [one's claims] will be baseless.[34])

I have pondered all the sutras and treatises of the Emptiness school. The Emptiness school can say that suchness is the true nature (實性) of the myriad dharmas ("True nature" corresponds to Reality; "suchness" is another name for Reality. "Myriad dharmas" refers to the mental and material dharmas, which are also collectively called dharma characteristics.) but definitely does not consent to saying that suchness transforms into the myriad dharmas. What is stressed in each statement is different, something that is of major import. Here are both statements juxtaposed:

(A) It is suchness that is the true nature of the myriad dharmas.
(B) Suchness transforms into the myriad dharmas.

In so contrasting the statements, their meaning is clearly different. Pondering statement A, we see that none of the myriad dharmas has self-entity and so should be said to be empty. What is the reason? Because it is suchness that is the Reality of the myriad dharmas, and it is not the case that removed from suchness the myriad dharmas separately have independent self-entity. (From

---

[33] "The nature of all dharmas is empty but because the inversions of ordinary people give rise to false dharmas, from their perspective they are real."
[34] Zhang Zai, "Zhong zheng" 中正 (Balance and Rectitude), *Zhengmeng*, p. 411: "If students stand upright on the way of balance, then they will have a position from which to expand that way. To attempt to expand [some teaching] in the absence of the way of balance would amount to a baseless [attempt] to exhaust [that teaching] to the greatest extent."

"It is not the case" to here, should be read without interruption.) Hence it is known that the myriad dharmas have only provisional names and actually are non-existent.

Pondering statement B, although the myriad dharmas do not have independent self-entity, it is not the case that they have no describable dharma characteristics. Dharma characteristics are all the various characteristics into which Reality transforms, the so-called myriad images of the cosmos. Accordingly, whereas statement B affirms dharma characteristics, statement A completely negates them. It should also be understood that statement B

[p. 47]

indicates that with regard to characteristics, *they* are the nature (即相即性), because it is not the case that outside of the characteristics there is the nature. A mature person of virtue once said: "There is nothing you touch that is not suchness." This is indeed understanding born of personal realization. (It is called "understanding born of personal realization" because it is understanding the truth and is not deluded speculation. Suchness is a name for dharma nature. Now, when I extend my hand to touch each of the things before me, in each case I am actually touching suchness. This explains what is meant by it is the characteristics that are the nature.)

The Emptiness school deems all dharma characteristics merely to be observing emptiness. The first assembly (會) [of teachings] in the *Perfection of Wisdom Sutra*[35] teaches that there are twenty [aspects of] emptiness (二十空) (*Kong* 空: non-existent. Hereafter, this gloss is the same.), such as "internal emptiness" (內空), "external emptiness" (外空) and so on.[36] (As for mental dharmas, because they arise and cease instant by instant and do not really exist, this is [what is referred to as] internal emptiness. Because the body is unreal, just like foam, it is also internal emptiness. External emptiness: because all the various things in the natural world unceasingly transform and change, they should be said to be empty.) The names and meanings of the twenty [aspects of] emptiness are particularly prolix. In general terms, observing emptiness simply amounts to observing the truth (諦觀) that each and every material and mental dharma (行) (For the character *xing* 行, see the "Explaining Transformation" chapter.) ceases in an instant and does not abide for a moment; that they are all non-existent (*Di* 諦 means "true." *Diguan* 諦觀 means that in observing the principles of things one grasps their truth.);

---

[35] The *Perfection of Wisdom Sutra* consists of sixteen such divisions of its contents.
[36] For the full list from this sutra, with links to glosses of each, see Charles Muller and Dan Lusthaus, "二十空," *Digital Dictionary of Buddhism*, http://www.buddhism-dict.net/cgi-bin/xpr-ddb.pl?q=%E4%BA%8C%E5%8D%81%E7%A9%BA.

and finally looking within to observe that the mental consciousness' (意)[37] conceptualizations (想) are still attached (取) to the characteristic of emptiness (空相) (Because the mental consciousness still makes the conceptualization that "everything is empty," that is, that the characteristic of emptiness exists, therefore the text says, "attached to the characteristic of emptiness." *Qu* 取 means "to be attached" [執].) and that this very characteristic of emptiness should also be refuted—this is called "emptying emptiness" (空空). With the characteristic of emptiness having been emptied, what else is there that exists!?

Ever since there has been reasoned argument, nobody has been able to match the Prajñā (般若) school in emptying all that exists; in being so unreservedly without attachment. (*Prajñā* [Ch. *bore*] is a transliteration and means wisdom [智慧]. The reason that the meaning was not translated [into Chinese] is because people are generally used to using the word "wisdom" and would not look for a deeper meaning [if it had been so translated]. Because the meaning of this word for wisdom is extremely profound and far-reaching it was transliterated in the hope that people would carefully reflect upon it.) Moreover, the Prajñā school did not just empty and remove (空除) dharma characteristics. (*Kongchu* 空除 is just like saying "remove completely.") Even though "*nirvāṇa* dharma nature" (涅槃法性) is utterly true and utterly real (The word *niepan* 涅槃 has such meanings as true and constant, quiescent and extinguished, and is another name for dharma nature. Here I have joined the two terms to use as a compound term.), out of concern that that people would become attached (執) to it, the Prajñā school taught that it is unconditioned emptiness (無為空). (*Wuwei* 無為 is yet another name for dharma nature. Dharma nature has many names, and these are not limited to suchness, *nirvāṇa*, and unconditioned. *Zhi* 執 is called *zhizhuo* 執着 in the vernacular because it has a sense of sticky adhesion [粘滯]. The meaning of *zhi* 執, however, is extremely profound and subtle, and difficult to convey in words. When we open our eyes and see things, our minds think that what we see are real things, and so unconsciously form attachments. When we think about a certain principle and affirm that the principle is indeed as such, then as soon as we make this affirmation, we simultaneously form an attachment yet are not conscious of doing so. When there are differences in thinking, this easily leads to fighting, and is due to attachments. In the past, readers of Buddhist texts did not seek to understand [the deeper import of] the character *zhi* 執. Mr Cai Diaomin 蔡刁民,[38]

---

[37] The sixth consciousness (*manovijñāna*): *yi shi* 意識; one of eight or nine recognized by Buddhists.
[38] A leading intellectual and educationalist, Cai Yuanpei 蔡元培 (1868–1940) was president of Peking University from 1917 to 1927. For an example of Cai's views on attachment, see his "Xin jiaoyu yijian" 新教育意見 (My Views on New Education) in Wen Di 聞笛 and Shui Ru 水如 eds., *Cai Yuanpei meixue wenxuan* 蔡元培美學文選 (Selections from Cai Yuanpei's Writings on Aesthetics)

[p. 48]
however, certainly had a deep understanding of it, realized through personal experience.) The *Perfection of Wisdom Sutra, juan* 556 states: "Then, the celestial beings [*devas*] asked Shanxian (善現):[39] 'Surely it is not possible that *nirvāṇa* is also like an illusion?' Shanxian replied: 'Even if there were a dharma that was more powerful than *nirvāṇa*, it too would be an illusion, so of course *nirvāṇa* is like an illusion.'"[40] (Shanxian 善現: the name of a buddha.[41]) This is the concealed meaning (密意) [of emptiness]. This is because, even though one maintains that there should not be attachment to dharma characteristics, if one then becomes attached to dharma nature, even though it is the dharma nature, it is also a characteristic. (If one becomes attached to dharma nature, then it is no different from being attached to dharma characteristics.) Hence, concomitant with both being refuted, everything is empty. (The [purport] of the entire *Perfection of Wisdom Sutra* depends on a deep understanding of the meaning of the twenty emptinesses. If, however, one does not read the entire *Perfection of Wisdom Sutra* and instead does no more than crudely toy with the nomenclature of the twenty emptinesses, then there will never be nothing to awaken to.) In eliminating characteristics, the Emptiness school ended up refuting [dharma] nature; function having been emptied and so Reality was emptied together with it. As such, the Emptiness school's method of refuting attachments is so severe it resembles that of a fierce general's charging the enemy, regardless of the costs, as he focuses on nothing more than the reckless pursuit of his goal. The great bodhisattvas (This is just like saying, "the great awakened ones.") had their aim focused on refuting attachments. To the very end, however, they did not (卒不) awaken to the fact that as they relentlessly [sought to] refute them completely, refutation itself became an attachment. (The sentence runs from the two characters, *zu bu* 卒不, to here.) Alas! I am unable to bring the bodhisattvas back to life and call them to account. Confucius said: "I would like to be without words."[42] One who has grasped the meaning of forgetting

---

(Taipei: Shuxing chubanshe, 1989), p. 4. Cai invited Xiong to teach Buddhism at Peking University in 1922. For a translation of Cai's foreword to Xiong's 1932 edition of the *New Treatise*, see Makeham, *New Treatise on the Uniqueness of Consciousness*, pp. 3–7.

[39] Shanxian or Subhūti was one of the Śākyamuni's ten main disciples. Presumably, Xiong takes the name to be a reference to a buddha is because the *Lotus Sutra* records that Śākyamuni had guaranteed that Shanxian would ultimately attain buddhahood after countless kalpas of rebirth; see *Miao fa lianhua jing*, T262.9, 21a19–20.

[40] Paraphrase of T220.7, 771a12–16.

[41] Subhūti is also rendered as Xuputi 須菩提.

[42] *Analects* 17.19:

words[43] is like Yu's 禹[44] guiding the waters, which required no effort.[45] Why be attached?

Someone asked about the following: "The *Perfection of Wisdom Sutra*, *juan* 562, states: 'All dharmas are gathered into the dharma nature; nothing is seen outside the dharma nature.'[46] ("All dharmas" refers to all mental and material dharmas, which are also collectively called dharma characteristics.) From this it can be understood that 'to empty dharma characteristics' [means] to gather all the dharma characteristics into the dharma nature—its fundamental meaning is not to empty the dharma nature."[47]

I replied: "If characteristics have already all been completely emptied, how can they be gathered into the dharma nature? Take the analogy of 'each and every wave is the ocean'—this is stated this way precisely because the waves are gathered into the ocean. As for those people who perversely say that the wave forms are non-existent, it would be out of the question that the waves are gathered into the ocean."

Mahāyāna ratifies Buddhist teachings with the three Dharma seals. (See above for "Dharma seal." The three Dharma seals: All things are impermanent; no dharma has an inherent self; and *nirvāṇa* is perfectly still.[48] Mahāyāna learning emerged after all of the Hīnayāna schools, and the Hīnayānists did not acknowledge that the Mahāyāna sutras are the words of the Buddha. As for the Mahāyānists, they used the three Dharma seals to ratify all sutras. Those that tallied were all [deemed to be] the words of the Buddha, otherwise they were not the words of the Buddha. As none of the Mahāyāna sutras runs

---

Confucius said: "I would like to be without words."
   Zigong said: "But if you did not speak, what should we disciples transmit from you?"
   Confucius said: "What does Heaven say? The four seasons move by it and the one hundred things issue from it. What does Heaven say?"

[43] Allusion to "forget about words when the meaning has been grasped" in "Wai wu" 外物 (External Things), *Zhuangzi*, p. 944.

[44] Legendary sage king, celebrated for his skills in flood mitigation.

[45] Allusion to *Mencius* 4B.26: "What is so detestable about the wise is the way they try to force their way through things. If the wise would just emulate the manner in which Yu guided the waters, there would be nothing detestable about their wisdom. In guiding the waters, he did so in a way that required no effort. If the wise could also guide things in a way that requires no effort, then their wisdom would be great indeed." Translation by Edward Slingerland, *Effortless Action: Wu-wei as Conceptual Metaphor and Spiritual Ideal in Early China* (New York: Oxford University Press, 2003), p. 152 mod.

[46] Paraphrase of T220.7, 627c14.

[47] Given Xiong's response to this comment, the premise here is that all dharma characteristics are able to be gathered into the dharma nature, because all dharma characteristics have been shown to be empty, to be non-existent.

[48] The three Dharma seals as identified in *Da zhidu lun*, T1509.25, 222a28–222b1: "The first is that all conditioned dharmas arise and cease in instant by instant—all are impermanent. The second is that all dharmas are no-self. The third is that *nirvāṇa* is calm extinction." See also T1509.25, 170a2–4 for a similar passage.

counter to the three Dharma seals there is nothing for the Hīnayānists to argue about.) The third Dharma seal is "*nirvāṇa* is perfectly still." (*Nirvāṇa* is another name for dharma nature.) It is thus clear that all [Mahāyāna] schools describe "nature-as-Reality" (性體) as perfectly still.[49]

[p. 49]

(Here the two characters *xing* 性 and *ti* 體 are combined to form a compound term. Subsequent examples are the same use.) Their words are indeed based on a correct view and definitely cannot be criticized in a cavalier manner. It must, however, also be understood that utter stillness is wondrous transformation (神化). (Because transformation is difficult to fathom it is described as wondrous; *shen* 神 here does not mean a heavenly deity.) Transforming but not creating, hence it is said to be still. Stillness cannot be said not to be transforming. (Where there is a conation to create then this is not stillness. Because the Reality of the myriad transformations has no conation it is devoid of creativity, and so the myriad transformations are all still.) Utter stillness is uncanny (譎) transformation. (*Jue* 譎: strange and unfathomable.) Transforming without being thrown into disarray, hence it is said to be still. Stillness cannot be said not to be transforming. (Reality, which undergoes myriads of transformations, moves with a natural regularity, and so is not in disarray. Hence, with regard to its moving, it is still [即動即靜]. When ordinary people see things move, they deem them not to be still; transformation is different from this.) Utterly still yet transforming, and so its stillness is not a barren (廢然) stillness but rather it dwells in stillness with the defining characteristic that is vigor. (Wang Chuanshan 王船山 rebuked the Principle-centered Learning's [理學] [account of] stillness, characterizing it as a barren stillness.[50]

---

[49] Here Xiong treats *xingti* 性體 as equivalent to *nirvāṇa* and dharma nature. Elsewhere in *Ti yong lun*, he also treats it as synonymous with "Ultimate meaning" and "unconditioned" (see p. 82.) Xiong widely used the term in his 1944 vernacular edition of *New Treatise*, where he defines it as follows (pp. 171, 173): "'Nature-as-Reality.' Although the nature has no form it is not non-existent. Because it is not non-existent, it is said to have self-entity. As soon as the nature is spoken of, it is with specific regard to the self-entity of the nature. The reason that the characters *xing* 性 and *ti* 體 are combined into a word is because it is precisely the nature that is Reality.... 'Mind-as-Reality' is another name for nature-as-Reality. As the origin of the cosmos' myriad existents, it is called nature-as-Reality. As that which controls my person, it is called mind-as-Reality." (性體者，性雖無形，而非空無。以非空無故，說有自體。方言性時，即是剋指性之自體而目之也，故以性體二字合而成詞，即性即體故。... 心體，即性體之異名。以其為宇宙萬有之原，則説為性體。以其主乎吾身，則説為心體。)

[50] The particular passage that Xiong refers to is probably the following: "When the Supreme Pivot moves, generating *yang*, this is movement in its active mode. When still, generating *yin*, this is movement in its passive mode. If it were barren, devoid of movement and stillness, by what means could *yin* be generated?" See Wang Fuzhi, *Si wen lu* 思問錄 (Records of Thinking and Questioning) in *Chuanshan quanshu* 船山全書 (The Complete Works of Wang Fuzhi) (Changsha: Yuelu shushe, 2011), vol. 12, p. 402. This contrasts with Zhu Xi's account of the relationship between the Supreme Pivot and movement and stillness. See the discussion of relevant passages in my chapter, "Monism and the Problem of the Ignorance and Badness in Chinese Buddhism and Zhu Xi's Neo-Confucianism" in Makeham, ed., *The Buddhist Roots of Zhu Xi's Philosophical* Thought (New York: Oxford University Press, 2018), pp. 311–316.

In Buddhist teachings this is even more acute.) Utterly quiescent yet transforming, and so its quiescence is not a desolate (曠然) stillness, but rather it animates stillness with the defining characteristic that is humaneness. (*Kuangran* 曠然 is like "barren" [廢然].) Vigor is a defining characteristic of production and reproduction (生德); humaneness is also a defining characteristic of production and reproduction. ("Defining characteristics of production and reproduction" [生生之德] are [also] called *sheng de* 生德.) "Vigor" and "humaneness" are different names for the same actuality.

The irrepressible, exuberant greatness of production and reproduction is called vigor. The absence of stagnation in the harmonious flourishing of production and reproduction is called humaneness. Accordingly, vigor is the lord (君) of stillness, and humaneness is the master (主) of quiescence. (*Jun* 君 is like "master" [主]. Because the defining characteristic that is vigor is the master of stillness, stillness is not stagnant. Because the defining characteristic that is humaneness is the master of quiescence, quiescence is not withered.) [By means of] "vast productivity" (大生) and "capacious productivity" (廣生) the myriad things are developed and nurtured. Human life uses this to continue Heaven's defining characteristics and establish ultimate human [norms]. ("Heaven" is [another] name for Reality. "Heaven's defining characteristics": Reality's defining characteristics. Humans are innately endowed with Heaven's defining characteristics, and because they are able to realize them and not lose them, the text says "continue." "Ultimate": the highest norms.) It is also precisely with this that human abilities are [developed] to the greatest possible extent [盡] and their Heavenly[-endowed] nature expanded. (*Jin* 盡 is like "to develop." "Heavenly[-endowed] nature" refers to Reality, what the Buddhists call dharma nature. The Buddhists say that because sentient beings are impeded by hinderances they are unable to see their nature, and so it is necessary to remove hindrances before the nature can be seen. Confucian learning, however, holds that human life should develop human abilities and that the Heavenly[-endowed] nature necessarily depends on human abilities before it can be expanded. <On human abilities, see the "Great Commentary" to the *Book of Change*.[51] People are innately endowed with the Heavenly[-endowed] nature. Since they are human, then they themselves bring to completion their special abilities. That is why they are called human abilities.> The myriad things are all endowed with the Heavenly nature but are unable to expand it. Only humans have what it takes to expand the Heavenly nature. In human life, humans should expand the nature. It is not enough simply to see the nature [見性].

---

[51] Probably referring to "Xici, shang," 7.12a: "That which continues [the Way] is goodness; that which brings it to completion is the nature. When the humane see it, they call it humaneness; when the wise see it and call it wisdom."

This is a major point of distinction between Confucians and Buddhists.) [Realizing] the non-duality of Heaven and humans is the ultimate [achievement] of the Confucians. The Buddhists deem nature-as-Reality merely to be quiescent, leading sentient beings to return together with them to the village of quiescent extinction (寂滅之鄉). Is that still the world of human beings? I have no way of knowing.

[p. 50]

(The "Guan niepan pin" 觀涅槃品 [Contemplation of *Nirvāṇa* Section] and other sections in the *Treatise on the Middle Way* say that *nirvāṇa* and the mundane world are not different from one another,[52] the purport being [to show] only that the transforming mundane world is quiescent extinction. Readers, however, do not search for any deeper meaning, and being fond of taking the words literally, think that it is the mundane world that is the transcendent world. How utterly confused they are! In fact, the meanings inherent in the term "quiescent extinction" [寂滅] are exceedingly profound. The character *mie* 滅 means that afflictions have been extirpated. Little do they realize that those who have the body of sentient beings are unable to sever afflictions. <"Sever" means to eradicate.> When bodhisattvas are about to become buddhas, their afflictions have nearly been extirpated <"Extirpate" is like eliminate.> However, because they have made a vow to save sentient beings, they still retain afflictions to nurture their own lives [留惑潤生] <The lives of sentient beings need afflictions to nurture them, just like the life of a sprout needs water to nurture it. The meaning of this is extremely profound and far-reaching, and I am unable to elaborate here. When bodhisattvas are about to extirpate their own afflictions they deliberately retain them to nurture their lives. They continue to appear in the bodily form of sentient beings and make connections with sentient beings.> From this it can thus be understood that if afflictions were extirpated then there would no longer be sentient being bodies. If the mundane world were to be transformed into quiescent extinction[53] would this still be the human world?)

Addendum. A mature person of virtue once said: "When the moon is high above, everything is silent."[54] ("Everything" is like saying "the myriad kinds of things." "When the moon is high above": The image of extreme purity. The myriad

---

[52] For example, T1564.30, 36a4–9.
[53] That is, *nirvāṇa*.
[54] Lang Shiyuan 郎士元 (c. 727–c. 780), "Huanzeng Qian Yuanwai 'Ye su Lingtai si' jianji" 還贈錢員外夜宿靈臺寺見寄 (Presented in Reply to the Poem "Spending a Night at Lingtai Temple" Sent to Me by Supernumerary Qian [Qi] [錢起 (c. 722–780)]), in *Jin Shengtan xuanpi Tang shi liubai shou* 金聖嘆選批唐詩六百首 (Jin Shengtan's Selection of Six Hundred Tang Poems with Notes) (Beijing: Lianjing chuban gongsi, 2018), p. 104.

kinds of things are all still, "quiescent and unmoving."[55]) This provides a glimpse into the quiescent aspect of "nature-as-Reality." A poem by Tao [Yuanming] states: "A cloudless sunset, the spring breeze fans gently."[56] Using this to describe "nature-as-Reality" comes close to it and is not inclined to the error of stagnation and quiescence. "A cloudless sunset" is stillness, while "the spring breeze fans gently" is the true agency (真機) of production and reproduction, and production and reproduction's defining characteristics of vigor and humaneness flow undifferentiated.

The Emptiness school had a profound understanding of the quiescent aspect of nature-as-Reality. Unfortunately, it failed to avert becoming stagnated in quiescence and mired in stillness, and, quite simply, it utterly annihilated the true agency of incessant production and reproduction, and endless transformation and change. The Existence school was certainly not being overly harsh in disparaging [the Emptiness school] for being perniciously attached to emptiness (惡取空). (*Kong* 空: non-existent. *Qu* 取: to grasp. *E* 惡: a term of reprimand. Because the school failed to awaken to its deluded attachment, it was berated for being "perniciously attached.") The Emptiness school says that *nirvāṇa* is also like an illusion (See above.), and also talks of "ultimate meaning emptiness" (勝義空) (Its meaning being the most excellent, it is called "ultimate meaning," and refers to dharma nature. "Ultimate meaning emptiness" thus refers to [the doctrine that] dharma nature is also non-existent.) and "unconditioned emptiness" (無為空).[57] (For "unconditioned," see above.) "Ultimate meaning" and "unconditioned" are both names for nature-as-Reality. *Nirvāṇa* is also a name for nature-as-Reality. Yet, can nature-as-Reality be said to be empty, to be like an illusion? To say that it is empty and like an illusion amounts to exterminating the seeds of production and reproduction. (Here "seeds" is a metaphor for the defining characteristics of nature-as-Reality's production and reproduction.) The bodhisattva Bhāviveka (清辨 [c. 490–570]) (A venerable master who appeared after the advent of Madhyamaka.) wrote *Zhang zhen lun* 掌珍論 (The Jewel in the Hand Treatise)[58]

---

[55] "Quiescent and unmoving" translates 寂然不動, a phrase from "Xici, shang," 7:24b: "Change is without thought and without [deliberate] action, quiescent and unmoving, but when it resonates it interconnects with all of the causes for everything under Heaven."

[56] Tao Yuanming, "Ni gu, qi qi" 擬古, 其七 (In Imitation of Old Poems, #7), in Wang Yao ed., *Tao Yuanming ji*, p. 91.

[57] "Ultimate meaning emptiness" (also called *diyi yi kong* 第一義空 and *zhenshi kong* 真實空) and "unconditioned emptiness" are two of the so-called "eighteen aspects of emptiness" (十八空). See *Mohe bore boluomi jing* 摩訶般若波羅蜜經 (*Pañca-viṃśati-sāhasrikā-prajñā-pāramitā*; The Perfection of Wisdom Sutra in 25,000 Verses), T223.8, 219c9–12.

[58] The full title is *Dasheng zhangzhen lun* 大乘掌珍論 (*Mahāyāna-hastaratna-śāstra*).

in which he set out the following inference (量) ("Inference" is a syllogism. The three parts are the thesis [宗], reason [因], and example [喻], the details of which are [to be found in] Buddhist "science of reasoning" [因明 (*hetu-vidyā*)].[59]):
[p. 51]

(Thesis) Unproduced and devoid of reality
(Reason) because it does not arise,
(Example) like sky flowers.[60]

The Existence school was extremely displeased with this inference for going so far as to deem unconditioned-nature-as-Reality (無為性體) to be sky flowers ("Unconditioned-nature-as-Reality" is a compound term.) For example, Dharmapāla (護法)[61] and our country's Kuiji both vehemently criticized Bhāviveka. (For details, see *Cheng weishi lun shuji*.[62]) If this is adjudicated in an even-handed manner, in his account of emptiness Bhāviveka was certainly perniciously attached to emptiness, but his point of view was indeed based on the *Perfection of Wisdom Sutra*, where it is clearly written that once dharma characteristics have been emptied, then the dharma nature is emptied. What blame lies with Bhāviveka? When reason sees what is true there is certainly no need to use intemperate words. If reason is indeed as such then it should be discussed accordingly—it is really quite simple. If, in the course of explaining one's reasoning, there is even a modicum of intemperance it will certainly become evident that the reasoning is one-sided and does not ring true. Of course, being opposed to human life, Indian Buddhists had little insight into the true agency that is nature-as-Reality's production and reproduction (性體生生真機), regarding it merely to be emptiness and quiescence (空寂).

In the *Analects* Confucius says: "What does Heaven say? The four seasons move by it and the one hundred things issue from it. What does Heaven say?"[63] The "Heaven" that Confucius spoke of is the name of nature-as-Reality

---

[59] *Yinming* is the Chinese interpretation of Buddhist reasoning and logic: *hetuvidyā* (science of reasoning). See Christoph Harbsmeier, *Language and Logic in Traditional China*, in *Science and Civilisation in China*, vol. 7, pt. 1 (Cambridge: Cambridge University Press, 1998), pp. 358–408.

[60] Based on *Dasheng zhangzhen lun*, T1578.30, 268b22. "Sky flowers" is the equivalent to the Western philosopher's "unicorns" or "round squares": actual things erroneously juxtaposed.

[61] Sixth-century Indian Yogācāra exponent.

[62] For example, T1830.43, 488a11, 490b16–17, 494b25. Because tradition followed Kuiji, whose commentaries on Xuanzang's *Cheng weishi lun* attributed all authoritative opinions to Dharmapāla, in subsequent East Asian treatments "Dharmapāla" effectively functions as a metonym for views expressed in *Cheng weishi lun*, which is typically labeled as Dharmapāla's commentary. Xiong follows this practice. For criticisms in *Cheng weishi lun* of the view that emptiness is the ultimate truth, see T1585.31, 16a6–13.

[63] *Analects* 17.19.

and is not saying that there is an Emperor of Heaven. Being without words describes its quiescence. Quiescent, yet the four seasons move and the hundred things issue; the four seasons move and the hundred things issue, yet it is still quiescent. As for those who talk about "unconditioned emptiness," how could they understand this reasoning? *Balance as the Norm* is the bequeathed words of Confucius. In praising the defining characteristics of nature[-as-Reality], he said: "The *Odes* says: '[Its] defining characteristics are as light as a feather' (德輶如毛). But a feather still has generic features (倫).[64] 'Heaven on high contains [the myriad things] yet has no sound or scent' (上天之載無聲無臭).[65] Perfect!"[66] *You* 輶 means light. A feather is a light object. *Lun* 倫 means markings (迹). "On high" means absolute. "Heaven on high" also refers to nature-as-Reality. *Zai* 載 means to contain. This is saying that it contains (含藏) the myriad existents. These lines from the *Odes* are cited so as to show that nature-as-Reality is insubstantial and formless. If it were compared to being as light as a feather, a feather still has generic features, [but nature-as-Reality] has nothing to which it can be compared. Sound and scent have both simply vanished in nature-as-Reality; indeed, it is ultimate emptiness and quiescence. Yet even though it has no visible form, it contains the myriad existents, is utterly true and real and so Confucius praised it as "perfect." How absurd are such notions that *nirvāṇa* is like an illusion!

There are no grounds for censure regarding the original intent behind the Emptiness school's particular concern that people will form attachments to nature-as-Reality.
[p. 52]
In the past, those who have discussed intrinsic Reality have, by and large, sought for the origin of the cosmos beyond the myriad things in Heaven and Earth. Like the blind men touching the elephant—none was able to verify (證) the truth. (*Zheng* 證 is like "to know" [知], but the meaning of this *zhi* 知 character is very profound. Here I am unable to go into the details.) If those blind men were to hear about *nirvāṇa*, not only would they perversely maintain false views, but they would even end up believing themselves. Although I certainly would not dare to look down upon the Emptiness school, I could never assent to its views. The Emptiness school did not just refute views based on [conventional] knowledge, it even bluntly stated that nature-as-Reality is empty and

---

[64] The line is from the ode, "Zheng min" 烝民 (The Multitudes) (Mao 260), *Shijing*, 18/3.15a.
[65] The line is from ode, "Wen Wang" 文王 (King Wen) (Mao 235), *Shijing*, 16/1, 14a, translated on the basis of Xiong's glosses.
[66] "Zhongyong," 53.18a. This passage is translated on the basis of Xiong's glosses.

like an illusion. In this kind of perverse refuting, refutation also becomes an attachment. This is not just being a little off target—it is a major error.

In the past, when Chan master Meizi 梅子 (Plum)[67] studied under Mazu 馬祖[68] he learned of the teaching, "With regard to the mind, *it* is awakening" (即心即佛).[69] (*Fo* 佛 means "correct awakening." It is our inherent mind [本心] that is correct awakening—it is not necessary to seek for correct awakening externally. It must also be understood that if the mind is separated from correct awakening then that will be false thought and not the inherent mind. Mazu's instruction was very incisive.) After he left Mazu, he lived in Meiling 梅嶺 in the Min 閩 area[70] for more than a decade. When one of Mazu's disciples visited him there, Meizi asked him about news of Mazu's recent teachings. The visitor said: "The venerable master at first had taught 'with regard to the mind, *it* is awakening,' but recently he teaches 'neither mind nor awakening' [非心非佛]." (Fearing that if people heard his early teaching they would then become attached to the mind and awakening as if they were numinous entities, he now negated both.) Meizi snorted, saying: "The old guy is at it again—greatly confusing everyone. Even if he negates both mind and awakening, I acknowledge only 'with regard to the mind, *it* is awakening.'" When Mazu heard about this, he said: "The 'plum' (Meizi) has ripened!"[71] This *gongan* 公案 is well worth savoring. Students, be sure not to misunderstand the Emptiness school, mistakenly thinking that nature-as-Reality is merely quiescent. What you must understand is that quiescence is production and reproduction; that absolute stillness is flow. If you truly see the origin, then you will immediately accept it [for what it really is]. For human life to develop perfectly, do not fall into deviant ways. These are the humble views I feel I must make clear.

Someone raised an objection: "Emptiness and quiescence are Reality; the incipience (幾) of unceasing production and reproduction and transformation and retransformation (生生化化) is function. (The first budding [始萌] of production and transformation is called "incipience.") For Indian Buddhists, seeing Reality is the ultimate, but the learning of Chinese Confucians talks only about function. Now, sir, you wander between Chinese and Indian learning,

---

[67] Master Fachang 法常 (752–839) from Mt. Damei 大梅.
[68] Celebrated Chan master Mazu Daoyi 馬祖道一 (709–788).
[69] In this story, *fo* 佛 is typically understood to refer to the Buddha rather than awakening per se.
[70] Today's Fujian Province.
[71] This account is based on *Jingde chuandeng lu* 景德傳燈錄 (Record of the Transmission of the Lamp Published in the Jingde Reign Period), comp. Daoyuan 道原 (fl. 1004), T2076.51, 254c2–20. On different versions of the story, see Jinhua Jia, *The Hongzhou School of Chan Buddhism in Eighth-through Tenth-Century China* (New York: SUNY, 2006), p. 56.

seeking to fuse Buddhism and Confucianism in a single furnace. As for those places that cannot be forcibly accommodated, then you use your own judgment as to whether to accept or to reject. In your critiques of Buddhism, is it not the case that you have formed a determined view that it is inferior?"

I replied: "What!? What are you talking about? If it were indeed as you presume then Reality would be Reality and function would be function—two distinct things. Function is the incipience of [ceaseless] production and transformation. How could you possibly say that it is not constituted of Reality. (This is like saying that the numerous leaping waves are not constituted of the ocean.) If Reality were merely emptiness and quiescence, and unable to be said [p. 53] to produce and to transform, then not only would it be a lifeless thing it would also be a useless thing. It should be understood that although Reality and function can be differentiated, actually they cannot be differentiated. Where they can be differentiated is that Reality is without distinctions (Like the ocean, it has always been a complete whole.) and function is a myriad particulars. (Like the way the numerous waves appear as individuated.) Where they cannot be differentiated is that with regard to Reality, *it* is function (即體即用) (Like the way the ocean completely becomes the numerous waves.), and with regard to function, *it* is Reality (即用即體). (Like the way there is no ocean apart from the numerous waves.) Accordingly, none of the profusion of the myriad existents is fixed and this should be called function. That which is undifferentiated and all-pervading (渾然充塞) and is without deliberate action yet there is nothing it does not do is intrinsic Reality qua the flow of great function. (*Hunran* 渾然 refers to its being an indivisible great whole; *chongsai* 充塞 refers to its being all pervading and omnipresent.) Function is constituted of Reality (This is analogous to all the countless wave forms' [漚相] being constituted of the ocean.), and Reality depends on being function to exist. (This is analogous to how the ocean does not transcend the countless wave forms to exist independently.) Wang Yangming said: 'As for Reality, function is determined by Reality; as for function, Reality is [manifest] as function.'[72] These words come from having [personally] verified the truth. Thus, although Reality and function can be differentiated, actually they cannot be differentiated. The import of this can be spoken only to people who have awoken; it is difficult to explain it those who do not know [the truth]."

---

[72] See "Superfluous Words," p. 11.

Within the lineage of the Mahāyāna Existence school, Master Xuanzang's learning is the most distinguished. In a memorial he submitted to Emperor Taizong 太宗 [r. 626–649] of the Tang dynasty, he wrote: "I have heard that although the six lines of the hexagrams are profound and mysterious, they are limited to the realm of arising and ceasing (Xuanzang is saying that the six lines of each hexagram in the *Book of Change* serve to elucidate the significance of transformation and change and so can be said to be profound and mysterious in their complexity; however, the *Book of Change* observes only arising and ceasing and talks only about dharma characteristics—it did not understand dharma nature.) and rectifying the names of the one hundred things did not touch upon the realm of suchness."[73] (Xuanzang maintains that the *Spring and Autumn Annals*'[74] tracing of the transformations in the principles of things and in human affairs began with [Confucius'] rectification of names.[75] However, the *Annals* did not touch upon the realm of suchness, and so its deficiency was the same as that of the *Book of Change*.) The venerable master Yihuang 宜黃[76] said that the Confucians talk only about function.[77] His claim was actually based on that of master Xuanzang. As for master Xuanzang's derision of Confucius for not perceiving Reality, and his exclusive revering of Buddhism for its [emphasis on] the personal realization of suchness, this was

---

[73] The passage is from Xuanzang's "Xie Taizong Wen Huangdi zhi 'Sanzang Shengjiao xu' biao" 謝太宗文皇帝製三藏聖教序表 (Memorial to Thank Emperor Taizong for Writing the "Preface to the Sacred Teachings [Translated by] the Tripiṭaka [Master Xuanzang of the Great Tang]", in *Shi shamen Xuanzang shang biao ji* 寺沙門玄奘上表記 (Memorials and Records Submitted by Monk Xuanzang), T2119.52, 819b6-7. Xiong has substituted two key characters. In the phrase 六爻探賾 (the six lines of the hexagrams delve into the mysterious) he substituted *tan* 探 with *shen* 深, changing the meaning of the phrase to "the six lines of the hexagrams are profound and mysterious." In the phrase 局於生滅 (being near to arising and ceasing) he substituted *ju* 局 with *ju* 拘, changing the meaning of the phrase to "limited to the realm of arising and ceasing." Dorothy C. Wong explains that the "'Da Tang sanzang shengjiao xu 大唐三藏聖教序 (Preface to The Sacred Teachings [Translated by] the Tripiṭaka Master Xuanzang of the Great Tang)' had been granted by Emperor Taizong as an encomium extolling Xuanzang's endeavours upon his completion of the *Yuqie shidi lun* 瑜伽師地論 (Skt. Yogācārabhūmi-śāstra; Treatise on the stages of yogic practice) in 100 fascicles at Hongfu Monastery in 648." See her *Buddhist Pilgrim-Monks as Agents of Cultural and Artistic Transmission: The International Buddhist Art Style in East Asia, ca. 645–770* (Singapore: NUS Press, 2018), p. 27.

[74] Traditionally regarded as having been compiled by Confucius.

[75] See *Analects* 13.3.

[76] Xiong's former teacher, Ouyang Jingwu; he was born in Yihuang county in Jiangsu province.

[77] Possibly referring to comments Ouyang makes in a short essay written in 1936, "Kong Fo" 孔佛 (Confucians and Buddhists), included in his *Kongxue zazhu* 孔學雜著 (Assorted Writings on Confucianism), in *Ouyang Jingwu xiansheng neiwai xue* 歐陽竟無先生內外學 (Mr Ouyang Jingwu's Buddhist and Non-Buddhist Learning), vol. 14, available at http://www.guoxue123.com/new/0002/bfehyx/043.htm. On this identification, see also Hu Yong 胡勇, "Jindai foxue gegu yu ti yong quanshi de chuangxin 近代佛學革故與體用詮釋的創新 (A Revolution in Modern Buddhism and Innovations in Interpreting *Ti* and *Yong*), in Cheng Gongran 程恭讓 and Miaofan 妙凡 eds., *2016 Xingyun dashi renjian fojiao lilun shijian yanjiu* 2016 星雲大師人間佛教理論實踐研究 (Studies from 2016 on Putting Venerable Master Xingyun's Humanistic Buddhism into Practice) (Gaoxiong: Foguang wenhua, 2017), p. 381, n. 20.

not a deliberate attempt to uphold a sectarian position. Master Xuanzang was fundamentally carrying on the learning of Indian Buddhism, which talked about suchness-cum-nature-as-Reality (真如性體)[78] only in terms of its being quiescent and would certainly not have allowed it to be said that, with regard its quiescence, *it* is producing and transforming and that with regard to its producing and transforming, *it* is quiescent. The learning that master Xuanzang carried on could talk about Reality only in terms of the defining characteristic that is emptiness (孔德) ("The defining characteristic that is emptiness" is a phrase from *Laozi*. Wang Fusi 王輔嗣 said: "*Kong* 孔 means emptiness [空]."[79] To take emptiness as a defining characteristic is called *kong de* 孔德.) and not in terms of the defining characteristics of production and reproduction (生德) (For *sheng de* 生德, see above.); and could describe Reality only in terms of being "stopped at the back" (艮背) (The Gen 艮 [Stopped] hexagram in the *Book of Change* says: "Stopped at the back."[80] The back is a place [on the body] that does not move. To be stopped at an unmoving place is called "stopped at the back."[81] When the Buddhists talk about Reality, they say that it is "constant and unchanging"; it is the same.) and not in terms of "The movement of thunder

[p. 54]

and rain [brings things to] fullness." (The Image for the *Zhen* 震 [Shake] Hexagram states: "The movement of thunder and rain [brings things to] fullness."[82] The Confucians used this to describe the flow of intrinsic Reality, the supreme greatness of which is difficult to conceive—an excellent analogy indeed. The Indian Buddhists, however, did not agree to talk about Reality in terms of flow.) Having been accustomed to Indian Buddhist doctrines would have been why Xuanzang did not understand the Way of Confucius.

The "Great Commentary" of the *Book of Change* states: "In the *Book of Change* there is the Supreme Pivot (太極)."[83] (The Supreme Pivot is the Reality

---

[78] In the abridged edition of *Xin weishi lun* (1953), p. 118, and *Yuan Ru*, p. 437, Xiong notes that this is a compound term.

[79] This is Wang Bi's *Laozi Dao de jing zhu* gloss on *Laozi*, *zhang* 21. Interpreted on the basis of Wang's gloss and Xiong's above comments, *Laozi* 21 can be translated as follows: "Only [by emulating] the receptivity of the defining characteristic that is emptiness can the Way be followed." (孔德之容，惟道是從。) Wang comments: "*Kong* 孔 means emptiness. Only by making emptiness one's defining characteristic can one act in accordance with the Way." See Lou Yulie, ed., *Wang Bi ji jiaoshi*, vol. 1, p. 52.

[80] *Zhou yi*, 5.26a.

[81] This explanation seems to be based on Zhu Xi's comments on the passage. See *Zhuzi yulei* 朱子語類 (Topically Arranged Conversations of Master Zhu), compiled by Li Jingde 李靖德 (fl. 1263) (Beijing: Zhonghua shuju, 1986), 73.1853–1854.

[82] The passage is actually from "Tuan" commentary to the Zhun 屯 hexagram in *Zhou yi*, 1.28a-b.

[83] "Xici, shang," 7.28b.

of the cosmos, and is also called "the origin of Qian" [乾元].) There are sixty-four hexagrams and 384 hexagram lines. Each hexagram line is the Supreme Pivot. (The hexagram lines reveal movement becoming things. "Movement": *yin* and *yang*. The Supreme Pivot is the Reality of *yin* and *yang*. Hence it is said that each hexagram line is the Supreme Pivot.) How could it be said that the *Book of Change* does not see Reality? The *Spring and Autumn Annals*' [practice of] establishing [a record] for the "origin" year [in the reign of a new Lu duke] (建元)[84] is based on the purport of [*yuan* 元] in the *Book of Change*. (In the "Zhong zheng" 重政 [Emphasizing Governance] chapter of *Chun qiu fan lu* 春秋繁露 [Luxuriant Dew of the *Spring and Autumn Annals*], Master Dong Zhongshu 董仲舒 [179-104]: said: "*Yuan* 元" is like "source/origin" [原].[85] The *yuan* of the *Spring and Autumn Annals* is precisely the *yuan* of Qian yuan 乾元 in the *Book of Change*.) Although Dong's is a unique perspective, the purport of the crux of the principle (宗要) involved is no different.[86] (*Zong* 宗 means "purport"; *yao* 要 means "the crux of a principle.") How could it be said that the *Spring and Autumn Annals* does not see Reality? Both the *Book of Change* and the *Spring and Autumn Annals* uphold the non-duality of Reality and function, which is vastly different from the Buddhists who, in their pursuit of Reality, discard function. In holding on to the views of one school, Xuanzang became blinkered by those views and so failed to understand the purport of the sage [Confucius] and his scriptures.

Above I already said: "That which is undifferentiated and all-pervading and is without deliberate action yet there is nothing it does not do, is intrinsic Reality qua the flow of great function."[87] "Being without deliberate action" is saying that Reality does not deliberately create things. "There is nothing it does not do" is saying that Reality's production and reproduction, transformation and retransformation (生生化化), are so of themselves and cannot help but be so. "There is nothing it does not do" is the fundamental irreconcilable difference between me and the Indian Buddhists. Try pondering the case of the Buddhist canon and its twelve divisions—when suchness is

---

[84] The formula used is "Duke X, origin year" (X公元年).
[85] Dong Zhongshu: "Only a sage is able to link the myriad things to the One and to bind them to the Origin. If ultimately you do not reach the root from which [the myriad things] proceed, and continue it, you cannot succeed in your endeavors. This is why the *Spring and Autumn Annals* alters the 'one' [in the first year of each reign] and designates it the Origin [*yuan* 元] year. *Yuan* is like *yuan* 原 (source)." Modified translation of Sarah A. Queen and John S. Major, eds. and trans. *Luxuriant Gems of the Spring and Autumn* (New York: Columbia University Press, 2016), p. 172; *Chun qiu fan lu*, 5.6a, *Sibu beiyao* 四部備要 (Shanghai. Zhonghua shuju, 1936).
[86] That is, like the *Book of Change*, the *Annals* provides correct insight into the principle of *yuan* 元.
[87] "Being without deliberate action (無為) yet there is nothing it does not do" is a famous line from *Dao de jing*, *zhang* 37. Xiong is playing both on the sense it has there and also on the sense of "unconditioned," of not generating, not producing an effect.

mentioned, can you find any reference to "there is nothing it does not do"? (As noted already, "suchness" is a name for Reality.) The Buddhists agree only to saying that suchness is without deliberate action; they definitely do not agree to saying that there is nothing it does not do. This is because ever since the advent of Hīnayāna, their fundamental goal has been to leave [the cycle of] birth and death, and so all that they personally realize about dharma nature is quiescence. When the Mahāyāna Emptiness school first arose, as its fundamental vow, it undertook not to abandon sentient beings (The fundamental vow of the Mahāyānists is to liberate all sentient beings. However, not all sentient beings can be liberated, and so the power of their vow also accompanies sentient beings eternally. Accordingly, they never abandon sentient beings.) and made [the commitment] to abide neither in cyclic existence nor in *nirvāṇa* as its great practice. (Hīnayānists feared cyclic existence and so [aspired to] enter *nirvāṇa* rather than abide in cyclic existence. This is called the doctrine of [pursuing] one's own awakening. As for Mahāyānists, they abided neither in cyclic existence nor in *nirvāṇa*. The defilements of delusion having ceased, they did not abide in cyclic existence; converting or transforming people according to the capacities of those people, they did not abide in *nirvāṇa*. This is why the practices of the Mahāyānists are great.) Although they vastly surpassed those of inferior capacities ("Inferior capacities" refers to the Hīnayānists.), they consistently aspired to save all sentient beings so as to free them from the ocean of cyclic existence,
[p. 55]
and simply could not bear to enter *nirvāṇa* alone. The [thought of the] Emptiness school is indeed thought about transcending the mundane world (出世思想). Hence, what [the masters of this school] personally realized about intrinsic Reality is only that it is without characteristics, without deliberate action, without creating and without devising; quiescent, utterly quiescent; and profound, utterly profound (From "without characteristics" up to here is all taken from the *Perfection of Wisdom Sutra*.[88]), but, to the end, they never realized its true agency of the unremitting flow of production and reproduction, transformation and retransformation. Therefore, they said only that it is without deliberate action but did not agree to say that there is nothing it does not do, and consequently made the mistake of doing away with function in the pursuit of Reality.

The "Fayong pusa pin" 法湧菩薩 (Dharmōdgata Bodhisattva Section) of the *Perfection of Wisdom Sutra* states: "[This is] because the suchness of all

---

[88] This is a loose paraphrase of T220.7, 898a13–15.

dharmas (諸法真如) is free of quantification, and because it does not have a nature. It is like a mirage or even a dream."[89] Suchness is the Reality of all dharmas and is inherently without characteristics, without that to which it stands in contrast, and further, is without quantification. ("Without characteristics": Suchness is not something with form, nor does it exist by itself separate from the myriad dharmas, and so it is said to be without characteristics. "Without that to which it stands in contrast": this is easy to understand.) However, to say that it does not have a nature, that it is like a mirage, like a dream, is most illogical. Suchness is the Reality of the myriad dharmas—what does it mean to say that it has no nature!? Mirages and dreams are both illusory objects—how can they be compared to suchness? Although [the Emptiness school] says that this is to refute attachments, how could it perversely refute to this degree? In his later years Xuanzang had a profound respect for the *Perfection of Wisdom Sutra*, [yet even so,] with regard to passages such as this, oddly, he provided no rectification. In my view, there is nothing to criticize about the Buddhists' observing emptiness (觀空); rather, what should be criticized is their obsession with emptiness. There is nothing to criticize in their taking refuge in quiescence; rather, what should be criticized is their being mired in quiescence. (What does "observing emptiness" mean? It means that there should be no deluded attachment to any dharma. "Emptiness" simply means the emptying of deluded attachments.[90] "To take refuge in quiescence" means to make quiescence one's foundation such that when there is movement one is not thrown into disarray. None of this should be criticized.) Being mired in quiescence, they did not awaken to the exuberance of production and reproduction, and, being obsessed with emptiness, they did not recognize the wondrousness of transformation and retransformation. What I do not agree with is the Buddhists' doing away with function in the pursuit of Reality.

The Buddhists wanted nothing other than to obstruct production and reproduction, and transformation and retransformation, so as to realize their ideals about transcending the mundane world. If we probe the fundamental aim of the Buddhists, originally they wanted to remove innate superfluous things: so-called defiled habituated tendencies (染污習氣). [The effects of] defiled habituated tendencies are enough to block nature-as-Reality, [and so] the Buddhists wanted to remove these kinds of superfluous things.

---

[89] T220.6, 68a6–7 has only the sentence "Because the suchness of all dharmas is free of quantification, and because it does not have a nature." The remainder is a selective paraphrase of T220.6, 1069a22–23.

[90] By realizing that there is nothing with inherent nature to become attached to in the first place.

Unexpectedly, however, this led to the obstruction of production and reproduction and transformation and retransformation.

Someone said: "Hīnayāna definitely obstructs the flow of nature-as-Reality ("Flow" refers to production and reproduction, and transformation and retransformation.) but Mahāyāna is not like this."

I replied: "The Mahāyānists' only difference from the Hīnayānists is that they do not adopt the doctrine of [pursuing only] one's own awakening. The power of their vow is immense—the vow to save all sentient beings. Yet not all sentient beings can be saved and so for long eons the [Mahāyāna bodhisattvas] also do not abandon the mundane world, do not abandon sentient beings—the greatness of Mahāyāna (the Great Vehicle)

[p. 56]

lies herein. If, however, one reads the entire Mahāyāna canon, seeking its purport, the consistent aspiration is to leave the ocean of cyclic existence—on this point, there is no room for confusion. Xuanzang said: 'The ninety-six kinds of [non-Buddhist] paths all seek to transcend [the cycle of] birth [and death] (超生).'[91] (There were ninety-six kinds of non-Buddhist sects. *Chao sheng* 超生 means to transcend birth and death.) It is thus evident that most Indians in ancient times embraced transcendent thinking, and it was not just the Buddhists who did."

The Buddhists say that nature-as-Reality is emptiness and quiescence—I would not be so presumptuous as to disagree. Nature-as-Reality has neither shape nor conscious deliberation (作意); with respect of these features, there is nothing wrong in saying that it is empty. It has always been pure and undefiled; with respect to these features, to say that it is quiescent [is appropriate because] it is indeed the case that it is quiescent. Regrettably, however, teachings about transcending the mundane world are able to grasp only emptiness and quiescence, and so the degree to which the Buddhists have turned their backs on true principle (真理) is great indeed. I maintain that being quiescent yet producing incessantly, and being empty yet transforming endlessly, are the potent functioning (德用) of the Reality of the cosmos, just as it is (自然), and that whereby it comes to be as such cannot be altered. Empty, yet transforming endlessly, hence [transformation's agency] does not cease for a moment. (See the chapter, "Explaining Transformation."[92]) Quiescent, yet producing incessantly, hence production is not bound to anything. (In the

---

[91] Cited in *Xu gaoseng zhuan*, T2060.50, 455c7.
[92] Chapter 1, p. 41: "Transformation's agency never stops for a moment."

immense flow of "vast productivity" [大生] and "capacious productivity" [廣生] the small self cannot be selfish. Mencius' statement, "Above and below flow together with Heaven and Earth,"[93] gives expression to the genuineness [真] of "vast productivity" and "capacious productivity" and of not being bound to the small self; this indeed is to have understood production.) It is by this means that the gentleman abandons himself to daily renewal and so ultimate authenticity (至誠) is unceasing. ("Ultimate authenticity" refers to Reality.)

2. The doctrines of the Existence school

Originally, the theses upheld by the Mahāyāna Existence school (Asaṅga and Vasubandhu's school.) were born of a desire to rectify the abuses of the Emptiness school, yet, by and large, the Existence school indulged in impressionistic constructions and was never able to make the Emptiness school defer to it. I will now provide an outline account of this school as follows.

The learning of the Existence school was originally based on that of the Emptiness school, but later the Existence school vigorously promulgated the "existence teaching" (有教) to stand in opposition to the Emptiness school. (It is called the existence teaching because the teaching was established on the basis of the claim that all dharmas do exist and are not empty.) If we examine the sutras on which this school is based, such as the *Jie shenmi jing* 解深密經 (*Saṃdhinirmocana-sūtra*; Sutra Explaining the Profound and Esoteric), we will see the Existence school made the determination that there were three periods of the Śākyamuni Buddha's teachings. (See the "Wu zixing xiang pin" 無自性相品 [Characteristic of Having No Self-Nature Section].[94]) The Existence school says that in the early period, for the sake of (為) the Hīnayānists, the Buddha taught the existence teaching. (*Wei* 為 here is read on the fourth tone. In what follows, this is the same.) In broad terms, he explained [the principle of] the emptiness of a person (人空) (This means that there never was a real person or real "me"; rather it is simply that, on the basis of the five aggregates,[95] there is mistaken attachment to there being a person or an "I.") but did not yet reveal the principle of the emptiness of dharmas (法空).[96] It was probably because the Hīnayānists' innate capacity

---

[93] *Mencius* 7A.13.
[94] T676.16, 697a23–b5.
[95] Cf. above, p. 62: "What is referred to as 'I' is merely a self that is falsely presumed on the basis of form, sensation, and the rest of the five aggregates. If I am separated from the five aggregates, just where am I?"
[96] That is, that even the five aggregates are empty.

was shallow that he refuted only attachment [to the belief] in the existence of an inherently existent self (人我執). (In the early period, when the Buddha taught for the benefit of the Hīnayānists, he refuted only the deluded attachment [to the belief] that there are real people and a real "I," but still did not reveal the principle that the five aggregates are all empty. In other words, the existence of mental and material dharma characteristics had yet to be refuted. Hence it is called the "existence teaching.")
[p. 57]

In the second period, for those who had aroused the aspiration to hasten to (發趣) the Mahāyāna [path], the Buddha taught the "emptiness teaching" (空教). (*Faqu* 發趣 is only to have aroused the aspiration [發心] to hasten to [趣向] the Mahāyāna [path], and is not yet to have entered the Mahāyāna [path]. From this we can see that when the Existence school arose, it vehemently deprecated the Emptiness school. The *Sutra Explaining the Profound and Esoteric* is the Existence school's earliest [attempt] at pretending to be the words of the Buddha so as to bolster its own self-esteem.) For example, the *Perfection of Wisdom Sutra* states that no dharma has self-nature[97]—that is, dharma characteristics are inherently empty—hence it is called the "emptiness teaching." However, [because] there is a superior teaching above this (有上), [that teaching must also] be included (有容), [and so] the emptiness teaching is not the definitive doctrine. (*You shang* 有上 means "because there is a superior teaching above it." *You rong* 有容 means "because the middle path teaching [中道教] must also be included [in the three-period doctrinal classification scheme].")

In the third period, for the benefit of the followers of Mahāyāna, the Buddha taught "the middle path teaching of neither existing nor empty" (非有非空). The "I" that deluded discrimination is attached to is inherently non-existent (空無) and should be said not to exist (非有). However, because dharma characteristics such as mental and material dharmas are conditionally arisen (緣生)[98] dharmas, they cannot be said to be non-existent (無). Moreover, all dharma characteristics have suchness as their true nature, and so [there is even further reason to insist] that they cannot be said to be empty. In sum, that to which deluded consciousness is attached, truly does not exist. However, dharma nature and dharma characteristics are certainly not empty. This teaching was very different from the exclusive focus on talking about emptiness in the *Perfection of Wisdom Sutra*, and so it was called "the middle path teaching of neither existing nor empty."

---

[97] For example, T220.6, 997b29–30; T220.7, 395a24; T220.7, 736a5.
[98] Arise from causes and conditions.

Having gone into the particulars of the so-called three periods of [the Buddha's] teachings, [we can see that] that there is this differentiation of three periods of teaching because, using the pretext that Śākyamuni had taught according to the capacity of his audience, the Mahāyāna Existence school [expanded this to the claim that Śākyamuni] had taught the Dharma for three types of people in three different periods, the depth of the teaching differing in each period. The Existence school deemed itself to be transmitting the supreme doctrine, and further determined that the teaching inherited by the Emptiness school was not the definitive doctrine. ("Not the definitive doctrine": because its doctrine was still shallow and not the pre-eminent doctrine.). Brazenly opposing the Emptiness school, in order to promote its own teachings, the Existence school falsified the words of Śākyamuni, passing them off as genuine. Although the intentions of the Existence school were always admirable [as evidenced] in its use of the "neither existing nor empty" teaching to counteract the harm brought about by the Emptiness school's exclusive focus on talking about emptiness, it is just a pity that the set of theories it developed fell into the old rut of views based on false discrimination (情見), making it particularly difficult for the Existence school to subdue the Emptiness school. Now, if we wish to adjudicate what it got right and what it got wrong, the matter must be investigated from two aspects: ontology (本體論) and cosmology (宇宙論).

I will first investigate the Existence school's doctrines from the aspect of ontology. In the *Baoxing lun* 寶性論 (*Ratnagotravibhāga*; Jewel Nature Treatise[99]) we can find evidence of where the Existence school and the Emptiness school are opposed to one another. (The *Jewel Nature Treatise* was translated by Indian Tripiṭaka Master Ratnamati.[100]) From this *Treatise*, I will base [my exposition] on "Wei he yi shuo pin di qi" 為何義說品第七 (The Purpose of Instruction Section, Number 7):

> Question: "The other sutras (修多羅) ([Note]:[101] *Xiuduoluo* 修多羅 means scriptural text.) all say that everything is empty. (Note: this is referring to the scriptural texts that the Emptiness school took as foundational.) So, in this *Treatise*, why does it teach that there is suchness,

[p. 58]

---

[99] Full title: *Jiujing yisheng baoxing lun* 究竟一乘寶性論 (*Ratnagotravibhāga-mahāyānōttaratantra-śāstra*; Jewel Nature Treatise), T1611.

[100] Ratnamati (勒那摩提; [d. u.]) undertook the translation in 511.

[101] These notes are Xiong's comments on the cited passages.

buddha-nature? (Note: The *Jewel Nature Treatise* is an Existence school text.[102] Buddha-nature is another term for suchness.) The verse says:

Everywhere the scriptures say that
Internally and externally, everything is empty,
(Note: For "internal emptiness" and "external emptiness," see above.)
Conditioned dharmas are like clouds,
And like dreams and illusions.
(Note: the above is with reference to the Emptiness school.)
Here [in this *Treatise*], why does it teach that
All sentient beings
Have suchness as their nature
And does not say that they are empty and quiescent?
(Note: the above is with reference to the Existence school.)

Answer: The verse says:

Because [sentient beings] have timid minds,
(Note: This is the first kind of shortcoming [caused by the Emptiness school's teaching.] When sentient beings hear the Emptiness school say that everything is empty they become afraid and think that there is nowhere to take refuge, and so they come to have timid minds.)
And because [the Emptiness school is] contemptuous of sentient beings,
(Note: this is the second kind of shortcoming. To say that everything is empty is to say that all sentient beings are devoid of suchness, buddha-nature, hence the Emptiness school is contemptuous of sentient beings.)
And because there is attachment to unreal dharmas,
(Note: this is the third kind of shortcoming. This is referring to the Emptiness school's saying that everything is empty, yet it does not have anything that is real to show people. Hence, non-Buddhists are all attached to unreal dharmas, but the Emptiness school has nothing to guide these people to enter [the path] of true principle.)
And because they speak ill of the true nature that is suchness,
(Note: this is the fourth kind of shortcoming. None of those who are attached to unreal dharmas knows that they have suchness as their nature, and so they wantonly malign [their true nature].)

---

[102] The *Ratnagotravibhāga* is widely recognized for its account of the *tathāgatagarbha* doctrine.

And because they presume that the body has a spirit-cum-*ātman*,
(Note: this is last of the five kinds of shortcoming. An example is that because non-Buddhists do not see [that suchness is their nature] they falsely presume that there is a spirit-cum-*ātman* in their body.)
Therefore, in order to cause these kinds [of people]
To be far removed from these five kinds of shortcoming
It is taught that [sentient beings] have buddha-nature.[103]

According to what the *Jewel Nature Treatise* states, it is not hard to see that in the scriptures transmitted by the Emptiness school, everywhere there is talk about emptiness and quiescence. Coming to the rise of the Existence school, the scriptures it venerated all talk about "suchness-Reality" (真如實相) (*Shixiang* 實相 is just like saying Reality [實體]. *Zhenru shixiang* 真如實相 is a compound term. The Existence school called dharma nature "suchness" (真如). *Zhen* 真 means "real" [真實]. *Ru* 如 means "unchanging" [不變], because it is constantly just as its nature is; it also means "real.") and so, it is vastly different from the Emptiness school. (The Emptiness school says only that dharma nature is emptiness and quiescence. The Existence school opposes this and says that dharma nature is real.) These points of difference that the *Jewel Nature Treatise* raises especially, are very much worth paying attention to.

The *Perfection of Wisdom Sutra* talks of seven and even twenty [aspects of] emptiness (See the first part of the *Perfection of Wisdom Sutra*.[104]) and of observing the emptiness (空觀) of all dharma characteristics.[105] (*Guan* 觀 is "to observe" [觀察]. To observe that all things have always been empty is called observing emptiness.) And so, when it came to dharma nature, so as to guard against people's becoming attached to it, the Emptiness school had no hesitation in saying that it was empty—this really was going too far. Later,
[p. 59]
the Existence school began extensively to use suchness to explain dharma nature. (See *Great Treatise* [大論], *juan* 77.[106]) For example, the *Sutra Explaining the Profound and Esoteric* and treatises such as *Great Treatise* and *Zhong bian [fenbie] lun* 中邊[分別]論 (*Madhyānta-vibhāga*; Treatise Distinguishing the Middle from the Extremes) all say that there are seven [aspects of] suchness,

---

[103] T1611.31, 816a20–16b1.
[104] For the twenty, see T220.7, 13b26–c28; T220.5, 13b22–26; see also above p. 74, n. 36. T220.7, 13c27, 29; T220.7, 435b15–16; and T220.7, 991b21 all refer to *qi kong* 七空 but do not provide a list.
[105] See, for example, T220.5, 209a29–30.
[106] A reference to the *Dazhidu lun*. See, for example, T1509.25, 599c20–21; T1509.25, 601b15–16.

and as many as ten [aspects of] "that which is real" (真實).[107] (*Zhenshi* 真實 is another name for suchness.) "Seven [aspects of] suchness" does not mean that suchness is divided into seven kinds. It is just that it has different aspects and so is given multiple names. For example, the first is called "suchness of the successive flow of turning over" (流轉真如) (*Liuzhuan* 流轉 refers to mental and material [dharmas'] flowing in succession as the prior ceases and the succeeding arises, instant by instant. Hence, they are called dharmas that are in the successive flow of turning over [流轉法].) and means that suchness is the Reality of the dharmas that are in the successive flow of turning over. It is for this reason that this name was created. It does not mean that the successive flow of turning over is itself suchness. As for the seventh, it is called "suchness of correct practices" (正行真如) (*Zhengxing* 正行 refers to the saints' [聖者] cultivation of the path of [eight kinds of correct practice],[108] in which they arouse the aspiration to undertake correct practices. The sutras also talk about "the truth of the Way" [道諦].[109] I am not going to cite [those passages] here, as I fear that my explanations would be excessively prolix.) and means that correct practices are able to arise because of suchness, hence the name. It does not mean that correct practices are themselves suchness. The ten [aspects of] "that which is real" vary according to the meaning [as determined by context][110] and I will not provide an account here. In short, in the two schools' accounts of dharma nature, one says that it is empty quiescence, and one names it as suchness. Their difference is obvious.

Someone raised an objection: "The *Perfection of Wisdom Sutra* had already talked about suchness—it was certainly not an innovation of the Existence school."

I replied: "In order to investigate the learning of each school fully, those who are skilled at learning must be fully informed about the main aim of each school (Note the word "each."); they cannot selectively choose phrases out of context and thereby lose the overall meaning. Although the *Perfection of Wisdom Sutra* does talk about suchness, crucially, its aim was fully focused on refuting characteristics. If there is attachment to suchness as a real existent, then this is also grasping (取) characteristics, and constitutes a

---

[107] Seven suchnesses: *Saṃdhinirmocana-sūtra*, T676.16, 699c19-25); ten aspects of "that which is real": *Madhyānta-vibhāga*, T1599.31, 455b1-4.
[108] The eight kinds of correct practice or "eightfold correct path" (八正道) was taught by Śākyamuni in his first sermon and is a foundation of Mahāyāna Buddhist practice.
[109] The fourth of the Four Noble Truths; it includes the path of eight kinds of correct practice.
[110] In other words, there is no definitive list of these ten names, unlike the seven names for suchness.

massive delusion. (*Qu* 取 is just like "to hold on to" [執]. If suchness is imagined to be something that really exists, then at that moment the mind gives rise to a kind of attachment to characteristics, and so it is said to be "grasping characteristics.") The main aim of the *Perfection of Wisdom Sutra* is to empty all characteristics completely, in the hope that people will thoroughly awaken to suchness without resort to words. Hence, the Emptiness school's exclusive focal point was personal realization that dharma nature is empty and quiescent. This focal point was the nexus interconnecting the myriad threads [of the Emptiness school's doctrines]. Only by acknowledging this can we avoid falling into the error of selectively choosing phrases out of context."

Although the Existence school vigorously called attention to that which is real (真實), it certainly also talked about emptiness and quiescence. For example, the *Sutra Explaining the Profound and Esoteric* and *Yuqie [shi di lun]* 瑜伽[師地論] (*Yogācārabhūmi-śāstra*; Treatise on the Stages of Concentration Practice) both state that there are seventeen [aspects of] emptiness,[111] and the *Xianyang shengjiao lun* 顯揚聖教論 (Acclamation of the Holy Teaching Treatise) (In *juan* 15.) and the *Treatise Distinguishing the Middle from the Extremes* both say that there are sixteen [aspects of] emptiness.[112] (See *Bian zhong bian lun shuji* 辯中邊論述記 [Commentary on the *Treatise Distinguishing the Middle from the Extremes*].[113]) In addition to these, there is also Paramārtha's [眞諦; 499–569] translation of *Shiba kong lun* 十八空論 (Treatise on Eighteen Aspects of Emptiness).[114] (These various aspects of emptiness were presumably taken from the Emptiness School's *Perfection of Wisdom Sutra* by the Existence school.) It is thus evident that the Existence school also talked about emptiness and quiescence, but its focal point was, after all, to [make people] understand that dharma nature is real. Students, if you choose any of the Existence school's important sutras or treatises

[p. 60]

and ponder its content you will see that the main aim of the doctrines it has posited is completely different from that of the Emptiness school.

---

[111] *Saṃdhinirmocana-sūtra*, T676.16, 701a10–28 lists ten. Woncheuk's 圓測 (613–696) *Hae simmil gyeong so* 解深密經疏 (Commentary on the *Saṃdhinirmocana-sūtra*), X21.369, pp. 253, 255, 262 refers to seventeen. *Dai Nihon zokuzōkyō* 大日本續藏經 (Kyoto Supplement to the Canon), CBETA Chinese Electronic Tripiṭaka Collection ebook edition, Taipei, www.cbeta.org. *Yogācārabhūmi-śāstra*, T1579.30, 726c11–27a1 and 826b8–12 yield a combined total of twenty-three aspects of emptiness.
[112] *Xianyang shengjiao lun*, T1602.31, 556a15–18; *Madhyānta-vibhāga*, T1600.31, 466a3–6.
[113] Kuiji, *Bian zhong bian lun shuji*, T1835.44, 7c27–9a9.
[114] This work (T1616) is a commentary on Vasubandhu's *Treatise on Discriminating the Middle and the Extremes*; author unknown.

Further, it should also be understood that Mahāyāna's discarding of function in order to pursue Reality was not without a background. It will be recalled that in transmitting the Dharma, when Śākyamuni first taught about the five aggregates (蘊) he used a method of breaking down or deconstruction, breaking apart material and mental phenomena one by one, [to show that] none is real. For example, when the leaves of a banana plant are completely peeled away, one by one, of course there is no banana plant to apprehend. In the same way, not just are the characteristics of personhood and the characteristics of a self both empty, so too are dharma characteristics. Hīnayāna, which carried on from Śākyamuni, also promoted the teaching of emptiness. Crucially, beginning from the time of Nāgārjuna and the others, thereafter everything was exhaustively emptied.

Whereas the Emptiness school regarded dharma nature to be merely emptiness and quiescence, the Existence school opposed this view, hoping to lead people to recognize that dharma nature is real. Particular attention should be paid to the fact that the two schools' understanding of dharma nature differ. Why then did the Existence school still not change the original purport of the teaching of transcending the mundane world? I maintain that, when all is said and done, the two schools share an unshakable fundamental belief: The Reality of the myriad dharmas (Dharma nature.) is devoid of production and reproduction, devoid of flow and movement, devoid of change and transformation (The phrase from "is" to here is to be read uninterrupted.), and this is why dharma nature is said neither to arise nor to cease. The Existence school was unwilling to change this fundamental belief. Although it quite properly proclaimed that dharma nature is real—in order to remedy the error of being mired in emptiness and drowning in quiescence—yet it was this alone in which the Existence school differed from the Emptiness school. It is no coincidence that the Existence school still resolutely upheld the teaching of transcending the mundane world. In essence, the Existence school was not different from the Mahāyāna Emptiness school (大空). ("Mahāyāna Emptiness school" is abbreviated as *da kong* 大空; this is the same below.)

On the one hand, the Existence school posited innate seeds as the initial cause of the myriad dharmas ("Myriad dharmas" is the collective term for mental and material dharmas. The term "seeds" was posited because of the productive function that seeds have. This is undoubtedly because the Existence school imagined that the myriad dharmas have an origin from where they arise and so they called it "seeds." That is, seeds were said to be the initial cause of the myriad dharmas. "Innate" is saying that that it is because the seeds originally existed and did not arise subsequently. They are also called "seeds that are so of themselves" [法爾種子]. *Faer* 法爾 means "self-so" [自然]. This is because the existence of these seeds is self-so, and one cannot ask where they came from.), yet, on the other hand, it still carried on the old doctrine, saying that suchness is the true nature of the myriad dharmas. [In doing so,] it gravely committed the error of having two tiers of intrinsic Reality (二重本體). The Existence school was unwilling to betray the old doctrine that suchness is a dharma that neither arises nor ceases. Hence in positing seeds to serve as the generative cause for (為) dharmas (*Wei* 為 is to be read on the fourth tone.) the Existence school was probably not aware that it had fallen into colossal error. (As the initial cause of the myriad dharmas, innate seeds

[p. 61]

must be said to be intrinsic Reality [本體]; yet, by additionally positing suchness as the true nature of the myriad dharmas, the school had two tiers of intrinsic Reality. Already at the outset, Asaṅga was in error, and so it should not be Vasubandhu alone who is criticized.)

Ever since the Hīnayānists, when Buddhists talk about all dharmas they break the conditioned (有為) (That is, dharmas that arise and cease.) and the unconditioned (無為) (That is, dharmas that neither arise nor cease.) into two fragments. [This division] already served as [the precursor for] that upon which the differentiation between nature and characteristics in later Mahāyāna cosmology was based. (The unconditioned is dharma nature; the conditioned is dharma characteristics.) As for the learning that meticulously examines the Reality (實相) of the myriad dharmas, and which occupies the highest rank among Buddhist teachings, it was only with the rise of bodhisattva Nāgārjuna, when he markedly raised the profile of Mahāyāna, that this supreme norm (極則) started to be promulgated. (*Shixiang* 實相 is just like saying "intrinsic Reality" [本體]. Although there should be a source for Nāgārjuna's learning, no doubt it was only with Nāgārjuna that Mahāyāna's profile started to rise. *Ji ze* 極則: *ji* is just like "ultimate" [至]; *ze* is just like "standard" [法]. The standard spoken of here, however, is referring to the ontology [本體論] that Mahāyāna first started to talk about. Because Mahāyāna promulgated Reality and fathomed principles to their ultimate, therefore it is called "supreme norm." It was Nāgārjuna who began to raise the profile of the Mahāyāna school of learning. At first, the name "Emptiness school" was never used. Later, however, the Existence school arose, opposing emptiness and talking about existence. It, too, was called Mahāyāna. Thereupon, Mahāyāna became divided into the two schools of Emptiness and Existence.) The *Treatise on the Middle Way* states: "Mahāyāna has only one Dharma seal and it is called the seal of Reality." (As seen above.[115]) It is thus evident that Nāgārjuna used the [Dharma] seal of Reality to ratify sutras such as (等) the *Perfection of Wisdom Sutra* and treatises such as the *Treatise on the Middle Way*. (Whenever *deng* 等 is used this is because there are too many examples to cite. The sutras subsequently revered by the Existence school, however, such as the *Sutra Explaining the Profound and Esoteric*, would certainly not have been among those that Nāgārjuna would have deemed to be Mahāyāna sutras.) He certainly would not have acknowledged that the sutras and treatises of the various (諸) Hīnayāna masters would have been able to investigate Reality exhaustively (窮) (*Zhu* 諸: this is because there were many branches of Hīnayāna. *Qiong* 窮 is "to investigate exhaustively" [窮究].) nor would he have acknowledged that they would have been able to talk about Reality. Because the realm created by Mahāyāna was indeed one that Hīnayāna had never climbed to, Nāgārjuna and the other masters had no other option than to single out the name Mahāyāna (Great Vehicle) in order to differentiate themselves from the lesser [school of] learning (小學). ("Lesser [school of] learning": the learning of Hīnayāna [Lesser Vehicle].) In sum, from the time of Śākyamuni's passing, Buddhist teachings developed from the twenty divisions (部) of Hīnayāna (*Bu* 部 is like "branch" [宗派].) to the rise of Nāgārjuna, who brought together the great works on ontology—a vast ocean of doctrines, truly the acme of perfection! (The *Perfection of Wisdom Sutra* was certainly not the product of one person, nor was it the collaborative effort of a few contemporaries. Nāgārjuna should be regarded as having collected the teachings of many early and later masters.)

When people who have no grounding in Buddhist teachings quickly peruse the *Perfection of Wisdom Sutra*, they find it to be dull and insipid, and cannot bear to continue reading it. When people who have long studied Buddhist doctrine [encounter the *Perfection of Wisdom Sutra*], not only do they not precipitously harbor views opposing [the *Sutra*], moreover, in pondering the path [disclosed] by the teaching of transcending the mundane world, they find that its line of reasoning is profound and far-reaching and are effusive in their praise. The Buddhist
[p. 62]
doctrine of Reality (實相之論) began with the Emptiness school, and attained comprehensive completion with the *Perfection of Wisdom Sutra* collection—it was perfect, with nothing more that could augment it. When the Existence school was in its initial ascendency, it produced the *Sutra*

---

[115] Xiong here misattributes the quotation. See note 21 in this chapter.

Explaining the Profound and Esoteric and, seeking to aggrandize itself, wrongly denigrated the *Perfection of Wisdom Sutra*—indeed, it had no sense of its own competencies. (It was unaware of [the limits] of its own competencies.) Ultimately, however, the brothers Asaṅga and Vasubandhu (These two masters were the progenitors of the Existence school.) found refuge in the *Perfection of Wisdom Sutra*. In his later years, Xuanzang devoted all of his energies to translating the *Perfection of Wisdom Sutra* (大經) (*Da jing* 大經 is an abbreviation of the *Perfection of Wisdom Sutra* [大般若波羅蜜多經].) and when he completed the translation his joy was boundless. In his *Commentary on the Demonstration of Nothing but Consciousness*, Kuiji refuted Bhāviveka,[116] yet later he said: "Bhāviveka's words should be studied and practiced."[117]

Although the Existence school had initially opposed the Emptiness school, with respect to ontology, the Existence school was unable to develop expositions that were independent of those found in the Emptiness school's sutras and treatises. In his later years, Vasubandhu wrote *Weishi sanshi [lun] song* 唯識三十[論]頌 (*Triṃśikā*; Thirty Verses on Nothing but Consciousness). The first twenty-four verses all talk about dharma characteristics, verse twenty-five talks about dharma nature, and the last five verses talk about the order of states of cultivation. (See [Kuiji's] *Commentary on Demonstration of Nothing but Consciousness*, juan 2, pages 5–6.[118]) If one were to undertake a balanced adjudication of the Existence school on the basis of these verses, three matters should be noted. First, in his early years, Asaṅga compiled the *Treatise on the Stages of Concentration Practice* (This treatise is a collection of doctrines drawn from many sources.) and also wrote ten supporting (十支) [treatises]. (On the basis of the *Treatise on the Stages of Concentration Practice*, he also wrote ten supporting treatises, called "the ten supports."[119]) His erudition was prodigious. In his later years, he wanted to establish the doctrine of nothing

---

[116] Bhāviveka was a Mādhyamika scholar and critic of the views of early Yogācāra scholars. In *Cheng weishi lun shuji*, T1830.43, 494b24–26, Kuiji criticized Bhāviveka for being "perniciously attachment to emptiness" (惡取空).

[117] I have not found this passage or a similar one in searches of Kuiji's writings. In his "Du Zhi lun chao" 讀智論鈔 (Reading notes on the *Treatise on the Great Perfection of Wisdom Sutra*), published in 1947–1948, Xiong makes reference to the same passage, additionally noting, "I seem to have read this in [Kuiji's] [*Cheng*] *weishi lun biechao* [成]唯識論別抄 (Digest of the *Demonstration of Nothing but Consciousness*). There is a clear record of this passage—I am not mistaken." See, p. 652. Despite Xiong's insistence, neither this passage nor any similar passage can be found in Kuiji's *Cheng weishi lun biechao*.

[118] It is not clear which edition Xiong is referring to. For the Taishō edition, see *Cheng weishi lun shuji*, T1830.43, 237b4–37c3.

[119] Xiong's attribution of all ten treatises to Asaṅga is problematic. For the list, see Charles Muller, "十支論," *Digital Dictionary of Buddhism*, http://www.buddhism-dict.net/cgi-bin/xpr-ddb.pl?q=%E5%8D%81%E6%94%AF%E8%AB%96.

but consciousness (唯識) but was unable to bring that task to completion and so he passed it on to his younger brother, Vasubandhu. It was also in his later years that Vasubandhu wrote the *Thirty Verses*, and in doing so more or less completed the doctrine of nothing but consciousness. At that point, although the learning of the Existence school now had a rigorous system, its scope was narrow. Second, only one of the verses in the *Thirty Verses* talks about dharma nature, just a few phrases. Clearly, when it came to ontology, Vasubandhu had no insights of his own. It would seem that what he had previously learned from Asaṅga lacked any ultimate referent (勝義). Third, twenty-four of the verses talk about dharma characteristics in detail. Clearly, from Asaṅga to Vasubandhu, the learning of the Existence school attached particular importance to proving that dharma characteristics really exist, in diametric opposition to the Emptiness school's aim to refute characteristics. In my humble view, there was nothing inherently wrong with the Existence school's opposition to the Emptiness school in matters of cosmology (Here "cosmology" is being used in a narrow sense to refer specifically to dharma characteristics or phenomena.), it is just a pity that its theoretical deficiencies (敗缺) were excessive. (Where the thesis one holds is imprecise and ill-considered this is called "deficient" [缺]; where that thesis lacks what is needed to attack the enemy, that is called "failure" [敗].) As a separate chapter, next I shall still continue to discuss the Existence school in general terms, but I will also elaborate my account of the Emptiness school with respect to matters I have more to talk about.

3
Buddhist Teachings, B

Only after having drawn on and intermixed Hīnayāna's "existence teaching" (有教) ("Existence teaching": the affirmation that all dharmas exist. Hīnayāna was originally separated into twenty divisions, and those that discussed emptiness were few. Most of the divisions discussed existence.) and rectified Mahāyāna's "emptiness teaching" (空教) did the brothers Asaṅga and Vasubandhu set out the discourses of their Mahāyāna Existence (大有) school. (Even though they [also] discussed existence, their views surpassed those of Hīnayāna [Lesser Vehicle] and so are called the Mahāyāna [Great Vehicle] Existence school.) During its initial ascendency, the mainstay of the Mahāyāna Existence school's affirmation of dharma characteristics was actually the deployment of a new doctrine of conditioned origination (緣起). (*Yuan* 緣 has two senses: "by means of" [由] and "rely on" [藉]. If you say that it is by means of depending on that thing that this thing is able to arise, or if you say that this thing begins to arise by relying on that thing, then that is called "conditioned origination"; it is also called "conditioned arising" [緣生].) This had already begun in treatises such as Asaṅga's *Discourse on the Stages of Concentration Practice*, with the system reaching completion in Vasubandhu's *Thirty Verses*. It is pity that he was unable to write explanations for the verses before he passed away. Coming to Xuanzang—from whom Kuiji personally received [instruction]—he assembled a collection of the doctrines of ten masters beginning from the time of Vasubandhu, to create *Demonstration of Nothing but Consciousness*.[1] Although he made a commendable contribution to preserving the learning

---

[1] *Cheng weishi lun* is a composite of commentaries on Vasubandhu's *Triṃśikā*. In order to buttress his own claim as rightful successor to a lineage through Xuanzang, Kuiji claimed that *Cheng weishi lun* was strictly based on ten Indian commentaries, with the opinion of sixth-century Indian Yogācāra exponent Dharmapāla invariably prevailing. Hidenori Sakuma and Dan Lusthaus, however, argue that it is often the interpretations of the seventh-century Yogācāra master Sthiramati that are the authoritative position (demonstrable by comparing Sthiramati's commentary, the only one of the supposed ten that is extant today, with *Cheng weishi lun*). See Hidenori Sakuma, "On Doctrinal Similarities between Sthiramati and Xuanzang," *Journal of the International Association of Buddhist Studies* 29, no. 2 (2006 [2008]): 357–382; Dan Lusthaus, *Buddhist Phenomenology: A Philosophical Investigation of Yogacara Buddhism and the Ch'eng Wei-shih Lun*, Curzon Critical Studies in Buddhism Series (London: Routledge, 2002), chapter 15.

of the Existence school, the [doctrines of] the ten masters all gave license to fanciful speculation, engaged in trivia, and are simply not worth paying attention to.

The doctrine of conditioned origination

Tracing back the doctrine of conditioned origination, it started with Śākyamuni and was further elaborated in the Hīnayāna scriptures. In discussing conditioned origination, several types of condition (緣) need to be posited (Here *yuan* 緣 is used as a noun and has the two senses of "by means of" and "rely on." See above. The same applies in subsequent uses.): causal condition (因緣 [*hetu-pratyaya*]), continuous sequence of sameness condition (等無間緣 [*samanantara-pratyaya*]), condition enabling an object to be taken as the cause of consciousness (所緣緣 [*ālambana-pratyaya*]), and contributory factors as condition (增上緣 [*adhipati-pratyaya*]).[2]

In their accounts of causal condition, the Hīnayānists never established [the notion of] seeds. What they meant by causal condition is simply that whenever dharmas arise, there must be a cause for this to be so. (The meaning of causal condition in Hīnayāna is extremely broad and is actually not so different from contributory factors as condition. When the Mahāyāna Emptiness school talked about causal condition its account was still not different from the Hīnayāna account.)

With respect to all dharmas, the prior is able to induce the subsequent (With respect to all dharmas, when the prior dharma ceases, the subsequent dharma arises. The reason this is uninterrupted is that just as the prior dharma arises, it has the power to induce the subsequent dharma to continue to arise.), hence it is said to be the condition that has [uninterrupted] sequence (次第緣).[3]

With respect to all dharmas, the cognizer (能緣)
[p. 64]
(Here *yuan* 緣 is like "having cognitive concern for" [思慮], but the characteristic of this cognitive concern is extremely profound and subtle. "Cognizer" refers to the mind.) necessarily[4] depends on external objects (外境) to arise (*Wai jing* 外境 means "external things."), hence it is said that there is the condition enabling an object

---

[2] The four conditions are central to Yogācāra accounts of causality, particularly for explaining the causal relationship between seeds, consciousness, and cognitive objects. See, for example, *Cheng weishi lun*, T1585.31, 40c20–41b6; translated in Francis H. Cook, *Three Texts on Consciousness-only* (Berkeley, CA: Numata Center for Buddhist Translation and Research, 1999), pp. 242–250.

[3] This is another term for the continuous sequence of sameness condition.

[4] Both the 2001 and 2019 editions of *Ti yong lun* mistakenly have *xin* 心 rather than *bi* 必.

to be taken as the cause of consciousness. (The mind is the cognizer and external things are that which is cognized. Only by means of there being that which is cognized can the cognizer be induced, hence, having external things "facing" [對] the cognizer, so to speak, is called the condition enabling an object to be taken as the cause of consciousness. The second *yuan* 緣 in *suoyuan yuan* 所緣緣 is a noun and has the same meaning as *yuan* 緣 in *yuanqi* 緣起 [conditioned origination]. However, it most certainly has a different meaning from the *yuan* 緣 in *nengyuan* 能緣 and *suoyuan* 所緣. Further, it must be understood that in my account here of "the condition enabling an object to be taken as the cause of consciousness" I have referred only to external objects. There is more to this, but I am unable to go into the details here.[5])

All dharmas exist through mutual dependence (A exists through dependence on B; in turn, B exists through dependence on C—an endless succession of mutual dependence.) and so it is said that there are contributory factors (增上) as condition. (*Zengshang* 增上 is like saying "additional" [加上]; that is, it means "to exist through mutual dependence." Take the example of an ink stone—it exists through dependence on a stone. The stone exists through dependence on a mountain. The mountain exists through dependence on this great land. And even the planet earth exists through dependence on the solar system.)

Buddhists from Hīnayānists to the Mahāyāna Existence school extensively distinguished all sorts of conditions, eventually bringing them together as four conditions. The *Treatise on the Middle Way* states: "All conditions are subsumed (攝) within the four conditions (*She* 攝 has two senses: "to include in" [收入] and "to contain" [包含]. All conditions are included in the four conditions—that is, the four conditions contain all conditions.) and it is by means of these four conditions that the myriad things (物) are able to arise."[6] As such, it is clear that the Mahāyāna Existence school's (大乘有宗) doctrine of conditioned origination (Hereafter, "Mahāyāna Existence school" will be abbreviated as *da you* 大有. The myriad things all arise in reliance on the four conditions; this is called conditioned origination. However, here "things" refers collectively to mental and material [dharmas]. Subsequent references all follow this. In the passage, "the myriad things are able to arise," quoted above from *The Treatise on the Middle Way*, the character *wu* 物 is treated as covering both mental and material [dharmas] and does not refer exclusively to things in the material world. References to conditioned origination in Buddhist texts are to both

---

[5] Already in his 1923 work, *Weishixue gailun* 唯識學概論 (A General Account of Yogācāra Learning), Xiong provided much more detail about these concepts. See John Makeham, "The Significance of Xiong Shili's Interpretation of Dignāga's *Ālambana-parīkṣā* (Investigation of the Object)," *Journal of Chinese Philosophy* 40:S (2013): 205–225.

[6] T1564.30, 2c2–3.

aspects, the mental and the material—do not be mistaken.) actually maintains that the myriad things all arise from the convergence of the four conditions. (It is not the case that there is an Emperor of Heaven who created the myriad things.) In other words, all dharmas arise by serving as conditions for each other. Because of conditioned origination there is a great power that enables the myriad images of the cosmos to flow and move, transform and change, and not to be extinguished. The respective cosmological standpoints of *da kong* 大空 (The Mahāyāna Emptiness school [大乘空宗].) and *da you* 大有 (The Mahāyāna Existence school [大乘有宗].), where one establishes and one destroys (The Mahāyāna Emptiness school's thesis that the five aggregates are all empty annihilates the cosmos. The Mahāyāna Existence school's conditioned origination doctrine establishes the cosmos.), are poles apart.

Someone asked: "The Mahāyāna Existence school's conditioned origination doctrine was originally passed on from Hīnayāna, yet you, sir, extol the Existence school for its new doctrine of conditioned origination. Why do say it was new?"

I replied: "An excellent question! Although the Mahāyāna Existence school's account of conditioned origination
[p. 65]
has aspects that were taken up from Hīnayāna (小) teachings (*Xiao* 小 [is an abbreviation for] "Hīnayāna" [Lesser Vehicle]; subsequent uses follow this.), it is actually vastly different from [conditioned origination] in Hīnayāna learning. First, Hīnayāna accounts of causal conditions were fragmented and lacked overarching categories. It was not until the Mahāyāna Existence school used the four conditions to subsume all conditions that the doctrine of conditioned origination constituted a grand and rigorous system. This is the first reason that it was a new doctrine.

Second, Hīnayāna accounts of causal condition did not posit seeds. When the Mahāyāna Existence school began to posit seeds it specifically stipulated that seeds are the causal condition of the myriad things. In particular, it stipulated that because there has been the creation of the myriad things from beginningless time, the initial cause is 'seeds that are so of themselves.'[7] (The term "myriad things" refers collectively to mental and material [dharmas]; see above. A mental phenomenon must have seeds as its causal condition—only then can it arise. A material phenomenon also must have seeds as its causal condition—only then

---

[7] In Chapter 2, p. 99, Xiong wrote: "[Innate seeds] are also called 'Seeds that are so of themselves' [法爾種子]. *Faer* 法爾 means 'self-so' [自然]. This is because the existence of these seeds is self-so, and one cannot ask where they came from."

can it arise. There is no dharma that is able to arise without a cause.) This development had already commenced in the *Treatise on the Stages of Concentration Practice* (大論) (In early times, the *Treatise on the Stages of Concentration Practice* was called *Da lun* 大論.) compiled by bodhisattva Asaṅga. (The *Treatise on the Stages of Concentration Practice*'s account of seeds was still not consistent—but that is a matter for a separate discussion. Nevertheless, when he composed the *She dasheng lun* 攝大乘論 [*Mahāyāna-saṃgraha-śāstra*; Compendium of the Great Vehicle], which he passed on to Vasubandhu, the doctrine of innate seeds [本有種][8] was already firmly in place, as was the teaching that seeds are real existents.) As Vasubandhu's *Thirty Verses* was transmitted to Dharmapāla, and subsequently to Xuanzang and Kuiji in China, the seeds doctrine became increasingly detailed, and can be compared to the theory of [metaphysical] pluralism (多元論) in Western philosophy. This is the second reason that it was a new doctrine." (Kumārajīva had introduced [to Chinese Buddhists] the learning of the Mahāyāna Emptiness school. The reason Xuanzang introduced the learning of the Mahāyāna Existence school was in order to remedy the error of being obsessed with emptiness.)

In their accounts of causal condition, the Hīnayānists particularly disliked being loaded down with trivial details and consequently they were unable to establish their doctrine. Hence, the Mahāyāna Emptiness school, taking the opposite tack, flourished by making use of the doctrine of conditioned arising (緣生) to refute dharma characteristics, and so annihilating the cosmos. (*Yuansheng* 緣生 is like saying *yuanqi* 緣起.) Take the example of the following [three-part] inference (量) set out by bodhisattva Bhāviveka. (Bhāviveka was a venerable master of the Mahāyāna Emptiness school. When an inference is set out in the "science of reasoning" [因明學 (*hetu-vidyā*)]), it is divided into three parts: thesis, reason, and example.[9])

[With respect to] the true nature [真性], conditioned [dharmas] are empty. (This is the thesis. "The true nature" is referring to Bhāviveka's purport in setting out this inference. "The true nature" is referring specifically to ultimate truth [真諦]. The Emptiness school distinguishes ultimate and conventional truth. See above. "Conditioned" means that all dharma characteristics arise through dependence on the four conditions, hence they are called "conditioned." "Empty": nonexistent. This is because, with respect to ultimate truth, conditioned dharmas should be concluded to be non-existent. How is this known?)

---

[8] Seeds that have been in the store consciousness since beginningless time.
[9] On Bhāviveka and *yinming*, see also Chapter 2.

This is because they arise from conditions. (This is the reason. It explains why conditioned dharmas are empty. All conditioned dharmas arise by depending on numerous conditions coming together, hence it is said that they arise from conditions. All dharmas arise from numerous conditions; that is, they do not have independent, real self-entity and so are empty.)
[p. 66]
Like an illusion. (This is the example. The various material images [物象] that illusionists make appear are actually non-existent. No conditionally arisen dharma has independent, real self-entity. Hence, only by using illusory things to demonstrate this reason [因] can a definitive case be made that conditioned dharmas are non-existent. <That is, the thesis.>)

Kuiji was extremely dissatisfied with this inference in which Bhāviveka strenuously refutes the "existence teaching" (有教).[10] However, according to the rules of the science of reasoning, Bhāviveka was not free of error. According to the old science of reasoning, only if the example part of the inference is an analogy can the inference be free of error. Beginning with Dignāga [陳那; ca. 480–540],[11] the example part changed to serve as proof of the cause and was no longer an analogy. The example, "like an illusion," cannot demonstrate what is explained by the reason. If one seeks to use conditioned arising as the reason to establish the thesis that conditioned dharmas are empty, then it will be necessary for the example part to require that all things of the same kind are conditionally arisen, and are also empty, with absolutely no room for a single exception. (If there is a conditionally arisen dharma that is not empty, then that is an exception and there are definitely no exceptions.) Only then could conditioned arising as the reason be demonstrated, and a definitive case be made that conditioned dharmas are empty. In this inference, however, because [the category of] "conditioned dharmas" includes [all] the myriad existents of the cosmos, therefore, it is only among conditioned dharmas that things of the same category as the example part can be sought.[12] Accordingly, "like an illusion" in the example part can serve only as an analogy and cannot [be used to] demonstrate conditioned arising as the reason. If examined in terms of Dignāga's new science of reasoning, Bhāviveka had committed a major error. (If Bhāviveka had not set out an inference,

---

[10] Kuiji, *Weishi ershi lun shuji* 唯識二十論述記 (Commentary on *Twenty Verses on Nothing but Consciousness*), T1834.43, 983c2–3.

[11] Famous Indian logician.

[12] An illusion is not an existent and hence cannot be a conditioned dharma.

but rather had simply presented "like an illusion" in the "discussions of doctrine" [論議] genre,[13] then there would have been no error.) Yet even though he had committed an error with this inference, his intended meaning was consistent with the orthodox tradition of the *Perfection of Wisdom Sutra*. As it would have been inappropriate for Master Kuiji to make open accusations against the *Perfection of Wisdom Sutra*, he directed his criticisms at Bhāviveka. His purpose in doing so was indeed very subtle.

The bodhisattva Nāgārjuna was the great progenitor of the Emptiness school. The *Treatise on the Middle Way* was the school's authoritative scripture (宗經), which it treated as its fundamental canon. (*Zong jing* 宗經: to take the *Treatise on the Middle Way* as basis.) The *Treatise on the Middle Way* proceeds directly to refute the four conditions, the details of which are set out in "Guan yinyuan pin" 觀因緣品 (Observing Causal Conditions Section).[14] I will not elaborate here. Later, when the bodhisattva Asaṅga founded the Mahāyāna Existence school, he revised the doctrine of conditioned origination, and first of all he posited seeds as the causal condition (因) of mental and material dharmas. (Causal condition is also abbreviated at *yin* 因.) Seeds are also called "productive power" (功能). (*Gong* 功 is like "power" [力]. *Neng* 能 is also like power. Because seeds have the function of being able to produce, they are given the other name of "productive power." Seeds have many other names as well, but I will not relate them here.) Next, he posited that the store consciousness (阿賴耶識 [*ālayavijñāna*]) stores all seeds (*Alaiye* 阿賴耶 means "store." Hīnayāna talked about only six consciousnesses, but when the Mahāyāna Existence arose it began to add the seventh consciousness, *mona shi* 末那識 [*manas*], and the eighth consciousness, *alaiye shi* 阿賴耶識. The eighth

[p. 67]

stores all seeds, hence it is called the store consciousness, which is abbreviated as *laiye* 賴耶. Seeds [種子] is abbreviated as *zhong* 種. Seeds are of many different kinds and so the text says "all seeds."), and so completed the doctrine of nothing but consciousness. (If it had been posited only that seeds are the cause of mental and material dharmas, and not also that the store consciousness contains the seeds, then the source of the cosmos would be nothing other than a multitude of seeds, which would amount to a doctrine of "nothing but seeds" and so the doctrine of "nothing but consciousness" would not have been able to have been established. Having considered this, Asaṅga maintained

---

[13] This refers to one of the twelve traditional genre divisions of the Buddhist canon, *upadeśa*, characterized by a question-and-answer format.

[14] "Observing Causal Conditions Section" is the opening chapter of the *Treatise on the Middle Way*.

that all seeds are concealed within the store consciousness and so brought rigor to his doctrine of nothing but consciousness.)

The *Compendium of the Great Vehicle* states:

If there is ignorance about [seeds] in the store consciousness' serving as the initial condition to effect arising (This is saying that the seeds in the store consciousness are the generative cause of the mental and material dharmas, or myriad dharmas, and so is called "the initial condition to effect arising." "Ignorance" means "failure to understand." What is meant here is that if one is unaware that the seeds in the store consciousness are the generative cause of the myriad dharmas, then this will give rise to the following false discriminations.) then some people will discriminate self-nature as cause (The Sāṃkhya [數論][15] posited self-nature as the cause of mental and material dharmas. What they referred to as self-nature was neither mental nor material.[16]); some will discriminate prior deeds as cause ("Prior deeds" refers to what had been done in a previous life; it is also called "karma from a previous life." For example, those such as Nirgrantha [尼乾子][17] maintained that there is prior karma and that it is the cause of all dharmas.); some will discriminate the transformations of Maheśvara (大自在天)[18] as cause (The Brāhmans and others maintained that Maheśvara exists, and because he is able to transform, this is the cause of all dharmas.); some will discriminate a real self as cause ("Real self" is like saying "true self" or "spirit-cum-*ātman*" [神我]. For example, the Sāṃkhya [僧佉] and others maintained that spirit-cum-*ātman* is the cause of all dharmas.[19]); and some will discriminate that there are no causes and no conditions. (Non-Buddhists who believe in spontaneous generation [自然外道],[20] [non-Buddhist] exponents of the view that there are no causes [無因論師],[21] and non-Buddhists who uphold the view of emptiness [空見外道],[22] all presume that the myriad

---

[15] A brahmanistic school of early Indian philosophy.

[16] This is referring to the Sāṃkhya concept of *prakṛti*.

[17] Fifth-century BCE founder of the Jain school. See, for example, *Da sazhe Niganzi suo shuo jing* 大薩遮尼乾子所說經 (*Mahāsatya-nirgrantha-sūtra*; The Sutra Explained by the Mahāsattva Nirgrantha), T272.9, 329c5–30a5.

[18] Hindu god who creates the world; epithet of Śiva.

[19] When referring to Sāṃkhya philosophy, this term is a rendering of *puruṣa*, which, together with *prakṛti*, produces the myriad things, although Xiong seems to this attribute this productive power directly to both *prakṛti* and *puruṣa* independently.

[20] See, for example, Daoxuan 道宣 (596–667), *Sifen lü shanfan buque xingshi chao* 四分律刪繁補闕行事鈔 (Summary of the Procedures of the Four-Part Vinaya, Abridged with Supplements) T1804.40, 150c28–151a1; Huiyuan 慧遠 (523–592), *Dasheng niepan jing yiji* 大般涅槃經義記 (Commentary on the *Great Nirvana Sutra*), T1764.37, 894a22.

[21] See, for example, Jizang, *Zhongguan lun shu* 中觀論疏 (Subcommentary on the *Treatise on the Middle Way*), T1824.42, 7a27–28.

[22] See, for example, *Yuqie shi di lun* (*Yogācārabhūmi-śāstra*), T1579.30, 311a17.

things do not have causal conditions.) Moreover, there are those who discriminate a [spirit-cum-]*ātman* that creates (The Vaiśeṣika school [勝論] posited the existence of a spirit-cum-*ātman*, saying that it has the power to create.[23]) and a [spirit-cum-]*ātman* that can sense. (The Sāṃkhya school posited the existence of a spirit-cum-*ātman*, saying that it can sense objects of form, sound, smell, taste, [and touch].[24]) This is like a group of men, all blind from birth (生盲), who have never seen an elephant (Being born blind is *sheng mang* 生盲.) and then someone showed them an elephant, telling them what it is. Some of the blind men touched its trunk, some touched its teeth, some touched its ears, some touched its feet, some touched its tail, and some touched its spine. Someone asked them, "What is an elephant like"? Some said it was like an ox plough; some said it was like a pestle; some said it was like a winnowing basket; some said it was like a mortar; some said it was like a broom, and some said it was like a mountain made of stones. If one does not understand the nature of conditioned origination, then ignorance will produce blindness. This is just like [the blind men guessing about the elephant]. ("The nature of conditioned origination": seeds in the store consciousness are the initial conditioned origination. Here this is referring to the [opening part of] the above passage. If one does not understand that seeds are the cause of all dharmas then there will be all sorts of false discrimination. That is, due to ignorance one becomes blind and does not awaken to true principle. Indeed, it is just like the blind men guessing what the elephant is like. "Ignorance" is also called "lack of understanding.")[25]

This passage by Asaṅga
[p. 68]
maintains that each philosophical school's account of the origin of the cosmos is conjecture and deluded conceptualization. His assessment is very scrupulous. In positing innate seeds as the initial cause of the cosmos, however, he ventured very close to the theory of [metaphysical] pluralism; and in further positing a store consciousness that stores all seeds, he came close to the theory of a spirit-cum-*ātman*. Did he really succeed in avoiding the errors of the other schools?

---

[23] Comments possibly based on Kuiji, *Cheng weishi lun shuji*, T1830.43, 262b28–c4.
[24] Possibly based on Kuiji, *Yinming ru zhengli shu* 因明入正理論疏 (*Commentary on the Introduction to the Science of Reasoning*), T1840.44, 129b3–11.
[25] Asaṅga, *She dasheng lun ben* 攝大乘論本 (*Mahāyāna-saṃgraha-śāstra*; Compendium of the Great Vehicle), T1594.31, 135a5–15.

On the one hand, the new doctrine of conditioned origination [formulated by] Asaṅga's school set up the Existence school by remedying [the errors of] the Emptiness school, and, on the other hand, established Mahāyāna by appropriating [doctrines] from Hīnayāna. (It appropriated Hīnayāna doctrines and sought to remedy the errors of the Mahāyāna Emptiness school, and so established the Mahāyāna Existence school.) In doing so, I believe that the school's intentions were laudable. The doctrines it posited, however, gave extreme license to subjective conceptualization and were deficient in many places. In what follows, I will briefly cite some examples.

Five doctrinal deficiencies of the Existence school

First is the matter of positing seeds stored in the store consciousness to be the initial condition to effect arising. Here the doctrine is quite close to the non-Buddhist doctrine of a spirit-cum-*ātman*. Xuanzang summed up the Mahāyāna Existence school (大有) [as being represented by] six sutras and eleven treatises (Mahāyāna Existence school is abbreviated as *da you* 大有. For details of the six sutras and eleven treatises, see [Kuiji's] *Commentary on Demonstration of Nothing but Consciousness, juan* 1.[26]) and also wrote a verse about the store consciousness, in which he says: "It comes first and departs last, as the master."[27] (This is saying that as a person starts to undergo birth, the store consciousness has already entered the mother's womb. It is not the case that it is only after the person is born that they begin to have this consciousness, and that is why it says, "comes first." When a person draws near to the end of their life, [the store consciousness] departs the body last of all, and that is why it says, "departs last." When a person is alive, [the store consciousness] resides in the person as the master, and that is why it says, "as the master." For the details, see Xuanzang's *Verses on the Structure of the Eight Consciousnesses*.[28] In the late Ming, Wang Chuanshan 王船山 [1619–1692] wrote an appraisal of Xuanzang's *Verses* but it was not transmitted.[29]) It is thus evident that even though the Mahāyāna Existence

---

[26] T1830.43, 229c28-28a3. See also the entry "六經十一論" by Charles Muller and Jing Yin, *Digital Dictionary of Buddhism*, http://www.buddhism-dict.net/cgi-bin/xpr-ddb.pl?q=%E5%85%AD%E7%B6%93%E5%8D%81%E4%B8%80%E8%AB%96.

[27] This line of verse is part of Xuanzang's *Ba shi guiju song* 八識規矩頌 (Verses on the Structure of the Eight Consciousnesses). Although not extant as a stand-alone text, the root-text and verses are cited in Putai's 普泰 (early sixteenth century) *Ba shi guiju buzhu* 八識規矩補註 (Supplementary Notes on the *[Verses on the] Structure of the Eight Consciousnesses*). The line Xiong cites is at T1865.45, 475c23.

[28] Xiong's explanation of the line is based on Putai's commentary, T1865.45, 475c23–24.

[29] The table of contents to the first *juan* of Zeng Guofan and Zeng Guoquan, comps., *Chuanshan yishu* lists the title *Ba shi guiju lunzan* 八識規矩論贊 (Discussion and Appraisal of [Tripiṭaka Master

school's doctrine of "nothing but consciousness" spared no effort in refuting non-Buddhist accounts of a spirit-cum-*ātman,* in fact there was no difference between the store consciousness and a spirit-cum-*ātman.* What must be criticized, however, is that even though the Mahāyāna Existence school and the non-Buddhists similarly believed in a spirit-cum-*ātman,* each gave license to subjective conceptualization in constructing their respective bodies of theory. Of course, this must be criticized. Scholars in our country have always lauded Buddhist teachings as atheism or "doctrine of no-*ātman*" (無我論). None has ever sought for explanations in the Buddhist texts and so they feel no shame in deceiving both themselves and others.

Second is the matter of innate seeds' being the initial cause ("Innate seeds" are also called "seeds that are so of themselves"; see the earlier note.) It is indeed the case that this teaching was first expounded in opposing the non-Buddhist doctrine that the transformations of Maheśvara [are the cause of everything]. (What the *Compendium of the Great Vehicle* refers to as "the initial condition to effect arising" is just like saying "initial cause"; see the earlier note.) Maheśvara is only one and there is nothing he depends on; to say that Maheśvara is able to transform and change is fundamentally illogical (不應理).³⁰ (*Bu ying* 不應 is like saying "does not correspond with" [不合].) The *Compendium of the Great Vehicle* posits that seeds in the store conscious are

[p. 69]

individuated and innumerable. (In *Yiye lun* 意業論 [Karma Produced by Mental Activity] the bodhisattva Qingyi 輕意 states:³¹ "The countless seeds are as numerous as rain drops."³²) This is the first point of fundamental difference between seeds and [the transformations of] Maheśvara. Even though all seeds are causal conditions whereby all mental and material dharmas come into existence, they must depend on other conditions coming together and only then are dharmas produced. Otherwise, even though there are seeds in place, by itself a solitary cause cannot produce. The *Compendium of the Great Vehicle* clearly

---

Xuanzang's] [*Verses on the*] *Structure of the Eight Consciousnesses*) but records it as not having been seen. Liang Qichao 梁啟超, *Qing dai xueshu gailun* 清代學術概論 (An Overview of Qing Dynasty Scholarship) (Shanghai: Shanghai guji chubanshe, 1998/2000), p. 20, lists the title as not having been engraved.

[30] Above Xiong commented: "The Brāhmans and others maintained that Maheśvara exists, and because he is able to transform, this is the cause of all dharmas."

[31] This work ceased transmission in the Tang period. I have been unable to find information about the identity or Sanskrit name of this author.

[32] Cited in *Yuqie lun ji* (*Yuga rongi*) 瑜伽論記 (Commentaries on the *Yogācārabhūmi*), T1828.42, 592b25–27, compiled by the Silla scholar Dullyun 遁倫 (ca. 650–730).

shows the six characteristics of seeds.[33] The fifth characteristic is that seeds depend on numerous conditions. This is the second fundamental difference between seeds and the fallacy that Maheśvara depends on nothing and yet is able to transform and change. (The Mahāyāna Existence school says that even though seeds are causal conditions, they still need to depend on numerous conditions. For example, in order for visual consciousness to occur at this very instant, there must be the seeds of visual consciousness as causal condition. It also requires that as the previous instant of visual consciousness ceases there is still the residual power that is able to induce continuation by the subsequent instant of visual consciousness so that there is no interruption. This is the "[uninterrupted] sequential condition" [次第緣].[34] Further, there must be an external thing that is able to draw forth visual consciousness at this instant, enabling this consciousness to be manifest. This is the "condition enabling an object to be taken as the cause of consciousness" [所緣緣]. Moreover, as auxiliary conditions, the optic nerve or intact cerebrum, as well as various dispositions [resulting from] past contact with the myriad things, right through to the light and so forth, all must have a bearing on this instant of visual consciousness. This is also called "contributory factors as condition" [增上緣]. This explanation is in terms of mental dharmas. If explained in terms of material [dharmas], then take the example of the sprouting of wheat shoots, which needs to have wheat seeds as its causal condition. Additionally, it needs to have water, soil, sunlight, air, fertilizer, the seasons, manual labor, and so forth as its "contributory factors as condition." If these other conditions are lacking, then even though the causal condition is in place, there will never be any sprouting. None of the myriad things and the myriad affairs arises without a causal [condition], yet equally they are unable to arise by relying on just the causal [condition] alone and not also on numerous conditions. This is the gist of the Mahāyāna Existence school's new doctrine of conditioned origination.) The Mahāyāna Existence school refuted the fallacy of "the transformations of Maheśvara" and was the first to expound the theory of the conditioned origination of the cosmos. ("Cosmos": the generic term for all mental and material dharmas.) If the cosmos is explained by focusing on the interconnection between all things, then the theory is indeed of indelible value. It is regrettable

---

[33] Vasubandhu, *She Dasheng lun shi* 攝大乘論釋 (Commentary to *Compendium of the Great Vehicle*), T1597.31, 329b28–c10, lists the following: seeds cease in an instant (剎那滅); seeds are simultaneous with their effects (果俱有); they always operate in conjunction with their corresponding consciousness (恆隨轉); they have a determinate karmic nature (性決定); they depend on numerous conditions (待眾緣); and they induce effects specific to themselves (引自果). For explanations of each, see under the entry "種子六義" by Charles Muller and Billy Brewster, *Digital Dictionary of Buddhism*, http://www.buddhism-dict.net/cgi-bin/xpr-ddb.pl?q=%E7%A8%AE%E5%AD%90%E5%85%AD%E7%BE%A9.

[34] This is a pre-Xuanzang rendering of *samanantara-pratyaya*. Xuanzang translates this term as *deng wujian yuan* 等無間緣 or "uninterrupted sequence of sameness condition."

that the Mahāyāna Existence school went so far as to devise a hidden place [in which to store] all seeds, which was tantamount to refusing to allow a heavenly deity (Maheśvara.) entrance through the front door, while ushering in a spirit-cum-*ātman* (Store consciousness.) through the back door. Is this not bizarre! As far as I am concerned, there was no harm in saying that seeds exist through mutual support but there was no need additionally to posit a store in which to store them. The reason that Asaṅga and the other Existence school masters did not awaken to this is simply because the basis of Buddhist teachings is, after all, religion. These masters were compelled to posit a spirit-cum-*ātman* in altered form so not to lose the traditional spirit [of Buddhism as a religion].

Addendum.[35] Someone asked: "In the *Collectanea* of Zhang Taiyan's 章太炎 [1869–1936] writings, there is an essay in which he takes the store consciousness to be that which is shared between sentient beings.[36] Is what he said an error?"

I replied: "This is a major error, not a minor error. Taiyan had no understanding at all of the basis and structure of *Demonstration of Nothing but Consciousness*;

[p. 70]

all he did was to pick a few fine phrases to savor. This was not unique to him—the temperament of literati has always been as such. (From the Wei-Jin period until recent times, none of those literati who were fond of Buddhism sought out its true meaning.) If the store consciousness were to be shared between sentient beings then it would be akin to what Zhuangzi called 'the vast and open wilds' (廣漠之野).[37] [As such,] how could it maintain the seeds of each and every person's karmic impressions such that the seeds did not scatter and disappear? Students, all you need to do is to examine carefully what is written in *Demonstration of Nothing but Consciousness*."

---

[35] The Chinese text has "Addendum 1" but as there is no Addendum 2, I have removed the numerical reference.

[36] The essay in question is "Jianli zongjiao lun" 建立宗教論 (On Establishing a Religion), in which Zhang writes: "All sentient beings share suchness in common and also share the store consciousness in common. Accordingly, the store consciousness is not limited to its own self-entity but is shared in common by sentient beings, where it is one, not two [i.e., separate from sentient beings]. If there were attachment to it as having self-entity, then the doctrine of nothing but consciousness would be no different from a [doctrine of] spirit-cum-*ātman*." See *Bielu, juan san* 別錄卷三 (Separate Category, *juan* 3), 24b, in *Taiyan wenlu chubian* 太炎文錄初編 (First Collection of Zhang Taiyan's Writings), *Zhang shi congshu* 章氏叢書 (Collectanea of Mr Zhang's Works), vol. 11 (Hangzhou: Zhejiang tushuguan, 1919).

[37] "Xiao yao you," p. 40. Xiong's point is that it would have no bounds.

[The person] asked: "If sentient beings each possessed an individual store consciousness, would it not then be the case that each sentient being was an individual cosmos?"

I replied: "The Mahāyāna Existence school treatises do indeed maintain that each sentient being is an individual cosmos. According to what is stated in treatises such as the *Treatise on the Stages of Concentration Practice*, each sentient being has eight consciousnesses and each consciousness can be broken down into an object part (相分) and a perceiving part (見分). Take the example of the visual consciousness. That which is able to discern material objects is the perceiving part of the visual consciousness, and the visual objects it discerns are the object part of the visual consciousness. This is how it is with the visual consciousness. The sounds that the auditory consciousness discerns are the object part and that which is able to discern is the perceiving part. This is the case all the way through to the store consciousness (Eighth consciousness.), which also can be broken down into an object part and a perceiving part. According to the various treatises, my body is the transformed appearance of my store consciousness' object part. The material cosmos that surrounds this body, such as the mountains, rivers, the earth right through to the sky and the various heavens are all called the 'container world' (器界); they too are all the transformed appearances of my store consciousness' object part. Accordingly, it can be understood that each sentient being's possessing an individual store consciousness is precisely each sentient being's being an individual cosmos. Each of the infinite cosmoses, however, thoroughly pervades the same locus, with none obstructing any of the others. Such is the overall purport [of those treatises]. I also have something to say on the matter. Although I also maintain that each sentient being is an individual cosmos, what I mean by this is fundamentally different from that of the Mahāyāna Existence school treatises. I maintain that the cosmos is extremely complex and the lives of the various sentient beings (有情) are also manifold and diverse. (What the Buddhists call *you qing* 有情 is an alternative term for sentient beings [眾生]. Sentient beings have deluded consciousness [含有情識], hence the name.) Hence, it should be said that each sentient being is an individual cosmos, but this is not referring to [the notion that] each [sentient being] possesses an individual store consciousness."

Third is the great confusion caused by dividing seeds into innate seeds and newly perfumed seeds.[38] After Asaṅga rebutted the cosmologies of each

---

[38] The newly created seeds formed by the imprint of the karmic impressions derived from the other seven consciousnesses on the store consciousness.

of the philosophical schools, he posited innate seeds as initial cause in his *Compendium of the Great Vehicle*. What he meant by seeds was those that have always been so of themselves (法爾) and innate. ("So of themselves": see the note above.) From Vasubandhu onward, however, the various masters changed to different

[p. 71]

theories, some teaching that there are only innate seeds, others teaching that the manifest activity (現行) [of the first seven consciousnesses] newly perfumes (熏) [the store consciousness]. ("Manifest activity" is another name for consciousness.[39] Here manifest activity refers to the first seven consciousnesses. *Xun* 熏 means "to perfume" [熏發]. When the first seven consciousnesses arise, a kind of impetus issues forth, which is deposited into the store consciousness to form new seeds. This impetus is also called "habituated tendency" [習氣]. Refer to *Compendium of the Great Vehicle*, *Demonstration of Nothing but Consciousness*, *Commentary on Demonstration of Nothing but Consciousness*, and so forth.)

Coming to master Dharmapāla, he was the first to reconcile the two teachings by positing both innate and newly perfumed seeds. According to his teaching, if innate seeds are not posited, then manifest activity, which is beginningless, would have no seeds [to account for its arising], and this would certainly amount to falling into (墜) into [the fallacious] theory of non-causality (無因論). ("Beginningless" is like saying Grand Primordium [太初].[40] Because it is not possible to estimate a temporal period for the Grand Primordium, it is said to be beginningless. *Zhui* 墜 is like saying "to fall into" [陷入].) Accordingly, [he decided that] innate seeds should be posited. (The *Compendium of the Great Vehicle* posited the seeds in the store consciousness to be the initial cause so as to refute theories that there are no causes and no conditions.[41] It is worth consulting.) As soon as manifest activity occurs, however, there is an impetus that in turn perfumes the new seeds concealed in the store consciousness. These new seeds will in turn become causes, giving rise to subsequent manifest activity. Accordingly, [he decided that] it was appropriate that newly perfumed seeds should be posited. (The Mahāyāna Existence school also called seeds "habituated tendencies," the

---

[39] More specifically, it is the activity of consciousness. Manifest activity is the appearance of things in their manifest aspect in the first seven consciousnesses as they emerge from seeds in the eighth consciousness.

[40] In Daoist cosmology, *taichu* 太初 refers to "a cosmogonic stage prior to phenomenal differentiation, prior to the inception of forms (*xing* 形) and matter (*zhi* 質), and prior to the emergence of the categories of time and space." See Zornica Kirkova, *Roaming into the Beyond: Representations of Xian Immortality in Early Medieval Chinese Verse* (Leiden: Brill, 2016), p. 150. See also Xiong's comments on p. 188.

[41] Possibly referring to *She dasheng lun ben*, T1594.31, 134c11–35a8.

name deriving from the newly perfumed seeds.) Although both Chinese masters, Xuanzang and his disciple Kuji, took Dharmapāla as the founder of their lineage, I must demure [with respect to Dharmapāla's views]. Given that Asaṅga had already posited innate seeds, it was nothing but utter confusion for Dharmapāla then further to claim that manifest activity engenders new seeds through perfuming. According to his theory of newly perfumed seeds, just as my manifestly-active-visual-consciousness ("Manifestly-active-visual-consciousness" is a compound term.) has just given rise to the discernment of a blue-green color, a [new] blue-green seed engendered through perfuming is deposited into the store consciousness. This new seed will in turn become a causal condition, giving rise to the ensuing blue-green color. Maintaining such a thesis is ludicrous.

The fourth concerns the matter of the Mahāyāna Existence school's taking each of the eight consciousness clusters (八識聚), and collectively naming each cluster as manifest activity. (*Ju* 聚 is like "category" [類]. That which Vasubandhu and others referred to as the eight consciousnesses were not eight simple entities; rather, each consciousness consists of multiple elements assembled as a single cluster. For example, the visual consciousness consists of the mind and each of the mental associates [心所] assembled as the visual consciousness cluster. The auditory consciousness consists of the mind and each of the mental associates assembled as the auditory consciousness cluster. For the olfactory and gustatory consciousness, right through to the store consciousness, this is the same. I maintain that Vausbandhu's school dissected the mind into fragments and then separately arranged the fragments into eight clusters. The technique it applied may be said to be fragmentation or dissection, but it cannot be called analysis. The technique of analysis is to apply the skill of intricate investigation to those places where there is a multiplicity of different orders of coherence. It is not to use one's own conjectures to dissect and then join together without any basis.) The term "manifest" (現) means "to be evident." The term "activity" (行) means "passing flow" (遷流). Each of the eight consciousness clusters has an image (象) that is evident, but it is not fixed; rather, it is a ceaseless passing flow, and so each cluster is collectively named as "manifest activity." (Someone raised the following objection: "Things have images but the mind has none." I replied: "This objection is incorrect.

[p. 72]

Your mind clearly has awareness; you can reflect within to check this for yourself. How can you say that it has no image? Surely it is not the case that only what the eyes see, and the hand touches, can be called images?") Each of the eight clusters of manifest activity has seeds, and the countless seeds are all concealed within the store consciousness. Such is the school's doctrine in general terms. Having thus examined the doctrine, [quite clearly] it simply separates the cosmos into a two-tier world of the concealed and the manifest. How can this not be deemed to be frivolous conceptual elaboration?

Addendum. The strangest aspect of Vasubandhu and the others' theory of eight consciousness clusters is that they maintained that the eight divisions of consciousness create the material world. For example, the visual consciousness transforms into the realm of visible material objects (色塵界) (*Chen* 塵: material.); the auditory consciousness transforms into the realm of sound; right through to the store consciousness, which transforms into the physical body and the container world. (For the "container world," see above.) This kind of fanciful theory is really very strange. Stranger still is that the Chinese people have consistently held it in esteem. From the *Treatise on the Stages of Concentration Practice*, as well as various scriptures translated by Paramārtha, I have detected that there was another school [that upheld the theory of] nothing but consciousness. That school's accounts of the store consciousness and seeds frequently differ vastly from those of Vasubandhu's school; and in its accounts of mind, mental factors, and even the Three Natures (三性),[42] there were no points of similarity with the Vasubandhu school. Moreover, that group's teachings are particularly intriguing, and largely consistent with the truth. I think the reason that Xuanzang did not introduce this school, instead excessively propagating [the teachings of] the Vasubandhu school, was simply because when Xuanzang was traveling in India, Vasubandhu's school was flourishing.[43]

Fifth, in treating seeds and suchness as two tiers of intrinsic Reality, the error was incalculable. Bodhisattva Asaṅga's *Compendium of the Great Vehicle* extensively refuted each school's cosmology (宇宙論) (Here "cosmology" is used in the broad sense, and refers both to intrinsic Reality [本體] and phenomena.) before

---

[42] Uncharacteristically, Xiong does not provide a note on the Three Natures. The first is the nature of existence produced from attachment to all-pervasive imaginative constructions, or the imaginatively constructed nature (遍計所執性; *parikalpita-svabhāva*). The second nature is the nature of existence arising from causes and conditions, or the other-dependent nature (依他起性; *paratantra-svabhāva*). The third nature is the nature of existence being perfect and true, or the consummate nature (圓成實性; *pariniṣpanna-svabhāva*).

[43] In his final book, *Cun zhai suibi* 存齋隨筆 (Notes from the Studio of Preserving [the Source]), published in 1963, Xiong further asserts that originally Asaṅga and Vasubandhu had suppressed this old school of "nothing but consciousness," and later Xuanzang had done the same, and so its writings became lost. See *Xiong Shili quanji*, vol. 7, p. 709.

revealing his own thesis, that is, that the seeds in the store consciousness are the cause of all dharmas (諸行). (*Zhuxing* 諸行: all mental and material dharmas; it is also a general designation for the myriad dharmas.) Asaṅga clearly took seeds to be the origin of the myriad dharmas, yet he also taught that suchness is the Reality of the myriad dharmas. As such, how was he able to avoid the error of two tiers of intrinsic Reality? Even if one were to use all the iron in the Nine Regions (九州) to cast it, it would still not be enough to make an error as huge as this! Because the learning of the Mahāyāna Existence school affirms that the myriad dharmas really exist, it therefore has to explain where the myriad dharmas come from. Its positing of innate seeds as the initial cause was certainly a theoretical necessity. If the Mahāyāna Existence school had not sought to add a layer of neither arising nor ceasing suchness in addition to innate seeds, would that not have been very appropriate? It is particularly regrettable that its deluded attachment to a spirit-cum-*ātman* was never destroyed and so it hastened toward quiescence, ultimately finding refuge in the neither arising nor ceasing.

The Mahāyāna Emptiness school talks about Reality, but by doing away with function, ultimately nature and characteristics are both emptied. This is due to the aspiration to enter quiescence (趣寂)—a view informed by false discrimination.

[p. 73]

(To transcend the ocean of cyclic existence and so enter quiescent extinction [寂滅]— hence "to enter quiescence." *Mie* 滅: all afflictions have completely ceased. Although the school does not say that intrinsic Reality also ceases, the sort of Reality it had in mind is merely one that is quiescent and devoid of production and transformation—how different is that from extinction?) The Mahāyāna Existence school arose succeeding the Mahāyāna Emptiness school, taking particular exception to the Emptiness school's refutation of dharma characteristics. Accordingly, it established a new theory of conditioned arising, posited seeds, and affirmed dharma characteristics. Now, while the aims of the school cannot be criticized, it is particularly regrettable that it was unable to perfect its theories. As for the five deficiencies adduced above, they reveal only the broad picture and I have not gone into the detail.

When I was young, I was fond of exploring cosmology. Seeking for understanding in [in the writings of] the Song and Ming Confucians proved futile. Seeking in the Daoist treatises (Laozi and Zhuangzi.), I delighted in their untrammeled and detached qualities, but as far as their analytical skills were concerned, I found very little to be inspired by. Seeking for understanding within the classics at that time I was not yet able to identify and correct instances of deliberate textual corruption, and when I perused the images of the hexagrams (卦象) in the *Great Change* I failed to grasp their wondrous import. Only then did I focus attention on Buddhist Mahāyāna, and with complete abandon (曠) investigated (觀) the Emptiness and Existence schools. (*Kuang* 曠: the mind has no constraints. *Guan* 觀: to investigate.) I was born with a feeling of compassion for the human realm. Before turning twenty, I read the "Great Commentary" to the *Book of Change* for the first time. When I first encountered the following passage—"the Way of Heaven arouses the myriad things but does not share in the worries of the sage"[44]—it suddenly brought forth a feeling of boundless inspiration that gripped my mind. It was not for no reason that when I later heard the Buddhist teachings, I felt the deepest affinity for the learning of the Mahāyāna Emptiness school. Eventually, however, I took the supreme doctrine that the sage "fashions and brings to completion [the Way of] Heaven and Earth,"[45] assists the myriad things, and, taking his place with Heaven and Earth, nurtures the myriad things,[46] to be the constant, ultimate principle (至理) (The ultimate principle is called *zhi li* 至理.) and the paramount standard (極則) for the human Way. (*Ze* 則: standard [軌則]. *Ji* 極: [This term is used] to acclaim that it cannot be changed.) Hence, I had always suspected that the *Perfection of Wisdom Sutra*'s [teaching] that nature and characteristics are both empty failed to correspond with true principle. (It is worth pondering again what I wrote above.) The Mahāyāna Existence school opposed the [doctrine of] emptiness and set forth the [doctrine that dharmas] exist. Although I applaud the overall aims of this school, the cosmology that the various masters constructed on the basis of their impressionistic indulgences suffered all manner of fragmentation, leaving them wide open to the ridicule of "drawing in the sky" (畫空). (It is popularly said that when a flock of wild geese flies in formation across the sky, the arrangement resembles calligraphy and painting. In a poem, Wang Chuanshan wrote: "Like birds drawing in the sky, leisurely flaunting their compositions."[47] Wang is implicitly ridiculing former and

---

[44] "Xici, shang," 7.12b–13a. The "Xici" has "the Way" rather than "The Way of Heaven" as the subject.
[45] See Chapter 1, note 29.
[46] See "Zhongyong," 12.1b, translated on the basis of Xiong's comments. "'Balance' is the great foundation of all under Heaven; 'harmony' is the all-pervading way of all under Heaven. Attaining balance and harmony is that whereby [the sage] takes his place with Heaven and Earth, nurturing the myriad things."
[47] The lines are adapted from "He Guishan 'Ci ri bu zai de shi tong xue'" 和龜山"此日不再得示同學" (In Response to [Yang] Guishan's [Poem] "Now I Am No Longer Able to [Do the Following]... As an Instruction to My Students"), *Jiangzhai shi ji* 薑齋詩集 (Collection of Wang Fuzhi's Poetry), 4.1a–b, in *Jiangzhai xiansheng shiwenji* 薑齋詩文集 Collection of Wang Fuzhi's Poetry and Writings), *Sibu*

contemporary scholars for resorting to fanciful speculations to support their theories, just like birds who depend on the sky (憑空)[48] to create their drawings—they have no solid basis.) I spent a long period examining the Mahāyāna Emptiness and Existence schools from the perspective of cosmology, but I found nothing I could agree with. Finally, near at hand, by drawing from my own person, and further away, by drawing from other things, I suddenly realized that Reality and function are non-dual. Recalling the significance of Qian 乾 and Kun 坤 in the *Book of Change* led me to lament even more my early failure not to have discerned what the former sages had created and elucidated long ago. Yet, if I had not exhaustively investigated the Emptiness and Existence schools, achieving understanding after uncertainty, being rewarded after being frustrated, then by what means might I have come to comprehend the purport of the sage?[49] I acknowledge that even though Buddhist teachings obstruct the great flow of the cosmos' "vast productivity" (大生) and "capacious productivity" (廣生),[50]

[p. 74]

those teachings are a remarkable kind of wisdom; nevertheless, they are indeed contrary to the ultimate Way. Those who have attained genuine understanding would not deem what I say to be in error.

Someone raised the following objection. "Laozi took 'the constant Way' to be the name of intrinsic Reality, and the Buddhists took 'suchness' to be the name (目) of dharma nature. (*Mu* 目 is like "name.") Hence, we know that Reality is true and constant (真常) and function transforms and changes incessantly. Now, sir, you say that Reality and function are non-dual, that with regard to Reality, *it* is function, and with regard to function, *it* is Reality

---

congkan chubian. The original reads: "Like those birds inscribing the sky, leisurely flaunting their compositions (如彼鳥篆空漫爾矜文章)." Xiong has omitted the character *bi* 彼; replaced the character *zhuan* 篆 with the character *hua* 畫; and replaced the character *jin* 矜 with the character *jing* 驚. The first two changes are of minor consequence. The substitution of *jin* 矜 with *jing* 驚, however, makes little sense in the context. This substitution is already made in Xiong's earlier writings, such as *Yinming dashu shan zhu* 因明大疏刪注 (Abridged Edition of *Large Commentary on Introduction to Science of Reasoning* with Notes), (1925), *Xiong Shili quanji*, vol. 1, pp. 274, 326; *Zun wen lu* 尊聞錄 (Record of What Has Been Respectfully Heard), (1930), *Xiong Shili quanji*, vol. 1, p. 579, and *Xin weishi lun* (1944 edition), *Xiong Shili quanji*, vol. 3, p. 485. This is odd, however, because when Xiong quoted these same lines in his 1933 essay, "Po 'Po Xin weishi lun'" 破《破新唯識論》(A Rebuttal of "A Rebuttal of *New Treatise on the Uniqueness of Consciousness*"), *Xiong Shili quanji*, vol. 2, p. 168, there is no such substitution, and Xiong's awareness of the significance of the character *jin* 矜 is apparent from his discussion on p. 167. In my translation, I have followed the reading with *jin* 矜.

[48] Xiong is using this term as a pun; its other meaning is "without basis."
[49] Confucius.
[50] See Chapter 2, p. 72 and n. 31.

(即體即用、即用即體). This being so, surely it is incorrect to talk of Reality in terms its being true and constant?"

I replied: "I maintain that 'true and constant' refers to the defining characteristics (德) of intrinsic Reality. Because it is not false, it is called 'true.' Because it does not change its nature, it is called 'constant.' (It is analogous to water's being able to transform into steam or freeze to become ice, yet its wet nature does not change. From this analogy it can be understood that intrinsic Reality constantly preserves without change its defining characteristics of robustness and vigor, utter goodness, and so forth.) 'True and constant' refers specifically to intrinsic Reality's defining characteristics; it does not refer to [some notion] that intrinsic Reality exists by itself, transcending the myriad images that transform and change ceaselessly. (Although I also use the term "suchness" [真如] [to refer to Reality], the sense in which I use it is vastly different from its original meaning.) The character *de* 德 is glossed [as follows]: '*De* 德 is "to get" (得).'[51] For example, if it is said that a white vase possesses the characteristic (德) of being white, then 'white' is that whereby the vase gets to be a white vase. Now, in referring to intrinsic Reality in terms of its defining characteristics of true and constant, right through to its myriad other defining characteristics, these defining characteristics are that whereby intrinsic Reality gets to be the intrinsic Reality of the cosmos. If there were no defining characteristics of true and constant and so forth, how could Reality start the myriad transformations and bring the myriad things to completion? The character *de* 德 contains two meanings: defining characteristics (德性) and potent functioning (德用). Intrinsic Reality's defining characteristics are those of being 'true and constant,' and its potent functioning is without limit, hence intrinsic Reality is called the source of the myriad things. The defining characteristics of true and constant interconnect the myriad defining characteristics with none omitted. Students, if you do not investigate this fully, you will be unable to talk about intrinsic Reality."

In this treatise, [I set out to show that] Reality is to be discerned by way of function (To recognize Reality in the flow of its great function is like recognizing the ocean in the leaping of the numerous waves.), hence I say that intrinsic Reality is called "capable of transforming" (能變) and is also called "productive power" (功能). (In this treatise, the term *gongneng* 功能 has a completely different sense from the Mahāyāna Existence school's use of *gongneng* as a name for seeds.) Having reflected

---

[51] See, for example, "Xin shu, shang" 心術上 (Techniques of the Mind, A), *Guanzi* 管子, *Sibu congkan chubian*, 13.3a: "Hence, *de* is to get. *De* means that which is obtained/gotten [for something] to be as it is." (故德者，得也；得也者，其謂所得以然也。)

profoundly on the fact that, in its pursuit of Reality, the Mahāyāna Emptiness school discarded function, and with function having been discarded, Reality also followed into emptiness; and that by refuting characteristics in order to reveal (顯) the nature, because characteristics had been refuted the nature could no longer be posited (*Xian* 顯 is like "to show."), I therefore seek to explain clearly that Reality and function are non-dual, making manifest the Great Way so as to distinguish it clearly for future worthies. I have never understood how one might find solace in [the idea that] by loathing and renouncing (厭離) the actual world, people will find refuge (皈依)[52] in a constant and unchanging world of quiescent extinction. (The term *yanli* 厭離 is taken from the Āgama sutras.[53] Śākyamuni took the mundane world to be an ocean of cyclic existence; loathing it, he sought

[p. 75]

emancipation.) In this treatise I uphold the principle that Reality and function are non-dual. I have not contrived to make its system rigorous, and yet it is rigorous in and of itself. This treatise is willing to accept all those [theses upheld by] any of one hundred schools of thought that are consistent with [this] principle. As for those that are not close to this principle, of course they are rejected, and there is unable to be any mutual understanding between us. In rectifying the shortcomings of the two Mahāyāna schools, it is truly because I had no other choice—I would not dare to disagree with them frivolously.

The learning of the Mahāyāna Emptiness school takes the emptying (空) of dharma characteristics to be pivotal (樞要). (*Shuyao* 樞要: This is like the seat of a central governing body's controlling [administrative] agencies in all directions. This is called "pivotal." *Kong* 空 is like "to refute" [破]. Thoroughly refuting all [dharma] characteristics amounts to all characteristics' being non-existent. Hence, when "to empty" [空] is spoken of, the sense of "to refute" [破] is already contained therein. When "to refute" is spoken of, the sense of "to empty" is also contained therein. This applies to other places in this treatise where these terms are used but no note is provided. The learning of the Mahāyāna Emptiness school is extremely profound and far-reaching. The purport of refuting dharma characteristics is pivotal to the immeasurable meanings [無量義] [of the school's teachings].) Practitioners of superficial learning do not search deeply for the meaning of "to empty." They mistakenly presume the "emptying" that

---

[52] Both the 2001 and 2019 editions of *Ti yong lun* incorrectly give the character *yang* 仰 instead of *yi* 依.
[53] For example, *Zhong Ahan jing* 中阿含經 (*Madhyamāgama*; Middle Length Āgama Sutras) T26.1, 779c16–20.

bodhisattvas speak about is merely giving free rein to subjectivity so as to get rid of everything. I maintain that the wise Mahāyāna Emptiness masters' talk about "emptying" was indeed based on investigating things and analyzing principles; it was not lacking in verification. To say that it gave free rein to subjectivity is truly excessive.

The Mahāyāna Emptiness school's three proofs for the doctrine of emptiness

In talking about the meaning of emptying, the bodhisattvas broke things down to set out three [proofs for their doctrine]. First, by breaking material things down into atoms, the appearance (相) of things is emptied. (When things are broken down into atoms and then broken down further, that is called *linxu* 鄰虛.[54] *Linxu* [literally] means "to be close to non-existent." At that point, material appearances [物相] are emptied. *Xiang* 相: appearance [相狀]. Subsequent uses of the character *xiang* all have this same meaning.) Second, by breaking time down into instants (剎那), material appearances and mental appearances are both emptied. (The appearance of continuity between past, present, and future is called temporal appearance. The appearance of North, South, East, and West [spatial] distributions is called spatial appearance. Mental appearances can be personally investigated within because they have the appearance of continuity. Material appearances can be discerned because they have the appearance of [spatial] distribution. When material appearances are broken down into atoms or into *linxu*, given that there is no longer any appearance of spatial distribution that can be referred to, how could there be any material appearances to discern? Having broken time down into instants, then if from this present interval of an instant one were to trace back to the past, at every instant [temporal continuity] would certainly have already been completely extinguished; and if one were to anticipate the future, at every instant [temporal continuity] would also be suddenly transforming, never preserving the past. As such, given that there is no appearance of temporal continuity that can referred to, how could there be any mental appearances to discern? Hence, to say that temporal and spatial appearances are refuted is precisely what "material appearances and mental appearances are both emptied" refers to.) Third, by observing that, in all cases, it is because numerous conditions come together that dharmas (This refers to mental and material dharmas.) arise, suffices to verify that dharmas do

---

[54] Xiong first introduced this technical term in Chapter 2, p. 62.

not have independent, real self-entity, and so it should be said that dharmas have always been empty.

As related above, in claiming that all dharmas are empty, the Mahāyāna Emptiness school provided three doctrinal proofs. This school exhausted the profound (玄) via the medium of things—how could it be frivolously denigrated? (The most universal and all-embracing principle, which is so utterly obscure and deep that it is difficult to fathom, is called

[p. 76]

xuan 玄.) Take, for example, the first doctrinal proof, which infers that atoms have no substance (實質), and names this *linxu*. This doctrinal proof refutes the non-Buddhists and the Hīnayānists for maintaining that atoms are round in appearance. In other words, it does not acknowledge that atoms are small granules. Here, the school's subtle (微) (*Wei* 微: subtle [隱微].) observation of things and the Confucian teaching about particles that cannot be broken apart (莫破質點), can [be seen to be] mutually illuminating. (*Balance as the Norm* states: "So small that nothing in the world can break it apart."[55] A Qing-dynasty scholar explained [atoms] as "particles that cannot be broken apart."[56] His explanation is certainly correct but is still incomplete. "Small" is when matter (質) begins to condense. When matter begins to condense, fundamentally it is something that is vital and active, and one cannot speculate that atoms are [merely] solidified matter. Hence, "cannot be broken apart."[57] After matter has already hardened it can be broken into fragments; before it becomes hardened it cannot be broken apart. The Mahāyāna Emptiness school does not agree that atoms have substance—this is quite compatible with the sense of "cannot be broken apart.") A shared conventional presumption is that all things have a fixed nature. ("Fixed nature": convention makes the false presumption that each of the myriad things has its own independent, real self-entity.) When the bodhisattvas broke things down to atoms, they additionally stated that atoms have no

---

[55] "Zhongyong," 52.7b. See also Chapter 1, p. 23 where this passage is also cited.

[56] The Qing scholar Xiong is referring to is Yan Fu 嚴復 (1854–1921). In Yan's translation of John Stuart Mill's (1806–1873) *A System of Logic* (which Yan published under the title of *Mule mingxue* 穆勒名學 in 1903), we find the following passage in describing the law of universal gravitation: "With large [things] it is evident among the stars, sun, and moon; among small things it exists within points so tiny that they cannot be broken apart. ('Cannot be broken apart': this is referring to atoms [*atun* 阿屯]. '*A* 阿' translates 'not'; *tun* 屯 translates 'break apart.')" (大之見於恆星日月之間，微之存在於纖尖莫破<莫破彼雲阿屯，阿譯言莫，屯譯言破也。>之內。) Further, in the glossary of translation terms at the end of the book, Yan lists *mopojian* 莫破尖 as the translation of "atom" and *mopozhidian li* 莫破質點例 as the translation of "atomic theory." See *Mule mingxue* (Beijing: Sanlian, 1959), pp. 327, 380, 384. The English term "atom" is ultimately derived from the Greek term *atomos* "not cuttable; indivisible": *a*- "not" + *tomos* "divided" [from *temnein*, "to cut"].

[57] See Xiong's related discussion below, where he writes: "In elaborating the purport of the *Great Change*, *Balance as the Norm* explains the reason 'particles that cannot be broken apart' cannot be broken apart is because they are productive and reproductive, pulsating, and not fixed."

substance. Thereupon, the fixed nature of the myriad things was completely stripped away, with nothing remaining. This is what is meant by "material appearances are emptied." (The Mahāyāna Existence school masters all say that atoms lack substance; their doctrine is actually based on that of the Mahāyāna Emptiness school.)

The second is the doctrinal proof of the instant. (The doctrinal proof of arising and ceasing in an instant. For details, see the chapter "Explaining Transformation." It is worth re-reading.) I often encounter people who do not understand this doctrinal proof and are full of doubts (疑) and objections (難) (*Yi* 疑: do not believe; *nan* 難: are critical of.). What they particularly fail to understand is that the myriad existents have two kinds of arising and ceasing. (See the Buddhist scriptures.[58]) The first is the arising and ceasing over one period (一期生滅). (From arising to ceasing, in which there is passage over several temporal phases, is called "one period.") For example, from when a person is born until the end of their life one hundred years later is called "arising and ceasing over one period." Another example is the white vase on this low table—from when it was first created it has undergone twenty years of annihilation without remainder. This also is arising and ceasing over one period. The second kind of arising and ceasing is "arising and ceasing in an instant" (刹那生滅). The myriad things all transform, change, and secretly move—none holds on to the old (故). (*Gu* 故 is like "the old" [舊]. Holding on to one's already formed shape and not transforming is called "holding on to the old." The nature of things is not like this.) In the interval of every instant (刹), they cease as soon as they arise, none abiding temporarily. (*Cha* 刹 is the abbreviation of *chana* 刹那.) In other words, to arise suddenly and cease suddenly in the interval of an instant is called "arising and ceasing in an instant." It was not only the Buddhists who perceived this; when the sage wrote the *Book of Change* ("The sage" is Confucius.) he said: "Swift yet not rapid; reaching without moving."[59] Certainly, he was already the first to have given expression to the doctrinal proof of arising and ceasing in an instant. (Each single instant suddenly arises and suddenly ceases. With respect to interconnecting multiple instants, [it is still the case that] each instant newly arises. Although the speed at which they do so is so great that it cannot be measured, it does not resemble

---

[58] See, for example, *Fo yijiao jing lunshu jieyao* 佛遺教經論疏節要 (Exegesis with Summary of the *Sūtra on the Buddha's Deathbed Injunction*), T1820.40, 850a10–11, with exegesis by Jingyuan 淨源 (1011–1088) and supplementary notes by Zhuhong 袾宏 (1535–1615).

[59] "Xici, shang," 7.25b: "不疾而速，不行而至。" Translation based on Xiong's explanation. In *Yuan Ru*, pp. 339–340, Xiong writes that it was based on the hexagrams created by Fu Xi 伏羲, as well as the Xia *Book of Change* and the Yin *Book of Change*, that Confucius refined and expanded the content as he undertook his own creative work on the text.

[p. 77]
the onset of human desires, which are rapid. Hence, "swift yet not rapid." The objects of the previous instants suddenly arise and suddenly cease; it is not the case that there is a previous object that moves to the subsequent [instant]. Nevertheless, the objects of the subsequent instants tightly follow the objects of the previous instants and so continue to arise, never being interrupted, just as if the previous object had the power to move to the subsequent [instant]. Hence, "reaching without moving.") According to Zhuangzi, Confucius said to Yan Yuan: "I [wish] always to be with you, arm in arm (臂), but it has disappeared (失)."[60] This is also talking about the unstoppable, sudden transformation of the myriad things, instant by instant. (See the "Tian Zifang" chapter of *Zhuangzi*. From the shoulder to the wrist is called the "arm" [臂]; *shi* 失 is "to disappear" [喪]. Confucius said to Yan Yuan: "Although I wish always to be with you and to take you by the arm and hold on to it, in the interval of time it takes to link arms, my arm and your arm have long already lost their former shape."[61] The ten thousand things are all [like] arms—is it likely that you can grasp them and hold on to them?) From afar, what the Buddhists said about "instants" matches what Confucius said, even though neither knew of the other's account. Is this not uncanny?!

Someone asked: "What sort of connection is there between these two types of arising and ceasing?"

I replied: "The myriad things are inherently without a fixed nature, instant by instant suddenly arising and suddenly ceasing, suddenly ceasing and suddenly arising. In this manner, pushing forward and shifting (推移), unceasingly producing and reproducing (*Tui* 推: pushing forward [推動]; *yi* 移: shifting [遷移]. Instant by instant, everything arises in constant renewal, with no previous object remaining, hence, "shifting.")—this is the inherent nature of the myriad things." ("Inherent nature" refers to the intrinsic Reality of the myriad things. It has always been producing and reproducing, transforming and re-transforming, inexhaustibly and unceasingly.)

But what about the arising and ceasing of a single lifetime? (This is raised as a question [that my interlocutor might have raised as an objection].) In order to provide an explanation for this objection, I would directly tell him that with respect to interconnecting multiple instants, the object of the subsequent instant tightly follows the object of the previous instant, continuing on yet altering (轉). (*Zhuan* 轉 has two meanings. 1. The object of the subsequent instant arises in succession to the object of the previous instant. 2. The succeeding arising must have altered

---

[60] "Tian Zifang" 田子方, *Zhuangzi*, p. 709. Translation based on Xiong's explanation.
[61] This is Xiong's interpretative paraphrase of the passage.

from what was prior, like a person from when they were an infant until from when they become a young child and onward. This is because, in the twinkling of an eye, the person changes.) It very much seems as if the object of the previous instant had never ceased, and just adds new vitality all the time, enabling it to pass through several temporal phases before finally ceasing. (From "It very much seems that" until here should be read without interruption.) Accordingly, it is said that there is the arising and ceasing over one period. This is what is accepted by convention, and there is no need to refute it. Because, instant by instant, things suddenly arise and suddenly cease, past [things] have already ceased (This is saying that past things have all completely ceased.) and the present also does not abide. (This is saying that things at this present interval of an instant also cease as soon as they arise. Here the word "things" is being employed in a figurative sense, one that includes both mental and material things. This sense applies also to those passages above where "thing" [物] is used without any note.) How is it possible not to say that material (物) characteristics and mental characteristics are both empty? (Here the character *wu* 物 is being used as the specific term for material things.) It is solely because ordinary people do not understand arising and ceasing in an instant that they are unable to observe emptiness in things. (Here "things" is again being employed in a figurative sense, one that includes both mental and material things.)
[p. 78]

The third is the doctrinal proof of conditioned arising (緣生). (It is also called the doctrinal proof of conditioned origination [緣起]. *Qi* 起 is like *sheng* 生.) The myriad dharmas arise through their reliance on numerous conditions (眾緣). ("Dharmas" is the collective term for mental and material dharmas. The four conditions include all conditions [一切緣], which are also called "numerous conditions.") For example, wheat grain is able to grow only by relying on wheat seeds as causal condition, and water, earth, sunlight, air, and human labor as auxiliary conditions. If any of these conditions were to be absent, then there would be no wheat grain. Heaven and Earth are large things, and their arising also has to rely on numerous conditions. Even such pure and spirit-like phenomena as seeing, hearing, being aware, and knowing are all unable to arise in the absence of causal conditions, as is detailed in the sutras and treatises.[62] Because the myriad dharmas begin to arise due to numerous conditions coming together, it is patently obvious that they have no real self-entity. Given that the myriad dharmas do not have real self-entity it therefore should be said that the myriad dharmas have always been empty. This theory upheld by the

---

[62] See, for example, *Yuqie shidi lun*, T1579.30, 289b13–21.

Mahāyāna Emptiness school is not lacking in proof with regard to the facts, nor is it logically in error, and cannot be lightly disparaged. Although the Mahāyāna Emptiness school masters had three doctrinal proofs for their account of emptiness, actually the main one was that of conditioned arising. This can be known by examining the four treaties. (The four treatises are: the *Treatise on the Great Perfection of Wisdom Sutra*, the *Treatise on the Middle Way*, the *One Hundred Verses Treatise*, and the *Twelve Gateways Treatise*.)

Assessment of the Mahāyāna Emptiness school's three proofs for the doctrine of emptiness

The foregoing is my detailed explanation of the Mahāyāna Emptiness school masters' three proofs for their account of emptiness. Now I should submit their account of emptiness to balanced adjudication. Ordinary people suspect that the bodhisattvas' account of emptiness, in which everything is removed, is simply giving free rein to subjectivity. ("Bodhisattva" is like saying "one who is properly awakened" [正覺者].) I will therefore [seek to] make it clear that it was not simply giving free rein to subjectivity, and that because the scriptural texts are all extant, [their accounts] can be verified. Although one should not calumniate wise men of the past, the three proofs for the bodhisattvas' account of emptiness are all in error. The first proof, for example, serves only to counteract ordinary people's deluded attachment [to the notion] that material things have a fixed nature, such as earth is nothing but earth, and water is nothing but water—how could they possibly be things that are suddenly transforming? Such is the delusion of ordinary people. Through their deep investigations into the nature of things, the Prajñā masters (般若家) understood that all things are inherently without a fixed substance. Hence, in order to counteract (對治) the delusions of ordinary people, they forthrightly stated that material things are empty. (*Duizhi* 對治: this is like the way a doctor treats illness. This term is based on [its use in] Buddhist texts. "Prajñā masters" refers to the Mahāyāna Emptiness school masters.) Yet, even though the fixed nature of material things is empty, material things most certainly cannot be said to be empty—the Prajñā masters failed to make this distinction. In elaborating the purport of the *Great Change*, *Balance as the Norm* explains the reason "particles that cannot be broken apart" cannot be broken apart is because they are productive and reproductive, pulsating, and not fixed. This is a characteristic of material things. It is not the case that to be named a material thing must entail [having] a solid, hard substance. (In the Qing dynasty, both Jiao Xun 焦循 [1763-1820] and Hu Xu 胡煦 [1655-1736] stated that *Balance as the Norm* was a book that elaborated the *Book of Change*.[63] As I have previously discussed in *To the Origin of the Ru*, however, *Balance as the Norm* was deliberately corrupted by people in Han times.[64]) The Prajñā masters

[p. 79]

hold that material things have no fixed nature, that is, that material things have always been empty. The reason that their doctrine is the diametrical opposite of that of the *Great Change* is because they suffer the fault of having sunken into emptiness and, moreover, they hold a biased view in their investigation of things.

Their second proof uses ceasing in an instant to show that material characteristics and mental characteristics are both empty. This also is completely different from [the teachings of] the *Great Change*. I have previously said that both Buddhist scriptures and the *Book of Change* elucidate the doctrine of arising and ceasing in an instant, but there is a fundamental difference. Seeing that [things] arise and cease in an instant, the Buddhists regard all of the endless succession of countless instants to be nothing other than unremitting cessation after cessation (滅滅不住). ("Unremitting" means that the ferocious power of extinction never ceases.) Seeing that [things] arise and cease in an instant, the *Great Change* regards all of the endless succession of countless instants to be nothing other than the unfathomability (不測) of production and reproduction. (*Bu ce* 不測 means that because the potency of production and reproduction is utterly fecund the wondrous speed with which the old ceases and the new arises is unfathomable.) Accordingly, whereas the Buddhists speak about ceasing in an instant (That is to say, in a single instant the myriad things cease as soon they arise. For example, at the initial interval of an instant they cease as soon as they arise, and the next interval of an instant they do the same ... all the way through to the countless instants it is the same. Hence it is called, "ceasing in an instant."), the *Great Change* talks only of production and reproduction. (What the Buddhists see is instant by instant of cessation, whereas when the sage wrote the *Book of Change*, he explained that instant by instant all arises anew.) Why does the *Book of Change* not talk about

---

[63] Jiao Xun, *Yi guang ji* 易廣記 (Extended Notes on the *Book of Change*), Qing edition held in Beijing University Library, 3.3b, available at https://ctext.org/library.pl?if=gb&file=94449&page=77; Hu Xu, *Gou deng yue zhi* 篝燈約旨 (Burning the Midnight Lamp [to Illuminate] the General Purport [of the *Book of Change*]), *juan* 45, 6b-7a, in his *Zhou Yi han shu, bieji* 周易函書別集 (Writings on the *Zhou Book of Change*, Author's Collected Works), *juan* 8, Qinding Siku quanshu.

[64] In *Yuan Ru*, pp. 328–329, 385 and elsewhere, Xiong claims that all Six Classics underwent deliberate textual corruption in the Han dynasty.

cessation? The cessation of the old is that thereby the new arises. If the old did not cease, then when something [first] arose in the beginningless (無始), it would have held onto its old [self] (*Wushi* 無始 is like saying "Grand Inception" [太始].[65] The start of Grand Inception cannot be traced, hence "the beginningless."), and, prospectively, there would certainly be no agency of arising anew,[66] and to the very end it would remain surrendered to the absence of arising. Surely, great transformation is not like this. It is because instant by instant the old is relinquished that instant by instant the new arises, and that whereby one cannot but help see the ceaseless abundance and flow of great transformation. The human way [entails] embodying (體) Heaven so as to realize human capabilities ("Heaven" is a name for great transformation and does not refer to a deity. *Ti* 體 is like saying "to actualize" [實現]. The human way consists of actualizing the potent functioning of great transformation and realizing the superior capabilities of humans. Indeed, as stated in the "Great Commentary" to the *Book of Change*: "The sage realizes his capabilities by himself."[67]); amending one's errors and moving toward the good without losing heart; being fully [committed] to renewing oneself daily without becoming exhausted; and merging the small self into the greater body (大體) to wander without limit. (*Dati* 大體, see *Mencius*.[68] If we are able to pursue humaneness, abandon self-centeredness, and be undifferentiated in the same body/whole as the myriad things in Heaven and Earth, then we will have awakened and entered into that which does not have that to which it stands in contrast [無對] from within that which does have that to which it stands in contrast [有對]. The small self does have that to which it stands in contrast and lives a life in dire straits. The greater body does not have that to which it stands in contrast and is forever inexhaustible.) How could [the Emptiness school] choose cessation and so drown in emptiness?

The third doctrinal proof uses conditioned arising to show that the myriad dharmas do not have real self-entity, that they are empty. ("Myriad dharmas" refers to mental and material dharmas.) This is the primary (第一) doctrinal proof in the Prajñā masters' account of emptiness. (Here, *diyi* 第一 is not

---

[65] As with Grand Primordium (太初), Grand Inception represents another stage in Daoist cosmography. According to Zornica Kirkova, *Roaming into the Beyond*, p. 150, n. 241, it represents "the inception of forms" (形之始) and precedes "the inception of matter" (質之始). Here Xiong is using the term in a non-technical sense.

[66] Cf. Xiong's earlier statement in Chapter 1: "When things temporarily abide, this would be [a state in which] the agency (機) of great transformation's removal of the old and creation of the new has already been suspended, so how could new things continue to arise?"

[67] "Xici xia," 8.24a. Translation based on Xiong's gloss of *cheng neng* 成能, *Ming xin pian*, p. 263. This passage is already cited in chapter 1 of *Ti yong lun*.

[68] *Mencius* 6A.14: "Those who follow their greater body are great persons; those who follow their small body are petty persons." Translation based on Xiong's following comments.

[p. 80]

talking about numbers [in a sequence], such as the first doctrinal proof, the second doctrinal proof, and so on. [Rather, what it means is that] of the Prajñā masters' doctrinal proofs for their account of emptiness, it is actually conditioned arising that is the main [主要] one. *Zhu* 主 is like the vernacular expression, "where the center of operation is located." *Yao* 要: "main point." This is why it is described as "primary.") As already stated above, because the myriad dharmas rely on numerous conditions coming together in order to begin to arise, it is evident that the myriad dharmas have no real self-entity, and so it should be said that the myriad dharmas are inherently empty. I maintain that in explaining that whereby the myriad things arise, the theory of conditioned arising is [posited] merely from the perspective that the myriad things rely on each other to serve as conditions. This is to focus only on the interconnectedness of the phenomenal world. Although philosophically it constitutes a distinctive account, crucially, it is not an exhaustively probing theory. Take the analogy of someone on the ocean shore gazing at the countless ocean waves. Wishing to find out what the productive cause [of the waves] is, someone else then explains that the numerous waves arise by pushing one another. (This pushing one another is to serve as conditions for each another.) I maintain that this explanation does not get to the root of the matter and is definitely unacceptable. I also maintain that even if this explanation is to some extent apposite, it certainly does not solve the problem. It must be understood that each and every one of the numerous waves takes the ocean to be itself (本身); it is not the case that apart from the ocean there separately exists an independent itself [for each wave]. If there were no ocean then there would be no numerous wave forms (相) (*Xiang* 相: form [相狀].), and so it can be said that the ocean is the cause whereby the numerous waves arise. In other words, the ocean is the source of the numerous waves. The understanding of the person who explained [that the numerous waves arise by pushing one another] was limited merely to the interrelationship between the numerous waves; this person did not take the next step of deeply probing their source. How could this suffice to solve the major problem of [identifying] the productive cause of the numerous waves? I have drawn his analogy to show how proponents of conditioned arising still find it difficult to talk about the learning that penetrates to the very bottom of the source of dharmas (徹法源底). I am not being unduly harsh in my criticism. (*Che* 徹: to probe thoroughly; *fa* 法 is like saying "things"; *yuan* 源: source; *di* 底: bottom. This is like probing to the very bottom of a tall and deep vessel so that the hidden contents can be completely understood. In the Buddhists' *Shengman* [*shizi hou yisheng da fangbian*

fangguang] *jing* 勝鬘[師子吼一乘大方便方廣]經 [*Śrīmālādevī-siṃhanāda-sūtra*; Sutra on the Lion's Roar of Queen Śrīmālā], *che fa yuan di* 徹法源底[69] means to probe thoroughly the true source of the myriad things and so come to know its inexhaustibly profound and mysterious secrets—this is philosophy's ultimate accomplishment.) What is, however, beyond dispute is that the point of the Prajñā masters' account of conditioned arising is unique and clearly cannot be talked about in the same breath as those Hīnayānists [who discussed] existents (小有) and who upheld a doctrine of conditioned arising. (*Xiao you* 小有 means those Hīnayānists who discussed existents; as seen above.) Whereas the Hīnayānists certainly erred in not fathoming the source, the Prajñā masters used conditioned arising to show that the myriad dharmas do not have real self-entity—that is, that dharma characteristics are inherently empty—so that people would thereby be able to awaken and enter into Reality (實相).[70] It was precisely their theory of conditioned arising that provided a beacon of wisdom for those who sought the origin. ("Their" is referring to the Mahāyāna Emptiness school masters. "Origin" is referring to the Reality of the myriad dharmas.) If it were claimed that they were not seeking the origin, do you think that those people would have been persuaded?
[p. 81]

Explanation of verse 18 in Nāgārjuna's *Treatise on the Middle Way*

The "Investigating the Four Truths Section" (觀四諦品) of the *Treatise on the Middle Way* states (*Pin* 品 is like "category" [類]. When the Buddhist scriptures discuss doctrine, they are divided into *pin*, which is more or less equivalent to *zhang* 章 ["section"] in the writings of the hundred schools of thought.):

Dharmas produced by the myriad causes and conditions,
I say they are empty.
And because ["empty"] is also a provisional name,
It is also that to which the middle way refers.

---

[69] The phrase is not found in the *Śrīmālādevī-siṃhanāda-sūtra*. It is, however, found, at *Hongzhi Chanshi guanglu* 宏智禪師廣錄 (Extensive Record of the Chan Master Hongzhi), Hongzhi Zhengjue 宏智正覺 (1091–1157), T2001.48, 78a20.

[70] As already noted, this technical term is synonymous with suchness, dharma nature, *nirvāṇa*, the unconditioned, and so forth.

136   TREATISE ON REALITY AND FUNCTION

众因缘生法　　我说即是空
亦为是假名　　亦是中道义[71]

This verse (偈) is the locus of the main purport (宗趣) of the *Treatise on the Middle Way*. (*Jie* 偈 roughly corresponds to the Chinese term *song* 颂 [verse].[72] When Indians wrote treatises in ancient times, they would first write a verse to summarize the main purport and then provide a detailed explanation based on the verse. This was called a treatise [论]. *Zong* 宗 is like "main" [主]; *qu* 趣: purport [旨趣]. The *Treatise on the Middle Way* extensively elucidates immeasurable meanings [无量义] and it is this single verse that is the basis for those immeasurable meanings and also where they converge. Hence it is said that this single verse [is the locus of] the main purport of the whole book.) In what follows, I will provide a summary explanation of the verse.

"**Dharmas produced by the myriad causes and conditions**" The two terms "causes" and "conditions" can be interchanged yet they are also differentiated. When interchangeable, then conditions are also able to be termed causes, and causes are also able to be termed conditions. This can be verified virtually anywhere in the sutras and treatises. When they are differentiated, then it is causes that have the closest relationship with the dharmas produced, whereas it is conditions that have a relatively remote relationship with the dharmas produced. Although the verse refers to both terms, causes and conditions, actually [even if] only "the myriad conditions" were referred to, it would still include causes. The "four conditions" is a case in point. (Of the four conditions, the first, causal condition, is both cause and condition. This can be verified in master Kuiji's *Commentary on Demonstration of Nothing but Consciousness*.[73]) Readers, be sure to understand this well, and do not be inflexible: "the myriad causes and conditions" can be abbreviated as "the myriad conditions." Between the characters *yuan* 缘 and *sheng* 生, the character *suo* 所 lies concealed.[74] In Jizang's subcommentary [the passage] reads, "the dharmas that are produced by causes and conditions" (因缘所生法)— this is correct.[75] (There would be nothing remiss if the sentence "Dharmas produced

---

[71] *Zhong lun*, T1564.30, 33b11–12. In the *Taishō* edition, the character *wu* 无 is used and not *kong* 空. In Piṅgala's (青目; fourth century) commentary on this verse, which is appended to Kumārajīva's Chinese translation of the *Mūla-madhyamaka-kārikā*, however, *kong*, not *wu* is used. Also, when Jizang, *Zhongguan lunshu*, T1824.42, 23a2–3, cites the verse, again *kong*, not *wu*, is used.

[72] *Jie* 偈, an abbreviation of *jieta* 偈他 (alt. *jita*), is one of several transliterations of the Sanskrit term *gāthā*.

[73] Xiong is referring to the way the term *yinyuan* 因缘 is generally used in that work.

[74] In other words, it is implicit.

[75] See, for example, T1824.42, 5c4. Elsewhere, however, Jizang also gives 众因缘生法. See, for example, T1824.42, 23a2.

by the myriad causes and conditions" were changed to "Dharmas that are produced by the myriad causes and conditions.") "Dharmas that are produced" is referring to mental and material dharmas (諸行). (For an explanation of the character *xing* 行, see the first section in the "Explaining Transformation" chapter. It is worth re-reading.) None of the myriad images of the cosmos falls outside the two aspects of the mental and the material. The mental is not produced because of some spirit-cum-*ātman* (神我)[76] nor is the material created by an Emperor of Heaven—both arise from the coming together of numerous conditions. The [early] Buddhists excelled in using the theory of conditioned arising to refute [the notion of] Maheśvara. As the Prajñā masters arose, they began to use conditioned arising to promulgate the doctrine of emptiness. Although they also venerated Śākyamuni and his teachings, the [purport of] the *Treatise on the Middle Way* is profound and far-reaching.

"**I say they are empty**" The author of the treatise is saying that the dharmas produced by the myriad conditions are empty. ("Empty": non-existent. "The author of the treatise": the author of the *Treatise on the Middle Way*, the bodhisattva Nāgārjuna.) Why does he say that they are empty? The dharmas (The dharmas produced by the numerous conditions. In what follows, I refer to them with the abbreviation "dharmas.") are all produced by relying on numerous conditions coming together. Accordingly, their generation is inherently without real self-entity [無實自體]. This is because it is [from the coming together of] these numerous conditions

[p. 82]

that they are constituted. ("Without real self-entity" means that none of the dharmas produced by numerous conditions, such as the mental and the material, has independent self-entity. Master Kumārajīva's disciple translated this as "without self-nature."[77] Here *xing* 性 [nature] should be interpreted as *ti* 體 [entity], [and the phrase "without self-nature"] is like saying "without self-entity." Xuanzang also continued to use "without self-nature."[78] The *Treatise on the Great Perfection of Wisdom Sutra* has "without definite characteristics" [無決定相],[79] in which *xiang* 相 [should] also be interpreted as *ti* 體 [entity].[80] *Jueding* 決定 is like "fixed' [固定]. Dharmas are produced from numerous

---

[76] See note 19 in this chapter.

[77] The phrase "devoid of self-nature" is taken from Piṅgala's commentary on this verse, T30. 1564, 33b15–22. Xiong is implying that the Chinese translation of Piṅgala's commentary was undertaken by one of Kumārajīva's students.

[78] See, for example, *Cheng weishi lun*, T31.1585, 47c24–c5; *Weishi sanshi lun song*, T31. 1586, 31, 61a20.

[79] The *Dazhi du lun* has several examples of the phrase *jueding xiang* 決定相 (e.g., T1509.25, 197b5; 503c3) but none of *wu jueding xiang* 無決定相.

[80] Presumably interpretating both as renderings of *sva-bhāva* (own-being).

conditions and so are without a fixed self-entity. Most Chinese translations of Buddhist scriptures represent *ti* 體 with either *xing* 性 or *xiang* 相, which is not easy for ordinary people to understood. I often use "without real self-entity" [無實自體] instead but the meaning remains unchanged.) Since dharmas are without real self-entity, the author of the treatise therefore asserts that they are empty.

"And because ['empty'] is also a provisional name" The intended meaning of the author of the treatise can be paraphrased as follows. "I am saying that dharmas produced from numerous conditions are empty so as to refute the stubborn attachment that deluded people have to [the view that] dharmas have real self-entity. Hence, saying that dharmas are empty is the means by which to free them from their attachments. If, however, when they hear me talk of emptiness they were, in turn, to give rise to the view of emptiness (空見), mistakenly presuming that everything is empty, that would further constitute a great mistake. It must be understood that the term "emptiness" is also a provisional name. ("Provisional name" is like "nominal explanation" [假說].) If, upon hearing the term "emptiness," one were profoundly to awaken to the understanding that dharmas are without real self-entity, and at the same time, moreover, one were no longer to abide (不住) in emptiness (*Bu zhu* 不住 is like saying "not fall into the view of emptiness" [不陷於空見].), then this would be like obtaining good medicine after a being ill for a long time, and to recover from the illness completely with no lingering afflictions. (Ordinary people mistakenly view dharmas as all being individual, fixed entities <That is, they are attached [to the mistaken view] that dharmas have real self-entity.> This is called "attachment to the view of existence" [執有之見], which is abbreviated as *you jian* 有見. If one mistakenly presumes that everything is empty, this is called "attachment to the view of emptiness" [執空之見], which is similarly abbreviated as *kong jian* 空見. These two views are both deluded and mistaken. Only by removing these two views is there correct insight and realization of the truth.) If, in panic (惶然), one were to reject attachment to the view of existence, instead falling into (墜) the view that everything is empty (Upon hearing the term "empty," in panic, a deluded person rejects attachment to the view of existence and instead falls into attachment to the view that everything is empty. *Zhui* 墜 is like "fall into" [陷]. *Huangran* 惶然 is like "confusion" [惑].), then that person's error would be even greater than that of being attached to the view of existence (執有). Accordingly, in order to refute the existence attachment (有執), Nāgārjuna said that dharmas are without self-nature, that is, dharmas are empty. (*You zhi* 有執: to be so firmly attached to the view that dharmas truly exist as to be unable to abandon this view.) So as to guard against his listeners turning instead to hold the view of emptiness, he further said that emptiness is also a provisional name. From this it is evident that Nāgārjuna himself clearly understood that the original intention [of the early Mahāyāna Emptiness school masters] was never [to promote] the thesis that all dharmas are empty[81] and yet its later adherents were even ridiculed for being perniciously attached to emptiness (惡取空)[82]—why? (*E* 惡 is term of reprimand. *Qu* 取 is like "attached to" [執]. [The later adherents] were attached to the view that everything is empty yet were unaware that they were wrong. Accordingly, they were reprimanded for being perniciously attached to emptiness.)

"It is also that to which the middle way refers" Emptiness is spoken of so as to (為) refute the existence attachment (有執). (*Wei* 為 is to be read on the fourth tone. My comment here elaborates the first two lines of the verse, "Dharmas produced by the myriad causes and conditions / I say they are empty." Ordinary people are deluded, and perversely attached

[p. 83]

[to the view] that dharmas really exist. That is what is termed *you zhi* 有執.) Once the existence attachment has been refuted, it should be understood that the word "empty" is also a provisional name, and that it cannot be said that everything is completely non-existent. (My comment here elaborates the third line, "And because ["empty"] is also a provisional name.") Because it is removed from the two extremes of existence and non-existence (有無二邊), it is called the middle way. (Being attached [to the view that dharmas] really exist is to be attached to one extreme; being attached [to the view that dharmas] are non-existent is also to be attached to one extreme. Now, since [the view that dharmas really] exist has been refuted, there is no inclination toward the extreme [of attachment to the view that dharmas really] exist; and since it has been further explained that "empty" is a provisional name, there is no inclination toward the extreme [of being attached to the view that all dharmas are] non-existent. Being now far removed from the two extremes of existence and non-existence is why it is called the middle way.)

This verse, as well as Jizang's subcommentary,[83] merely serve to confuse people. [Piṅgala's] *Treatise on the Middle Way* commentary states:

"Dharmas produced by the myriad causes and conditions / I say they are empty." (In the past it was said that here Nāgārjuna was citing the *Hua shou jing*

---

[81] Xiong, Chapter 2, p. 68: "the original intention of the Mahāyāna Emptiness school masters was to refute characteristics to reveal the nature."

[82] Xiong, Chapter 2, p. 81: "The Existence school was certainly not being overly harsh in disparaging [the Emptiness school] for being perniciously attached to emptiness."

[83] *Sub-commentary on the Mūlamadhyamaka-kārikā*.

140 TREATISE ON REALITY AND FUNCTION

華首經.[84] I, however, maintain that this is Nāgārjuna's teaching. Mahāyāna sutras are all falsely attributed [to the Buddha]. One cannot claim that because the *Hua shou jing* has this passage[85] therefore this proves that it is the words of the Buddha.) What is the reason? (This is posited as a question.) When the numerous conditions are fully combined then things are produced. Because these things belong to causal conditions they do not have self-nature. ("These things" refers to the things produced through the combination of numerous conditions. Since they are produced through the combination of numerous causal conditions, then such things should belong to the numerous causal conditions, and it should not be said that these things have real self-entity.) Not having self-nature, therefore they are empty. (The above explains the first sentence [first two lines].) Emptiness is also empty. (Although it is said that dharmas produced by causal conditions are non-existent, nevertheless one cannot be perversely attached to [the view] that dharmas are definitely non-existent, hence he says, "Emptiness is also empty.") It is only for the purpose of leading sentient beings [not to be attached to emptiness] that [emptiness is] used as a provisional name. (["Empty"] in the above explanation ["emptiness is also empty"] also functions as a provisional name.) To be free of the two extremes of existence and non-existence therefore is called the middle way. (Take note.) Because these dharmas have no [self-]nature (無性) ("These dharmas" refers to dharmas produced by causal conditions. *Wu xing* 無性 is a contraction that should read, "have no self-nature" [無自性].) they cannot be said to exist (Because they have no self-nature they are empty. How can they be said to exist?); yet because they are not nothing (Emptiness is also merely a provisional name.) they cannot be said to be non-existent. (Emptiness is also empty hence they cannot be said to be non-existent. Summarizing the above: By attaining correct insight into the dharmas produced by numerous conditions, one does not fall into either of the extreme views of existence and non-existence, and so this is the middle way.) If dharmas "had [real] self-entity" (有性相) then they would exist without depending of causal conditions. (The two characters *xingxiang* 性相 are a compound term; both characters are to be interpreted as "entity" [體]; *you xingxiang* 有性相 is like saying "to have real self-entity" [有實自體]. If dharmas have real self-entity, then each is independent, each is a fixed thing—what need is there for them to be produced by depending on conditions?) Yet, if dharmas were not produced

---

[84] Also known as *Hua shou jing* 華手經 and *Fo shuo hua shou jing* 佛說華手經 (*Kuśalamūlasamparigraha*) (T657), translated by Kumārajīva in 406.
[85] *Fo shuo hua shou jing*, T657.16, 127c25–26 has a similar but not identical passage.

by depending on conditions, then there would be no dharmas. (If one were to seek dharmas that were not produced by depending on conditions, then there would be no such dharmas. In other words, there has never been a single dharma that was not produced from causal conditions.) And for this reason, there are no dharmas that are not empty. (Since there is not a single dharma that is not produced from causal conditions, dharmas produced from causal conditions are empty. Hence, he says, "there are no dharmas that are not empty." The above all cites [Piṅgala's] explanation of the text in the "Investigating the Four Truths Section" of the *Treatise* [*on the Middle Way*].)[86]

This
[p. 84]
passage cited from the *Treatise* [*on the Middle Way*] first explains that dharmas produced by causal conditions are empty. Next it explains that emptiness is also empty and is spoken of only as a provisional name. Following this, it explains that being removed from the extremes of existence and nonexistence is called the middle way. Finally, it asserts that there has never been a dharma that was not produced from causal conditions, and for this reason there are no dharmas that are not empty. The conclusion thus returns to the opening of the verse: Dharmas that are produced by causal conditions are empty and that is all.

In composing the *Treatise on the Middle Way* Nāgārjuna took the *Perfection of Wisdom Sutra* as his main authority. (Although he took the *Perfection of Wisdom Sutra* as his main authority, [the content of] its six hundred *juan* is extremely vast and its limits are beyond measure. Nāgārjuna brought the immeasurable meanings [無量義] together into a comprehensive understanding, making his own judgments and determinations—this is indeed a magnificent creative work. Of the main texts of the Mahāyāna Emptiness school, the *Treatise on the Middle Way* would have to be the foremost.) The system Nāgārjuna employs to set out his teaching is grand and rigorous, but actually it is the doctrine of emptiness that is its deft pivot (靈樞). (A centrally positioned post controlling internal-external communications is called a pivot [樞]. *Ling* 靈: deft [靈活], a term of esteem.) The *Treatise* states:

Because of the doctrine of emptiness, all [dharmas] are able to be established. / Without it, nothing would be established (一切則不成).[87]

---

[86] T1564.30, 33b15–21.
[87] Nāgārjuna's verse, T1564.30, 33a22–23.

(Between the characters *qie* 切 and *ze* 則 the character *fa* 法 [dharma] is concealed.[88]) Because there is the doctrine of emptiness, all mundane and supramundane dharmas are established. If there were no doctrine of emptiness, then none would be established.[89] (For the above passage, see the "Investigating the Four Truths Section" in *Treatise on the Middle Way*.)

From this passage it is evident that the doctrine of emptiness is the pivotal teaching of the Mahāyāna Emptiness school. (The doctrine of emptiness is that all dharmas depend on it to be established, hence it is said to be pivotal.) Despite this, students would often raise the following objection with me, [asking,] "What does it mean to say that all dharmas depend on it in order to begin to be established?"

Basing myself on the *Treatise*, I would reply as follows: "If you do not believe in the doctrine of emptiness then you do not believe in causally conditioned dharmas (The *Treatise* states: "Dharmas produced by the myriad causes and conditions / [I say] they are empty." Hence, the doctrine of emptiness is stated with respect to causally conditioned dharmas. If you do not believe in the doctrine of emptiness then you do not believe in causally conditioned dharmas.); and if you do not believe in causally conditioned dharmas then surely you would be presuming (計) that dharmas have a fixed nature (定性)? (*Ji* 計 is like "to conjecture" [猜度]. The character *xing* 性 in *ding xing* 定性 should be understood as *ti* 體 [entity]. "To have a fixed nature" means that each and every dharma is independent, that each and every dharma is a fixed real thing.) Nāgārjuna said: 'If dharmas had a fixed nature then the various mundane appearances (相) (*Xiang* 相: appearance [相狀].)—Heaven, humans, animals and the ten thousand things—should all neither arise nor cease, should abide forever, and should never be destroyed. Why is this? Because if they had real nature they would be unable to change, yet each of the manifest ten thousand things has changing appearances (相). (*Xiang* 相 has the same meaning as above.) Because they arise, cease, and change they should not be said to have a fixed nature.' (See the "Investigating the Four Truths Section" in *Treatise on the Middle Way*.[90]) Nāgārjuna is very clear in this passage: If you do not believe in the doctrine of emptiness then you do not believe in causally

---

[88] In other words, it is implicit.
[89] Piṅgala's commentary on the verse, T1564.30, 33a22–23.
[90] This passage is actually Piṅgala's commentary; see T1564.30, 34b26–29. The charitable interpretation is that Xiong takes Piṅgala's comments to be an accurate restatement of Nāgārjuna's intended meaning as set out in the accompanying verse T1564.30, 34b24–25.

conditioned dharmas; and if you do not believe in causally conditioned dharmas then you will be sure to speculate that each of the myriad things [p. 85] has a fixed nature, that none arises or ceases, abiding forever and never being destroyed, when actually this is certainly not the case. Each of the manifest myriad things has a changing appearance: arising, ceasing, and changing. Thus, it is known that the myriad things are produced from numerous conditions, and therefore they have no fixed nature and should be said to be empty. It is only because there is the doctrine of emptiness that the existence of the myriad dharmas [can be accounted for]. If there were no doctrine of emptiness then the cosmos would eternally be neither arising nor ceasing, so from where would the myriad dharmas be produced? The purport of the *Treatise* is patently clear. What further doubts could you entertain?"

Next, the *Treatise* states: "If a person sees that all dharmas arise from numerous conditions then that person will be able to see the Buddha (見佛) and the dharma body (法身)."[91] (This is also a passage from the "Investigating the Four Truths Section" [in *Treatise on the Middle Way*]. "To see the Buddha and the dharma body" are two goals.[92] Students of Buddhism look forward to truly understanding the Buddhist path, hence "to see the Buddha." I will explain "dharma body" later.) What does [the verse] mean in saying that "to see conditionally arisen dharmas is to see the dharma body?"[93] ("Conditionally arisen dharmas" is an abbreviation of "dharmas that are produced from numerous conditions." "Causally conditioned dharmas" is an abbreviation of "Dharmas that are produced from causal conditions." Although the words differ slightly, the meaning is actually the same.) I maintain that having compiled the *Perfection of Wisdom Sutra* (The six hundred *juan Perfection of Wisdom Sutra* is certainly not the product of the hand of one person or several people; much less is it the work of one period. Undoubtedly, Nāgārjuna completed its compilation.) Nāgārjuna then summarized the essentials (綱要) of the *Perfection of Wisdom Sutra* to complete the *Treatise on the Middle Way* (中觀論). (*Gang* 綱: outline [綱領]; *yao* 要: essence [精要]. *Zhongguan lun* 中觀論 is abbreviated as "*Zhong lun* 中論.") Being concerned that Hīnayāna [accounts of] existents (小有) had failed to awaken [to the truth] (*Xiao you* 小有 means Hīnayāna accounts of existents.) and in order to remedy [the situation in which] Hīnayāna [accounts of] emptiness (小空)

---

[91] Again, it is Piṅgala's commentary, T1564.30, 34c8–9. The line actually reads: "If one sees that all dharmas arise from numerous conditions, then one will be able to see the Buddha's dharma body."

[92] Here Xiong emphasizes that these are two goals, not the single goal of seeing the Buddha's dharma body as stated in Piṅgala's commentary.

[93] This is taken from the verse, slightly modified; see T1564.30, 34c6–7.

remained insufficiently developed (*Xiao kong* 小空 means Hīnayāna accounts of emptiness.) he initiated Mahāyāna learning, in which the elucidation of Reality (實相) alone was his objective. In doing so, he transcended the Hīnayāna school and surpassed the hundred schools, and so fathomed deeply to the very bottom of the source of the myriad dharmas (源底). (On *yuan di* 源底, see the *Sutra on the Lion's Roar of Queen Śrīmālā*; an explanation is provided above.[94]) This was his unique achievement. In Hīnayāna accounts of existents, when those masters discussed conditioned arising they merely explained the mutual dependence of all dharma characteristics ("Dharma characteristics" is like saying phenomena.) but did not take the next step of fathoming the source. As already stated earlier, this is analogous to a child who sees only the numerous wave forms but does not understand that it is the ocean that is the source of the numerous waves. This comes down to Hīnayāna accounts of existents being lost in superficiality. Nāgārjuna's treatise, however, is different from this. He states that "if one sees that all dharmas arise from causal conditions, then one will see the dharma body." His fundamental point consists of [the thesis that] by investigating conditioned arising one will thoroughly understand the true nature (實性) of dharmas (*Shixing* 實性 is like saying "Reality" [實體].) and so, he did not err by failing to fathom the source.

Someone asked: "What does 'if one sees that all dharmas arise from causal conditions then one will see the dharma body' mean? I hope you can explain."

I replied: "So as to dispel your puzzlement, I first need to explain some of the terms. Here 'all dharmas' is the collective term for mental and material phenomena (行).
[p. 86]
(This is the same in those other places where I speak of dharmas or the myriad dharmas.) *Xing* 行 means 'passing flow' [遷流]. The passing flow of the mental and the material is unceasing, hence they are called *xing* 行.[95] All phenomena lack real self-entity, hence they are also called 'dharma characteristics' (法相)."
(The character *xiang* 相 in *faxiang* 法相 means "appearance" [相狀] and is like saying

---

[94] P. 134. As already noted on p. 134, n. 69, the term *che fa yuan di* 徹法源底 does not appear in this sutra; nor does the term *yuan di* 源底.

[95] Cf. the opening sentence of Chapter 1, "Explaining Transformation": "In ancient times, Indian Buddhists called all mental and material phenomena '*xing* 行.' The word *xing* 行 has two senses: passing flow and appearance." As I noted there, "Inter alia, the term *xing* translates the Sanskrit terms *saṃskāra, ākāra, carya*, and *pratipad*. *Saṃskāra* refers to conditioned phenomena; and *ākāra* can refer to both appearance and defining activity. *Carya* and *pratipad* have senses associated with movement, travel, carrying out."

"manifest image" [現象]. The term "dharma characteristics" is posited in contrast to "dharma nature.")

[This person] asked: "'Dharma characteristics' is the collective term for mental and material phenomena. If we check the scriptures this is indeed the case, but there is something that puzzles me. Material phenomena certainly have appearances, but do mental phenomena have appearances?"

I replied: "Clearly, the mind is self-illuminating and self-aware; illuminating awareness is its appearance. If one is stubbornly fixed to one particular category, and exclusively deems only those things that the eyes can see and the hands can touch to have appearance, then there are surely very few of the myriad existents that you are able to discern."

[I then continued my explanation of terms:] "Dharma body (法身) is also called dharma nature (法性) (*Shen* 身 is like Reality [體]. The character *xing* 性 is also to be interpreted as Reality.); it is like saying 'the Reality (實體) of the myriad dharmas.' 'Guan niepan pin' 觀涅槃品 (Investigating *Nirvāṇa* Section) of the *Treatise on the Middle Way* states: 'The Reality (實相) of dharmas (Here the character *xiang* 相 is to be interpreted as Reality [體] and not the same as the *xiang* 相 in *faxiang* 法相 [dharma characteristics].) is also called constantly so (如) (*Ru* 如: because it is constantly just as its nature is, it refers to not changing. For example, when fire is used to smelt gold, the nature of the gold never alters. When Xuanzang began translating, he translated [suchness; *tathatā*] as *zhenru* 真如 and did not use just the single character *ru* 如. Early translations [of *tathatā*] also occasionally used *ruru* 如如.), dharma nature (See above.), Reality-apex [實際] (This is like saying "Reality" [真實].[96]), and *nirvāṇa*.'[97] (*Nirvāṇa* means "quiescent extinction" [寂滅]. This gloss is based on the *Treatise on the Middle Way*. Later, however, it seems that followers of the Mahāyāna Existence school embellished the *Nirvana Sutra* [涅槃經],[98] in which the meaning slightly differed by not particularly emphasizing the sense of "quiescent extinction.") The 'Investigating *Nirvāṇa* Section' lists only these five terms. (From "constantly so" to "*nirvāṇa*" are four but if "Reality [實相]" is included then there are five. Actually, there are more than five, with still many other individual terms. The term "dharma body" is not listed in the "Investigating *Nirvāṇa*" chapter. <When referring to Reality [實相], "dharma body" is also named "dharma nature.">)

Terms in the Buddhist scriptures are excessively prolix. If readers do not search out the correct interpretation of all the terms and fail to discern those cases where the actual [referent] is the same but it has different names, they

---

[96] Chapter 1: "'Reality' (真實) refers to intrinsic Reality (本體)."
[97] T1564.30, 36b14–15.
[98] Generic name for a group of sutras called *Mahāparinirvāṇa-sūtra*.

will certainly become confused at every turn and so have no means by which to investigate the arrangement, system, and meaning of Buddhist teachings."

Now that I have finished explaining terms, next I should explain what "if one sees that all dharmas arise from causal conditions, then one will see the dharma body" means. At first, I thought that a fundamental teaching must lie herein, that is, that even though nature and characteristics can be separated, actually they are

[p. 87]

non-dual. ("Nature" is an abbreviation of "dharma nature," the Reality of all dharmas. "Characteristics" is an abbreviation of "dharma characteristics," the collective term for all dharmas. In other words, all dharmas are collectively called dharma characteristics. Nature and characteristics must be spoken of separately, but they cannot be split to form a two-tier world.) In the past, when philosophers talked about Reality and phenomena, they have always dissected them in two. ("Reality" is like dharma nature, and "phenomena" is like dharma characteristics referred to here.) Reality is what is real (真實), phenomena are changing; Reality has nothing to which it stands in contrast (無對), phenomena have that to which they stand in contrast. Dissected as such, they cannot be combined at all. Actually, what is real is itself transforming and changing (This is analogous to the ocean water's changing to become the incessantly arising and ceasing numerous waves.); it is change itself that is real. (This is analogous to every wave appearance itself being the ocean.) That which has something to which it stands in contrast is precisely that which has nothing to which it stands in contrast. (Analogous to seeing an undifferentiated body of water in the myriad waves, that which has something to which it stands in contrast is precisely that which has nothing to which it stands in contrast.) That which has nothing to which it stands in contrast is precisely that which has something to which it stands in contrast. (That which has nothing to which it stands in contrast cannot be sought for apart from that which has something to which it stands in contrast.) The cosmos is an undifferentiated Great Unity (渾然太一) (*Hunran* 渾然: cannot be divided. The *yi* 一 in *taiyi* 太一 means "whole" [大全] and is not the number "one.") If students were each to rely on the presumptions of their mental consciousness (意計)[99] to break apart this Great Unity, I would not know what to do with them. (To use the mental consciousness to conjecture is called *yiji* 意計; this term is based on Buddhist texts.)

When I started to study Buddhism I began with the Mahāyāna Existence school's doctrine of nothing but consciousness (唯識論). Upon examining

---

[99] The sixth consciousness (*manovijñāna*): *yi shi* 意識.

the school's account of nature and characteristics, [I learned that] suchness is dharma nature and is said to be a dharma that neither arises nor ceases; and that manifest activity (現行) is dharma characteristics and is said to be dharmas that arise and cease. (*Xianxing* 現行 is another name for consciousness.[100] The doctrine of nothing but consciousness maintains that consciousness controls all things, clearly manifesting them as the myriad images. Hence, the consciousnesses are also called manifest activity. Although there are many explanations of the term manifest activity, here I am using it in the sense of manifesting [顯現].) Dharmas that arise and cease and dharmas that neither arise nor cease are completely divided into a two-tier world in which there is no interaction between the two tiers.

Taking deep exception to this, I went back to carry out my own free investigation, whereupon I suddenly awakened to the non-duality of Reality and function. Despite this, I still did not dare immediately to posit a thesis upholding this view. In the interim, I went back to before the advent of Yogācāra to explore the learning of the Mahāyāna Emptiness school. While paying attention to the *Treatise on the Middle Way* I read the following lines in the "Investigating the Four Truths Section": "If one sees that all dharmas arise from causal conditions, then one will see the dharma body." I sighed in admiration: "So, early on, Nāgārjuna had already given expression to the principle of the non-duality of nature and characteristics! Otherwise, how could the dharma nature be seen in all dharmas." ("Nature" is like "Reality"; "characteristics" is like "function.") At first, I was confident that I had a good grasp of what Nāgārjuna meant, but before long, as I carefully pondered the *Treatise on the Middle Way*, I came to understand that early on, the Mahāyāna Emptiness school had already [also upheld] the distinction between dharmas that arise and cease and dharmas that neither arise nor cease. The Mahāyāna Emptiness school had undoubtedly adopted without alteration the Hīnayānist's surviving teaching that distinguishes conditioned and unconditioned dharmas. The Mahāyāna Emptiness school never changed the foundation [of all Buddhist schools] in the teaching of transcendence [p. 88] and because that which it pursued was, of course, a Reality that neither arises nor ceases, it would certainly never come to the awakening that nature and characteristics are non-dual. When I first read the *Treatise on the Middle Way*, my own views undoubtedly led me to misinterpret it. Only later did

---

[100] As already noted, manifest activity is the appearance of things in their manifest aspect in the first seven consciousnesses as they emerge from seeds in the eighth consciousness.

I became aware of my error, and after pondering the *Treatise* again, I started to grasp the hidden intent (密意) of its refutation of characteristics. The *Treatise* states: "If one sees that all dharmas arise from numerous conditions, then one will see the dharma body." (Cited above.) Here the crux is "produced from numerous conditions." Conditioned arising is the doctrine of emptiness. The *Treatise*'s elucidation of the doctrine of emptiness is extremely profound and far-reaching. Here I will briefly adduce three of the doctrine's teachings, summarizing their essential features.

Three teachings of the doctrine of emptiness

The first teaching is that emptiness is non-existence. All dharmas arise from numerous conditions and have always lacked an individuated, independent, fixed self-nature ("Self-nature" is like saying "self-entity."), hence it is said that dharmas have always been empty and are devoid of anything that exists. This is what the text above refers to as refuting characteristics so as to reveal (顯) the nature. (*Xian* 顯 is like "to show.")

The second teaching is that emptiness does not obstruct existents. Nāgārjuna used the doctrine of conditioned arising to show that it is dharmas' lack of a fixed nature that is emptiness. (If the expression "lack of a fixed nature" were to be translated using the vernacular language of today, we would say that all dharmas lack individuated, fixed self-entity. It is thing's lack of a fixed nature that is emptiness. The Buddhists by no means deem this kind of theory to be illogical.) [By the same token,] the doctrine of emptiness provides the sole avenue by which to establish that all things exist, hence it is said that emptiness does not obstruct existents. Nāgārjuna maintained that opposing the doctrine of emptiness is to oppose the doctrine of conditioned arising, and once the doctrine of conditioned arising has been opposed, there will certainly be grave error. If the myriad things did not have causal conditions, then there would be no means for them to arise, and not having arisen there would be no ceasing either. To neither arise nor cease is to be without conditioned dharmas—if this is not a grave error, then what is it? Hence, to oppose emptiness is to oppose conditioned arising, which ends up with the annihilation of existents. To observe emptiness is to perceive conditioned arising and is not to reject the myriad existents. (It is to acknowledge that the myriad existents are produced from numerous conditions, that the teeming myriad existents cannot be denied.) This is the profound purport of Nāgārjuna's combining the doctrine of conditioned arising with the emptiness doctrine. (See the "Investigating the Four Truths Section" of the *Treatise on the Middle Way*. Someone asked: "Is [the doctrine that] 'emptiness does not obstruct existents' compatible with Laozi's 'existence is produced from non-existence'?"[101] I replied: "The fundamentals of the Buddhists and the school of Laozi are completely different and cannot be confused.")

Having now explained the first two teachings, I should proceed to the third. The third teaching explains that dharma nature is empty (法性空), which is also expressed as *xing kong* 性空. For the interim, I will not directly discuss the third teaching but rather will first explain why the first two teachings are the reason whereby the third teaching is realized.

The first teaching explains that because all dharmas arise from numerous conditions and have no fixed nature, they are absolutely empty, and so
[p. 89]
refuting dharma characteristics is merely to be on the verge of awakening and entering dharma nature. ("Dharma characteristics" is like saying "phenomena." "Dharma nature" is like saying "the Reality of the myriad dharmas.") "Guan fa pin" 觀法品 (Investigating Dharmas Section) states: "Before one has [awakened] and entered into Reality (實相), one discerns each and every dharma as separate. [As one awakens, one discerns] that all dharmas are unreal and it is only because the myriad conditions gather together that there are [dharmas]." (See Chapter 18 of the *Treatise on the Middle Way*.[102] The passage says that before one has awakened, one is merely deludedly attached to each and every dharma as an independent and fixed thing, and because of this it is not possible to awaken and enter into Reality through dharmas, hence it says, "Before one has [awakened] and entered into Reality." <*Shixiang* 實相 is another term for dharma nature.> Before one has awakened yet seeks to become awakened, one only has to apply analytical method and investigate each and every dharma separately, then one will see that no dharma is real and that it is only because numerous conditions gather together that there are dharma characteristics that appear. The passage concludes by saying, "it is only because numerous conditions gather together that there are [dharmas]," proving that although there are dharmas they are not real. Because all dharmas are unreal it should be said that dharmas have always been empty.) With the refutation of dharma characteristics, "dharma nature Reality" (法性實相) is manifest (顯). (*Xian* 顯: manifest [顯現]. The two terms "dharma nature" and "Reality" are here combined and used as a compound term.) It is like when the clouds and

---

[101] *Dao de jing*, *zhang* 40. I have translated this in the sense in which I believe Xiong was adapting it. The original meaning is more likely to be invoking notions of having characteristics (有) and not having characteristics (無), rather than abstract notions of existence and non-existence.
[102] T1564.30, 25a21–22. This passage is translated on the basis of Xiong's following explanation.

mist have dissipated, the sky's appearance (相) is manifest. (Here *xiang* 相 is like what in the vernacular is called "appearance" [相貌].) Hence, when the *Treatise* states, "[if a person] sees that all dharmas arise from causal conditions, then that person will be able to see the dharma body," undoubtedly this is saying that to perceive conditioned arising is to perceive that dharmas are absolutely empty. Dharma characteristics having been refuted, then dharma nature is manifest. This is to realize the third teaching by means of the first teaching.

The second teaching shows that emptiness does not obstruct existents. How is it that the third teaching is realized by means of it? (The third teaching is that [dharma] nature is empty [性空]. The second teaching accepts that all dharmas exist—how then is the third teaching realized by means of it? It is quite understandable that one might have some doubts.) Here I will briefly explain two reasons. The first teaching explains that causally conditioned dharmas are empty. Concerned that those who hear this teaching will fall into (墜) attachment to the view of emptiness (空見), mistakenly presuming that everything is empty (*Zhui* 墜 is like "fall into" [陷]. If it is said that everything is empty, then dharma nature is also empty.), is why this [second] teaching accepts that [all dharmas] exist—this is the first reason. Dharma characteristics have no fixed nature, hence are said to be empty. However, the reason that emptiness is spoken of is to refute deluded attachment. Although dharma characteristics are not real existents, because they are accepted (極成) by ordinary people (Ordinary people's collectively agreeing that dharma characteristics are real existents is called *jicheng* 極成.) they cannot be said not to exist.[103] Moreover, there are supramundane dharmas only if there are mundane dharmas. If mundane dharmas are not established, then supramundane dharmas cannot be established (The *Treatise on the Middle Way* strenuously upholds this explanation; it is worth referring to.[104]) is why this teaching accepts that [all dharmas] exist—this is the second reason. These are the two reasons that account for why it is by means of the second teaching—which shows that emptiness does not obstruct existents—that the third teaching is realized. If there were no second teaching, then one would certainly fall into the erroneous view that everything is empty—in that case, what dharma nature would there to be speak of?

---

[103] That is, they "exist" in the sense that they are objects of people's beliefs/attachments.

[104] As translated above (and cited by Xiong) the *Treatise on the Middle Way* states: "Because of the doctrine of emptiness, all mundane and supramundane dharmas are established. / Without it, nothing would be established." Nāgārjuna's verse, T1564.30, 33a22–23. Xiong's point is that the emptiness of dharmas must first be realized before the non-emptiness of supramundane dharmas (dharma nature; Reality) is realized, but in order for that to be possible, mundane dharmas must first be posited.

[p. 90]

Having explained [how] the third teaching is realized by means of the first and second teachings, I should now discuss the third teaching. The third teaching directly shows that dharma nature is quiescent extinction (寂滅). Ji 寂: quiescent (寂靜); mie 滅: all afflictions are completely extinguished. Without acting, without creating, without arising, unchanging (如如) and unmoving (Ruru 如如 is an adjective; it means "unchanging." For all these terms, see the Perfection of Wisdom Sutra.), without form and without image (Although dharma nature is without form and image it is not non-existent.), it is beyond what can be seen or heard and cannot even be conceived, hence [this teaching] is called [the teaching that shows that dharma] nature is empty (性空). (Xing 性 should interpreted as "Reality" [體]. "Guan rulai pin" 觀如來品 [Investigating Rulai Section] of the Treatise on the Middle Way states: "The nature being empty as such, it cannot even be conceived."[105] Rulai 如來 means "coming from nowhere" [無所從來][106] and originally was another term for dharma nature. Generally, however, it was also used as an epithet for Śākyamuni, because he was able to bring to completion the potent functioning of inherent nature,[107] and so he was referred to by recalling the original meaning of the term.)

The Treatise on the Middle Way's account of Reality (實相) as quiescent extinction, and that the views of [existence, non-existence, eternalism, and nihilism] do not apply to it, is indeed very engaging in its line of reasoning. (Shixiang 實相 is another name for dharma nature.) The "Investigating Dharmas Section" states: "Here, because there are no dharmas to grasp or refute, it is called quiescent extinction Reality (寂滅相)."[108] (Xiang 相 is like "Reality" [體]. This passage is like saying that if you give rise to attached views about this Reality [實相] spoken of here, if you treat it as something that really exists, something that seems as if it can be grasped, then you will be in error. Reality is not a thing, so how could it be grasped? On the other hand, if, on the basis that there is nothing to be grasped, you choose not to believe that the myriad dharmas have Reality, and so you reject Reality and no longer seek to fathom it exhaustively, then this too is a type of attached view, albeit merely an attached view with an altered orientation. Reality's existence is so of itself (法爾) <Faer 法爾 is like saying "self-so" [自然].>; it does not begin to exist because you believe it exists, nor does it not exist because you reject it. If you believe it exists and seek to grasp it, that is your own self-delusion—how could it be grasped? If you do not believe it exists and you reject

---

[105] T1564.30, 30c24.
[106] See, for example, Jin'gang bore boluomi jing, T235.8, 752b4–5. "Coming from nowhere" is also a gloss on "beyond what can be seen or heard and cannot even be conceived."
[107] In other words, this potent functioning is the potent functioning of dharma nature (= Reality).
[108] T1564.30, 25b7–8.

it, that also is your own self-delusion—how could it be rejected?) This is saying that whether scholars perversely give rise to grasping or to rejecting, this will have no bearing upon Reality. (Reality is not affected by your impositions.) This is analogous to the way clouds and mist are all around, yet space is not encroached upon. This is why Reality is constant (恆) quiescent extinction. (Note the character *heng* 恆.) This example is cited to illustrate how the views of [existence, non-existence, eternalism, and nihilism] do not apply [to Reality.] In the course of daily human living, with regard to all things, we constantly give rise to the views of existence, non-existence, eternalism, and nihilism. (Sometimes when we look for something and do not find it, we then think that it does not exist; other times when we look for something and find it, we then think that it exists. When we look up at the sky and down at the earth, we think that they constantly abide. When we fell a tree for firewood, after its ashes have completely burned away, we then presume that it has been annihilated.) Over time, the views of existence, non-existence, eternalism, and nihilism gradually form the norms for how we distinguish things. (The same applies to [the norms we use for determining] cause and effect, sameness and difference, and so forth.) When scholars talk about the Reality of the myriad dharmas, they do so on the basis of the norms they use to distinguish things, presuming that the myriad dharmas either have Reality or on the contrary do not. If they say that Reality does not exist,

[p. 91]

this is, of course, an erroneous view and does not apply to Reality. If they presume that it does exist, although this view is different from the erroneous view, it wrongly imputes the view of existence. How is this the case? Reality has never not existed, so why should there additionally be a need to give rise to the view of existence? This, too, is something that does not apply to Reality. There are those who presume that because the myriad things cease, Reality should likewise cease. (This is called the view of nihilism [斷見].) And there are those who claim that although the myriad things arise and cease, the Reality of the myriad things is absolutely eternal. (This is called the view of eternalism [常見].) Here I have compared the views of nihilism and eternalism. Since the doctrine of nihilism acknowledges that the myriad things have Reality[109] then it cannot be said that Reality ceases along with the myriad things. This

---

[109] Otherwise, why would this view hold that "because the myriad things cease, Reality should likewise cease"?

is because Reality and the appearances of each and every thing should be differentiated.[110]

Someone raised the following objection: "The view of nihilism is certainly erroneous, but we should not deem the view of eternalism to be mistaken. This is because the Buddha said that *nirvāṇa* has the quality of being eternal."[111] (*Nirvāṇa* is another name for Reality; see above.)

I replied: "It is so of itself (法爾) that Reality is without cessation. It is not possible for the view of eternalism additionally to arise with respect to it. ("It" refers to "Reality.") For the view of eternalism additionally to arise with respect to Reality is called the view of imputation (增益見), and is not something that additionally applies to Reality. (For the view of imputation, take the example of seeing the color white. Silently, one directly realizes [親證] it. <"Directly realize": one's seeing and the white color are an undifferentiated unity; no analysis such as, "white or not white," is made.> This is a realm of silent understanding. If, in addition to the white color, one also gives rise to a kind of discriminating, such as "this is white, it is not blue-green or yellow," then at that moment one is already imposing a subjective element on top of the white color, such as the functions of memory and striving after [something desirable]. This is the view of imputation. If we conceive of the Reality of the myriad things as either existing or non-existing, if we conceive of it as either eternal or annihilated, these are all [examples of] taking what are called the views of eternalism and nihilism [formed] when we encounter things in everyday life and augmenting [增加] Reality with them—hence it is called the view of imputation [增益]. What I have explained here integrates [the accounts in] the "Investigating *Nirvāṇa* Section," "Investigating Dharmas Section," and "Investigating *Rulai* Section" of the *Treatise on the Middle Way*. The "[Investigating] *Nirvāṇa* Section" had already taken Reality as quiescent extinction, [holding that] the sixty-two kinds of mistaken views cannot be applied to it, rejecting popular non-Buddhist theories of the day.[112] Here I have not cited the text—I have made do by citing the examples of the views of existence, non-existence, eternalism, and nihilism so as to reveal the [main] purport.) The *Fahua jing* 法華經 (Lotus Sutra)[113] states: 'Final *nirvāṇa*[114] is itself (相) eternal quiescent extinction, and ultimately reverts to emptiness.'[115] (Here the character *xiang* 相 should be interpreted as the character *ti*

---

[110] Given that Reality is not the same as the appearance of things then there is no basis for claiming that it should also cease along with appearance of things.
[111] This is one of four qualities attributed to *nirvāṇa* in *Da ban niepan jing* 大般涅槃經 (*Mahāparinirvāṇa-sūtra*; Northern Edition of the *Great Nirvana Sutra*): eternal, blissful, Self, and pure. See T374.12, 544c.
[112] T1564.30, 36b10.
[113] Abbreviation of *Miaofa lianhua jing* 妙法蓮華經 (*Saddharma-puṇḍarīka-sūtra*).
[114] After which there is no more rebirth.
[115] T262.9, 19c4–5.

體. This is saying that *nirvāṇa* is itself [涅槃自體] quiescent extinction—this is what was previously described as without acting, without creating, without arising, without form, and without image. Although the term "emptiness" does not mean "non-existent," it is not much different given that it is without acting and without arising.) This is why the various [mistaken] views and all manner of conceptual elaboration (戲論) cannot be applied to it."

Evaluation of the Prajñā school's doctrine of emptiness

The foregoing has talked about the three teachings of the doctrine of emptiness. From this account, the doctrinal system of the Prajñā school and its marrow can be glimpsed. Next, I will provide a brief evaluation.

1. When Śākyamuni left home to learn about the Way, his first thought was to loathe and renounce (厭離) the mundane world. (*Yanli* 厭離 is a term that comes from the

[p. 92]

Āgama sutras; see above. This is completely different from world-weariness, which is merely to be dispirited. Loathing and renouncing [the mundane world], in contrast, is untrammeled, transcendent awakening, with heroic powers enough to obliterate space and submerge the land. However, the later and degenerate stages of Buddhist teaching remained incapable of talking about this.) Six hundred years after the passing of Śākyamuni, Nāgārjuna founded the Mahāyāna Emptiness school. In terms of developments in scholarly thought, he certainly far surpassed Śākyamuni. However, the reason he still venerated Śākyamuni as the great patriarch is undoubtedly because his own ideas about human life still retained Śākyamuni's purport in renouncing the world. The transmission of [teachings] from teacher to teacher had its origin and Nāgārjuna did not forget where this transmission came from. After all, Nāgārjuna's thought is that of renouncing the world and this must be acknowledged.

2. Nāgārjuna began with the theory of conditioned arising to start [his account of] the emptiness doctrine. (Mental and material dharmas all depend upon numerous conditions to arise, and this is called "conditioned arising." Equally, it can be said that because dharmas arise by serving as conditions for one another that it is called conditioned arising.) The reason that conditioned arising can be said to be emptiness is because the myriad dharmas are produced from numerous conditions and no dharma has real self-entity. ("Myriad dharmas" is also the general term for mental and material dharmas.) Little did Nāgārjuna realize, however,

that his account still had two errors. First, it did not investigate the true source of the myriad dharmas. Second, it cannot be claimed that because the myriad dharmas do not have self-entity that they are therefore empty.

I will begin with the first error. Those who advocated the theory of conditioned arising focused their attention on the interconnections between the myriad dharmas, claiming that the myriad dharmas are produced from numerous conditions. This is merely to catch a glimpse of the superficial and fails to fathom the true source of the myriad dharmas. It is like a dull-witted person on the ocean shore looking at the numerous waves unceasingly turning and leaping and then saying that the numerous waves arise by pushing one another—this is all that person sees. In fact, each of the numerous waves takes the ocean as itself; in other words, the ocean is the true source of the numerous waves. To the very end, however, the dull-witted person does not thoroughly investigate this. As I already stated above, those who advocated the theory of conditioned arising failed to fathom the source.[116] Nāgārjuna's point, however, is that even if one wanted to use conditioned arising to show that dharma characteristics are ultimately empty, that would [still only] be on the verge of awakening and entering Reality. Nāgārjuna's perspective would seem to be poles apart from those Hīnayānists who failed to fathom the source. However, it must further be understood that [Nāgārjuna also insisted that] causally conditioned dharmas are dharmas that arise and cease whereas Reality is a non-arising and non-ceasing dharma. Causally conditioned dharmas and Reality are different from one another and constitute a completely disconnected two-tier world. (The "Investigating Dharmas Section" of the *Treatise on the Middle Way* states: "The Reality of dharmas is without arising and also without ceasing."[117] "The Reality of dharmas" is like saying "the Reality [實體] of the myriad dharmas.") He says that a dharma that neither arises nor ceases is the Reality of dharmas that arise and cease—this is a case of name and actuality failing to correspond with one another. ("He" refers to Nāgārjuna.) Hence, we can understand that, in the end, Nāgārjuna's account of conditioned arising did not investigate the true source of the myriad dharmas, and his error cannot be concealed. (How could a dharma that neither arises nor ceases possibly be said to be the Reality of dharmas that arise and cease? And

---

[116] P. 143.
[117] T1564.30, 24a3–4: "The Reality of dharmas / is severed from mental operations and language / is without arising and also without ceasing / and is quiescent extinction."

[p. 93]

because the Buddhists failed to realize this, then of course their teaching of transcendence required that Reality be non-arising and non-ceasing. Although theoretically this made no sense, they did not take this into consideration.)

Second, with respect to the claim that conditionally arisen dharmas are empty, again I must demur. I maintain that nature and characteristics are inherently non-dual. ("Nature" is like Reality [體]; "characteristics" is like function.) All of the profusely and multifariously differentiated dharma characteristics are the process of the flow of great function. If one focuses exclusively on the myriad particulars and does not fathom the source of dharma characteristics, then even though it can be said that all dharmas arise by taking one another as conditions, they have no real self-entity, and all are empty. (The theory of relativity held by philosophers and the Buddhist theory of conditioned arising are similar. More than thirty years ago when [Bertrand] Russell came to China to lecture, I had heard a little about his introduction [to philosophical problems] but felt his picture of the cosmos was somewhat empty and lacking in generative vitality.[118]) As for [initially] regarding all dharmas as lacking individual, independent self-entity (This is also called "being without a fixed nature.") and then undertaking a deeper investigation into that which is intrinsic to all dharmas, one will come to see that even though all dharmas are profusely and multifariously differentiated, actually it is undifferentiated Reality in its entirety that is transforming and moving without interruption, flowing incessantly; as the old passes away, completely relinquished (捐), the new arises ever anew; vast productivity (大生), capacious productivity (廣生)—the undifferentiated whole of limitless great existents (大有). (From "As for" to here is to be read as one long sentence. Sun 捐 is like "discard" [捨去]; for both *da sheng* 大生 and *guang sheng* 廣生, see the "Great Commentary" to the *Book of Change*.[119] *Da you* 大有: there is the "Da you" hexagram in the *Book of Change*,[120] which acclaims the abundance of the cosmos' myriad images.) The Mahāyāna Emptiness school masters failed to have insight into

---

[118] Bertrand Russell and Dora Black arrived in China in October 1920 and stayed nine months, based in Beijing, and gave lectures across the country. Xiong began to teach at Peking University in 1922. In one of his lectures, titled "Zhexue wenti" 哲學問題 (The Problems of Philosophy), Russell remarked that "nothing in the world is more real than momentary things." See Song Xijun 宋錫鈞 and Li Xiaofeng 李小峰, comps., *Luosu ji Bolake jiangyan ji* 羅素及勃拉克講演集 (Collected Talks of Russell and Black) (Beijing: Weiyiri baoshe, 1922), p. 11. In Xiong's 1932 edition of *Xin weishi lun*, while expounding the Buddhist doctrine that "dharmas do not abide even momentarily," he singled Russell out for maintaining "what is temporary is real." See *Xin weishi lun*, p. 43; Makeham, trans. *New Treatise on the Uniqueness of Consciousness*, p. 101.

[119] "Xici, shang," 7.14b–15a. See also Chapter 2, n. 31 in this volume.

[120] Hexagram 14.

this, instead saying that all dharmas arise from numerous conditions, that they lack self-entity, that they are empty. This, however, is to observe the exterior of all dharmas but not investigate what they contain; it is to see their myriad differentiations but not awaken to the great whole. [Thereby,] the doctrine of emptiness is devoid of a foundation.

Nāgārjuna said that dharmas arise from numerous conditions, that is, they are empty. Pondering this matter further, however, [he realized] that this would certainly commit the fallacy [of asserting] that everything is empty and so he further stated that emptiness is also a provisional teaching. The ingeniousness of the position he upheld lay in synthesizing the doctrine of emptiness and the doctrine of conditioned arising. He thereby boasted about his teaching precisely because the doctrine of emptiness was able to be established. (See above for my account.) In the end, however, Nāgārjuna's error was one that could not be concealed. After all, the main tenet of the Mahāyāna Emptiness school is emptiness. The *Perfection of Wisdom Sutra* has the following verse:

All conditioned dharmas
Are like dreams, illusions, bubbles, shadows.
They are like dew, and they are also like lightening,
Such is how they should be regarded.[121]

(Conditioned dharmas are the mental and material dharmas. Because they are produced from numerous conditions, they are a called conditioned dharmas.) This verse explains that although conditionally arisen dharmas exist they are not real; they exist merely in the way that dreams, illusions, bubbles, shadows, dew, and lightning exist. Nāgārjuna inherited
[p. 94]
this view and so said that conditionally arisen dharmas are empty. It is certainly evident that his main authority was the *Perfection of Wisdom Sutra*. Subsequently, the Mahāyāna Existence school [masters] similarly inherited [this view] from Nāgārjuna, and they also all maintained that dharmas that originate through dependence on other things (依他起法) are illusory existence (幻有). (*Ta* 他 refers to conditions; *qi* 起 is like "to arise" [生]. Dharmas originate by depending on numerous conditions, hence they are called dharmas that originate

---

[121] The verse is from *Jin'gang bore boluomi jing*, T235.8, 752b28–29, a text included in the ninth "assembly" (會) of teachings in the *Perfection of Wisdom Sutra*.

through dependence on other things and means the same as conditionally arisen dharmas. *Huan you* 幻有: although something exists, it is not real, and so is illusory existence. It is like an illusionist who makes something appear—there never was a real thing, only an illusory appearance. Conditionally arisen dharmas are not real and so "illusion" is chosen as an analogy.) As such, even though Nāgārjuna said that emptiness does not obstruct existents, what he referred to as "existents" were illusory and not real. I wonder how much difference there is between the meanings of "illusion" and "emptiness"?

I maintain that the cosmos' myriad changes, myriad transformations, myriad things, and myriad affairs, are real, vibrant, and inexhaustibly abundant. The human way [lies in] the great enterprise of fully exhausting the capabilities of the mind; utilizing the abundance of things; and fully manifesting the grand enterprise [in which the sage] takes his place with Heaven and Earth, nurturing the myriad things. This is why the sage [Confucius] exclaimed "great existents" rather than taking existents to be illusions.[122] ("Takes his place with Heaven and Earth....": see *Balance as the Norm*.[123] Fashioning and bringing to completion [the Way of] Heaven and Earth's transformative nurturing,[124] so that "Heaven and Earth interact perfectly, constituting [the image of] greatness,"[125] is what "taking his place [with]" refers to. The myriad things truly will be equal and support one another; [the goal of] "sharing all under Heaven" [天下為公] will have been achieved; and consummate fullness [as auspicious as a] flight of dragons with no leader[126] will ensure their nurturing.) The theory of illusory existents runs counter to the principle of being so of itself and abandons the people's capabilities—we Confucians must set this right.

The *Treatise on the Middle Way* states: "To see that all dharmas arise from numerous conditions is to see the dharma body."[127] ("Dharma body" is another name for dharma nature.) To see conditioned arising is to see that all dharma characteristics are empty. Since dharma characteristics are empty then of course dharma nature is empty. The *Perfection of Wisdom Sutra* says that suchness, an unconditioned dharma ("Suchness" and "the unconditioned dharma" are other names for dharma nature.), is without arising, without creating, like a

---

[122] On p. 156 of this chapter, Xiong comments: "There is the 'Da you' [大有] hexagram in the *Book of Change*, which acclaims the abundance of the cosmos' myriad images."
[123] See note 46 in this chapter.
[124] See Chapter 1, n. 29.
[125] "Xiang" commentary to the Tai 泰 hexagram, *Zhou yi*, 2.21a.
[126] Qian hexagram, *Zhou yi*, 1.5b–6a: "When one sees a flight of dragons with no leader this is auspicious."
[127] T1564.30, 34c8–9: "If one sees that all dharmas arise from numerous conditions then that person will be able to see the Buddha's dharma body."

mirage (燄), like a dream. (*Yan* 燄: beneath high mountains there is a large marsh and when the sun first appears, in the middle of the marsh a moist vapor floats above it. In the vernacular this is called a "mirage" [陽燄] and actually is not water. Gazing at it from a distance, deer think that it is water and race toward it to drink.) The *Treatise on the Middle Way* says that Reality is quiescent extinction ("Reality" is another name for dharma nature.) and that because dharma characteristics are seen to be empty, when one then investigates dharma nature, one will be certain to see that it is empty. Dharma characteristics being empty then it goes without saying that [dharma] nature will of course be devoid [of existence]. Having carefully pondered the learning of the Mahāyāna Emptiness school, it would have been difficult [for this school] to have avoided the error [of holding that] nature and characteristics are both empty. Even if it were to be said that the school's aim was to refute attachments (執着), in its relentless and exhaustive refuting, it was still attached to (着) the view of emptiness. (In Buddhist writings, when the term *zhi* 執 is used, sometimes it is combined with the character *zhuo* 着 and sometimes just the character *zhuo* is used.[128] *Zhuo* is like *zhi*.) In my opinion, the problem of nature and characteristics is a fundamental philosophical problem that has always been difficult to solve.

[p. 95]

(What the Buddhists call nature and characteristics is like what I call Reality and function.) For a very long time, there have been many who have been convinced by the Mahāyāna Existence school's solution to this problem. I, nevertheless, have always felt that it [suffers from] all sorts of fragmentation. Although the Mahāyāna Emptiness school's [teachings] are profound and far-reaching, when I closely [examined the doctrine that] nature and characteristics are both empty, I found it even harder to endorse.

The non-duality of Reality and function

Over the course of my life, I wandered between Buddhism's two Mahāyānas ("Two Mahāyānas": the Mahāyāna Emptiness school and the Mahāyāna Existence school.) before finally returning to undertake my own free investigation. Further away, I drew from other things, and near at hand, I drew from my own person. After building up a body of inferences over a long period of time, suddenly I understood that Reality and function are non-dual. This

---

[128] More commonly, the character *zhuo* 著 is used.

experience triggered [an awareness of] the profundities of *Great Change*, and only then did I understand that already in antiquity the former sages had elaborated on the non-duality of Reality and function. From then on, I studied the *Book of Change* as well as the *Spring and Autumn Annals*, and ritual and music texts in which remnants of the doctrine were preserved by chance. I teemed with joy [in the knowledge that] no matter whether it is the four cardinal directions and above and below, or the four seasons;[129] no matter how small or large, fine or coarse, there is nowhere that [the doctrine of the non-duality of Reality and function] does not apply. From this point on, my learning had a principle to uphold, and I would not waver. (It was in the context of cosmology that I came to realize that Reality and function are non-dual. [When the application of this principle] is extended to human life discourse [人生論],[130] then Heaven and humans are one. <"Heaven" refers to intrinsic Reality not an Emperor of Heaven. With specific reference to we humans, [this means that] Heaven is our true nature and does not transcend us, existing alone, and so Heaven and humans have always been one.> This is to be without religious delusion, to be without such errors as leaving society, renouncing the world, or cutting oneself off from all dealings with others. Equally, it does not amount to being so mired in material desire that one loses one's spiritual life. This is because in the course of their life, people are, after all, not ignorant of their human nature. When extended to discourse on transformation through institutions [治化論][131] then the Way and instruments [道器] are one. <*Qi* 器 refers to the physical world. *Dao* 道 is the intrinsic Reality of the myriad images, hence the Way and instruments are non-dual.> By "fashioning and bringing to completion [the Way of] Heaven and Earth"[132] and "by going out of one's way to enable all people to develop [their nature fully]"[133] is how the container world [器界] is made to thrive <*Qijie* 器界 is a term borrowed from Buddhism.[134]>, which is how the great Way is made magnificent. If, however, there was

---

[129] In other words, space and time.

[130] Here Xiong is using the term in a broad sense rather than referring to *Lebensphilosophie*. As he explains in *Yuan Ru*, p. 647, it includes investigating our innate human nature; the way of bringing both oneself and things to completion (成己成物之道); socio-political thought; and scientific (格物) thought.

[131] Again, one of Xiong's own technical terms. It refers to the idea of an institutional structure grounded in Confucian ethical norms, which in turn serve to guide the application of scientific principles to ordering human life. See *Yuan Ru*, pp. 311–312.

[132] See Chapter 1, note 29.

[133] This is Xiong's idiosyncratic interpretation of the phrase *qu cheng wan wu* 曲成萬物 in "Xici zhuan, shang," 7.10b, as set out in a gloss provided in Chapter 4, "Forming Material Things," p. 235: "*Qu cheng* 曲成: All people accord with the good beginnings of their Heaven-bestowed nature and their individual competencies to support and exhort one another so that their natures are also fully developed." See also related glosses of *qu cheng* in *Ming xin pian*, p. 203 and *Cun zhai suibi*, pp. 742–743.

[134] The term means the world in which humans live.

awareness of instruments [器] but their origin was not fathomed, then human life would strive solely to facilitate the indulgence of desires and overlook the learning dedicated to knowing the nature and preserving the nature. This is why Zhuangzi berated Huizi 惠子 [Hui Shi 惠施] for chasing after the myriad things, never turning back.[135] <"Never turning back" means that he did not return to seek the Way.> By understanding that the Way and instruments are one, one will neither abandon instruments in the pursuit of the Way, nor will one look at things but remain ignorant of their origin. Only in this way is neither root nor tip omitted. These days, however, it is a challenge to discuss the meaning of this with those who talk about scholarship.)

The "Great Commentary" to the *Book of Change* states: "It is manifested as humaneness, hidden within its functioning (顯諸仁藏諸用)."[136] How profound and far-reaching! This single utterance expresses the profundity of the non-duality of Reality and function. What is "manifested as humaneness"? Ceaseless production and reproduction is called humaneness and it is the functioning of the Great Ultimate (太極). (The Great Ultimate is the name of the intrinsic Reality of the cosmos. The *Zhou Yi bian tong jie* 周易變通解 [Explaining the Principle of Succeeding by Adjusting to Changing Circumstances in the *Zhou Book of Change*], by the now deceased Confucian master, Wan Shuchen 萬澍辰 [Wan Yuyun 萬裕澐; fl. 1873], who hailed from the same county as I, states: "The Way of Heaven takes humaneness as its function."[137] Note: "The Way of Heaven" is a term for intrinsic Reality and must not be misunderstood as an Emperor of Heaven. Usually, humaneness is to be understood as a quality of the mind; here, however, it is used in a more general sense. All of the myriad phenomena of the cosmos are the flow of the true agency [真機] that is ceaseless production and reproduction. It is precisely this that is named humaneness and it is precisely this humaneness that is the functioning of the Great Ultimate. *Xian* 顯: manifest [顯著].

[p. 96]

This says that it is precisely the function of unceasing production and reproduction that is the manifestation of the Great Ultimate, which is what is meant by "with regard to Reality, *it* is function" [即體即用].) What is "hidden within its functioning"? "Function" refers to humaneness, which, as described in the above text, is unceasing production and reproduction. "Hidden" shows that the Great Ultimate does not exist independent of its functioning. ("Great Ultimate" is a term for Reality. In the text below, I use just "Reality.") It is really difficult to explain what this means

---

[135] "Tianxia," *Zhuangzi*, p. 1112.
[136] "Xici shang," 7.12b.
[137] Wan Shuchen, *Zhou Yi bian tong jie*, in *Zhonghua congshu* 中華叢書 (China Book Series) (Taipei: Zhonghua congshu bianshen weiyuanhui, 1960), *juan* 5, p. 207, slightly misquoted.

and so I will give some examples to elucidate. When *ti* 體 and *yong* 用 are discussed in cosmology, *ti* is an abbreviation of *shiti* 實體 and *yong*, function (功用), is the name (目) of the myriad mental and material images. (*Mu* 目 is like "name.") The two terms, *ti* and *yong*, are mutually entailing. If it were said that there is *ti* but no *yong*, then *ti* would be empty and non-existent. If that were the case, then how could the term *ti* be posited? If it were said that there is *yong* but no *ti*, then *yong* would have been without an origin, suddenly appearing out of emptiness, just like a tree that emerges without a root or a river that flows without a source. [Or yet again, imagine] a myriad-tier building being constructed in the sky, even though nothing can take the sky as its foundation. Where in the cosmos would such strange things be possible!? Likewise, it must be understood that without *ti*, the term *yong* cannot be posited. As I have stated previously, although *ti* and *yong* can be differentiated, in fact, they are non-dual. Near at hand, by drawing from my own person, and further away, by drawing from other things, I built up a body of inferences and verifications, finally achieving this realization—this is not some baseless theory in which I give license to subjective conceptualization. (Someone raised the following objection: "Above, your use of such analogies as root and source seems inappropriate because there is a difference between the root and the tree-trunk, and between the source and the river flow." I replied: "According to Buddhist science of reasoning [因明], [in a three-part inference], in all cases, the example [喻] chosen can be only partially similar [with the thesis] and cannot be completely similar.[138] That *yong* must have *ti*, is analogous to a tree must have roots, a river must have a source, and a building must have a foundation—in each case there is some similarity [with the thesis, "*yong* must have *ti*"].") Both in this treatise and in *To the Origin of the Ru*, I have often used the metaphor of the ocean and the numerous waves in my discussion of *ti* and *yong*. (The ocean is a metaphor for Reality and the numerous waves are a metaphor for function.) Reality's transformation into the countless functions of unceasing production and reproduction is analogous to the ocean's transforming into the numerous incessantly leaping waves. (The principle of "with regard to Reality, *it* is function [即體即用]" can be realized from this.) The countless functions all take Reality as their self (自身). (Someone objected: "Given that function arises from Reality then it is not identical to Reality." I berated him, saying: "So, what you have in mind is a creator!" He quickly awakened. The *Book of Change* states: "Transformation and movement are unceasing."[139] This refers both to the mental and the material. The mental

---

[138] See Xiong's discussion above, pp. 82.
[139] "Xici zhuan, xia," 8.18b.

is the functioning of Reality, its transforming and moving are unceasing; the material is also the functioning of Reality, its transforming and moving are unceasing. The mental and material are simply the two aspects of function and cannot be broken down into two [entities]. The reason that function's transforming and moving are unceasing, and its moment-by-moment abandonment of the old and advancement to the new is inexhaustible, is precisely because "the itself" of all functions is Reality.) Take the example of the numerous waves—each takes the ocean as itself. (The itself of wave A is the ocean, [p. 97] the itself of wave B is also the ocean, and this is the case right through to all of the countless waves. From this we can realize the principle of "with regard to function, *it* is Reality" [即用即體]. "With regard to function, *it* is Reality" means that it is function that is Reality [功用即是實體], just as that it is the numerous waves themselves that are the ocean.) Hence, [in explaining] the meaning of the non-duality of Reality and function, only the metaphor of the ocean and the myriad waves comes quite close to the mark. It serves to lead people to awaken to and enter correct principle (正理) and hopefully corrects the various fallacies of those who have previously discussed cosmology or ontology. There is good reason that I am never reluctant to talk at length, reiterating that Reality and function are non-dual. Whenever I read the passage in the *Book of Change*, "It is manifested as humaneness, hidden in its functioning," I really feel that the choice of the word "hidden" (藏) is wonderful. "Hidden" serves to show that Reality does not exist outside function, hence "hidden in its functioning." The word "hidden" describes only the non-duality of Reality and function and must not be mistaken to mean that "this" is hidden within "that."[140] How could Reality and function possibly have a relationship of "that" and "this"? Here, comparisons must not be drawn with those things we are used to seeing in everyday life—the wise should reflect on this.

Someone raised the following objection: "The learning of the Mahāyāna Emptiness school eradicated everything and was detached and dissociated from human life.[141] It stands as a uniquely extraordinary contribution to human wisdom and should not be looked down upon."

I replied: "When the sage proceeds on the path of great transformation, assisting the myriad things, there is no self-interest, so what attachments could there be? Yet it is surely not the case that he strives to eradicate everything."

---

[140] Reality is not something that lies concealed within function: Reality is function. Our experience of Reality, however, is as function.

[141] In other words, there is no attachment.

Someone asked: "Sir, your treatise explains that great function (大用) has two aspects, the mental and the material. (*Da* 大: a term of acclamation; *yong* 用: the abbreviation of *gongyong* 功用.) In other words, the mental and the material are both function. Why then do you separately talk of Reality?"

I replied: "You have not yet understood the meaning of the non-duality of Reality and function. I will first explain function to you. Function is a term for transformation. Transformation does not arise alone; it must have that to which it stands in contrast, hence it is said that the flow of great function has two aspects, the mental and the material, [a principle that is] so of itself (法爾). (*Faer* 法爾 is like saying "self-so" [自然].) At the end of the day, those people who are [metaphysical] idealists (唯心者) cannot deny that there is matter, but they seek to explain that matter is only a by-product [of the mental.] At the end of the day, those people who are [metaphysical] materialists (唯物者) cannot deny that there is the mental/mind, but they seek to explain that matter is only a by-product [of the mental/mind]. The authority for [my learning] is the teaching of Qian and Kun in the *Book of Change*, which explains that the mental and the material are two aspects of great function, and that they are not two entities. These two aspects have always been the great flow that endlessly produces and reproduces, transforming and changing without exhaustion. From the perspective that its properties are not singular (單純),[142] function is explained in terms of the two aspects of the mental and the material. From the perspective that instant by instant it abandons the old and generates the new, without interruption, without stopping, it is explained as great flow. Such is a brief account of that whereby function is function.
[p. 98]

How should Reality be explained? Great function has always been the general term for the myriad mental and material images. The myriad mental and material images are not manifest based on nothing—they definitely have Reality. But this Reality neither towers above the myriad mental and material images nor lies concealed behind the myriad mental and material images—rather, it must be understood that Reality is precisely 'the itself' (自身) of the myriad mental and material images. It is analogous to the way the ocean is 'the itself' of the numerous waves. (The numerous waves are a metaphor for the myriad mental and material images; the ocean is a metaphor for Reality.) To

---

[142] In Chapter 1, p. 22, Xiong explains: "*Dan* 單 means 'solitary' and 'not having that to which it stands in contrast.' *Chun* 純 means 'pure' [純一] and 'without contradiction.'"

seek Reality beyond the myriad mental and material images is like [believing in] the Absolute Spirit that idealistic monists talk about, which is [nothing more than] an Emperor of Heaven in an altered guise. This is unacceptable. Those who, opposing the idealists, separately constitute the materialists, take matter as the foundation of the cosmos. What they fail to understand is that matter has always been phenomena[143] or function—how could it serve as a foundation? This too is a doctrine without Reality, and again I must demur. To affirm the [existence] of the myriad images yet not acknowledge that they have Reality is to regard the cosmos as if it were floating clouds that had no source (源底)—this is absolutely preposterous. (*Yuandi* 源底; see above for a passage cited from the *Sutra on the Lion's Roar of Queen Śrīmālā* for an explanation of the term.[144] Here "cosmos" is a collective term for the myriad mental and material images.) Seeking Reality beyond the myriad images is a remnant custom originating in ancient people's religious sentiments and must be abandoned. I was able to affirm the doctrine of the non-duality of Reality and function only after looking up and observing Heaven, looking downward and investigating Earth. Near at hand, I drew from my own person, and further away, I drew from other things, building up a body of inferences over a long period of time, and then examining them in the light of *Great Change*, where I pondered the sage's words deeply. I did not dare casually or lightly to have confidence in my views.

Having awoken to the non-duality of Reality and function there is not much to be said about Reality itself; rather, it is only from great function's flow (That is, the myriad images of the cosmos.) that one can probe into the hidden (隱) from the manifest. (Starting from those manifest aspects that can be readily investigated to probe into that which is profoundly subtle, recondite, and difficult to exhaust fully, is what "probing into the hidden from the manifest" means. *Yin* 隱 has two meanings. 1. Profoundly subtle. For example, in the physical world there are undoubtedly countless examples of the extremely subtle that have yet to be explained; the same is true of mental functions. 2. Recondite. For example, Reality does not exist by itself, separated from the myriad images of the cosmos. Those who are able to understand this recondite principle are few indeed!) The-whole-that-is-Reality (全體) transforms into great function (*Quanti* 全體 is also a name for Reality. It is named as such because Reality is a whole. Reality's transforming into function is analogous to the ocean's transforming into the myriad waves.) The daily renewal that manifests in function

---

[143] Literally, "manifest images," *xianxiang* 現象.
[144] As already noted, the term *yuandi* 源底 does not appear in that sutra.

is the endless unfolding of expansion (闢) in Reality. There is no gap between the manifest and the subtle because external and internal are non-dual." ("Manifest" and "external" refer to function; "subtle" and "internal" refer to Reality. Here "subtle" is what is meant by "recondite.")
[p. 99]

Addendum. The two names, "phenomena" and "function," are different, but their actuality is the same. From the perspective of its incessant transforming and moving it is called function; from the perspective of its incessant transforming and moving, in which it apparently (宛然) has an obvious appearance, it is called phenomena. (*Wanran* 宛然 is a descriptive term. This is saying that although it has an appearance, that is not fixed.) Hence, I said that the names are different, but their actuality is the same. The two names, phenomena and function, appear frequently in *To the Origin of the Ru* but I did not provide a note. Here I have provided a note because quite a few people have asked about this.

Those who study cosmology must affirm the doctrine of the non-duality of Reality and function. To maintain that the phenomenal aspect is the basis (Such as the two schools of idealistic monism and material monism.) would actually amount to falling into [the mistaken] doctrine that there is no Reality. In China, this kind of thinking is rare. (The Ming Confucian, Tang Ning'an 唐凝庵 [1538–1619] was quite a strong proponent of materialism.[145] Master and disciple, Liu Jishan 劉蕺山 [1578–1645] and Huang Zongxi 黃宗羲 [1610–1695] are well-known as members of the school of Wang Yangming, but actually continued the line of Ning'an.[146] Because Principle-centered Learning [理學][147] has been in decline over the past three centuries, no-one has noted this.) Since the Qin and Han periods, the orthodox transmission of Confucius' studies on the *Book of Change* had [already] been usurped by Tian He 田何 [second century BCE].[148] When Confucians discuss

---

[145] Ning'an was Tang Hezhang's 唐鶴征 sobriquet (號). Tang held that the universe is constituted exclusively of *qi* 氣. See, for example, his *Taoxi zhaji* 桃溪劄記 (Reading Notes from Taoxi), in Huang Zongxi 黃宗羲 (1610–1695), comp., *Ming ru xue an* 明儒學案 (Case Studies of Ming Confucians), 26.14a–15b, *Qinding Siku quanshu*.

[146] Xiong's point is that Wang Yangming is celebrated as one of the founders of the School of Mind or Mind-centered Learning (心學), yet Tang advocated a *qi*-based monism.

[147] Associated with the Cheng brothers and Zhu Xi and contrasted with Mind-centered Learning.

[148] In *Yuan Ru*, p. 332, Xiong relates that in the "Yiwen zhi" 藝文志 (Bibliographic Treatise) in the *Han shu* 漢書 (History of the Former Han Dynasty), Ban Gu 班固 (32–92) states: "With the rise of the Han, those who discussed the *Book of Change* all based their accounts on Tian He." (The passage is actually based on "Ru lin zhuan" 儒林傳 [Biographies of Classicists], *Han shu* [Beijing: Zhonghua shuju, 1983], 88.3597.) Xiong then comments: "It can thus be known that Tian

the origin of the cosmos it is rare for them not to introduce the Emperor of Heaven (天帝) into their accounts—such is the poison of absolute monarchy!

With specific reference to great function (Note the words "with specific reference to."), expansion (闢) is the impetus of vigor, advancement, and unfolding—it is what is called "the pure and spirit-like" (精神). Contraction (翕) is the impetus of condensing, constricting, and hastening toward closure—it is what is referred to as the material (物質). With contraction, there is differentiation by which the myriad things become discrete. With expansion, there is undifferentiated unity (一) that pervasively moves through all matter, with no fixed locus yet there is nowhere where it is not there. (Here *yi* 一 means "unable to be split apart," and not the number "one.") Great function has these two aspects, by means of which they mutually oppose to mutually complete[149]—this is [an example of] the principle of being so of itself. (For "the principle of being so of itself," see Buddhist texts.[150] When a principle is fathomed to its ultimate, and nothing further can be asked about how something came about, it is simply "so of itself" that it is as such. Laozi's statement that "The Way takes the self-so as it model"[151] is also referring to this principle.)

Evaluation of the Mahāyāna Emptiness school's and the *Book of Change*'s respective views on the myriad phenomena and human life

The doctrine of emptiness so vigorously expounded (宣) by the Mahāyāna Emptiness school masters (*Xuan* 宣: to expound [闡明].) is the polar opposite of China's Confucian *Book of Transformation* (變經)—this is because their respective views on human life are fundamentally different. (The *Book of Change* is also called the *Book of Transformation* because it explicates the principles of the myriad transformations, myriad changes, myriad things, and myriad affairs.) Buddhist

---

He began a lineage of transmission based on numerology and it had no connection with Confucius' *Book of Change*. Moreover, [Sima] Tan's 司馬談 teacher, Yang He 楊何, was Tian He's second generation student [*Shiji*, 67.2211], and so Tan was completely ignorant of Confucian learning." Xiong also held that during the reign of Emperor Wu of the Western Han, the genuine Six Classics had been replaced by false versions and it was those false versions that were transmitted to posterity. See *Yuan Ru*, p. 329.

[149] Cf. Chapter 1, p. 34: "It is by mutually opposing that they mutually complete, and it is through this process that Reality transforms into great function."

[150] The "principle of being so of itself" is one of four principles of reasoning taught in the *Saṃdhinirmocana-sūtra*, T676.16, 709b11–10a18. Examples of this principle would be that fire burns or that water moistens, and that this must be accepted as simply how things are.

[151] *Dao de jing*, zhang 25.

thought is, after all, opposed to human life. It brazenly impedes the immense flow of "vast productivity and "capacious productivity," showing no reluctance, no fear in renouncing [human life]. Ever since Śākyamuni promoted the doctrine of conditioned arising (Śākyamuni taught that humans arise from the twelve [links of] causal conditions, such as ignorance and so forth. The details are in such sutras as the *Ahan [koujie shier yinyuan] jing* 阿含[口解十二因緣]經 [Sutra on the Oral Explanation of the Twelve (Links of) Causal Conditions in the Agamas][152] and the *Yuanqi jing* 緣起經 [*Pratītya-samutpādādivibhaṅga-nirdeśa-sūtra*; Sutra on Conditioned Origination].)[153]—according to which, if one follows the flow, one sinks into cyclic existence (If one follows

[p. 100]

the continuous flow [of the cycle] of ignorance and the other conditions, this is to sink into the ocean of cyclic existence.) and if one opposes it then one returns to cessation (Not to continue following the flow [of the cycle] of ignorance and the other conditions is called "oppose.")—this became the basis of both Mahāyāna and Hīnayāna [teachings]. In Hīnayāna, however, it is up to the individual to deal with cyclic existence, and so Hīnayānists even think nothing of "turning the body to ashes and annihilating cognition."[154]

With the rise of bodhisattva Nāgārjuna, he stopped the Hīnayāna practice of leaving matters to the individual to deal with, and laid out the magnificent foundation of Mahāyāna, taking an oath to liberate (度脫) all sentient beings forever (窮未來). (*Qiong* 窮 is like "to the end" [盡]. This says that he undertook to liberate all sentient beings from now until the very limit of the most distant future. *Du* 度 is "to save and convey to deliverance" [救度]. *Tuo* 脫 is "to be removed from the ocean of cyclic existence" [脫離生死海].) Hence it is said that craving, antipathy, and ignorance are awakening (菩提) (*Puti* 菩提 means correct awakening. Craving, antipathy, and ignorance are the basis of numerous mental afflictions and the origin of a myriad unwholesome qualities; they are called the three poisons. However, the three poisons themselves have never had a root [根] and so transforming craving into no craving, antipathy into no antipathy, and ignorance into no ignorance is true awakening.) and that the mundane world is *nirvāṇa*. (For this doctrine, see the "Investigating *Nirvāṇa* Section"[155] and the "Investigating Dharmas Section"[156] of the *Treatise on the Middle Way*. Scholars in the Qing dynasty misunderstood this doctrine and thought that the learning

---

[152] An Shigao 安世高 (fl. 148–170), trans. (?), *Ahan koujie shier yinyuan jing*, T1508.
[153] T124.
[154] That is, to remove all the sufferings of body and mind so as to achieve "*nirvāṇa*-without-remainder."
[155] T1564.30, 36a4–12.
[156] T1564.30, 25a9–13.

of the Mahāyāna Emptiness school was not a teaching of transcending the mundane world. Undoubtedly this is because when they read the sutras and treatises they failed to look for the true explanation; I will not dispute their interpretations here.) "While there remains even a single sentient being who has yet to become a buddha, I will never enter *nirvāṇa*."[157] So powerful was this vow that in forming a connection with unlimited numbers of sentient beings now and into the future, [a bodhisattva] would definitely not break the vow nor lose heart on the grounds that sentient beings are difficult to save and convey to deliverance. Although this is similar to the great wisdom and great virtue of the sage who fashions and brings to completion [the Way of] Heaven and Earth, and assists the myriad things,[158] nevertheless, whereas the sage's energies are focused on the actual world, the way of the Mahāyāna Emptiness school seeks to remove sentient beings from the ocean of cyclic existence, because it is, after all, a world-renouncing religion. (Although Buddhism is rich in philosophical thought, it is, after all, a religion.)

There is no question that Confucianism and Buddhism are different paths. In elaborating the doctrine of emptiness, Nāgārjuna sought to lead the myriad things[159] to return to limpid, quiescent extinction, to destroy the cosmos, and oppose human life. (People often do not believe that the way of the Mahāyāna Emptiness school is like this. In fact, the reason that the Mahāyāna Emptiness school created and elucidated [the teaching of] "not abiding in *nirvāṇa*" was precisely because for eternity [the bodhisattva] does not abandon the mundane world, does not abandon sentient beings. The fundamental aim was to be able eventually to save and convey [all] sentient beings to deliverance. All of the sutras talk of *nirvāṇa* in terms of quiescent extinction, and the *Treatise on the Middle Way* is no exception. What does quiescent extinction mean? The *Treatise on the Middle Way* had already provided an explanation, but the purport is subtle, the language terse, and so it is likely that only a few could understand. A verse in the *Nirvāṇa Sutra* reads:

All dharmas are impermanent,
They are dharmas that arise and cease.
When arising and ceasing has come to an end,
The quiescent extinction is a joy.[160]

---

[157] Paraphrase of *Dasheng ru lengqie jing* 大乘入楞伽經 (*Laṅkāvatāra-sūtra*; Sutra on the Buddha's Entering the Country of Lanka), T672.16, 597c15–16.
[158] This is based on the "Xiang" commentary to the Tai 泰 hexagram, *Zhou yi*, 2.21a.
[159] Here to be understood as referring to sentient beings.
[160] T7.1, 204c23–24.

The meaning of this verse is exceedingly clear, yet no scholars have searched for its true explanation. I would like to undertake a separate, detailed interpretation, but it is not convenient to do that here as it concerns too many other issues.) [In doing so, he showed] great compassion, selflessness (It was in response to the suffering of sentient beings that he aroused great compassion. Because he was never [attached] to the view of the existence of inherent selfhood, he therefore had a sense of communion with sentient beings who share the same Reality/body [體].), great heroism, and fearlessness. Although his teachings are problematic as models, crucially, no matter how indescribably long-lasting, complicated, dangerous, and polluted

[p. 101]

the mighty environment in which humans live might be, [Nāgārjuna's teachings are proof] that there is also a remarkable wisdom that arises of its own accord, transcending the mundane world. [Nāgārjuna] observed that nothing has a fixed nature, which he called emptiness, and so he had the courage to defy creative transformation (造化), to extinguish the cosmos, and [to undertake] the great vow [to save and convey all sentient beings to deliverance]. (*Zaohua* 造化 refers to the great power of production and reproduction, transformation and retransformation, in the cosmos. The Buddhists alone oppose and resist it.) By these means he guided sentient beings, joining with them to save them, advancing unrestrained, fearless, and spirited. This is undeniably a uniquely glorious display of human wisdom. Ordinary people are constantly in a state of dithering confusion but if they were to keep the doctrine of emptiness firmly in mind (服膺) (*Fuying* 服膺 means to hold something firmly in mind and not let it go.) then they would suddenly and fully awaken, and in the clear dawn, afflictions would suddenly cease. (If a person is able to empty his or her mind of defilements, then, just like the clarity of dawn, afflictions will cease by themselves.) There is no escape for delusion in the illumination of sapience. (Defilements having been emptied, sapience illuminates [delusions and habituated tendencies] and makes [them] manifest. In the clarity of illumination, no hidden delusions and residual habituated tendencies can remain concealed.) Having awoken to the fact that what is past is beyond repair, one realizes that what is to come can still be pursued. Then, not only would one not dare to create bad karma in the human world, moreover, the courage to bring humaneness to realization and to choose what is right would surge forth, so of itself, unrestrained, one not being able to stop oneself.

A sage is robust and vigorous so as to realize fully the path of life. In bringing himself to completion he brings all things to completion, and so develops and enhances the defining characteristics of the Reality he shares in common with all things. (What we Confucians refer to as "sage" is of two types. The first refers exclusively to Confucius. The second is to [one who] establishes norms for the human way so that people know what to aspire to. The text here is referring to this second type. Being robust and vigorous is how the sage controls bad practices such as selfish motives, selfish desires, and laziness—this does not mean using force to make other people submit. Using force to make other people submit is violence and this is not being robust and vigorous. In short, being robust and vigorous is to use strength to cultivate one's person and is not to use strength to make others submit. It can also be said that being robust and vigorous is to use strength to advance virtue and carry out one's tasks. If the sage was not robust and vigorous he would be without the means to bring all things to completion by bringing himself to completion and be without the means to expand his defining characteristics,[161] and so would lose that whereby he lives, lose the true [and constant defining characteristics] of the Reality he shares in common with all things.) The inversions (顛倒)[162] of fools (愚人) serve to harm the very principles [that enable them] to live (*Diandao* 顛倒: see Buddhist texts. If we were to provide a gloss to explain the term, it refers simply to the loss of correct awareness, but its underlying meaning is profound and subtle, and unless one has genuine personal experience of human life one will never understand the implicit meaning of this term. *Yuren* 愚人 does not mean a person who lacks ability and intelligence. When viewed through the wisdom eye (慧眼),[163] all those throughout history who had great talents but committed heinous acts were fools. If Qin Hui 秦檜 [1090–1155] had had any wisdom he most certainly would not have earned his reputation as a traitor for eternity. Prince Yue 岳王 [1103–1142],[164] whose good name lives on forever, had true wisdom.[165] Yao 堯 and Shun 舜 possessed sagely wisdom and so boldly opened the doors to the four quarters to meet with [men of talent] from all over the realm.[166] Lü Zheng

---

[161] That is, "the defining characteristics of the Reality he shares in common with all things." As Xiong relates above, Reality's defining characteristics include robustness and vigor, utter goodness, and being true and constant.

[162] The term "inversion" refers to the false and illusory being taken as the true and real.

[163] Here the term is being used in a non-technical sense to mean capacity for correct discernment.

[164] Yue Fei 岳飛; posthumous title, Prince of E 鄂王.

[165] Senior official at the Southern Song court, Qin Hui [alt. Qin Kuai], is known to history as a traitor for executing his enemy, the general Yue Fei 岳飛 (1103–1142). Yue Fei had fought against the invading Jurchen army, whereas Qin Hui supported suing for peace but at the price of ceding northern China to the non-Han Jurchens.

[166] Yao and Shun were two mythical sage emperors. This is alluding to accounts such as the following two. (1) "Shun dian" 舜典 (Canon of Shun), *Shangshu* 尚書 (Book of Documents), *Shisan jing zhushu*, 3.19b: "On the first day of the first month, Shun went to the temple of the accomplished progenitor(s). He deliberated with the [Officer of the] Four Peaks to open the gates of the four [directions], to clear the vistas of the four [directions], to penetrate what could be heard from the four [directions]." Translation of Martin Kern in "Language and the Ideology of Kingship in the 'Canon of Yao,'" in Martin Kern and Dirk Meyer, eds., *Origins of Chinese Political Philosophy: Studies in the Composition and Thought of the Shangshu* (Classic of Documents) (Leiden: Brill, 2017), p. 47. (2) Wang Fu 王符 (78–163) "Ming an" 明闇 (Clear-sightedness and Blindness), *Qian fu lun* 潛夫論

呂政[167] lacked wisdom and believed that the people should be kept ignorant.[168] One can further generalize on the basis of these few examples. All people are born endowed with true principle. After they are born, they become controlled by the body and habituated to inversions, and so harm their innate true principle.) Even though the world
[p. 102]
is a burning house,[169] people are unaware of it. (People all [suffer from] inversions, suspecting one another and harming one another. The powerful even use tactics and might to bully the majority of weak people. Laozi lamented that the myriad things were but straw dogs,[170] and the Buddhists are saddened that the world is a burning house—if it were not for inversions, it would not have come to this.)

The Buddha felt compassion for sentient beings for being deluded and so wanted to block the great flow of production and reproduction to transform

---

(Discourses of a Recluse), *Sibu congkan chubian*, 2.1b: "During their reigns, Yao and Shun opened the gates of the four [directions] to clear the vistas of the four [directions], to penetrate what could be heard from the four [directions]. By thus bringing the whole world together like spokes on a wheel, there is nothing about which the sage is not illuminated."

[167] Lü Zheng is the First Emperor, Qin Shi Huang 秦始皇 (r. 221–210). According to *Shiji*, his mother, Zhao Ji 趙姬 (Consort Zhao; c. 280–228), had conceived the future emperor while she was still a concubine of the merchant Lü Buwei 呂不韋 (290–235) and before becoming the consort of King Zhuangxiang of Qin 秦莊襄王 (281–247). It is for this reason that he was later disparagingly referred to as Lü Zheng. (Zheng is his given name.) "Lü Buwei liezhuan" 呂不韋列傳 (Biography of Lü Buwei), *Shiji*, 85.2508.

[168] This is probably referring to the notorious "burning of books and burying of scholars" (焚書坑儒) attributed to Qin Shi Huang (but repudiated by modern scholars.) and the traditional belief that this was connected with ideas about statecraft earlier developed by political adviser in the state of Qin, Shang Yang 商鞅 (d. 338 BCE), in particular, the idea of keeping the people ignorant, such as in the following passage from the "Ken ling" 墾令 (Orders to Cultivate Wastelands) chapter, *Shangzi* 商子 (also known as *Shang Jun shu* 商君書 [Book of Lord Shang]), *Sibu congkan chubian*, 2.2a–2b, attributed to Shang Yang: "Do not fix ranks, responsibilities, or offices according to foreign powers: then the people will not esteem learning and will also not despise agriculture. If the people do not esteem learning, they will be ignorant; if they are ignorant, they will have no external ties; if they have no external ties, the state will be at peace and will not be endangered." Translated by Yuri Pines in *The Book of Lord Shang: Apologetics of State Power in Early China* (New York: Columbia University Press, 2017), pp. 125–126. As Pines notes, p. 3: "Even though this attribution is not entirely correct because portions of the book were composed long after Shang Yang's death, the *Book of Lord Shang* remains a major testament to the ideas of Qin reformers, the architects of the future Qin Empire (221–207 B.C.E.)."

[169] The parable of the burning house is from the *Miaofa lianhua jing*, T262.9, 12b13–13c18. As Charles Muller explains: "The suffering of sentient beings is likened to a burning house, in which some children (representing sentient beings) are obliviously playing. Their father, unable to get them to come out, tries to lure them out by telling them that they he has three carts prepared for them, one drawn by a goat, one drawn by a deer, and one drawn by an ox. These three represent the three vehicles 三乘 of *śrāvaka* 聲聞, *pratyekabuddha* 緣覺, and *bodhisattva* 菩薩, respectively. When they come out, there is only actually one large white oxcart, which represents the ultimate reality of the One Buddha-Vehicle 一佛乘." See the entry "火宅喻" in *Digital Dictionary of Buddhism*, http://www.buddhism-dict.net/cgi-bin/xpr-ddb.pl?q=%E7%81%AB%E5%AE%85%E5%96%A9.

[170] *Dao de jing, zhang* 5: "Heaven and Earth are heartless, treating the myriad things as straw dogs." "Straw dogs" is interpreted as objects used in sacrifices or ceremonies that are discarded when no longer needed.

the mundane world into the village where there is nothing, or the wilderness of quiescent extinction.[171] Although this is a different path from that of we Confucians, nevertheless just as water and fire destroy one another, they also generate one another.[172] Would it not be wonderful if the Mahāyāna bodhisattvas' great vow to liberate sentient beings, and their strength in resisting creative transformation, were able to be used in fashioning and bringing to completion [the Way of] Heaven and Earth and assisting the myriad things!? (Here "myriad things" refers to all of humanity. The path of the sage consists of nothing other than of looking forward to all of humanity's supporting one other, and there being no leader who controls the masses.) Would it not be wonderful?! Buddhist teachings and world-weary sentiments are absolutely different. Whether in ancient times or modern, dispirited persons often grow world-weary. In the late Zhou period, even the expansive and profound [thought] of the Daoists was unable to avoid this. People from Tang times onward revered the Daoists as forming the third leg of a tripod together with the Confucians and Buddhists—this was an error due to a lack of learning. (For my whole life I have been very fond of Tao Yuanming's poems, [even though] they are redolent with world-weary sentiments. That which I draw positively on are their qualities of being untrammeled, carefree, and self-so; as for those places where they come near to being dispirited, I draw on this as a stern warning.)

Addendum 1. Someone enquired about the following: "Sir, you say that the learning of the Mahāyāna Emptiness school advocates the extinction of the cosmos—I doubt that this was original purport of Nāgārjuna and the other masters."

I replied: "Students must single-mindedly and meticulously inquire into the integrated system of Buddhist doctrine by first breaking down the overall arrangement and then summarizing the main purport—only then will they believe that what I say is not tendentious. However, this question is too large, and in my advanced years I do not have the energy to

---

[171] This is an appropriation of a description in the "Xiaoyao you" chapter of *Zhuangzi*, p. 40; Burton Watson, trans., *The Complete Works of Chuang-tzu*, p. 59: "Now you have this big tree, and you're distressed because it's useless. Why don't you plant it in Not-Even-Anything Village or the field of Broad-and-Boundless, relax and do nothing by its side, or lie down for a free and easy sleep under it?"

[172] According to Five Phases (五行) theory, wood generates fire; fire generates earth; earth generates metal; metal generates water; water generates wood; and the cycle is repeated. In this cyclical sequence, water and fire indirectly generate each other. In turn, wood overcomes earth; earth overcomes water; water overcomes fire; fire overcomes metal; metal overcomes wood; and the cycle is repeated. In this cyclical sequence, water directly overcomes fire and fire indirectly overcomes water.

write a monograph [to explain it properly]. I would really like to reduce the scope of the problem to something miniscule, carefully select [the relevant] materials, and write some reading notes, but I do not have time even to do this. As a last resort, in order to dispel the doubts of worthies (賢者),[173] for the interim I will cite a verse in the *Nirvana Sutra*: 'All dharmas are impermanent, / They are dharmas that arise and cease. / When arising and ceasing have come to an end'[174] and so forth. Note: 'all dharmas' is a general term for mental and material dharmas. With mental dharmas, as soon as a previous thought-moment ceases the following thought-moment arises. It is the same with material dharmas: moment by moment, as the former ceases the following arises. Hence, Buddhists call the mind and things 'dharmas that arise and cease.' What ordinary people refer to as the myriad images of the cosmos[175] is actually what the Buddhists refer to as dharmas that arise and cease. As for the line in the verse, 'When arising and ceasing have come to an end' (生滅滅已) ('Dharmas that arise and cease' is also abbreviated

[p. 103]

as 'arising and ceasing.' This can be checked in Buddhist texts. *Yi* 已 is like *liao* 了 in the vernacular. 'When arising and ceasing have come to an end' is like saying 'when dharmas that arise and cease have come to an end.'), if it is not interpreted to mean that the myriad images of the cosmos are annihilated, then how should it be interpreted? I have always known that devout believers of Buddhist teachings will certainly take 'When arising and ceasing have come to an end' to mean that because the Buddha felt compassion for ordinary people who form attachments to dharmas that arise and cease he was strenuously refuting their attachments and was certainly not saying that dharmas that arise and cease can be annihilated. What these devout believers have particularly failed to understand is that if the Buddha's refutation of ordinary people's attachments should be taken to be refuting only their deluded sentiments, then what need would there be to say, 'When arising and ceasing have come to an end'? If, without exception, there is complete annihilation, in the end one sinks into emptiness. If everything in the cosmos and human life is viewed as empty, then how is this not opposing human life and destroying the cosmos? I have deeply pondered

---

[173] "Worthies" here seems to refer most immediately to Xiong's students.
[174] See n. 160 above.
[175] In "Superfluous Words" Xiong noted that "'The myriad images of the cosmos' is a generic term for all kinds of material and 'pure and spirit-like' phenomena."

[those writings] of the Confucian school that talk exclusively of 'reflecting on authenticity' (思誠) and 'establishing authenticity' (立誠), where the inherent meaning of the character *cheng* 誠 cannot be exhausted.[176] *Cheng* 誠 means 'real' (真實). The myriad images of the cosmos are real and are not non-existent; human life is real and is not non-existent. If one thinks about people on the basis of this and takes a firm stance on the basis of this, then there is no way for any erroneous view to arise. What emptiness is there? It is, moreover, not the case that I am someone opposed to Buddhist teachings. Not only was I fond of the learning of the Mahāyāna Emptiness school in my youth, to this day I have never stopped being fond of it. The Prajñā masters regarded the cosmos to be absolutely empty and quiescent, and they were detached and dissociated [from human life]. We Confucians regard the cosmos to be dynamically (活躍) productive and reproductive, replete with (充然) great existents (大有)[177] (The *Book of Change* states: "vast productivity" and "capacious productivity";[178] it also states: "production and reproduction is called change"[179] and "transformation and movement do not abide [不居]."[180] *Bu ju* 不居 is difficult to describe and so reluctantly I use "dynamically" [活躍]. *Chongran* 充然: abundant [豐富].), and to be unimpeded and without limits. I firmly believe that observing emptiness must yield to 'reflecting on authenticity' and 'establishing authenticity.'"

Addendum 2. A visitor asked about the following: "It seems that you think that it was wrong for Xuanzang to have introduced the Mahāyāna Existence school [into China]."

I replied: "No, no. The learning of the Mahāyāna Existence school indeed has many areas of strength, but here it is not convenient to deal with too broad a range of issues, so I have not discussed them. There are three reasons that Xuanzang focused his efforts on introducing the Mahāyāna Existence school. First, Kumārajīva had already translated the canon of the Prajñā masters and so Chinese scholars had known about the doctrine of emptiness for a long time.[181] Second, when Xuanzang journeyed to the

---

[176] In Chapter 2, p. 91, Xiong noted: "'Ultimate authenticity' refers to Reality."
[177] See p. 156.
[178] "Xici, shang," 7.14b–15a.
[179] "Xici, shang," 7.13b.
[180] "Xici, xia," 8.18b.
[181] Xiong's implication is that because Chinese scholars had long known about the doctrine of emptiness, they sought to learn about newer developments in Buddhist doctrine.

West[182] this was the period when the Mahāyāna Existence school was at its height. Third, the hundred schools of Chinese scholarship were all derived from the *Great Change*, and there had never been thinking that annihilated production and transformation.[183] Xuanzang, of course, had the innate character of a Chinese person and so it was easier for him to approach the teachings of the Mahāyāna Existence school. (The seeds in the store consciousness produce and reproduce without cease. The backbone of Asaṅga and

[p. 104]

Vasubandhu's doctrinal system is the theory of conditioned origination, and the backbone of the theory of conditioned origination is [the analogy of] real seeds as causal conditions. The basis of opposition to emptiness and demonstration of existence lies in this, which is why Xuanzang and Kuiji had a singular affinity [for the analogy of seeds as causal conditions]!) In his later years, however, Xuanzang developed a singularly deep affinity for the *Perfection of Wisdom Sutra*,[184] evidencing that by then he had already attained a high level [of awakening]—certainly one that the learning of the Mahāyāna Existence school could not attain and hold on to."

That none of the myriad things has a fixed nature (Not having a fixed self-entity is called "not having a fixed nature.") is something that both the sage[185] and the Prajñā masters had observed. (The "Great Commentary" to the *Book of Change* states: "The numinous has no locale and change has no body [無體]." It also states: "The unfathomability of *yin* and *yang* is called 'the numinous.'"[186] Hence, "the numinous" is referring to how it is through the mutual opposition of *yin* and *yang* that transformation is accomplished. "No locale" means "no location." *Wu ti* 無體 means "has no physical body" [無形體]. This is saying that the myriad things have always been without a fixed nature, that their transforming is unfathomable, and that is all. Having neither locale nor body is what "none of the myriad things has a fixed nature" means. That which the Prajñā masters had observed is the same.) In the myriad things' lacking a fixed nature, however, the sage saw vitality and dynamism, that everything is real. This is why early on the doctrine of the non-duality of Reality and function was expounded in the *Great Change*. In regard to the myriad things' lacking a fixed nature,

---

[182] He arrived in India in 633 (the journey having taken several years) and returned to the capital in China, Chang'an, in 645.

[183] Xiong's implication is that the doctrine of emptiness remained "foreign" to Chinese scholars.

[184] Xuanzang devoted much of his last few years to complete his translation of this 600-fascicle sutra (which is actually a collection of sutras), T220.

[185] Confucius.

[186] "Xici, shang," 7.10b, 7.13b.

the Prajñā masters declared that things are like an illusion or a conjurer's trick. This is why the thesis that nature and characteristics are both empty was especially advocated in the *Wisdom* (般若). (The *Perfection of Wisdom*.) Having inherited Śākyamuni's world-renouncing thought, the Prajñā masters sought to defy the immense flow of "vast productivity" and "capacious productivity." Viewing the nature and characteristics of the myriad dharmas to be illusory was an aberrant (變態) development in the intellectual world. [This exemplifies] what *Balance as the Norm* refers to as the wise being excessive,[187] which is why their views are problematic as models. How superb the *Book of Change* is! It is perfection! (The term *biantai* 變態 is usually used to refer to a psychological disorder. Here the term is certainly not being used in that particular sense; rather, it is simply referring to thought that opposes human life and annihilates the cosmos. It is really a bit too odd.)

At this point, this chapter should be concluded. Next, I should elaborate on dharma characteristics. (The mental and the material are collectively called "dharma characteristics.") This elaboration is roughly divided into two chapters: "Forming Material Things" (成物) and "Explaining Mind" (明心), and related in that order.

---

[187] "Zhongyong," 52.3b: "The Master said: 'I know why the Way is not put into practice: the wise are excessive and those who lack talent fall short.'"

4
Forming Material Things

I remember one occasion, before I had yet turned twenty, I had climbed up to a high place and was gazing upon the dense profusion of the cosmos' myriad images when suddenly I had a feeling of incalculable wonder. From then on, I was always greatly puzzled by how the material cosmos had come to be but was unable to find an explanation. It was only later, when I had acquired a modest ability to read and my knowledge gradually started to expand, that I became aware that throughout history there were indeed many wise men who had entertained this same puzzlement. Now, if we were to summarize their explanations, in general, they fall into two camps. The first camp [upholds] the clustering of minute parts/atoms thesis (細分和集論). (Henceforth, this will be abbreviated as *xifen lun* 細分論. In their account of atoms [極微][1] the Indian Vaiśeṣikas [勝論], also called them "minute parts" [細分].[2] I will also adopt this name [for atoms]. *Heji* 和集: many small parts in a single locale in close proximity [近附] to one another. <*Fu* 附: like being near to one another.> *Ji* 集: although many atoms are intermixed they are still separated from one another and are not undifferentiated as one. This is analogous to many troops gathered together to form an array. The array is a whole. Within this whole, however, the many troops are actually still individuals and quite separated from one another. It is also analogous to many trees gathered together to form a forest. The forest is a whole. Within this whole, however, the many trees are each distinct and quite separated from one another by a considerable distance. Countless atoms separately cluster together to form the multifariously differentiated numerous things, and even the myriad things cluster together to form the great whole that is the material cosmos.) Already in ancient times the clustering of minute parts thesis had developed an account of atoms (極微、元子).[3] If we compare the elucidation of atoms and electrons by modern scientists with that of the ancient account,

---

[1] *Jiwei* 極微 is Xuanzang's translation of *paramāṇu*.
[2] Vaiśeṣika was an early non-Buddhist school. Xiong's claim that the Vaiśeṣikas referred to atoms as "parts" seems to be based on the Kuiji's description of the Vaiśeṣika understanding of atoms in *Weishi ershi lun shuji*, T1834.43, 992c3–4.
[3] Here Xiong uses both terms to refer to atoms.

even though in terms of detail they are very far apart, when it comes down to it, both are theories of the clustering of minute parts. The emperor's carriage began with a spokeless wheel, but with the accumulation of experience over time, later on, the excellent qualities [with which it was subsequently embellished] became increasingly apparent. (Someone asked: "With respect to atoms' combining to form a large entity, then it is enough simply to use the term 'combine' [和合]; why, then, is *ji* 集 [in *heji* 和集] added instead?" I replied: "Whether referring to atoms [極微] or to atoms and electrons [元子電子], even though it is claimed that they combine to form large entities <"They" is referring to atoms or atoms and electrons; the use is the same below.>, it is not, however, claimed that they are finely blended together like the hundred flavors [of the ingredients] mixed together to form a ball of [traditional Chinese] medicine, so thoroughly integrated that the flavors cannot be distinguished. <From "it is not" to here is to be read uninterrupted.>
[p. 106]
After all, between the atoms, there is a large distance and so the term *ji* 集 is added. 'Clustering' [和集] is just like many troops forming an array, or many trees forming a forest.")

"Holism"/the "Reality qua whole thesis"

Those who uphold "holism"/the "Reality qua whole thesis" (全體論) maintain that the myriad images of the cosmos are not the clustering of many, many atoms, but rather are the differentiation of an absolute and all-encompassing (一大) power—perfect (圓滿) and consummate, flowing everywhere unimpeded, its potent functioning inexhaustible (Attention must be paid to the two characters, *yi* 一 and *da* 大. *Yi* means "has nothing to which it stands in contrast" [無對]; it is not the number "one." *Da* 大 means that it is so immense that nothing lies beyond it. *Yuanman* 圓滿 means that it is able to arouse a myriad changes, give rise to a myriad transformations, and that it is that from which the myriad qualities and myriad principles emerge.), flood-like and surging (浩然油然)—as it forms the myriad particular entities. (*Haoran* 浩然: tremendous [盛大]; *youran* 油然: animated [生動].) This is analogous to the ocean's becoming differentiated as countless wave forms. (The numerous wave forms are a metaphor for the myriad things. Although each of the myriad things develops a different form, they all transform and change incessantly, and it was never the case that they are each an independent entity. For this reason, the metaphor of waves is used. The ocean is a metaphor for the Reality of the myriad things; this is Reality qua whole [全體]. Reality has nothing to which it stands in contrast, it incessantly produces and reproduces, and as an undifferentiated great whole, it has no divisions. For this reason, the metaphor of the ocean is used.) Because Reality qua whole is productive, reproductive, and dynamic (It is not a stiff, dead body.), it constantly (恆) gives rise to differentiation. (The character *heng* 恆 is crucial. There being no time when it is not giving rise to differentiation is why "constantly" is used.) This is what the "Great Commentary" to the *Book of Change* means when it states: "Kun transforms to become matter" (坤化成物).[4] I will explain the meaning of this in detail below. The earliest source to give expression to "holism"/the "Reality qua whole thesis" is China's *Great Change*, and with Confucius the thesis became more precise and meticulous.

Those who espouse "holism"/the "Reality qua whole thesis" maintain that the myriad images of the cosmos do not suddenly arise out of thin air. To arise out of thin air amounts to generating something from nothing—an impossibility. Hence it is said that the cosmos must have Reality. Take the analogy of watching the dynamic, numerous waves and knowing that they are the ocean. This is something that an adult is a capable of doing, whereas when a small child sees the numerous waves, he or she will not realize that it is the myriad waves themselves that are the ocean. This is because small children lack the ability to discern. If a scholar were to acknowledge only the myriad images of the cosmos and not believe that there is Reality, then what difference would his/her lack of awareness be from that of a small child?

The most miniscule [units of] matter are called atoms. (See above.) If we speak in terms of the development of matter, the largest things begin with the tiniest. The *Book of Change* gave prominence to the image of treading on frost and solid ice, [evidencing] that already very early on the sage had talked about large things beginning as small things. (The first line of the Kun hexagram states: "The frost one treads on reaches its ultimate stage as solid ice."[5] This is describing how, by treading on frost, a person knows that hard ice will

[p. 107]

follow. Frost is something very minute but eventually it becomes hard ice; and so, what starts as minute eventually becomes huge. All things develop from the minute to the massive. The first line of the Kun hexagram's elucidation of the principles of things is indeed

---

[4] "Xici, shang," 7.3a reads 坤作成物. Xiong uses 坤作成物 in *Yuan Ru*, p. 691ff. but glosses this as 坤化成物. It might also be noted that Hui Dong 惠棟 (1697–1758), *Zhou yi shu* 周易述 (Comments on the *Book of Change*), 12.22a, *Qinding Siku quanshu*, uses the phrase 坤化成物. He does, however, note that Yao Xin 姚信 (fl. 267; author of *Zhou yi zhu* 周易注 [Notes on the *Book of Change*]; not extant) states that *hua* 化 should be *zuo* 作.

[5] "Xiang" commentary, Kun hexagram, *Zhou yi*, 1.23a; Richard John Lynn, trans., *The Classic of Changes*, p. 145.

worth pondering.) Atoms are nothing but productive and reproductive, dynamic, and extremely lightly pulsating (輕動) matter. (The term *qingdong* 輕動 is borrowed from Buddhist texts. *Qing* 輕 refers to atoms' being different from dense and turbid things; *dong* 動 refers to their incessant pulsating.) The "Commentary on the Images" for the first line of the Kun hexagram states: "*Yin* begins to condense."[6] This is explaining that atoms were never fixed, materially obstructive things (質礙物).[7] (The *Book of Change* uses either Kun or *yin* as the collective term for matter and energy [質力]. The "Great Commentary" states this clearly; see my account in *To the Origin of the Ru, juan* B.[8] Matter and energy have always been non-dual but there is no harm in talking of them separately. Of course, although they are talked about separately, they cannot be conjectured to be two types of entity. It is only by clearly discerning this point that the phrase "*Yin* begins to condense" can be understood. Here, *yin* refers to matter. It must, however, be understood that what is referred to as matter is never fixed matter; rather, that it can be said to be matter is only by virtue of its dependence on contraction's [翕] condensing impetus. At the start of this condensing, there would have been extremely lightly pulsating tiny particles, what *Balance as the Norm* calls "small."[9]) Despite this, there have always been scholars who maintain that atoms are numerous discrete entities, each of which has a materially obstructive nature (質礙性) (For example, those who discussed atoms in ancient times claimed that atoms are round entities;[10] and in modern times there are also those who take atoms and electrons to be small particles.)—their contrary account is indeed far removed from the innovative insights of the *Book of Change*! If it is understood that atoms are nothing but lightly pulsating matter, then the following conclusion can be drawn: It is not the case that atoms each have a fixed, materially

---

[6] *Zhou yi*, 1.23b.
[7] The Buddhist notion of *zhiai* 質礙 means that different material things cannot occupy the same locus.
[8] *Yuan Ru*, p. 697: "The 'Great Commentary' states, 'Kun transforms to become matter' (坤作成物) followed by, 'By being firm and focused, Kun [becomes] energy' (坤以簡能).* *Wu* 物: matter (物質); *neng* 能: energy (能力). The sage explained that Kun is matter, is energy, and so it is evident that energy and matter cannot be separated: when matter is spoke of, there is energy there; when energy is spoken of, there is matter there." *"Xici, shang," 7.3a. Xiong provides detailed exegesis to support these interpretations, including his idiosyncratic gloss of *jian* 簡 as "firm and focused"; see *Yuan Ru*, pp. 696–698. See also his discussion below, p. 188.
[9] In Chapter 1, p. 23, Xiong wrote: "The extreme ferocity of condensing's might is such that, quite unexpectedly, it becomes countless tiny particles. These are what in the *Zhongyong* 中庸 (Balance as the Norm) explains as being 'so small that they cannot be broken apart.'"
[10] For example, in both Paramārtha's and Xuanzang's quite different translations of Dignāga's (sixth century) *Ālambana-parīkṣā* (Investigation of the *Ālambana*) atoms are described as round. See Paramārtha's translation, *Wuxiang si chen lun* 無相思塵論 (Treatise on Considerations [of the Fact That] Objects of Thought Have no Characteristics), T1619.31, 883a17; and Xuanzang's translation, *Guan suoyuan yuan lun* 觀所緣緣論 (Treatise Investigating the Conditions for the Causal Support of Consciousness), T1624.31, 888c11.

obstructive nature, and it is also most definitely not the case that they illusorily manifest out of thin air. Extrapolating from this it can be categorically stated that atoms are formed through the differentiation of Reality qua whole. (Reality [實體] is also called Reality qua whole [全體] because it is perfectly complete and has no boundaries.)

I use "the flow of Reality" and "it is by means of contraction and expansion that transformation is accomplished" to elucidate "the myriad mental and material images." An overview of the key points already appears in the "Explaining Transformation" chapter. Now, so as to forestall any misunderstanding, here I will briefly separate out and then integrate (疏會) [the component senses of] the terms "flow" and "contraction and expansion." (*Shuhui* 疏會: to separate out [疏析] and then to integrate [融會].) Take the phrase "the flow of Reality." Some people might think that "flow" refers to the functioning (功用) that issues forth from Reality. (I say "some people" because I am not going to cite their names. *Gongyong* 功用 is like saying "powerful functioning" [力用].) Undoubtedly, what they mean ("They" is referring to "some people.") is that Reality is independent and that because functioning issues forth from Reality, Reality itself is not function. In other words, Reality itself is not flowing. If this claim were deemed to be correct, then Reality would be no different from a creator—how could there be such delusion?!
[p. 108]

What I mean by "the flow of Reality" has always been that it is precisely Reality that is this flow. (Take note of this.) It is analogous to how it is precisely the ocean that is the numerous leaping wave forms (相). (*Xiang* 相 is to be read as the *xiang* 相 of *xiangzhuang* 相狀 [form; shape]. The ocean is an analogy for Reality. The numerous wave forms are an analogy for function. Because Reality's transforming into countless functions is just like the glistening of a myriad images, therefore it is compared to numerous wave forms.) If, failing to understand this, one were to seek for Reality beyond the flow, this would be like seeking for the ocean beyond the numerous leaping waves. Unless one was terribly stupid, things should not come to such a pass.

Contraction and expansion

What are contraction and expansion? Reality's transforming into function is definitely not a matter of singularity (單純) (*Dan* 單 is like "solitary" [獨]. *Chun* 純 is "pure" [純一], is without that to which it stands in opposition [相反].); there must be both aspects of contraction and expansion so that transformation is accomplished through their mutual opposition. As contraction moves it condenses, as expansion moves it ascends (升). (*Sheng* 升 has many meanings; broadly speaking, there are two: "to open up" [開發] and "to ascend" [向上].) Contraction is *zhi* 質, is *wu* 物; expansion is *jing* 精, is *shen* 神. ([From time to time,] I break both *jingshen* 精神 and *wuzhi* 物質 in two; it all depends on where the context makes it convenient to do so.) Reality transforms into function. That is, within this function there are already two opposing incipient tendencies (幾), which then give rise to contraction and expansion, the two aspects of evident differentiation. (*Ji* 幾: the subtlest of movement. They move from the subtle to the evident.) From this the myriad transformations [proceed] inexhaustibly. (*Yin* and *yang* having been differentiated, this animates the myriad transformations and so there is no exhaustion.) Contraction becomes only [material] things. The shape of each thing is different, just as the myriad things before us are spread out (散) as discrete entities (殊). (*San* 散: because all things are apart from one another. *Shu* 殊: because all things differ from one another.) Through the operation (運) of the supreme "pure and spirit-like" (至精) (*Zhi* 至 is a term of exaltation. *Jing* 精 is an abbreviation of *jingshen* 精神. The pure and spirit-like can be said to be a kind of special power. The reason that the *Book of Change* does not refer to it as a power but rather calls it "pure and spirit-like"[11] is because its powerful function is so immense that it cannot be measured, so sublime that it is difficult to describe, [and hence] cannot be named a power. *Yun* 運 has two meanings: "to operate" [運行] and "to function" [運用].) expansion pervasively penetrates all things, pervasively includes (遍包) all things, and even though it has no fixed locus there is nowhere it is not. Thus, whereas as matter becomes differentiated it multiplies, the pure and spirit-like is indivisible (渾然) and cannot be differentiated (*Hunran* 渾然 means it cannot be dissected.) As matter spreads out as discrete entities, there is none in which the pure and spirit-like does not pervasively operate (運). (*Yun* 運: see above.) That which Master Hui [Hui Shi 惠施] called "the largest one"[12] was named (目) with reference to the pure and spirit-like. (*Mu* 目 is like "to name" [名].) The pure and spirit-like pervasively penetrates all [material] things, pervasively includes all [material] things, and even though it has no fixed locus there is nowhere it is not. (Someone asked: "How do you explain 'pervasively includes . . . '?" I replied: "*Bian* 遍 means 'pervading everywhere' [普遍]; *bao* 包 means 'to contain' [包含]. The pure and spirit-like permeates the great

---

[11] Xiong provides an explanation for this claim below.
[12] "Tianxia," *Zhuangzi*, p. 1102.

[p. 109]

cosmos, and all dispersed, discrete material entities are contained within it—hence 'pervasively includes.'") Hence, although the material world appears to be dispersed as discrete entities, in fact the powerful function of the supreme pure and spirit-like (至精) pervasively operates within those dispersed discrete material entities, which are controlled by it. (For *zhijing* 至精 see the explanation above.) Ultimately, the material world is not [one in which material things] are apart from one another—scholars must deeply fathom the purport of this! Take the case of organisms—a small animal is actually connected with nature (大自然) as one body, and certainly does not live in isolation. A green leaf absorbs sunlight, air, [nutrients from the] soil and so on—it too does not live alone separated from nature. Take the case of celestial phenomena—the countless heavenly bodies in space also support one another and so constitute a whole; it is actually not the case that each one is independent. Although scholars are able to talk about such principles, nevertheless they are able only to say that all things are interconnected as a whole. Today's scholars affirm only that there is matter and do not acknowledge that there is the pure and spirit-like. As such, the whole that they refer to ultimately lacks generative vitality.

I must truly be dim-witted for stubbornly wanting to hold on to the teachings of the wise men of the past. The Qian hexagram of the *Book of Change* first of all elucidates the meaning of "six dragons control heaven" (六龍御天).[13] The six dragons are the image (象) of Qian-Yang (乾陽) (*Xiang* 象 is like "metaphor." Six dragons: the six lines of the Qian hexagram are all *yang* lines, hence it is said "six dragons." In ancient times, the dragon was deemed to be an extremely dynamic creature, and so the dragon served as a metaphor for Qian-Yang. <Qian is also called Yang; here I use Qian-Yang as a compound term.> The *Book of Change* takes Qian-Yang to be the pure and spirit-like. Yao Xin 姚信 stated: "Qian is called the pure [and spirit-like] (乾稱精).[14] <The "Jingji zhi" 經籍志 (Treatise on Bibliography) in *Sui shu* 隋書 (Book of Sui) lists the title, *Jiu jia Yi jie* 九家易解 [Nine Commentaries on the *Book of Change*], which collects nine commentators' explanations of the *Book of Change*: Xun Shuang 荀爽 [128–190], Jing Fang 京房 [77–37 BCE], Ma Rong 馬融 [79–166], Zheng Xuan 鄭玄 [127–200], Song Zhong 宋衷 [fl. early third century], Yu Fan 虞翻 [164–233], Lu Ji 陸績 [188–219], Yao Xin, and Di Zixuan 翟子玄 [d. u.].[15] Accordingly, Yao Xin was

---

[13] "Commentary on the Judgments" to the Qian hexagram, *Zhou yi*, 1.16a.

[14] On Yao Xin, see note 4 in this chapter. This passage is cited in Li Dingzuo 李鼎祚 (active in the Tang dynasty), *Zhou yi jijie* 周易集解 (Collected Explanations of the *Book of Change*), 15.18b, *Qinding Siku quanshu*, but rather than 乾稱精, Li gives 陽稱精.

[15] "Jingji zhi, shang" 經籍志上 (Treatise on Bibliography, A), in Wei Zheng 魏徵 (580–643) et al., comps., *Sui shu* (Beijing: Zhonghua shuju, 1973), p. 909, simply lists the following title: *Zhou yi Xun*

undoubtedly a leading authority on the ancient *Book of Change*. *Jing* 精 is an abbreviation of *jingshen* 精神. The *Book of Change* took Qian-Yang to be the pure and spirit-like and Kun-Yin 坤陰 to be matter. Here Yao Xin was simply passing on the ancient meaning of the *Book of Change*.> In this treatise, I take expansion to be the pure and spirit-like. What I mean by expansion is just like Qian-Yang of the *Book of Change*. *Yu tian* 御天: *yu* means "to control"; *tian* means "the various heavenly bodies in space." This is saying that the powerful function of Qian-Yang controls the various heavenly bodies. I also note that "heavenly bodies" includes all of the myriad things. "Six dragons control heaven" is undoubtedly saying that Qian-Yang pervasively operates within those dispersed discrete material entities and controls them.) Qian-Yang is the name of the pure and spirit-like. The pure and spirit-like pervades all those dispersed discrete entities, which are controlled by it, just as the mind is the controller of the five viscera and one hundred parts of my body. (As for the pure and spirit-like in my body, it is also called "mind.") The pure and spirit-like and matter were never two entities and cannot be dissected. As Reality transforms into function, within this function differentiation occurs, forming the two aspects of contraction and expansion. Expansion is the pure and spirit-like; contraction is matter. Matter is dispersed discrete [entities] whereas the pure and spirit-like

[p. 110]

is "the largest one" (大一).[16] By mutually opposing, contraction and expansion return to unity, thereby completing the development of "Reality qua whole" (全體). This is why the "Great Commentary" to the *Book of Change* exclaimed that its potency is consummate![17]

In holding the thesis that Reality as a whole becomes differentiated, I actually take the *Book of Change* as my main authority—this thesis is not simply my own conjecture. (Reality is a great whole, which is why it is said, "Reality qua whole.") The *Book of Change* explains (明) that the origin of Qian (乾元)[18] differentiates to become Qian and Kun. (*Ming* 明 means "to explain" [闡明].

Shuang jiu jia zhu, shi juan 周易荀爽九家注十卷 (*Zhou Book of Change* Annotated by Xun Shuang and Eight Other Commentators, in Ten *Juan*) and no further details. These commentators are, however, listed in the preface to Xun Shuang 荀爽 (128–190) (attrib.), *Jiu jia jizhu* 九家集注 (Collected Commentaries [on the *Book of Change*] of Nine Commentators), no longer extant, as cited in a note by Lu Deming 陸德明 (556–627), *Jingdian shiwen* 經典釋文 (Explanations of the Texts of the Classics), 1.14b, *Chizao Tang Siku quanshu cuiyao* 摛藻堂四庫全書薈要 (Essentials of *The Complete Collection of the Four Treasuries* from the Chizao Hall) (Taipei: Shijie shuju, 1986–1989).

[16] On "the largest one," see the note 12 in this chapter.

[17] "Xi ci zhuan, shang," 7.12b–13a: The Way "arouses the myriad things but does not share in the worries of the sage. Its consummate potency and its great achievements are supreme." For Xiong, the Way is but another term for Reality.

[18] Qian *yuan* 乾元 is taken from the "Commentary on the Judgments" to the Qian hexagram, 1.18b.

Qian yuan 乾元 means "the origin of Qian." It is not the case that Qian itself is the origin. The origin of Kun is the origin of Qian. It is not the case that Kun has a separate origin. The origin of Qian is also called Taiji [Supreme Pivot]; it is the Reality of Qian and Kun.) Although Qian and Kun are differentiated, in fact they are mutually inclusive. (The Qian hexagram has images of Kun, which show Qian-Yang actively controlling Kun—this is Yang being inclusive of Yin.[19] The Kun hexagram has images of Qian, which show Kun-Yin receiving Qian and moving—this is Yin's being inclusive of Yang.[20]) Qian and Kun cannot be dissected into two entities (They are only the two aspects of function, not a duality.); much less can one arbitrarily select one aspect or the other, such as the conceptual elaborations (戲論) of idealistic monism and material monism. (Idealistic monists exclusively choose the pure and spirit-like for their monism, which amounts to having Qian but no Kun. Material monists exclusively choose matter for their monism, which amounts to having Kun but no Qian.) If there were no opposition in the flow of great transformation (大化之流), then there would be no means for transformation to be accomplished. If it were not extremely complex, then how could it develop? (*Da hua* 大化 is like saying "great function." *Liu* 流: flow [流行]. Qian-Yang and Kun-Yin accomplish transformation through mutual opposition. This can be checked in the *Book of Change*.[21]) It is beyond question that this [is an instance of] the principle of being so of itself (法爾道理). (*Faer daoli* 法爾道理 is seen in Chinese translations of Buddhist texts and is like saying "self-so principle" [自然之理].[22]) In this treatise, my account of the meaning of contraction and expansion is established on the basis of [the meaning of] Qian and Kun in the *Book of Change*. Once the truth of a principle is perceived then there is correspondence between the former and the later. (Correspondence in the understanding shared by later scholars and former wise men.) How could I [possibly dare to propose] my own new standard?!

---

[19] Xiong does not provide an explanation of this claim here, but he does in *Yuan Ru*, pp. 692–693: "Within the Qian hexagram there are images of Kun and within the Kun hexagram there are images of Qian. Anyone with a modicum of knowledge about the images in the *Book of Change* would know this. For example, the 'Commentary on the Judgments' to the Qian hexagram states: 'The clouds move, the rain disperses; the categories of things flow and take form.' (Clouds and rain have form and are both images of Kun. 'To move' and 'to dispense' both mean movement and are images of Qian. This is saying that Qian moves within Kun, and that Kun receives Qian and transforms. Hence, as Qian and Kun flow together the myriad things take form therein. Form is also an image of Kun.)"

[20] Neither here nor in *Yuan Ru* does Xiong provide a similar example to explain "within the Kun hexagram there are images of Qian." In *Yuan Ru*, p. 693, he simply proffers the following recommendation: "If you reflect on it then you will come to understand."

[21] "Xici, shang" 7.28a: "Closing the door is called Kun and opening the door is called Qian. One closing and one opening is called transformation."

[22] See note 150 in Chapter 3.

Addendum. Someone enquired about the following: "With regard to the phrase 'Reality transforms to become (變成) function,' it seems it would be better to change *bian cheng* 變成 to *bian qi* 變起."

I replied: "No, no. If it were rephrased as you have suggested, it would certainly be understood to mean that Reality itself transforms to give rise to a function that acts externally [to Reality]. If this were the case, then Reality would be just like a creator and not itself be function. The reason I use only *bian cheng* and not *bian qi* is so as to avert misunderstanding. You need to understand that as soon as transformation is mentioned, then it is Reality itself that initiates transformation and movement, and the sense of 'giving rise to' is already implicit, obviating the need to repeat it. As for *cheng* 成, it indicates that as Reality initiates transformation, it

[p. 111]

completely transforms itself to become the functions of contraction and expansion. This is analogous to how when the ocean initiates transformation then it completely becomes the numerous turning and leaping waves. Only *cheng* 成 reveals the non-duality of Reality and function—there must be no misunderstanding."

Matter and energy

The scientific analysis of the myriad things categorizes them all as fundamentally being either matter or energy (質力). (Matter [物質] and energy [能力].) [For a long time,] I was always puzzled as to whether matter and energy could be divided in two. Unwilling to make a hasty decision, I remained puzzled by this for several decades. Having no grounding in the natural sciences, I certainly did not dare to indulge in conjecture and casually make a judgment. Drawing from what is near at hand, however, [I made the following observations]. From when I was born, to when I was young and strong, through to being old and infirm, every day I would absorb animal and plant matter (Medicines also mostly contain inorganic matter.), which, having been processed through the stomach's power to digest, are transformed into all kinds of energy. This energy then newly generates my body matter. This is clear proof that matter can transform into energy, and energy can transform into matter. Externally, I drew from other things [to make the following observations]. Water is flowing matter. When heated by the sun it transforms into steam and ascends; that is, it transforms from matter to energy. When it subsequently encounters cold air then it condenses to form raindrops and descends—energy re-transforms into matter. There are countless examples like this. If matter and energy are two things (物), how is that they are able to transform into one another? (Here *wu* 物 is being used as an empty term [虛字][23] and refers to both matter and energy.)

The "Great Commentary" to the *Book of Change* states: "By being firm and focused, Kun [becomes] energy" (坤以簡能).[24] (*Jian* 簡: firm and focused. These are qualities of Kun.) It also states: "Kun transforms to become matter" (坤化成物).[25] Take note that what the "Great Commentary" calls *wu* 物 is an abbreviation of *wuzhi* 物質 (matter), and what it calls *neng* 能 is an abbreviation of *nengli* 能力 (energy). Thus, the *Book of Change* took Kun to be matter and energy (坤為質力). ("[Took] Kun to be matter and energy" means that Kun is [即是] matter and energy. This is simply different terms for the same reality. Qian's being [為] the pure and spirit-like is the same.[26]) Thus, it is patently evident that the *Book of Change* maintained that matter and energy are not two things. When I checked the *Apocrypha to the Book of Change*, there is a passage that states: "The Grand Primordium is the genesis of *qi* (太初氣之始也)." In his commentary, Zheng Xuan glosses *qi* 氣 as *yuan qi* 元氣 (primal *qi*).[27] (*Tai* 太: great [大]; *chu* 初 is like "beginning" [始]. This is saying that primal *qi* is the beginning [始基; *arche*] of the material cosmos.) Extrapolating the purport of Zheng Xuan's gloss, undoubtedly it is primal *qi* that is Kun, and so to show its respect for Kun, this apocryphal writing called it "Grand Primordium." Zheng Xuan lived in the Eastern Han period [25–220 CE] and was still [able to] inherit the surviving teachings of the western capital.[28] The western capital[29] was still not far [removed in time from the period of] the six states,[30] and there were many surviving [works written by] the students of the seventy masters[31] who transmitted the doctrines of the *Book of Change*. There must have been a source for Zheng Xuan's gloss. It is a pity that since the Han period, those

---

[23] In Chinese grammar "empty term" refers to function words, words with a purely grammatical function, such as prepositions, conjunctions, auxiliary words, and interjections. Xiong is using "empty term" simply to mean that "things" is not to be taken literally.

[24] See note 8 in this chapter.

[25] See note 4 in this chapter.

[26] Xiong's point is that the use of *wei* 為 in this sentence has the same meaning as *ji shi* 即是.

[27] See *Yi wei: Qian zuodu*, A.5b. The original text reads 太初者氣之始也.

[28] Chang'an 長安, the capital of the Western Han (202 BCE–9 CE).

[29] That is, the Western Han period.

[30] This is a loose reference to the Warring States Period (475–221 BCE). The six states refer to the six warring states apart from Qin 秦: Qi 齊, Chu 楚, Yan 燕, Han 韓, Zhao 趙, Wei 魏. In 264 BCE, Qin first conquered Qi, and, in the following decades, it conquered the other five states.

[31] A reference to Confucius' "seventy" disciples.

who have worked on the *Book of Change* have not sought for the correct interpretation of the word *qi* 氣 and have discussed it only vaguely. (The word *qi* 氣 referred to here is not the *qi* of *kongqi* 空氣 [air] or *fengqi* 風氣 [ethos/mores] and [p. 112] other such meanings of the word.) What I call *qi* 氣 is a descriptive term. It is only because matter and energy lightly flow that I therefore describe them as *qi*. (*Qi* is a descriptive term for matter and energy; it is also another term for matter and energy.) The "Great Commentary" states: "By being firm and focused, Kun [becomes] energy." Undoubtedly this is saying that due to its qualities of being firm and focused, Kun is able to become energy, that Kun itself is energy. [The "Great Commentary" also] states: "Kun transforms to become matter"; that is, Kun itself is matter. Is it likely that primal *qi* existed before matter and energy? Can it be said that Kun is primal *qi*? According to the "Great Commentary," *qi* is matter and energy—can this view be abandoned? The meaning of the term *qi*, as used by people in ancient times, was very vague and must be inspected and corrected. For this reason, in taking primal *qi* to be another term for matter and energy, I have effectively remained faithful to the "Great Commentary." Ancient Yin-Yang specialists (The forebears of astronomers.) inferred that at the very beginning of the cosmos primal *qi* had not yet differentiated and was nothing but hazy vastness (濛鴻). Not yet having differentiated, none of the stars, clouds, or heavenly bodies had yet condensed and formed, hence "hazy vastness." (*Meng* 濛: nothing can be distinguished. *Hong* 鴻 is like "large." Hazy and indistinguishable—the image of a vast wasteland. [For a description of] primal *qi* before it has yet to be differentiated, see *Chunqiu ming li xu* 春秋命歷序 [(Apocryphon to the *Spring and Autumn Annals*: Enumerating the Sequence of Mandated Terms of Rule].[32]) At that time, there was only inchoate matter and energy, lightly flowing, dispersed throughout space. This is how the name "primal *qi*" came about. (Someone inquired about the following: "Energy is definitely not something that is coarse and heavy but rather can be said to be lightly flowing. There should, however, be a difference between matter and energy." I replied: "Your enquiry simply conceives of matter and energy as two things. In fact, matter and energy are not two things and cannot be split apart. When astronomers enquire into the beginning of the cosmos, before the stars, clouds, and various heavenly [bodies] had coalesced and formed, when was matter ever something coarse and heavy? How could it be said that it was not light? At that time, space was a diffuse, vast

---

[32] Xiong is presumably referring to the following passage: "The unseen stem has no form, hazy vastness portending, murky and opaque." (冥莖無形, 蒙鴻萌兆, 渾渾混混。) Cited in Xiao Tong 蕭統 (501–531) et al., comps., Li Shan 李善 (630–689), annot., *Liu chen zhu wenxuan* 六臣註文選 (Selections of Refined Literature Annotated by Six Scholar-Officials), 12.15b, *Sibu congkan chubian*.

wasteland, where not even a single thing ever existed, and where even energy had no concentrated locus. Not being concentrated, energy was light and subtle. You must understand that matter and energy have always been light and flowing. When they coalesced to form the various large things in Heaven and Earth, they never altered their light and flowing self-nature. This is analogous to water's being a liquid thing—when it coalesces to form hard ice, when did it ever change its self-nature of liquidity? Why do you doubt what I say?")

Later, as matter and energy developed, [the characteristics of differentiation] and the myriad things were formed, and the cosmos no longer was an image of hazy vastness. That which in ancient times was called "primal *qi*" can be taken only to be another name for matter and energy, and it is actually not the case that there was primal *qi* before matter and energy. Matter and energy were never two things, yet the agency and impetus of each aspect are markedly different. The matter aspect has an impetus that hastens toward solidification; the energy aspect quickly [advances] via the agency of diffusion. When energy vigorously swirls,[33] it assists in the solidification of matter. (It is like when incense and joss paper are burned, if they are swirled with vigorous energy, then a fire-wheel will appear. Having been assisted by the energy of the vigorous swirling, this fire-wheel is firelight that has coalesced into the image of a wheel. From this example it can be understood that matter condenses and contracts to become things, and this condensing and contracting needs to rely on

[p. 113]

the vigorous energy of swirling.) If energy is excessively diffused, then matter will gradually disappear. (If the internal energy of a thing has been excessively diffused then that thing must cease to exist—this is so for all things.) The two aspects mutually oppose and mutually complete. (The solidification of matter and the diffusion of energy have always been in mutual opposition. Mutual opposition, however, is precisely what is required for mutual assistance, and so the myriad things are formed.) This is how the myriad things come to be profusely and multifariously differentiated, surging, as moment by moment the old is abandoned and the new arises, never ending. In the teachings of China's ancient *Book of Change*, matter and energy are not deemed to be two things, nor does the *Book of Change* acknowledge that matter has an obstructive (對礙) nature. (For the term *duiai* 對礙, see Buddhist texts. There is a common belief among ordinary people that all [physical] things have material substance. [They maintain that] examples such as being able to be seen with the eyes and touched with the hand can prove that matter has a

---

[33] Amending *fa* 發 to *xuan* 旋 on the basis of a comment made by Xiong in "Da Ren Shuyong xiangsheng," appended to *Ming xin pian*, p. 311.

robust obstructive nature. And because matter is obstructive, one thing and another thing cannot both be contained in the same locus. This is to be obstructive and is why ordinary people firmly believe that matter has an obstructive nature. *Book of Change* specialists, however, maintain that the inherent nature of matter has always been unceasing transformation and movement. After it has become particular things, even though it seems to be obstructive, crucially that is not how it inherently is. Each hexagram in the *Book of Change* consists of six lines. These lines elucidate the unceasing transformation and movement of the myriad things. If it were said that all things inherently have an obstructive nature, then what transformation and change would there be to speak of? When the sage created the *Book of Change*, his investigation of things was profound.) Because matter does not have an obstructive nature, this further suffices to evidence that matter and energy have always been non-dual.

[**Addendum.**] The "Great Commentary" to the *Book of Change* states: "Transformation and movement do not abide."[34] "Do not abide" is key; it means "not stopping even temporarily." Unless someone has a profound understanding of the meaning of [instant] by instant of arising [and ceasing] then it would be difficult to have a discussion with them about this. In his commentary to the second line of the Qian hexagram in the *Book of Change*, "When a dragon appears in the fields (見龍在田)," the Qing dynasty Confucian scholar, Yao Peizhong, noted: "*Zai* 在: to be there temporarily."[35] In the whole of his commentary on the *Book of Change*, only these few words are of value.[36] From the past until now it has been rare for any of the many Confucian scholars to have understood this point. I will say it again: instant by instant the myriad things abandon the old and give rise to the new. What Mr Yao meant by "to be there temporarily" is that it is only for the interval of an instant that they arise.

The "Commentary on the Judgments" (彖) to the Kun hexagram (*Tuan* 彖: settle/decide [斷]. To decide on [斷定] the meaning of a hexagram.) states: "The mare belongs to the category of Earth and so moves across the Earth without restriction."[37] The hexagram statements and line statements in the *Book of Change* both draw on images (象) to elucidate (顯) principles. (*Xian* 顯

---

[34] "Xici, xia," 8.18b.
[35] Yao Peizhong, *Zhou yi Yao shi xue*, 1.4a.
[36] See also Xiong's earlier criticisms of Yao in Chapter 1, p. 48.
[37] Translated on the basis of Xiong's following comments.

is like "to explain it" [說明之也]; *xiang* 象 is like "metaphor" [喻].)[38] The first two hexagrams established in the *Book of Change* are Qian and Kun. As for why Qian is deemed to be *yang* in nature and Kun is deemed to be *yin* in nature, that is a matter for a separate discussion. As for ordinary people's use of *yin* and *yang* to distinguish various categories of things, because Earth is below Heaven, it belongs to the category of *yin*. Female horses also belong to *yin* and so it is said that mares

[p. 114]

are of the same category as Earth. "Moves across the Earth without restriction (疆)": According to *Shuowen jiezi* 說文解字 (Explaining Simple and Analyzing Compound Characters), *jiang* 疆 was originally written as 畺, which means "boundary" (界).[39] "Boundary" means "restriction." Horses are strong and powerful, move with utmost vigor, and have no restrictions, hence "no restriction."

Someone asked: "In explaining (明) Kun (*Ming* 明: to explain.) the Kun hexagram employs the two images of a mare and the Earth. What do they signify?"

I replied: "The reason it employs the images of a mare and the Earth is because mares belong to the *yin* category and so this serves to explain that Kun is *yin* in nature. Because they are powerful and strong, horses are employed as the image of Kun, which serves to explain that Kun is energy. The reason it employs the image of the Earth is no doubt because the Earth has material substance, and so employing the Earth as the image of Kun serves to explain that Kun is matter. The 'Commentary on the Judgments' to the Kun hexagram shows that 'the itself' of Kun (坤的自身) is nothing but an aggregation of matter and energy. The 'Great Commentary' states: 'By being firm and focused, Kun [becomes] energy (能)' (*Neng* 能: energy [能力].) and 'Kun transforms to become matter (物).' (*Wu* 物: matter [物質]. These two sentences show that Kun is both energy and matter, and matter and energy cannot be severed in two.) Both sentences are issued in accord with the 'Commentary on the Judgments' and [hence] both commentaries can [be seen to] verify one another."

Someone asked: "What does 'Moves across the Earth without restriction' mean?"

I replied: "I have already talked about how horses are taken as the image of energy and the Earth is taken as the image of matter. Because the mare and

---

[38] I have moved the closing bracket from after the character *ye* 也 to after the character *yu* 喻.
[39] See, for example, https://www.zdic.net/hans/畺.

the Earth are the same category, this intimates (隱示) that matter and energy are not different in nature, are not two different entities. (*Yinshi* 隱示: matter and energy are not explicitly referred to but only indicated [示] using images, hence *yin* 隱 [concealed].) 'Moves across the Earth without restriction,' [is explained as follows.] Because the image of horses moving across the Earth intimates that energy is contained within matter, and if this energy is activated and issues forth it is able to modify matter's occlusion, just like the vigorous movement of a horse is unable to be restricted, therefore it is said 'without restriction.' Further, just as energy issues forth with sudden intensity and its awesome power is at its peak, and whatever confronts it is destroyed, so too this is like war horses moving across the battlefield, carrying all before them. Hence, if people skillfully control and utilize energy, which is self-so (自然), in accord with the great and proper Way, then they will create their own good fortune, but if they employ it in the absence of [the proper] Way, then humanity will destroy itself."

In this treatise I employ [the insight that] "it is by means of contraction and expansion that transformation is accomplished" to explain where the myriad images of the cosmos originate. What I refer to as contraction actually follows [the account of] Kun in the *Great Change*: contraction is both energy and matter. Take the small knife on my table. If we investigate how it came to be formed, then [we will discover] that it also was formed through contraction's coalescing [impetus]. (The "Great Commentary" states: "Kun transforms to become matter." Note: Kun in the *Book of Change* is actually what, in this treatise, I refer to as the great flowing aspect [of function] that is contraction. Contraction is nothing other than the reconciliation of the antagonism [冲和] between matter and energy's giving rise to [p. 115]

a kind of condensing function, hence the name "contraction." Through contraction things are formed. *Chong he* 冲和: *chong* 冲 is interchangeable with *chong* 衝 [conflict]; "mutual antagonism" [相忌] is called *chong*. Matter is suited to condensing and energy maintains diffusion. This is the mutual antagonism of the agencies of the two aspects. Eventually, however, both revert to harmonious coalescence because their mutual antagonism is able to be reconciled, and because they are reconciled, things are formed.) This small knife is short and thin in shape and has power that is useful in cutting. The power that is useful in cutting is energy. The short and thin shape is matter. It is obvious that matter and energy have always been non-dual. Fathoming principle through things [can be undertaken with things] that are as close as those in front of you. This is hardly a baseless theory in which I give license to subjective conceptualization.

Addendum. In the Qing dynasty, the first translated writings on physics (格致) that I read were all pamphlets (In the Qing dynasty, physics [物理學] was called *gezhixue* 格致學[40] and drew its meaning from the phrase "to extend knowledge through the investigation of things" [格物致知] in the *Great Learning* [大學)].[41]) and through them I learned a little about accounts of matter and energy. At the time, the following question occurred to me. Is it the case that although matter and energy are naturally distinct from one another, they nevertheless influence one another, or is it the case that a thing contains two agencies that are mutually antagonistic? (Here the word "thing" is being used figuratively; it implicitly refers to contraction.) Before long, I took part in revolution[42] and, for a few years, gave up my studies. Later, I devoted myself exclusively to studying Chinese philosophy, and again pursued this question. Beginning with the ancient books and proceeding through to the various schools of the Han and Song periods [I discovered] that none had addressed this question. I put a lot of effort into [studying] Buddhism's Great Vehicle [Mahāyāna], but it proved to be even less relevant. Only when I had left Buddhist teachings to return to the *Great Change*, deeply pondering the ocean of meaning (義海) of expansion and contraction (Their meaning is extremely profound and vast, and so the metaphor of an ocean is used.) did I first affirm that matter and energy are not two things. Although my learning is limited, nevertheless for several decades I have reflected on this, and my understanding has led me to take the *Great Change* alone as my authority. (Someone asked: "Sir, why is it that in your writings you often refer to both the mental and the material [心物] or to the pure and spirit-like and matter [神質], but you rarely mention the word 'energy'"? I replied: "If one has perceived that matter and energy are inherently non-dual, then when the material or matter is referred to, this already includes energy within it.")

---

[40] *Gezhi* 格致 or *gezhixue* was also used to translates "science" (until it was replaced by *kexue/kagaku* 科學, one of many neologisms attributed to Nishi Amane 西周 (1829–1897). Eikoh Shimao dates Nishi's coinage to 1874; see Eikoh Shimao, "Some Aspects of Japanese Science, 1868–1945," *Annals of Science*, 46:1 [1989]: 71, n 4.). On the variety of ways of translating "physics" in late imperial China, see Iwo Amelung, "Naming Physics: The Strife to Delineate a Field of Modern Science in Late Imperial China," in Michael Lackner and Natascha Vittinghoff, eds., *Mapping Meanings: The Field of New Learning in Late Qing China* (Leiden: Brill. 2004), pp. 197–233. Joachim Kurtz cites the example of the missionary Joseph Edkins's (1823–1905) use of the term *gezhi lixue* 格致理學 to translate "physics" in 1886; see Kurtz, *The Discovery of Chinese Logic* (Boston: Brill, 2011), p. 111.

[41] "Daxue," *Liji*, 60.1b: "Those who sought to make their intentions sincere first extended their knowledge, and the extension of knowledge lies on the investigation of things."

[42] See "Foreword," p. 9.

When matter and energy begin harmoniously to coalesce and become things, undoubtedly through differentiation they form immeasurable (無量) small things. (*Wuliang* 無量 has two meanings. [The first is that] because there are numerous small things that cannot be counted therefore they are said to be countless. [The second is that] there are small things that are so extremely minute that there is nothing smaller than them. Are they extremely minute particles? Are they pulsating microwaves? Because, after all, they have no fixed image, they are also called immeasurable. It is because they are difficult to fathom that they are called "immeasurable.") Early records state: "The largest things necessarily arise from the small." (*Han Feizi* has this passage.[43] Undoubtedly, it was taken from

[p. 116]

an ancient saying.) "Small": the beginning [始基; *arche*] of the material cosmos. *Balance as the Norm* states: "What is referred to as small [means that] the whole world [acknowledges that] it cannot be broken apart." (語小, 天下莫能破焉。)[44] (*Yu* 語 is like "to say/speak" [說]. When speaking of a small thing, then it is acknowledged by people everywhere that it cannot be broken apart. *Mo neng po* 莫能破 has two meanings. The first is that the most miniscule of things cannot be further broken apart. If something could be further broken apart, then that thing would still not [be able to] be termed "small." The second is that the small thing constantly arises and ceases, is dynamic and does not abide even momentarily, and certainly is not of a fixed appearance [相] <This character *xiang* 相 is to be read as the *xiang* of *xiangmao* 相貌 [appearance]. In other places [where *xiang* is used] and I have not provided a note, then context should be used to discern the meaning.>, and also cannot be broken down.) I maintain that it is only those who have attained the utmost precision in the technique of investigating things are able to probe deeply into the small in their observation of things. The Fu 復 (Return) hexagram in the *Great Change* was the first [source] to elucidate the technique for discerning the small in things. (See the "Wai wang" 外王 [External Kingliness] chapter of *To the Origin of the Ru*.[45])

---

[43] "Yu Lao" 喻老 (Illustrating Laozi), Han Fei 韓非 (d. 233 BCE), *Han Feizi* 韓非子 (Master Han Fei), 7.2a, *Sibu congkan chubian*: "In the category of [things] that have form, the large necessarily arise from the small." (有形之類，大必起於小。)

[44] Translated on the basis of Xiong's gloss. Cf. Chapter 1, p. 23: "These are what the *Zhongyong* 中庸 (Balance as the Norm) explains as being 'so small that they cannot be broken apart' (小莫能破), and what Master Hui [Hui Shi 惠施] called 'the smallest ones' (小一). (Each single particle can be said to be a small unit in the constitution of a large object, hence they are called smallest ones.) This is how the material cosmos began."

[45] *Yuan Ru*, p. 464: "'The Fu hexagram shows that it is the small that is to be distinguished in things.' (See "Great Commentary, Part B," *zhang* 7.*) Note: The Fu hexagram consists of a solitary *yang* line below a group of *yin* lines,** and so is said to be small. (Of the six lines of the Fu hexagram, the first line is a *yang* line, and all five lines from the second line and above are *yin* lines. Hence, the solitary *yang* line at the bottom has the image of being small.) . . . Hence, in the case of the Fu hexagram, the sage particularly

It is regrettable that [the authentic versions of] the classics and their commentaries were lost and can no longer be examined. Hui Shi's theory of "the smallest ones" (小一) was undoubtedly based on Confucian learning, but being embellished with his own ideas it should not be deemed to lack originality. (*Xiao yi* 小一 is what *Balance as the Norm* refers to as "small." Because the Confucians' account preceded this, we know that Master Hui posited his thesis on the basis of the Confucians' account. Master Hui had a detailed understanding of the principles of things [物理] and so his explanation of "the smallest ones" must have had some new findings.) It is especially regrettable that Zhuangzi did not provide a description of Master Hui's theory. (The Confucians were the first to talk about the "small" and so must have had a detailed explanation of its meaning. Unfortunately, the commentaries disappeared, and Master Hui's writings were also lost. People in modern times say that [ancient] India had theories about atoms [極微論], which were the origin [權輿] of [modern] accounts of atoms [元子] and electrons, and that from ancient times onward China alone never had such a theory. <The *Erya* 爾雅 (Approaching Refinement) glossary states that *quanyu* 權輿 means "beginning" [始].[46]> Little do they realize that although it was never planned that what the Confucians referred to as "small" and what Master Hui referred to as "the smallest ones" should correspond with the theory of atoms, nevertheless, from far away, the different methods they employed had the distinction of tallying with that theory. Clear passages of text suffice to confirm this, why not examine this issue yourself?)

The two referents of "the smallest ones"

Someone asked: "What is the referent of the term 'the smallest ones'?"

I replied: "Master Hui undoubtedly took each and every small thing that constitutes a large thing to be an independent thing (This is analogous to a brick,

---

highlighted the method of the learning concerned with the investigation of things (格物學),*** saying that 'it is the small that is to be distinguished in things.' Distinguishing the small is the method of analysis. The principles of things (物理) are extremely profuse, and if they are not analyzed then it is difficult to probe the differences in what they share in common and what is the same among their differences. The principles of things are indistinct and slight, making them difficult to fathom; unless they are analyzed then no-one will be able to move from the exterior into the interior, from the coarse to the refined." *"Xici, xia," 8.17b. **☷ *** N.B. *Gewuxue* was one of the terms used to translate "physics" in the nineteenth century. See, for example, Iwo Amelung, "Naming Physics," p. 389, n. 30.

[46] *Er ya zhuzi suoyin* 爾雅逐字索引 (Concordance to *Erya*), D. C. Lau (Liu Dianjue 劉殿爵), et al. eds. (Hong Kong: Shangwu yinshuguan, 1995), 1.1/1/3.

a tile, and a piece of timber each being an independent thing, which [collectively] constitute a large building.) and that is why he called them the 'smallest ones.'"

On the basis of the *Book of Change*, I have deduced that, broadly speaking, "the smallest ones" has two referents.

1. Instant by instant (剎那剎那), "the smallest ones" suddenly arise individually (別別); dynamic, none abides even temporarily. (*Chana* 剎那 is reduplicated so as to refer collectively to a continuous succession of countless instants; it does not refer exclusively to the duration of one instant. *Biebie* 別別: at every instant each of "the smallest ones" separately suddenly arises. This is because it is not the case that "the smallest ones" of the preceding instant are able to extend to the subsequent instant. Someone asked: "Given that the 'smallest ones' of the preceding and the subsequent instant each separately suddenly arises, does this mean that between the preceding and subsequent instants must be empty and that there is nothing there?" I replied: "Just as 'the smallest ones' of the previous instant have ceased, 'the smallest ones' of the subsequent instant tightly follow, arising anew—what gap is there? It is like the way

[p. 117]

your body instant by instant abandons the old and generates the new. At the moments that new replaced the old, were you ever aware of any gap in between?")

The significance of the *Book of Change*'s six lines is to explain the unceasing (不居) transformation and movement of the myriad things. (The meaning of *bu ju* 不居 is extremely profound: instant by instant there is no abiding, even temporarily.) This discovery was made possible only by looking up to observe [the configurations of Heaven] and looking down to examine [the patterns of Earth], personally investigating things (體物) in the minutest detail. (The *ti* of *ti wu* 體物 means "personally investigate" [體察].) This is not something that a crude understanding is able to catch a glimpse of. The Confucians' and Master Hui's theory about "the smallest ones" would have been based on the *Great Change*. Based on its meaning in the *Great Change*, I affirm that "the smallest ones" are things (物) that unceasingly transform and change (Here the word *wu* 物 is used figuratively; it implicitly refers to the preceding "the smallest ones.") and most definitely this is not a case of me imposing my own subjective interpretation. The *Book of Change* is fully available, and its great meaning is patently evident.

Someone asked: "Sir, according to what you have said, 'the smallest ones' are nothing but energy—was matter never involved?"

I replied: "No, no. As I have said many times, energy and matter are inherently one thing (物) and cannot be dissected into two. (Here the word "*wu* 物" is used figuratively; it implicitly refers to matter and energy.) That which unceasingly transforms and changes is certainly energy, yet it is not the case that there is no matter. If there were never any matter but only energy, how could energy by itself be able to become things that are obstructive? It has always been the case that when scholars probe into the beginning of the myriad things they like to maintain a one-sided perspective. This is a great mistake. (Take the case of idealistic monists. They maintain that matter is a manifestation of the pure and spirit-like, and that energy is also based on the pure and spirit-like. This is to maintain a one-sided [perspective]. As for material monists, they maintain that the pure and spirit-like is the effect of matter or a form of matter's development. This also is to maintain a one-sided [perspective].) The myriad things are formed from the harmonious coalescence of matter and energy. This truth is obvious, and the unbridled proliferation of contrary views cannot be allowed. As undifferentiated matter and energy, 'the smallest ones' are, of course, lively and dynamic things (物). (Here the word "*wu* 物" is used figuratively; it implicitly refers to "the smallest ones.") If one were to speculate that "the smallest ones" are exclusively the manifestation of energy, and that they have always been devoid of matter, then this would be a mistake of one's own making. And although it was never the case that the 'the smallest ones' are devoid of matter, one cannot mistakenly presume that matter has a fixed obstructive nature. I maintain that matter lightly flows, and that together with energy is undifferentiated as one. I am confident that I am not mistaken."

Addendum. When people in the past talked of the six lines of a hexagram they also called them the "six positions" (六位). Actually, although the second to the fifth of the six lines were distinguished as being either in the correct position or not in the correct position, in all cases, the main consideration was given to what was appropriate in terms of human affairs and it was simply for purposes of expedience that a line was said to be in the correct position or not. We can know that the six lines actually did not have fixed positions because the first and sixth lines had no sense of position [attributed to them].[47] The "Great Commentary" to the *Book of Change* states: "The lines imitate (效)

---

[47] See Wang Bi's 王弼 (226–249) discussion of why the notion of appropriate position was not applied to the first and sixth lines but it was applied to the other lines, in his "*Zhou yi* lüeli" 周易略例 (General Remarks on the *Zhou Book of Change*); translated in Richard John Lynn, *The Classic of Changes*, pp. 33–34.

[p. 118]

actions in the world."[48] *Xiao* 效 is like "imitate" (倣). Having investigated the incessant transformation and movement of the myriad things, [the reason that] the six lines were established in imitation of that transformation and movement was so that scholars would ponder the six lines and so come to understand the principles [of transformation and movement]. Why can it be said that the six lines are six positions? Position is spatial. Space is the form in which the myriad things exist. If we talk specifically in terms of everyday experience, then we can affirm that the existence of the myriad things has position that can be referred to.[49] If one wanted to investigate exhaustively the arcane aspects of the principles involved, then that is best left for a separate discussion. The *Great Change* originally used the six lines to show the incessant transformation and movement of the myriad things, and these lines cannot be said to have [fixed] positions.

2. How can "the smallest ones" be collected together to form large things? The [attached exegetical] traditions and commentaries on the Six Classics were either lost or are incomplete and cannot be examined. (Sima Tan said that the scriptures and [attached exegetical] traditions of the six disciplines number to the thousands and ten-thousands.[50] By the time of the Western Han, however, they had already been completely lost or were incomplete.) Hui [Shi's] book was not transmitted either. Extrapolating on the basis of the principle of "things are divided according to group" (物以群分) in the "Great Commentary" to the *Book of Change*,[51] however, its broad outlines can still be traced. At the Grand Primordium stage of the cosmos, matter and energy were undifferentiated, drifting and scattered throughout space. This can be referred to as [the period] before primal *qi* (元氣) had yet been differentiated. Although this was conjecture on the part of ancient astronomers, the key elements of what they said is of course close to the truth of the matter, and they should not be criticized. When matter and energy coalesced and underwent differentiation to form the innumerable "smallest ones," this marked the beginning of their being things. Given, however, that all of these "smallest ones" were scattered throughout space, each solitary and unconnected with others, then although

---

[48] "Xici, xia," 8.8b.
[49] In other words, human existence has spatial dimensions that define it, such as bodily form, physical location, movement, and so forth.
[50] See "Superfluous Words," p. 5.
[51] "Xici, shang," 7.2b.

they were numerous, ultimately, they were unable to gather together to form large things, and so there was really little difference from that of the [state of] hazy vastness at the Grand Primordium [stage of the cosmos]. Having meticulously investigated the matter of how the cosmos came to be, I am deeply intrigued by the principle of "things are divided according to group." Things must group together otherwise they would be unable to cluster (和集) to form large things. (*Heji* 和集 is explained in the opening section of this chapter; it is worth re-reading.) Having grouped together there must be divisions, otherwise that which fills space would be merely an undifferentiated mass (一合相) devoid of the myriad particulars. (*Yi he xiang* 一合相 is a term borrowed from the Chinese translation of the *Diamond Sutra*, but its meaning here is not necessarily the same as its meaning in that text.[52] Here the term means a huge thing that is a singular mass devoid of any differentiation; clod-like, it cannot be distinguished, and so it is called "an undifferentiated mass.") As such, if there were no transformation and movement, no production and reproduction, what sort of cosmos would that be? For this reason, things must group together, and having grouped together there must be divisions. These two principles are so immense that nothing lies outside them (None of the myriad things lies outside of these two principles and is still able to be a thing.); profound and far-reaching, they are supreme. (Everyone takes the two principles of grouping and dividing as plain and unexceptional, when actually the utterly profound and the utterly far-reaching lies precisely within the utterly plain and utterly insipid. Those of shallow understanding fail to be aware of this.)

[p. 119]

Someone asked: "What do the two principles of group and division mean (云何)?" (*Yun he* 云何: to ask how these principles should be explained.)

I replied: "Innumerable 'smallest ones' are scattered throughout the six enclosures (六合). If several of the 'smallest ones' cluster together in a given locale such that they form a homogeneous, harmonious system, then this is called a group. (*Liu he* 六合 means north, south, east, west, above, and below. Although it refers to space, talking about the "six enclosures" better enables one to talk figuratively about such and such a locale within the six enclosures. The reason I say only "several" is

---

[52] *Jin'gang bore boluomi jing*, T235.8, 752b12–14. In his translation of the relevant passage, A. Charles Muller translates *yi he xiang* 一合相 as "composites: "World-honored One, that which the Tathāgata calls 'all the worlds in three thousand galaxies' are actually not worlds. Therefore, they are called worlds. Why? To the extent that these worlds really exist, they do so as composites. The Tathāgata teaches that composites are not composites. Therefore, they are called composites." "Subhūti, a composite is something that is ineffable. Only immature beings attach to such phenomena." See http://www.acmuller.net/bud-canon/diamond_sutra.html under "30. The status of composite things" [T 235.8.752b06]."

because it is difficult to conjecture just what a definite number might be. Each of these countless "smallest ones" is an independent micro-entity. When they cluster to form a homogeneous, harmonious system, this is the clustering of a number of the "smallest ones" to form a new thing. For the interim, I will call this a "grouping of the smallest ones" [小一群].)

Each of these countless 'groupings of the smallest ones' also clustered together, gradually forming a great trichiliocosm (三千大千世界) of the teeming, myriad particulars. ("Great trichiliocosm" is borrowed from Buddhist teachings. Here it is used merely to describe that the [number of] worlds is not one. Nor is it the case that [the number of worlds] is limited to one billion.[53]) The minutest are like tiny particles; the largest are like the heavenly bodies in space. All are formed by the clustering of countless 'groupings of the smallest ones,' hence I said, 'having grouped together there must be divisions.'

The countless 'groupings of the smallest ones' that are scattered throughout the six enclosures separately cluster to form all things with their assorted different modes and properties—how is that they avoid becoming inchoate and undifferentiated? The reason for this is, of course, difficult to fathom. Most probably, in the case of a minority of the 'groupings of the smallest ones,' when they cluster together, they are unable to form large things. As for the majority of the 'groupings of the smallest ones,' when they cluster together, simply as a matter of course they become the largest things. When things are formed from the clustering of several 'groupings of the smallest ones,' of course their structure or arrangement cannot all be consistent, and so their assorted modes and properties cannot all be the same. Here I will stop with what I am able to outline in general terms. As for a detailed account, that lies outside of my present discussion." (Someone asked: "Is it the case that none of the 'smallest ones' has a differentiated nature?" I replied: "There was never anything in the old texts to verify this. If we extrapolate on the basis of *yin* and *yang* in the *Book of Change*, then the 'smallest ones' can be divided into the two categories of *yin* nature and *yang* nature. My above account has followed the ancient doctrine. I have been rigorous in my deliberations on this matter.")

As I previously stated, at the Grand Primordium stage of the cosmos, matter and energy were undifferentiated, lightly drifting, filling space—this is what is referred to as primal *qi* (元氣). After they had become differentiated, they became countless "smallest ones," which clustered to form

---

[53] $1000 \times 1000 \times 1000 = 1{,}000{,}000{,}000$.

[p. 120]
the myriad things. Once the myriad things had been formed, the material aspect hastened toward solidification, and appeared as if it offered material obstruction. (Offering material obstruction is not its inherent nature, hence "appeared as if.") As for the energy aspect, it had all of the material entities there to serve as loci for it to be concentrated. Hence, when the right conditions come together and it becomes animated, the extreme might of its power is more than enough to topple mountains and overturn the oceans. The functioning of matter and energy is simply extraordinary! Through their opposition, condensing and diffusing complete one another, [and so] the myriad transformations, the myriad changes, the myriad things, and the myriad affairs produce and reproduce in profusion, inexhaustibly and endlessly—how utterly strange!

Resplendent, the myriad things are dispersed throughout space. (Here the term "myriad things" includes all that exists. The countless heavenly bodies, as well as all things or all humans, are all included without exception.) Even though each seems (若) to be independent (Ruo 若 is like saying "it seems to be like this" in the vernacular.), actually, they are an interlinked, interconnected whole (整體) (Zheng 整: "entirety." The myriad things are a single great complete body. It is like the five viscera and one hundred parts of we humans—they have always been a single body.)—this is the material cosmos.

Someone asked: "Sir, you are an advocate of 'holism'/the 'Reality qua whole thesis' (全體論). Now you maintain that individuated 'groupings of the smallest ones' cluster to form the countless large and small things, and, further, that all of the large and small things in space also cluster together to form a great, complete whole. How is this different from atomism?"

I replied: "In their fundamentals they are different. Atomists maintain that at the Grand Primordium stage of the cosmos there were only numerous small things, which gradually accumulated to become large things. (For example, the theory of atoms [極微 (*paramāṇu*)] in ancient India was, in general terms, undoubtedly like this.) This marked the beginning of materialism. Materialists fail to awaken to the Reality of the cosmos and uphold that it is matter alone that really exists. In this treatise, I take the *Book of Change* as my authority, the non-duality of Reality and function as my main tenet, and maintain that Reality transforms into function. (Take the analogy of the ocean, which completely transforms to become the incessantly leaping myriad waves that arise and cease in impermanence. Here the ocean serves as an analogy for Reality and the myriad waves serve as an analogy for function [功用]. Function is also referred to as "powerful function" [力用].

Matter and the pure and spirit-like are both the function of Reality.) Precisely within this function there are concealed two opposing incipient tendencies, which manifest (顯) as the two aspects of contraction and expansion. (Expansion refers to the pure and spirit-like. It is called expansion because it has qualities such as robustness and vigor, opening up, and ascending. Contraction refers to matter. In this treatise, however, matter includes energy within it; see above. *Xian* 顯 means "to appear" [著現]; from hidden to apparent.) This is
[p. 121]
the beginning of the differentiation of Reality qua whole (全體). (*Quanti* 全體: because Reality is a great whole and there is nothing to which it stands in contrast, it is also called "Reality qua whole.")

Now, at this point, it is appropriate to discuss contraction alone. Contraction: because matter and energy coalesce (凝斂), this is called contraction. (*Ning* 凝: to coalesce or solidify. *Lian* 斂: to gather together and not disperse; it is also like *ning*.) It is one aspect of function. (The pure and spirit-like is the other aspect; it is worth re-reading "Explaining Transformation" on this point.) When matter and energy are undifferentiated, they flow lightly. When they coalesce to form things (成物), they become differentiated to form countless 'smallest ones.' The 'smallest ones' are the first appearance (見) of things. (*Jian* 見 is to be read as *xian* 現. This is like saying when things first appear. The word *wu* 物 in the above phrase, *cheng wu* 成物, and in the statement here that the "'smallest ones' are the first appearance of things [物]," both refer to things in the natural world. In Chinese, the word *wu* has both a non-figurative and a figurative use. When used figuratively, then it can be used expediently in a turn of phrase, such as Laozi's "The Way is a thing that is...."[54] Here the word "*wu*/thing" is used figuratively to refer implicitly to the "Way" at the beginning of the phrase and is not saying that the Way is matter or something in the natural world. I thus deem its usage here to be figurative. Examples such as this are too numerous to mention. There is also a distinction in the word's use in the non-figurative sense. 1. The term *wuzhi* 物質 [matter] is also abbreviated as *wu*, such as in the *Book of Change* where Kun is taken to be matter. The passage states that Kun is matter; that is, that from which each of the particular things in the natural world is formed. 2. The *Book of Change* states: "Kun transforms to become matter/things" [坤化成物] and so the word *wu* here refers to each particular thing in the natural world. The word *wu* in both cases names real things and is certainly not being used figuratively. It should, however, further be understood that although there is this distinction in the non-figurative use of the word *wu*, each particular thing in the natural world is matter. Nevertheless, when referring specifically to semantic

---

[54] *Dao de jing*, zhang 21.

demarcation, it is apt that there is this distinction in the non-figurative use of the word *wu*. In this treatise, whenever the word *wu* appears, its meaning must be determined on the basis of context. I have not noted this elsewhere.) This is the general account [as set out] in this treatise. In fathoming and elucidating that whereby the material universe came to be formed, I have always upheld the thesis that Reality as a whole becomes differentiated. When compared to those who [uphold the] clustering of parts/atoms thesis, not only are two positions worlds apart, fundamentally they cannot be reconciled." (Here "things in the natural world" refers to Heaven and Earth or to all material phenomena.[55])

Someone asked: "Sir, when you said that the 'smallest ones' become things, why did you use the meanings of both *he* 和 and *ji* 集 to explain this?"[56]

I replied: "This is simply the self-so nature of things. Each 'smallest one' is a small thing and when multiple 'smallest ones' combine to become a relatively larger thing, this is certainly not a case of their being indistinguishably blended to form a mass. Each 'smallest one' still retains its individuality and characteristics, hence I said that they 'cluster' (和集). *He* 和 refers to their being in close proximity (親附) to one another. (*Qinfu* 親附: it is just as if they were fond of one another and so joined together.) *Ji* 集 refers to

[p. 122]

[the idea that] among them, none loses its individuality and characteristics. This is analogous to the sun and the large planets that make up the solar system. (This "system" is just like a "grouping of the smallest ones" [小一群]. The sun and the planets are just like various "smallest ones"; neither the sun nor the planets lose their self-[identity].) Further, the reason the system does not collapse and dissipate is because of the constancy of the natures of these things. Although the myriad things are said to be individual, ultimately, they are a great whole, like the way the five viscera and one hundred parts constitute a single body. This principle can be drawn from what is near at hand—it is certainly not at far remove from one. Only when individual things develop together does the whole become immense—this is an immutable principle. Individuals, however, cannot develop by themselves, separated from the whole. Think about it—if Heaven and Earth were on the verge of being extinguished, would there still be a single atom that could haughtily exist alone in space? You should understand that individual things cannot exist separated from the great whole."

---

[55] This note would seem to be out of place.
[56] See the opening paragraph of this chapter.

Addendum. By extrapolating from the case of the clustering of the myriad things to [the formation of] human society, the way of order (治道) can be divined. The Six Classics have the following four great precepts: "The world is to be shared by all equally" and "The world is one family." (The economic system [set out] in the *Zhou guan* 周官 [Classic of the Offices of Zhou] takes the equitable [distribution of resources] to be an inviolable principle and norm.[57] The *Great Learning* states that the fundamentals for bringing the world to order are all to be traced to the great way of peace.[58] If there is anywhere in the world that has not attained peace or any affair that has not been peacefully [resolved] then it cannot yet be said that [the world] is shared by all equally or that the world is one family.) These two precepts are saying that clustering is the way that protects the stability of humankind as a whole. "Everyone gets what they need."[59] (From each according to his ability, to each according to his needs.[60]) "A flight of dragons with no leader."[61] (Each and every member of humankind is his or her own master, yet they also put themselves in the shoes of others (恕). <*Shu* 恕: "Do not do to others what you do not want done to yourself."[62]> Hence, [we can infer] that every person in those times was sound and sturdy, just like a flight of dragons. In ancient times, dragons were numinous creatures. In those times, there were none who served as leaders, and so it says, "with no leader.") These two precepts are talking about the way whereby every member of humankind preserves his or her individuality and characteristics. [Based on these precepts, it can be divined that] from now onwards, the way of order will increasingly become one of great equality and supreme peace, and because individuals within the whole body [of society] will each attain unrestricted freedom, yet not overstep the mark, this will be the fullest flourishing of the human way!

The "smallest ones" never had any fixed [quantum] of matter. Their lively animation is simply their sudden transformation, instant by instant, in which

---

[57] *Zhou guan* = *Zhou li* 周禮 (Rites of Zhou); see *Zhou li zhuzi suoyin* 周禮逐字索引 (Concordance to the *Zhou li*), D. C. Lau (Liu Dianjue 劉殿爵) et al. eds. (Hong Kong: Shangwu yinshuguan, 1993), 2.31/27/1, 2.40/28/6.
[58] "Daxue," 60.1a–1b.
[59] "Qin ce" 秦策 (Qin Stratagems), *Zhanguo ce* 戰國策 (Stratagems of the Warring States), *Sibu congkan*, 3.69a.
[60] Slogan popularized by Karl Marx.
[61] See Chapter 3, n. 126. Cf. Xiong's earlier gloss of "no leader" (無首) in this phrase in his 1945 publication, *Dujing shiyao* 讀經示要 (Revealing the Main Points in Reading the Classics), *Xiong Shili quanji*, vol. 3, p. 618: "'No leader': the flourishing of ultimate order, no racial divisions, no national boundaries, everyone is free, everyone is equal. There is no-one wielding political control over the masses, hence 'no leader.'"
[62] *Analects* 15.24.

they do not hold on to any former constancy. ([Understanding] this requires carefully examining the meaning of "arising and ceasing instant by instant." It is worth again pondering [the account set out in] "Explaining Transformation."
[p. 123]
The [principle that] the myriad things arise and cease instant by instant was first given expression in the *Book of Change* but because it was only a few words, the meaning was not obvious. It was *Zhuangzi* that elucidated the meaning, but scholars of *Zhuangzi* have never sought to understand it deeply. In my work on Mahāyāna learning, [I discovered] that Mahāyāna learning had made quite a detailed analysis of this meaning—only then did I thoroughly awaken to the profound purport of the *Book of Change* and *Zhuangzi*. Thirty years ago, I elaborated expansively on this meaning in the first draft of the "Explaining Transformation" chapter of my treatise,[63] but most readers were unconvinced. At the time of the national calamity[64] I entered Sichuan. Han Yuwen 韓裕文 from Laifu 萊蕪 accompanied me on my travels in Sichuan, and from time to time we discussed this matter.[65] Yuwen said: "Scholars today say that the vibrations of an electron certainly do not follow a set pattern. Electrons are always jumping back and forth between many orbits. They suddenly vanish from this orbit only to be suddenly generated once again in a different orbit. Nor is it the case that some external force causes them do so." Examining what he said, it is evident that modern scholars have discovered that electrons suddenly vanish and then are suddenly generated once again. Although they did not say that in the interval of an instant, electrons suddenly arise and cease, and suddenly cease and arise, nevertheless the meaning of what they said is close to this. I can still remember when Yuwen said this. It is pity that he had the misfortune of dying young.) In the past, I thought about the following [question]. The "smallest ones" leap about incessantly, arising and ceasing in impermanence (無常) (*Wuchang* 無常: instant by instant, suddenly transforming and not having a permanent nature.)—then how is it that they are able to form all those things everyone has experienced that offer material obstruction? This question very much warrants attention. In my humble view, if each of the "smallest ones" was dispersed and not clustered together then it should be the case that there would be no possibility for things to be formed, and the cosmos would forever be nothing more than a hazy, great vastness.

[63] Xiong is referring to the "Transformation" (轉變) chapter of the 1932 edition of *New Treatise*.
[64] The Japanese invasion of China in 1937. See Chapter 1, n. 6.
[65] According to Xiong's preface to the second folio of the first draft of his vernacular edition of the *New Treatise* (dated 1942), Han Yuwen joined Xiong in Sichuan in 1939 and assisted in "translating" the first folio of the *New Treatise* from literary to vernacular Chinese. (This was not so much a translation but a major rewriting of that material.) See *Xin weishi lun* (1944 edition), *Xiong Shili quanji*, vol. 3, p. 5.

[What I infer actually happens is that] each of the countless "smallest ones" independently clusters to form countless "groupings of the smallest ones" (小一群). Each of these "groupings of the smallest ones," in turn, independently clusters, and this is how all things come to be formed. The "smallest ones" inherently lack a materially obstructive nature. When multiple "groupings of the smallest ones" cluster to form things, however, then they manifest a materially obstructive nature. The reason for this is perhaps because when each of the countless "groupings of the smallest ones" independently clusters, it is so of itself (自然) that they form all sorts of models of arrangement or structural models. It is likely that the force (動力)[66] and matter of the "smallest ones'" accords with those multifarious models of arrangement or structural models, transforming to appear as different shapes and different natures, right through to all manner of variegated things. This inference is probably not too far removed from what actually happens. Nevertheless, regardless of which type of model the "smallest ones" [accord with], and the fact that their metamorphoses are varied, they have one major feature in common. Since they have been molded (范) on a model (See the addendum below.) and have already become various sorts of things, then their matter [aspect] should of itself hasten toward solidification, and their energy [aspect] should also be contained within the bodies of those things. Thereupon, all things have a materially obstructive nature. This is the major common feature that is evident in all things.

[p. 124]

When we humans observe things from their exterior, we are certainly not aware that they are multiple "groupings of the smallest ones" that have always been incessantly leaping about, arising and ceasing in impermanence. Is it not extremely odd that all we see are things that have a materially obstructive nature?

> **Addendum.** *Fan* 范: In making vessels in ancient times, the bamboo used as a mold was called *fan* 范. The making of vessels depended on molds. Here I am saying that when multiple "groupings of the smallest ones" cluster, "it is so of itself that they form all sorts of models of arrangement or structural models." (It is not the case that the formation of these various models is a deliberate act of creation, but rather is nothing other than so of itself [自然]. *Ziran* 自然: not

---

[66] This is the only time that Xiong uses this term in this book. Its pairing with matter suggests that Xiong is treating it as a variant of, or as being subsumed within, the concept of energy (能力; 力). It is noted that he reverts to the terms *li* 力 and *zhi* 質 a few lines below.

caused to be so through planning but rather is happenstance. Expressed in the vernacular, this is like saying "nobody came to design it and make it like this, rather, it just so happens that is how it is." Hence it is said to be "so of itself.") A model is like a mold. At this point, [when each of the countless "smallest ones" independently clusters to form countless "groupings of the smallest ones,"] the transformation and movement of the "smallest ones" must accord with the model, just as a vessel is made by relying on the mold.

Originally, the "smallest ones" were that which was formed as the torrent of undifferentiated matter and energy became differentiated. (Although the torrent of matter and energy became differentiated as countless "smallest ones," this torrent and the "smallest ones" cannot be differentiated as two. This is because there are no "smallest ones" beyond the torrent, just as there is no torrent beyond the "smallest ones." Readers must not let misunderstanding lead to jumbled [thinking].) Hence, their arising and ceasing in impermanence is precisely what the "Great Commentary" to the *Book of Change* refers to as "Unceasingly transforming and moving, they flow throughout the Six Voids (When space is figuratively broken into [the categories of] above, below, and the four cardinal directions, this is called the "Six Voids.") and no constant norms (典要) apply to them (*Dian yao* 典要 is like laws. Their transformation and movement have never had fixed laws.), as they proceed to transformation alone."[67] (The great flow of a myriad inexhaustible transformations has always been devoid of conscious deliberation. Hence when the "smallest ones" transform, they cannot hold back, abandoning themselves to that where their impetus hastens, inexhaustibly. Hence, "they proceed to transformation alone.") Having deeply investigated great transformation, Zhuangzi exclaimed at how strange it was—could it have been this that he was referring to?[68]

As for when the "smallest ones" cluster, they already form various models to form things (It is worth re-reading the previous passages on this matter. When the "smallest ones" cluster is precisely when models are formed to form things. It is not the case that first there is clustering and only subsequently are models formed to form things. In regard to this matter, there should be no speculation about temporal sequences.), then at that point the myriad things are already complete. In one respect, each thing has individuated, singular features; in another respect,

---

[67.] This is a paraphrase of a longer passage at "Xici zhuan, xia," 8.18b–19a. See also Xiong's gloss of *wei bian suo shi* 唯變所適 on p. 232 of this chapter.

[68] Xiong is presumably referring to Zhuangzi's butterfly dream and what Zhuangzi called "the transformation of things" (物化). See "Qiwu lun" 齊物論 (Discussion on Making All Things Equal), *Zhuangzi*, p. 112.

[p. 125]

all things have categories [that they belong to]. (For example, dirt, stones, and so forth all belong to the inorganic category, whereas such things as animals and plants belong to the organic category. If they are further sub-divided, then the categories become so numerous that it is difficult to determine an end point.) Accordingly, if things are investigated with respect to their individuated features, then because things have a constitutive form (成型) [it can be seen that] they easily grow and develop. (*Chengxing* 成型 means that all things have their form, which, once constituted, does not change.) Moreover, because they have a form, ultimately there is a limit to their development, and they must revert to extinction. (For all things within inexhaustible time, even a thousand years is like the interval of an instant—how could they last long?) Nevertheless, even though there is no individual thing that is long-lasting, their categories are all long enduring. Although mountains can collapse and rivers run dry, unless the great earth is completely destroyed, the categories of mountains and rivers will not come to an end. Each of the trigrams in the *Book of Change* is used to show that the myriad things have three periods: beginning, maturity, and end. (See the *Apocryphon to the Book of Change*].[69]) For things, the start of life is called "beginning," following the beginning then there is "maturity," and following maturity then there is the "end." The end refers to extinction. The various heavenly bodies and the earth are the largest of things and their lifespan is extremely long, but extrapolating from the significance of the trigrams, even though the heavenly bodies and the earth are large, ultimately there is to be a period when they will come to an end. There is no thing that has form that does not revert to extinction; and because there is extinction, thereby the new is generated. It is only because the old passes away and does not remain that the new is endlessly renewed. Therefore, the fully realized person understands from experience that the Way is daily renewal and is able to overcome deluded attachment to his/her individual body or small self and so participate directly in great transformation—so what "end" is there? ("The Way" is referring to the principle of transformation. The flow of great function does not hold on to any former constancy—this is called great transformation. The fully realized person is not deludedly attached to the small self and so directly participates in great transformation. Great transformation has no end.)

---

[69] See *Yi wei: Qian zao du*, A.6b.

Three major fallacies in cosmological accounts of Reality

Someone asked: "Sir, in your treatise you call the coalescence of matter and energy 'contraction' and [say that] through contraction things are formed. If that is the case, then it would be enough to hold a doctrine of contraction-based monism (唯翕之論). Why do you further call the pure and spirit-like 'expansion' and say that great function (大用) has the two aspects of expansion and contraction? (*Gongyong* 功用 is abbreviated as *yong* 用 [function]; *da* 大 is a term of praise.) As such, are you not giving excessive license to subjective conceptualization?"

I replied: "How odd that you vigorously prosecute objections rather than direct your energies to fathoming the root of principles (理根)." (When principles are investigated to their ultimate, then [what is found] is the source of the myriad transformations, the root of the myriad things, that to which the myriad principles return. In his *Notes to Zhuangzi*, Guo Xiang called it "the root of principles."[70]) Hitherto, in cosmological accounts of intrinsic Reality, broadly speaking, three major deluded fallacies (迷謬) have been entertained. (*Mi* 迷: delusion so acute that it is difficult to discern principles; *miu* 謬: to be in error yet afraid to change.)

(1) To seek the absolute outside of the relative. This was the chronic malady of ancient monotheism.
[p. 126]
(Being unable to escape delusion is just like being unable to cure a chronic malady.) Later on, although scholarship flourished, [scholars] remained stuck in the same rut and had no idea that the absolute is a term for Reality and that the relative refers to the myriad things. Reality is "the itself" of the myriad existents (萬有的自身). This is analogous to the ocean's being "the itself" of the myriad waves. If scholars had been able to understand this, they [would have known that] the absolute and the relative are inherently non-dual, yet are also differentiated; although differentiated, actually they are non-dual. This is patently clear—what further doubts could there be? The truth is plain and unexceptional and there has never been anything strange about it. Despite this, as scholars create their own fog of delusion, they become increasingly distanced from the truth. Like wanderers far away from home who have lost their bearings and have no way to return—is this not lamentable?! (It is indeed lamentable that those who discuss intrinsic Reality do not see the truth. As for [those who

---

[70] See Han Yuankai's Foreword, p. 2.

would] engage in philosophy yet disdain ontology, this [leads to the mistaken belief that] the cosmos and human life do not have an origin—is that not even more lamentable?!)

Hitherto, scholars who have discussed Reality and phenomena all say that whereas phenomena transform and change, Reality is what is real. As such, phenomena and Reality constitute a two-tier world. If, however, [the matter is considered] on the basis of my account that Reality and function are non-dual, then it is Reality that is phenomena (This is analogous to the ocean's being the waves.) and that it is phenomena that are Reality. (This is analogous to there being no ocean that is apart from the numerous waves.) The arising and ceasing in impermanence of phenomena is precisely the arising and ceasing in impermanence of Reality. (This is analogous to how the arising and ceasing in impermanence of the numerous waves is precisely the arising and ceasing in impermanence of the ocean.) The incessant jumping about of phenomena is precisely the incessant jumping about of Reality. (This is analogous to the how incessant jumping about of the numerous waves is precisely the incessant jumping about of the ocean.) Accordingly, it should not be said whereas phenomena transform and change, Reality is what is real. Although phenomena and Reality are differentiated, ultimately, they cannot be split in two—this doctrine is definitive. It should be said that Reality and phenomena have always been one, that it is precisely that which transforms and changes that is real, and that it is precisely that which is real that transforms and changes. My treatise's investigation and rectification of the errors of the various schools is not limited to one or two aspects—here I broadly address [only] the key issues.

(2) Putting to one side the case of [those areas of] Western learning that do not discuss ontology, it remains the case that even those [areas] that do discuss ontology do so solely by indulging in bias, which in the end amounts to the doctrine that there is no Reality (無體之論). Ever since there was philosophy in the West, even though there were disagreements among the various schools, these schools never fell outside of the two antagonistic traditions of idealistic monism and material monism. In resolutely maintaining that the pure and spirit-like is the sole origin (一元) of the myriad existents, idealists must excise matter. However, because material phenomena cannot, after all, be denied, idealists incorporate them into the pure and spirit-like, and simply treat matter as a byproduct of the pure and spirit-like. In resolutely maintaining that matter is the sole origin of the cosmos, materialists must excise the pure and spirit-like. However, because pure and spirit-like
[p. 127]

phenomena cannot, after all, be denied, materialists incorporate them into matter and simply treat the pure and spirit-like as a byproduct of matter. In the [late] Qing period, when I first heard about the theses of these two traditions, I was very skeptical. From the middle period of my life and thereafter, the reason I deemed them to be fundamentally in error was actually because they failed to discern Reality and function (用). (*Gongyong* 功用 is abbreviated as *yong* 用. Function is the name for endless transformation. As transformation arises, it necessarily has form that is manifest and so it is also called "phenomena/manifest images" [現象].) The pure and spirit-like and the material are both the brilliance (燦然) of great function. (*Canran* 燦然: conspicuous appearance.) I dare to assert that the flow of great function does not suddenly arise out of thin air; much less is it like an illusion or a conjuring trick. I dare to assert that the brilliance of great function definitely has Reality [as its self], analogous to the way that the numerous waves in their disarray definitely have the ocean [as their self]. Reality is the itself of great function. This is analogous to the way that the ocean is the itself of the numerous waves. To observe the myriad existents and yet not exhaustively fathom their Reality (實相) ("The myriad existents" is another term for great function. *Shixiang* 實相 is the same as Reality [實體]; see the previous chapter.) is analogous to a child's looking at the numerous wave forms and yet not realize the ocean—how is this acceptable?! The pure and spirit-like and the material are both function. In other words, both are brilliant manifest images. Idealistic monists hold that the pure and spirit-like is the sole origin [of the myriad existents] whereas the material monists hold that matter is the sole origin. This amounts to splitting apart the cosmos, with each grasping one aspect of the flow of great function, which they deem to be the fundamental origin (本原). (*Benyuan* 本原 refers to Reality.) In fact, both converge in [espousing] the thesis that there is no Reality.

When I first began focusing my efforts on cosmology, I experienced a great many changes in my exhaustive investigation of Reality. In broad terms, there were three key changes. By the time of the third change, I had begun to formulate a definitive thesis. Concerning the first change, I [started by] tentatively conjecturing that there was a creator. Because in my youth I had become accustomed to the old books' references to *tian* 天 (Heaven) and *di* 帝 (god) I was unable suddenly to dismiss those references, but, at the same time, I did not dare readily to believe in a creator. From further away, I drew from other things, and near at hand, I drew from my own person, exhaustively fathoming principles everywhere but was never able to verify a creator. At that point, I abandoned this conjecture, which marked the first change [in my exploration of Reality]. (What I experienced in this period was extremely complex and also convoluted, but I will not go into that here.)

Concerning the second change, since [my conjecture about] a creator could not be established, next I tentatively conjectured that the myriad things had no origin. I maintained that since the genesis of the cosmos, the myriad things are each generated from one another through forms[71] (This is saying that the various types of things metamorphize.) yet each conforms with its category (類). (For example, inanimate things and animate things each conforms with its category.) No matter how unequal the myriad things are, they are equal—this is achieved by entrusting to that which is so of itself. (Things are each generated from one another through forms and so they are unequal; by each conforming to its kind, however, although unequal they are equal!) At this time

[p. 128]

my thinking was focused on putting in order the various categories of things so that a single large category could be attained through inductive reasoning. Rather than fathoming the source in some abstruse realm, I preferred to set the question of origin to one side and not pursue it, which amounted to a doctrine of no origin. Before long, I began to wonder whether breaking down and differentiating the myriad things to search for their unifying category was merely an undertaking in natural science. I almost gave up [my pursuits in] cosmology, as I was unable to reach to the vast and the great and fully reveal the fine the subtle.[72] While any attempt to fathom the source in some abstruse (玄冥) realm was definitely not an option (*Xuan* 玄: obscure; *ming* 冥 also means obscure. Wherever there is thinking that is fond of engaging in empty abstraction and unable to illuminate the subtle, it is ridiculed as being abstruse. In such cases, the term is used derogatively. There are, however, profound and far-reaching principles that are also described as abstruse. In such cases, the term is used to convey a sense of excellence. Here I am using the term in its derogatory sense.), if I were to have been so careless as to have falsely asserted that the myriad things have no origin, rejecting the possibility of such an origin and not pursue it, then this would be wishing to alienate myself [from that origin] and not regret being far removed from true principle (真理).[73] How could that be acceptable?

---

[71] Cf. "Zhi bei you" 知北遊 (Knowledge Wanders North), *Zhuangzi*, p. 741: "The myriad things are generated from one another through forms. Thus, those with nine holes are born from a womb, those with eight are born from an egg."
[72] "Zhongyong," 53.8b: "Therefore by esteeming his virtuous nature the gentleman follows the path of enquiry and learning, reaching to the vast and the great and exhausting the fine and the subtle."
[73] *Zhenli* 真理 here and in the next paragraph is synonymous with Reality.

Accordingly, once again I engaged in the learning [that is aimed at] exhaustively fathoming the origin. Near at hand, I drew from my own person, and further away, I drew from other things. I became profoundly aware and profoundly confident that the Reality of the myriad existents is the itself of the myriad existents. (This is analogous to how the ocean is the itself of the myriad waves. This analogy is the most incisive—without it, it would be very difficult to explain this principle.) Reality most certainly neither lies hidden behind the myriad existents nor does it transcend them. Moreover, it most certainly is not eternal and unchanging, separated from things and existing by itself. Having thoroughly awoken to this, [I realized that] every manner of thing is the pervasive manifestation of true principle. Shit, piss, tiles, and rubble—they are nothing other than purity as it inherently is. (Zhuangzi said: "The Way is in shit and piss"; "the Way is in tiles and rubble."[74] This is because, with regard to their Reality, it has always been purity as it inherently is—what filth is there?) As for the great enterprise of the sages and wise men of ancient China, who, having clearly perceived the great root, cherished and nurtured the virtuous wisdom (德慧) of the single body that is the myriad things in Heaven and Earth ("Great root" refers to Reality. When morality and wisdom are combined, this is called *dehui* 德慧.) to fashion and bring to completion [the Way of Heaven and Earth], and to assist (輔相) [the myriad things]—all of this was undertaken without any self-interest so as to bring to completion the inherent nature of the single body that is the myriad things in Heaven and Earth. (The *Book of Change* states: "To fashion and bring to completion [裁成] the [Way of] Heaven and Earth," "Assists the ten thousand things."[75] Note. *Cai cheng* 裁成: to modify the cosmos. Zhuangzi had a profound understanding of the *Book of Change* and said that when Great Peng flew high in the sky, its wings were like clouds suspended from Heaven.[76] [This account] already predicted space travel. Perhaps in the future, when the weather is unseasonable, there will be methods to control air currents. Confucius' lofty ideal would then finally be realized.[77] *Fuxiang* 輔相 means that on the basis of the spirit of equality and loving concern, all humans support one another, there is great equality and supreme peace, each thing fully expresses its nature, and the many ways [群道] are unhindered.) This [ideal of bringing to completion the inherent nature of the single body that is the myriad things in Heaven and Earth] is in the true lineage of transmission of the learning of the sage. I hope that people

---

[74] "Zhi bei you," *Zhuangzi*, p. 750, slightly misquoted.
[75] Loose paraphrase of the "Xiang" commentary to the Tai hexagram; see Chapter 1, n. 29.
[76] "Xiao yao you," *Zhuangzi*, p. 2.
[77] Xiong attributes a key role to Confucius in compiling and editing the *Book of Change*.

in the future will continue to preserve and nurture it, and not let it be severed. When my learning reached this point, this marked the third change.

(3) Material monism takes matter to be the sole origin [of the myriad existents], with the pure and spirit-like becoming a
[p. 129]
byproduct. Because people are easily persuaded by this doctrine, I must say something. The pure and spirit-like is neither a god nor a spirit but rather is our innate numinous nature. People all have free will (Confucius said: "The Master said, 'The commander of the Three Armies may be taken by force, but the will of even a commoner cannot be taken from him.'[78] [The fact that] the will cannot be taken away suffices to show [that there is] free will.), profoundly intricate thought, and rich feelings. These are all pure and spirit-like phenomena. To say that they are the byproduct of matter is like saying that beans can produce hemp—cause and effect are confused. How could such a doctrine make sense?"

Someone raised the following objection: "Psychological phenomena had to wait for organisms to have evolved [to a certain stage] before they gradually appeared, and organisms appeared quite late [in the process of evolution]. At the Grand Primordium stage of the cosmos, there were only inorganic things—the basis for this deduction is extremely [solid] and beyond doubt. Matter first existed and the pure and spirit-like appeared subsequently—this is a fact. Now, sir, in your treatise you hold that Reality transforms into function, [and in doing so] you avoid the error of bifurcating Reality and function—very deft indeed! However, [you also] say that function has the two aspects of contraction and expansion, where expansion is the pure and spirit-like and contraction is matter and energy. On this account, the pure and spirit-like and matter both existed right from the beginning of the cosmos. Sir, have you not committed the error (過) of indulging in abstruse thinking rather than being grounded in facts? (*Guo* 過 is the same as "mistake" [誤].)"

I replied: "It is actually you who is in error, but you have yet to awaken to this. I will itemize my responses as follows:

(i) The *Book of Change* states: 'His knowledge fully extends to (周) the myriad things.'[79] (*Zhou* 周: all pervasive [遍]. This says that the human mind's knowledge can comprehensively extend to the principles of the myriad things.) The *Great Learning* states: 'The extension of knowledge lies in the investigation of

---

[78] *Analects* 9.26.
[79] "Xici zhuan, shang," 7.10a.

things.'80 The learning of the sages established these two great precepts; they can never be changed. If a person engages in learning yet fails to seek verification in [actual] things, then they must certainly be indulging in fantasy or even delusion and should be severely admonished. Abstruse thinking, on the contrary, is indispensable. With abstruse thinking, numinous agency (靈機) suddenly moves, taking things as cognitive objects (緣物) without becoming impeded (不滯) by things. (For the term *yuan* 緣, refer to Buddhist texts. *Yuan* means to give rise to thought by taking [攀援; lit. "clamber on"] all things as cognitive objects.[81] The two characters *bu zhi* 不滯 are crucial but their meaning is difficult to express.) The most universal principles (大理) (*Da li* 大理 is the same as "principles" [原理].) and the most subtle inklings are always attained within abstruse thinking. If abstruse thinking were to be disdained then in the future there would be no more scholarship worth speaking about. Those competent at abstruse thinking, however, need to satisfy two conditions. First, in the course of everyday life, that they concentrate on the lofty and do not sink into the mundane. (When the mind constantly applies its thinking to fathoming principles through the investigation of things, then this is [to concentrate on] the lofty.) Second, although abstruse thinking is suddenly manifest, it actually comes about through the accumulation of learning. When compared to the first condition, this second condition

[p. 130]

is not very different. It is just that whereas the first is referring to everyday life, the second is referring to the achievements of accumulated learning.

(ii) There is fundamentally no way for you to deny the existence of the pure and spirit-like, [and so you] simply maintain that matter first existed and that the mind appeared subsequently, thereupon perversely leading you to presume that the pure and spirit-like is a byproduct of matter. In what follows, I will briefly raise several related issues to ask you about.

First, you hold that the appearance of mental functions comes after [there is] matter, and then perversely assert that the pure and spirit-like never existed until the appearance of the mental functions. What you fail to understand is that at the Grand Primordium stage of the cosmos, [space] was a diffuse, vast wasteland; there were not yet any heavenly bodies, so what stars and clouds would there have been? Chan master Huineng 慧能 [638–713]

---

[80] See note 41 in this chapter.
[81] The Buddhist technical term for this is *panyuan* 攀緣.

said: 'There never was a single thing.'[82] These words a well worth savoring. Suppose there was somebody over there who asserted that at the Grand Primordium stage there never was any matter that existed—would you be willing to concur? If you did not concur, then how could you [expect to be able to] force people to believe you when you now assert that the pure and spirit-like never existed until the appearance of mental functions? Before mental functions appeared they were simply concealed (隱) and not yet revealed, and cannot be said not to have existed. (*Yin* 隱: hidden. Here the word is not to be interpreted as "secret" [隱密].) 'Hidden and revealed' and 'existing and not existing' are two completely different sets of meaning. It most certainly cannot be said that [because mental functions were] hidden and had not yet been revealed therefore they did not exist.

The myriad transformations, myriad changes, myriad things, and myriad affairs of the cosmos necessarily follow a key rule: that which exists cannot be generated from that which does not exist. As for the transformations of all things, regardless of how complex or how strange they may be, if we were to take any one of those things and trace its cause, then there would be endless layers of cause and effect that in all cases can be sought. If we trace back from the present, the present stands in relation to the prior as effect, and so this effect has a prior cause that can be sought. Going back further and even further, if we were to trace back layer upon layer of prior [cause and effect relations], then [those layers of] cause and effect would be endless. If we trace forward into the future, the present stands in relation to the future as cause; moreover we can predict there will be endless layers of cause and effect [relations] in future futures (未來之未來). It is not only things in the organic world that undergo metamorphosis, and which have causes that can be sought; even in the inanimate world there are examples such as the oceans' transforming land masses. Although this happened in the extremely distant past, there are old traces that can be sought—it is definitely not the case that there was absolutely no prior cause yet by chance there was transformation into land. What was the prior cause? It was the soil that came from other places and most certainly was not a case of the ocean water's being able to transform into a land mass. (In identifying soil as the cause here, it is with respect to its being the direct cause [正因] of the formation of

---

[82] *Liu zu dashi fabao tan jing* 六祖大師法寶壇經 (The Sixth Patriarch, Great Master Huineng's Dharma Treasure Platform Sutra), T2008.48, 349a8.

a land mass; if the flow of the ocean water pounds against soil in other places, causing it to fall into the ocean, then that is a case of the ocean's being a supporting cause [旁因] in the formation of a land mass. In the vernacular a supporting cause is referred to as an external condition [外緣]. Without external conditions there would certainly not be the soil that comes to form the land mass;

[p. 131]

yet that which forms the land mass is necessarily the soil and so the soil is the direct cause.) There definitely are no chance occurrences in the cosmos. What ordinary people regard as chance, if examined carefully, is indeed not chance. I will not go into this here as I fear it would be prolix. In sum, the myriad transformation, myriad changes, myriad things, and myriad affairs [of the cosmos] cannot be generated into existence from that which does not exist. This key rule can actually be personally experienced [by observing the operation of] the law of cause and effect in all things. If that which does not exist were able to generate that which does exist, then the weird things in the cosmos would be so unimaginable that it would be impossible for science to be established. It that really how things are?

The reason I dare not readily believe that the pure and spirit-like is a by-product of matter is that there can be no cause and effect between the pure and spirit-like and matter, for the simple reason that they share absolutely no similar features. Causes are distinguished as direct and supporting. Direct cause is also called 'cause of the same kind' (自類因). It directly exerts power on the effect that is produced, and so cause and effect definitely have similar features. For example, bean seeds produce beans and hemp seeds produce hemp—these are both causes of the same kind. (Cause of the same kind [can be explained as follows.] Take the example of a person's lifetime. [Over the course of a life], from beginning to end, I do not know how many times the former "me" died and a new "me" was born. Even if one does not believe in [the notion of] arising and ceasing instant by instant, nevertheless, from youth to maturity, to old age, and on to infirmity clearly there was no former me who continued throughout—this is undeniable. So too for all people, just as the former me extinguishes a new me arises, and for this reason I am the direct cause of the newly arisen me. This is also called "cause of the same kind." Matter's producing matter is [an example of] a cause of the same kind, and so too the pure and spirit-like's producing the pure and spirit-like is [an example of] a cause of the same kind.) Supporting causes are also called external conditions but they have an influence only on the effect and do not have the power to produce the effect directly. For example, mandarin oranges (橘) [grown south of] the Huai River become trifoliate oranges (枳) [when grown north of] the Huai

River.[83] Mandarin oranges serve as the cause of the same kind for trifoliate oranges. The transformation of mandarin oranges into trifoliate oranges is due to the climate north of the Huai River's serving as supporting cause or external condition."

Someone said: "Trifoliate oranges are produced from mandarin oranges but because they have already transformed it would seem inappropriate to maintain that mandarin oranges serve as the cause of the same kind."

I replied: "That is not so. After mandarin oranges have transformed into trifoliate oranges, trifoliate oranges are still quite close [to mandarin oranges], and the traces of this can clearly be examined. They have certainly not suddenly transformed into completely dissimilar [plants such as] lotuses or brambles—how can you say that mandarin oranges do not serve as the cause of the same kind?"

Accordingly, now that supporting and direct causes have been clearly differentiated, [we can see that] matter cannot serve as the cause of the same kind for the pure and spirit-like just as the pure and spirit-like cannot serve as the cause of the same kind for matter. (Idealism holds that matter is the byproduct of the pure and spirit-like—this also is to fail to understand the law of cause and effect.) My statement that there cannot be a cause-and-effect relationship between the pure and spirit-like and matter is definitely seeking truth from facts and is not [due to some] selfish motive to take an unconventional position. The pure and spirit-like and matter share no similar features—this is patently evident. I have long wanted to write a book on the
[p. 132]
psychology of philosophy to explain this in detail. Regrettably, my energy has already been depleted and I can no longer hold a pen.

Two unique features of the pure and spirit-like

With regard to the unique features of the pure and spirit-like, here I will outline two of the most evident. First, it goes without saying that matter has boundaries; the pure and spirit-like, however, has no boundaries. ("Has no

---

[83] Yan Ying 晏嬰 (sixth century BCE), attrib., "Nei pian za xia" 內篇雜下 (Inner Chapters, Miscellaneous Tales, Part 2), 13b, *Yanzi chunqiu* 晏子春秋 (The Spring and Autumn Annals of Master Yan), *Sibu congkan chubian*: "Mandarin oranges grown south of the Huai River are mandarin oranges; when grown to the north of the river, they become trifoliate oranges. Only the leaves resemble one another; they differ in taste."

boundaries" is saying that because it has neither form nor image, no fixed location, yet is everywhere, therefore it is without borders, without sections.) Mencius said: "He flows together with Heaven above and Earth below."[84] This is referring to the pure and spirit-like in one's person, but it is not limited to one's person as it includes (包) and interconnects (通) Heaven above and Earth below, circulating everywhere without interruption. (*Bao* 包: to include; *tong* 通: to interconnect comprehensively.) It is analogous to the circulation of blood in the five viscera and one hundred parts of the body—there is nowhere it does not include and interconnect. Thought pervasively connects (遍緣) with the myriad things (*Bian* 遍: pervasively; *yuan* 緣 includes such senses as "to contact," "to infer," "to experience personally."), and the emotions merge into nature (大自然)—there is clear evidence of both.

Second, the speed at which the pure and spirit-like operates cannot be measured. For example, when we see a white vase, we always think that as soon as we see it, we immediately have awareness of a white vase. Actually, in the interval of the instant in which we are seeing a white vase, all such functions as recollection, imagination, and inference have yet to be involved. At this juncture, given that the seeing and the white vase are indivisible and undifferentiated, is it possible to say that as soon as we see a white vase, we immediately have awareness of a white vase? By the time we do have awareness of a white vase, numerous mental functions (Such as memory, imagination, inference, and so forth.) have already all gathered together. Given this extreme complexity, it would thus seem that it is necessary for a long passage of time to have passed before it is possible [to have awareness of a white vase]. Despite this, we each think that as soon as we see a white vase then immediately awareness occurs, just as if this were possible without an instant of time's having passed. This is for no other reason than that the operation of the pure and spirit-like is extremely rapid, and so it seems as if we are able to do this even before an instant has passed. Whereas the movement of matter can be measured in terms of such units as speed, strength, and so forth, the movement of the pure and spirit-like cannot be measured. For example, when people cogitate, sometimes we strenuously explore multiple aspects [of a problem] in order to find a solution—how could the intensity of that be measured? Having outlined these two features, it is evident that the pure and spirit-like and matter absolutely lack similar features and so cannot be said to be in a cause-and-effect relationship. The facts are as such—how could there

---

[84] *Mencius* 7A.13.

FORMING MATERIAL THINGS   221

be any confusion? ("Cause" here refers to "cause of the same kind"; elsewhere I adopt the same usage.)

Someone asked: "Sir, in your treatise you maintain that between the pure and spirit-like and matter there cannot be a cause-and-effect
[p. 133]
relationship. Let me ask you the following. At the time before organisms had appeared, there is certainly no clear evidence that the pure and spirit-like existed. How do you deal with this objection?"

I replied: "The cosmos develops ceaselessly. After the sage [Fuxi][85] had personally experienced this principle by looking upward and observing [Heaven], and looking downward and investigating [Earth], then in the *Book of Change* he revealed the principle of the cosmos' development: 'manifesting that that which was originally concealed.'[86] (In citing this passage, scholars often explain it as a method of thinking. Although this is not contrary to [its meaning], the fundamental purport of the *Great Change* is certainly to elucidate the principle of the cosmos' development.) The Qian hexagram is at the head of the *Book of Change*'s sixty-four hexagrams and their 384 lines. The first line of the Qian hexagram takes its image from a hidden dragon.[87] (In ancient times dragons were considered to be numinous creatures and so this image was taken as a metaphor for transformation, in the hope that from this image people would awaken to the principle of transformation.) 'Hidden' means concealed (隱) and not yet manifest (見). (*Yin* 隱: concealed. *Xian* 見 is like "manifest"; it is to be read as *xian* 現, as in *faxian* 發現. This is analogous to fruit's containing immeasurable vitality, which in the vernacular is called *ren* 仁 [kernel of fruit] and is hidden. Later it develops into sprouts, roots, trunk, branches, leaves, and right through to flowers and fruit—each of these endlessly emerging layers gradually becoming manifest. Crucially, all subsequently arising endless manifestations inherently have the fruit kernel as cause; it can also be said that they inherently have these various potentialities, it is just that their cause is concealed and not yet manifest. Being concealed, it is as though it does not exist, but actually it is not the case that it does not exist.) Reality's transformation into great function inherently contains immeasurable possibilities. The first line's image of the 'hidden dragon' reveals this meaning. All of the myriad transformations and myriad changes [represented by] the 384 hexagram lines arise from the first line of the Qian hexagram. In the first line of the Qian hexagram, [the dragon] is concealed and not yet manifest—this is

---

[85] The reference here is to Fuxi; see *Yuan Ru*, pp. 636–637.
[86] Paraphrase of a passage in "Sima Xiangru zhuan" 司馬相如傳 (Biography of Sima Xiangru), *Shiji*, 117.2609.
[87] Qian hexagram, line statement, *Zhou yi*, 1.1b.

the mother of immeasurable developments. Before organisms had appeared, the structure of inorganic things was exceedingly simple, and although the pure and spirit-like was latently operating in inorganic things, it remained concealed and unable to be manifest. This is just like the hazy vastness at the Grand Primordium stage of the cosmos, where matter was also concealed and had never been manifest. All of this [is captured in] the image of the concealed [dragon] in the first line of the Qian hexagram. Self-so principles (自然之理) are neither odd nor strange. What is the point of deluding oneself by perversely presuming that before organisms had appeared, the pure and spirit-like did not exist? 'Manifesting that which was originally concealed' is the great principle of the development of the cosmos. For those who study cosmology, their methods of thinking should of course proceed in accord with this principle, for only then will they align with the objective facts. If they do not, then although they will be able to see the pure and spirit-like when manifest, but when hidden it will be difficult to be aware of it. If they do not trace the manifest to the hidden, then they will certainly give free play to subjective opinion to dismember the cosmos—I simply do not know how this is acceptable."

Two features of the Reality of the cosmos

If we understand that the cosmos is ceaselessly developing, and if we want to investigate deeply the great principle of "manifesting that which was originally concealed,"
[p. 134]
then there are also two features [of the Reality of the cosmos] we need to pay attention to.

1. Reality cannot be denied (What I call "Reality" does not transcend high above the myriad things in Heaven and Earth, nor is it another world concealed behind the myriad things in Heaven and Earth. It is absolutely different from "noumena" talked about in Western learning. This must be noted.) otherwise everything would be rootless, and so what basis would there be to speak of its being concealed? The *Book of Change* established [the concept of] the "origin of Qian" (乾元)[88] (The origin of Qian is a name for Reality.) hence the first line of the Qian hexagram talks of a hidden [dragon]. I believe that no matter how perfectly nature

---

[88] See Chapter 1, note 33.

(大自然) and human affairs may come to be developed, if we focus on we humans and the myriad things, then of course it should be just as Confucius said: "It is humans who are able to expand the Way."[89] In other words, by our own effort we humans can develop the Reality of the cosmos and expand it. (It is also through their own effort that the myriad things develop. Here, I have cited only the example of humans to talk about this because human effort is pre-eminent.) If we focus on Reality, then, with respect to the myriad things and we humans, all of the creations, all of the transformations, and all of the [acts conducive to] the flourishing of virtue and [achieving] great merit, and which are richly endowed with daily renewal, should all be traced to this inexhaustible storehouse that is Reality.[90] There is no tree in the world that suddenly develops a thousand branches and a myriad leaves if it does not have roots; there is no river in the world that suddenly [becomes] an inexhaustible raging torrent if it does not have a source. It is indeed the case that the non-duality of Reality and function thesis I uphold was attained everywhere through personal experience: further away I drew from other things and near at hand I drew from my own person. ("The ocean and the myriad waves" is the [most] appropriate metaphor [to convey the idea of the] non-duality of Reality and function. The root and source metaphors are not entirely like [the non-duality of Reality and function]; see my previous account of this.[91])

2. Never severed, the cosmos-of-the-myriad-existents (宇宙萬有) is a complete whole that, from the past to the present, has been hastening to the future. ("Cosmos" is another term for the myriad existents. Here the two terms, "cosmos" [宇宙] and "myriad existents" [萬有] are combined as a compound term. Generally, however, they are employed separately as two individual terms.) Philosophy should view the cosmos in a comprehensive manner, supplemented with analytical method—only this way can indulgence in misguided conceptual elaboration be avoided. The intrinsic Reality of the cosmos contains immeasurable potential (This is what "concealed" [隱] refers to.) that is expressed at all times (隨時). (The purport of the Sui 隨 [Following] hexagram in the *Book of Change* is profound and far-reaching.[92]) This is analogous to [water] constantly emerging from a

---

[89] *Analects* 15.29.
[90] See also note 101 below.
[91] Chapter 3, p. 161.
[92] In *Dujing shiyao*, p. 590, Xiong writes: "*Great Change* established the Sui (Following), Ding 鼎 (Cauldron), and Ge 革 (Overturning) hexagrams to elucidate the meaning of 'overturning the old at all times in order to draw forth the new.' (The Sui hexagram states: "The meaning of 'at all times' is great indeed!"* The "Za gua" 雜卦 [Commentary on Assorted Hexagrams] states: "Ge [Overturning] is to get rid of the old; Ding [Cauldron] is to draw forth the new."**)." *Zhou yi*, 3.1b. **Zhou yi*, 9.15b.

deep spring (Deeply hidden there is a water source, and this called a deep spring. This source is replete and never becomes exhausted.); it is certainly not [something] that runs dry after discharging once. Wang Yangming said: "Creative transformation should have a sense of its being gradual (漸)."[93] Such a great line! I have already talked about [transformation's being gradual] in the "Explaining Transformation" chapter. The Grand Primordium stage of the cosmos was desolate and devoid of things; although matter and energy were hidden and not immediately manifest, it cannot be said that originally there was no matter. Before organisms had appeared, although the pure and spirit-like was hidden and not immediately manifest, it cannot be said that originally the pure and spirit-like did not exist. The pure and spirit-like does not exist alone separated from matter.

[p. 135]

Because it was not easy for it to be manifestly expressed, however, it needed to wait for inorganic things to evolve into organisms so that (為) a means for the pure and spirit-like to rely on (資具) was prepared in order for it to be manifestly expressed, after which the pure and spirit-like function was fully manifested. (*Wei* 為 is to be read on the fourth tone; *zi* 資: to rely on; *ju* 具: means. The pure and spirit-like needed to have a means it could rely on, otherwise it would be difficult to have been manifested by itself.)

The three major modifications undergone by living entities

Having carefully pondered the matter of the gradual modifications in living entities, it is virtually [impossible] that they are random. Please verify [this claim in the light of the following] three matters. (1) Transitioning from being fixed to moving. When plants first suddenly transformed from inorganic things they were still fixed to their birthplace and unable to shift (移轉). (*Yizhuan* 移轉 is the same as "to move" [運動].) Plants remained unable suddenly to change from the inert and fixed nature of inorganic things. When they evolved to become animals then they began to move. This was an extremely important phase in the evolution of plants without which it would have been

---

[93] This would seem to be a loose paraphrase of the following passage from Wang Yangming, *Yulu yi* 語錄一 (Record of Sayings, One), *Chuanxi lu*, p. 26: "Humaneness is the principle of creative transformation's producing and reproducing endlessly. Although it is all-pervasive and omnipresent, the expression of its flow is only gradual, and so it produces and reproduces endlessly."

very difficult for the pure and spirit-like ever to have been manifested by itself. When carefully investigated, these matters are intriguing, but I will not go into further detail here. It is not the case that plants lack a vague awareness but simply that due their being fixed and rigid the pure and spirit-like is unable to be expressed.

(2) From moving in a crouched manner to standing erect. In the evolution of plants to animals, initially there were things that are difficult to distinguish as animal or plant. This phase was probably very brief. After this then there were lower-order animals. Then, after many transformations, [the stage of] of higher-order animals was reached. In the transition from lower-order animals to higher-order animals, although very early on there was a change from a stationary mode of existence to an active one, nevertheless for long period [animals] were stuck in [a state where they] moved in a hunched manner. Although animals still evolved to have feet, because they moved in a hunched manner, the [posture of] their bodies was not conducive to standing erect and so they moved bent down facing the ground. Although higher-order animals had awareness, the reason that their mental functions were never well-developed was simply that they were stuck in [a state where they] moved in a hunched manner.

Someone asked about the following: "Birds have wings and fly in the sky, and so it would seem that they are not part of the category [of animals] that move in a hunched manner."

I replied: "Although birds fly high, their bodies are bent downward facing the surface of the earth and they are unable to stand erect, unable to face upwards. Hence, the category [of animals that] fly should also be included in [the category of animals] that move in a hunched manner—there is no need to establish a separate category for them."

When higher-order animals evolved to become humans, their bodies were modified appropriately and did not have the defect of being either too large or too small. On the one hand, they changed from being animals impeded by moving in a hunched manner; on the other hand, they still retained [the characteristic] of the upright trunk of plants, free-standing and towering in poise. Hence, the rise of human beings changed from the hunched movement of animals to being erect (挺然) and standing upright,
[p. 136]
their movement even more mysterious. (*Tingran* 挺然: to be straight; it also means unique.) The modification [represented by] this phase can be said to be extremely distinctive. With human beings, the pure and spirit-like became

manifest, grandly displaying its radiance. This is because the means for it to do so had already improved. (The evolution of higher-order animals into human beings did not happen all at once. For example, although with effort apes and monkeys can stand upright, they are unable to do so consistently.)

(3) The structures of the nervous system and the brain increasingly became more compact and keener. Having evolved to this point, living entities are almost perfect. Earlier scholars have already clearly explained this point, but it would seem that no attention has been paid to the first two points.

As described above, only after living entities had undergone three major modifications did the pure and spirit-like attain an excellent means such that it could manifestly express its own power. It is absolutely not the case that these three major modifications occurred randomly. Since they cannot be said to have been random, then it must be acknowledged that ever since the Grand Primordium stage of the cosmos, matter and the pure and spirit-like have always been an immense flow, undifferentiated as one. It must also be acknowledged that vis-a-vis the matter aspect, the pure and spirit-like has always had an active function. (The significance of Qian and Kun in the *Great Change* is that Qian is the pure and spirit-like, Kun is matter, but it is Qian that is active.) After the desolation[94] was opened up and the various heavenly bodies and all of the inorganic things had [each] coalesced and come into existence, however, for a long period of time organisms had not given manifest expression to the pure and spirit-like and, moreover, were unable to do so. The reason for this is none other [than the following]. Before matter had coalesced into various actual entities, it had been lightly drifting in space. Before matter had become apparent, the pure and spirit-like had nothing to depend on and so no means to be manifestly expressed. Once matter had coalesced into various actual entities, then it also gradually lost its original (本然) lightly drifting [appearance]. (*Benran* 本然 is the same as saying "original appearance.") Hence, all inorganic things have the nature of being closed and sinking, and so within them the pure and spirit-like has no means suddenly to be manifestly expressed—this is a necessary principle of things. (In explaining the Sui 隨 [Following] hexagram, Wang Chuanshan said that as soon as the *yin* impetus flourishes it is quite capable of blocking *yang*. [When this occurs] *yang* also temporarily accords with matter but slowly plans a turnaround.[95] *Yang* is the pure and spirit-like; *yin* is matter.

---

[94] That is, the Grand Primordium stage of the cosmos.
[95] Wang Chuanshan (Fuzhi), *Zhou yi da xiang jie* 周易大象解 (Explanation of the Great Images in the *Book of Change*) in *Chuanshan quanshu* bianji weiyuanhui 船山全書編輯委員會 ed., *Chuanshan quanshu* 船山全書 (Complete Writings of Wang Fuzhi) (Changsha: Yuelu shushe, 1988), vol 1, p. 707. "When lightning enters deeply into the marsh, it intends not to be active. The elder

In the period [when there were only] inorganic things, the pure and spirit-like was unable suddenly to be manifest—this precisely was its according with matter.) It nevertheless remains the case that hidden within matter the pure and spirit-like was moving and commanding, taking control as it accorded with conditions, [such that] eventually matter had to follow the perfect and unadulterated (純粹) pure and spirit-like and transform together with it. (*Chuncui* 純粹: see above.[96]) Accordingly, when inorganic things had developed to the point [where everything needed] was in place (For example, conditions suiting the existence of organisms such as the solar system being in place, the temperature of the earth, and so forth.), then within matter the pure and spirit-like

[p. 137]

manifested its active power, leading to changes in the configuration of the structure of matter, so that organisms suddenly appeared next after inorganic things. After organisms had appeared, they continuously modified their bodies, making it increasingly convenient for the development of the pure and spirit-like.

Some general remarks on the development of the cosmos

Accordingly, observing the cosmos from the past to the present and on into the future, it has always been a continuously developing whole. In the development of this whole, from everything being inorganic to the evolution of organisms, the pure and spirit-like started from being hidden to being suddenly manifestly expressed. And once organisms had appeared, they continued to evolve continuously until they reached [the stage of] higher-order animals. When ultimately humans arose, the pure and spirit-like was like a newly rising sun certain to reach its peak. By interconnecting the past, present, and future to gain a comprehensive view of the cosmos as a

---

follows the younger, *yang* follows *yin*. This is of no use to the gentleman and so he can only [bide his time] and by resting in the evening he can thus cease being active and do what he is told, thereby according with normal expected behavior." (雷入澤中，意在不動。長從少，男從女，陽從陰，君子無所用之，唯以向晦入宴息，則可息動而從說，以順人情。) The Sui hexagram consists of the Dui 兌 trigram above, the image of which is a young girl; and the Zhen 震 trigram below, the image of which is an adult male. Moreover, the Zhen trigram consists of a *yang* line at the bottom and two *yin* lines above, thus reinforcing the idea of a suppressed *yang*.

[96] Despite Xiong's instruction to "see above," the term does not appear anywhere else in the text. He does, however, gloss the term in *Ming xin pian*, p. 167, as follows: "*Chun* 純 has two meanings. 1. Unadulterated. 2. Simple and unable to be broken down; nowhere yet everywhere. *Cui* 粹 is the same as perfect."

whole, it is thus evident that from the desolation [that characterized the Grand Primordium], the cosmos began to develop ceaselessly, and it was precisely the pure and spirit-like within matter that eliminated its closure, striving to be active so as to transform and modify[97] matter, ceaselessly advancing without constraint. If the pure and spirit-like were not acknowledged then the cosmos would merely be a lump of matter, a world of inorganic things, eternally so (恆恆爾), perpetually so (常常爾), and devoid of all transformation—what development would there be to speak of? (*Er* 爾 is the same as saying "like this." *Hengheng er* 恆恆爾 is just like the vernacular "like this forever." *Changchang* 常常 is also the same as *hengheng*. These phrases are all borrowed from Chinese translations of Buddhist texts.) As we know from ordinary experience, however, the cosmos actually does not stop at the world of inorganic things; rather, the pure and spirit-like actively guides matter, causing the cosmos to develop without end. Is this not strange indeed!?

As already stated above, the development of the cosmos follows the great principle of manifesting that which was originally concealed. With this principle, the sage observed the great whole and did not become attached to some minor part (一曲) thereof. (*Yiqu* 一曲 means to take a partial observation and fail to see the whole.) He observed transformation (化) from the very beginning to the very end and did not demarcate any one period and become obsessed with it (*Hua* 化: transformation [變化].) Therefore, the way to get a glimpse of the development of the cosmos lies precisely in [discerning] the principle of manifesting that which was originally concealed. Now, if you wish to understand the principle of manifesting that which was originally concealed it is first necessary to affirm the Reality of the cosmos. If Reality were denied then the myriad transformations, the myriad things, and the myriad affairs would all lack a source, and the principle of manifesting that which was originally concealed would lose its highest basis. (The principle of manifesting that which was originally concealed comprehensively includes the myriad transformations, the myriad things, and the myriad affairs, and is omnipresent. It is like the countless worlds that begin as "the smallest ones," which I have already explained above. "The smallest ones" are concealed. When more exhaustively investigated,

[p. 138]

"the smallest ones" certainly do not exist randomly and so there should further be something concealed. Organisms begin with protoplasm. Protoplasm is concealed. Protoplasm does not exist randomly and so there should further be something concealed. The

---

[97] Translating *cai cheng* 裁成 based on Xiong's gloss of this term on p. 214.

ingenious craftsmanship of vessels is manifest. As for their principle (理), it certainly already pre-existed [any particular vessel] and so is concealed. There are countless such examples. As for an example concerning human affairs, such as the great enterprise of revolution, when those of foresight first aroused the idea of revolution, this was certainly "concealed," but this idea did not arise without a cause. If [such factors as] former social trends, political institutions, and so forth were retrospectively examined, then the "concealed" would be even more complex. Thus, the principle of manifesting that which was originally concealed is extremely widespread and ubiquitous. My thesis here, however, explains that in the context of cosmology the development of the cosmos occurs precisely by being in accord with the principle of manifesting that which was originally concealed, and so I cannot deny Reality. It was by profoundly pondering the [purport of] the *Great Change* that I discerned this principle.) I hold that Reality's transformation into function has always been the great flow of the pure and spirit-like and matter and energy, undifferentiated as one. (Reality transforms itself completely into ceaselessly productive and reproductive function. <This is analogous to how the ocean completely transforms itself into the numerous turning and leaping waves.> Function has the two aspects of contraction and expansion; expansion is the pure and spirit-like, contraction is matter. <When matter is referred to, this also includes reference to energy.> Hence, so-called function has always been the great flow of the pure and spirit-like and matter and energy undifferentiated as one.> Reality is not identical to function. <In other words, Reality is not identical to the flow of the undifferentiated [unity of] the pure and spirit-like and matter and energy.> This is analogous to how the ocean is not identical to the numerous waves. <The ocean is a metaphor for Reality and the numerous waves are a metaphor for function or the flow of the undifferentiated [unity of] the pure and spirit-like and matter and energy.> And yet, separated from function or the flow of the undifferentiated [unity of] the pure and spirit-like and matter and energy, there is no Reality. This is analogous to how separated from the numerous waves there is no ocean. [In claiming that] the five aggregates are all empty,[98] the Prajñā masters emptied [空去] function or the flow of the undifferentiated [unity of] the pure and spirit-like and matter and energy in order to see Reality [實相]. <*Shixiang* 實相 is the same as *shiti* 實體.> In doing so, however, they merely saw Reality as empty and quiescent—what difference is there between this and [the view that all dharmas] are non-existent [空無者]?[99] I dare to assert that the principle of the non-duality of Reality and function is beyond any doubt.) **With respect to the matter and energy aspect, the pure and spirit-like has an**

---

[98] See the discussion in Chapter 2, pp. 61–62.
[99] See Xiong's discussion of the two extreme views of existence and non-existence, Chapter 3, p. 139.

active function. This is not some baseless theory in which I give license to subjective conceptualization.

The development of the cosmos interconnects the past, present, and future into one great whole. Now, viewing this whole comprehensively, from the coalescence of inorganic things right through to the appearance of organisms, then, with the subsequent gradual evolutionary development into human beings, the cosmos developed to its highest peak. Because human beings possess the great treasure of the pure and spirit-like, by bringing to completion their abilities by themselves, they are able to expand the Reality of the cosmos (That which Reality has given to us humans is nothing other than unlimited possibilities. <The quantity of possibilities is unlimited.> After we are born, although Reality is absolutely unable to provide us with even an iota of assistance, nevertheless, given that we depend on the existence of the Fundamental (根本) <*Genben* 根本 refers to [p. 139] Reality.> to be able to self-strengthen, and by richly accumulating the power [gained from self-strengthening] we are able to accomplish countless virtuous acts and meritorious deeds. Hence, everything that Reality has not given to us humans is created by us through our own effort. Accordingly, it is through receiving [the support] of we humans that Reality increasingly expands. Indeed, as Confucius said: "It is humans who are able to expand the Way." <"The Way" is a name for Reality.>), and create and modify the cosmos, as exemplified by the various kinds of [acts conducive to] the flourishing of virtue and [achieving] great merit, which Confucius referred to as "fashioning and bringing to completion the [way of] Heaven and Earth" and "assisting the ten thousand things."[100] (See the "Yuan wai wang" 原外王 [To the Origin of External Kingliness] chapter of *To the Origin of the Ru*.[101]) The reason that humans' realization of their capacities (成能)[102] by themselves is so magnificent is because they possess the treasure of the pure and spirit-like. Taking a comprehensive view of the cosmos as a whole, from within matter, the pure and spirit-like commanded and moved (斡運) (*Woyun* 斡運 has two

---

[100] Loose paraphrase of the "Xiang" commentary to the Tai hexagram; see Chapter 1, n. 29.
[101] *Yuan Ru*, p. 466, Xiong cites and comments on the following passage from "Xici, shang," *Zhou yi*, 7.13a–b (my translation of the passage is based on Xiong's commentary): "To have it in abundance is called great merit. (People are able to embody the vigor of the movement of Heaven to have an abundance of creative ability, and so frequently achieve great merit.) Daily renewing it is called the flourishing of virtue. (People's wisdom, virtuous acts, right through to all institutions, such as historical records, administrative institutions and apparatus, and so on, are all [evidence of] daily renewal and not holding on to the old—this is the flourishing of virtue.)" Although it is incongruous that historical records are cited as an example of not holding on to the old, Xiong's point seems to be that historical records bear evidence of change over time.
[102] Translation based on Xiong's gloss of *cheng neng*, *Ming xin pian*, p. 263.

meanings: [1] "to command"; and [2] "to move."); gradually, it eliminated matter's closure, and a tremendous flame was spat out. (The flame refers to the pure and spirit-like.) Before organisms appeared, although the pure and spirit-like was concealed and had yet to be manifest, it is not the case that originally it did not exist. After organisms had appeared, for a long time the pure and spirit-like was manifested but not fully because it had still not completely stopped being concealed. By the time that humans [appeared], the pure and spirit-like was fully manifested. It is abundantly evident that the development of the cosmos followed the great principle of "manifesting that which was originally concealed." With the most refined and most precious of things, in all cases, the longer they are concealed the more magnificent they are when manifestly expressed. If we were to gather together examples drawn from the principles of things and human affairs and tested them, there would be none that are not like this. How could it be blithely asserted that before the appearance of organisms, the pure and spirit-like originally did not exist? If originally it did not exist, how was it later able to exist? Since it is undeniable that it does exist, if one were then to maintain that it is a byproduct of matter, this would be a failure to understand that matter has always been matter, and that judged on the basis of the law of cause and effect, matter absolutely cannot be the mother for (為) the pure and spirit-like (Wei 為 is to be read on the fourth tone. "Mother" is like "cause."), as has already been discussed above. Failing to realize that the cosmos is an incessantly developing whole, scholars go so far as to divide it into given periods, asserting that before the appearance of organisms the pure and spirit-like originally did not exist. How could this possibly be a thesis that testifies to the truth?! In short, the schools of idealistic monism and material monism in Western learning both failed to investigate Reality thoroughly; rather, each holds onto one aspect of phenomena, deeming it to be the sole origin. ("Phenomena" is another a name for function; see above. Idealists take the pure and spirit-like to be the sole origin, subsuming matter into the mind. Materialists take matter to be the sole origin, subsuming the mind into matter.) Little do they realize, both mind and matter are transformed from Reality. Reality is the great origin of the myriad transformations and the myriad existents. Its properties are definitely not singular, and its potent function necessarily stores unlimited potential. Hence, it transforms and moves to become the great flow of the undifferentiated unity of the pure and spirit-like and matter and energy,
[p. 140]

and the myriad transformations and myriad existents [emanate] from this inexhaustibly. (The great flow of the pure and spirit-like and matter and energy is collectively called function. The pure and spirit-like and matter and energy are the two aspects of function.) This principle is so-of-itself and one cannot inquire into that whereby it came to be as such. Above it was already stated: "If there were no opposition [in the flow of great transformation], then there would be no means for transformation to be accomplished. If it were not extremely complex, then how could it develop?" This is an immutable principle. As for idealistic monism and material monism, both split phenomena apart, each holding onto one side, deeming it to be the source of the cosmos. To study cosmology but not exhaustively investigate Reality results in such blindness. In the Ming dynasty, Master Yangming said: "In learning, one must be cognizant of one's brain."[103] The purport of this is profound and far-reaching, and it should never be abandoned.

Someone asked: "With regard to the development of the cosmos, the pure and spirit-like gradually transformed matter, eliminating its closure. As such, does the pure and spirit-like have a goal?"

I replied: "No, no. The pure and spirit-like cannot be treated like what is called a spirit in religions, in order to conjecture and make comparisons. How could it be said that it has a goal? The myriad mental and material images all transform and move unceasingly. The *Book of Change* states: 'That to where they proceed is transformation alone (唯變所適).' (See the "Great Commentary" to the *Book of Change*.[104] *Shi* 適 is the same as "to go to" [之], "to proceed towards" [往]. In moving forward, the action of great transformation is merely to let things take their own course. Never having had a plan, of course it has no predetermined goal, and so the *Book of Change* states: "That to where they proceed is transformation alone.") If, as you say, the pure and spirit-like has a goal, then there would certainly be no transformation and development to talk of. How is this so? If transformation were to follow a predetermined [course], then the cosmos would be a pre-established arrangement—what transformation would there be to talk of? If the myriad things and myriad affairs were all pre-established, then what development would there be? The *Book of Change* states: 'That to where they proceed is transformation alone.' In observing transformation, the sage was meticulous, and so attained the truth of the matter. The thesis that [transformation has] a goal certainly cannot be sustained. It can, however, further be argued that

---

[103] Paraphrase of *Chuan xi lu*, p. 116.
[104] "Xici zhuan, xia," 8.19a.

although the pure and spirit-like has no goal, it does, after all, have an impetus to take control as it accords with conditions. On the one hand, it is possible that the inorganic world possibly did not block the growth of organisms, and so organisms thus appeared. On the other hand, however, the various modifications that organisms underwent (See above.) are all clear evidence of the pure and spirit-like's having taken control as it accorded with conditions. 'Taking control as it accorded with conditions' [means the following.] On the unrestrained (蕩然) (*Dangran* 蕩然: not fixed [不定].) and unpredictable long path of 'that to where they proceed is transformation alone,' [the pure and spirit-like] accorded with the circumstances it encountered yet in doing so had control and freedom. This is absolutely different from a teleology (目的之論). [Having a] goal (目的) is to hang up a fixed target (的) (*Di* 的 is like the target [鵠] set up by archers in ancient times.) so as to determine the means necessary [to realize] the future that has yet to come and that it will necessarily be reached, and that different routes deviating from [this approach] will be unacceptable. (If we suppose that there was a god who created the world,

[p. 141]

then this is how he is likely to have created it.) Since there never was a creator (作者) of the flow of great transformation, how could there be anything like this? ("Great transformation" is just the same as saying "great function." *Zuozhe* 作者: see Chinese translations of Buddhist texts; it is like *zaowu zhu* 造物主.) 'That to where they proceed is transformation alone'—the sage's words are profound and far-reaching in the extreme. I am simply unable to praise them highly enough." (A detailed examination of teleology would be an extremely complex undertaking, and I will not go into the details here. During my life I have paid particular attention to this passage from the *Great Change*: "The Way of Heaven arouses the myriad things but does not share in the worries of the sage."[105] This passage concerns the greatest questions about the cosmos and human life, and it would take another book to expound this properly. The reason that the sage had such sublime and far-reaching ideas as "fashioning and bringing to completion the [way of] Heaven and Earth" and "assisting the ten thousand things"[106] was due to his having had worries. The term *gu* 鼓 in "The Way of Heaven arouses [鼓] the myriad things" is used ingeniously, its inherent meaning inexhaustible. The potent functions of "vast productivity" and "capacious productivity" can be seen therein. The Way of Heaven is not a creator, that to where they proceed is transformation alone, hence

---

[105] See Chapter 3, n. 44.
[106] See Chapter 1, n. 29.

the myriad things are not equal. The worries of the sage are not something that ordinary people can fathom.)

Concluding remarks

Having written up to here, I find that I no longer have the energy to sustain me and so I should conclude. There is so much that I want to say but I can no longer bear to hold a pen. During my life I have been extremely fond of philosophy, deeply reflecting on things while in solitude. Science, of course, is a partial view of the cosmos. The responsibility to view the cosmos comprehensively, deeply penetrating the very bottom of the source (源底), must lie exclusively with philosophy. (*Yuan* 源: source; *di* 底: innermost secret [底蘊].) Personally, I hope that the various branches of learning concerned with matter and energy, biology, mathematics, dialectics, as well as the exploration of all kinds of theories will increasingly broaden and deepen. There are indeed treasures in the texts bequeathed by ancient wise men in the East and I particularly hope that scholars will painstakingly study them in detail. (The *Book of Change* is the most important.) It is my great hope that in the future there will be a flourishing of philosophers who will integrate the above branches of learning to create a cosmology for a new philosophy. The *Book of Change* established "the origin of Qian" (乾元), which is the great origin of the myriad mental and material images. (*Qian yuan* 乾元: the Reality of production and reproduction.[107]) The *Book of Change* says that all matter transforms and moves unceasingly and that there never was hard obstructive matter. I maintain that if the various branches of learning concerned with matter and energy, as well as biology, were each to penetrate to the depths thoroughly, to investigate the incipient (幾), then as a matter of course they would surely gain a thorough understanding of the origin of Qian. (*Ji* 幾 is like "subtle" [微]. When the various branches of learning concerned with matter and energy have reached the extremely profound and far-reaching, the extremely subtle, they can then open up a path to the origin of the cosmos. When biology investigates and enters the profoundly subtle it will then be understood that the pure and spirit-like is active in opening-up the development of things.) To discuss cosmology and yet be unable to integrate biology and the various branches of learning concerned with matter and energy—even if the thesis being upheld were that of a renowned expert—would, after all, have

---

[107] Production and reproduction represent function.

nothing to do with the bottom of the source (源底) of the cosmos, and those of discernment would be sure to dismiss such talk. (*Yuan* 源: source; *di* 底: innermost secret [底蘊]. The myriad transformations and myriad changes, the myriad things, and myriad affairs—these are not like an illusion or a conjuring trick; they have a source and a bottom. The *Great Change* takes Qian to be the pure and spirit-like and Kun to be matter and energy. As for the principles of biology as well as those of the various branches of learning concerned with matter and energy, the *Great Change* was the first to expound all of them.

[p. 142]

Matter is not something that is inert. In Western learning this was not discovered until very late. The *Book of Change*'s discussion of generative vitality [生命] is extremely profound and far-reaching. Mencius said: "The myriad things are all contained in me."[108] <Here Mencius does not use the word "me" to refer just to himself. The principle [involved] is the same, no matter which person. This applies even to a grain of sand. It must be understood that a grain of sand and the great cosmos are the same body, the same generative vitality.> Mencius also said: "He flows together with Heaven above and Earth below." <See above.> This is also [based on] insight into the *Book of Change*. Laozi's and Zhuangzi' doctrines of generative vitality also originated in the *Book of Change*, albeit with some modifications. It is a pity that they were done poorly, but I will not go into this here. I surmise that the late Zhou Confucians must have had major works on biology. Former wise men were the earliest to have discovered that the various types of things metamorphize. Now that I am old, infirm, and forgetful, however, I am unable to put these kinds of materials into order.)

The *Book of Change* arranges odd and even numbers to form sixty-four hexagrams, [totaling] 384 lines. It is the first of the most ancient works of mathematical philosophy in the world. It uses odd and even [to reveal how] transformation is accomplished. (Qian [is represented by] odd numbers; Kun [is represented by] even numbers.) It shows how (1) that whereby the myriad transformations and myriad changes, myriad things, and myriad affairs are generated, as well as how (2) although [the myriad things] ceaselessly transform and change in utter profusion, they cannot be thrown into disarray, both have their laws. (From "It shows" to here is one sentence. Every word here is based on the text of [the *Book of Change*].)[109] Ultimately, this all comes down to "fashioning and bringing to completion the [way of] Heaven and Earth" and "assisting the ten thousand things." (See the "To the Origin of External Kingliness"

---

[108] *Mencius* 7A.4.
[109] Largely interpretative paraphrases.

chapter in my *To the Origin of the Ru*.[110]) As for the multifarious transformations and changes that humans undergo, the *Book of Change* was the first to express the rule that "when [change] reaches a limit then there is transformation, with transformation there is continuity, and with continuity there is endurance."[111] Ultimately, this all comes down to the flourishing of "going out of one's way to enable all people to develop [their nature fully]" (曲成萬物) and "a flight of dragons with no leader." (*Qu cheng* 曲成: All people accord with the good beginnings of their Heaven-bestowed nature and their individual competencies to support and exhort one another so that their natures are also fully developed.[112] For "a flight of dragons," see above. The passage is worth reading again.) The theories and institutions [set out in] the *Spring and Autumn Annals*, "Li yun" 禮運 (The Operation of Ritual) [chapter of the *Book of Rites*], and *Zhou guan* 周官 (Offices of Zhou)[113] were all derived from the *Book of Change*. The *Book of Change* is magnificent! Whereas there is that which even the transformations of Heaven and Earth and the movement of the four seasons do not encompass, there is nothing that the *Book of Change* does not encompass (周). (*Zhou* 周: all-encompassing [周遍]. Before the War of Resistance against Japan [1937–1945], Zhang Ertian 張爾田, [style] Mengqu 孟劬 [1874–1945]),[114] once said to me: "There are three great treasures in the world: the *Book of Change*, the *Analects*, and *Laozi*. I hope that you will write new commentaries on them." I replied: "The *Analects* and *Laozi* cannot be placed on the same level as the *Book of Change*." I had known Mengqu only for two years when the War of Resistance against Japan broke out. I entered Sichuan[115] and Mengqu passed away in grief and anger in Peking. I still mourn him and cannot bear to forget him. During my life I have engaged in useless learning; I did not dare to seek knowledge from my contemporaries; and I had no students to teach. Although new prospects have opened up, I am already in my dotage and have not carried out what Mengqu asked of me. He had innovative ideas about the filiation of Chinese scholarship. His book, *Shi wei* 史微 [The Little Things in History],[116] was published very early. In his late years, his learning was extremely refined and encyclopedic but, unfortunately, he did not put it on paper.)

---

[110] See note 101 above.
[111] "Xici, xia," 8.6a.
[112] See also related glosses of *qu cheng* in *Ming xin pian*, p. 203 and *Cunzhai suibi*, pp. 742–743.
[113] That is, *Zhou li* 周禮 (Rites of Zhou).
[114] Historian and elder brother of philosopher and public intellectual, Zhang Dongsun 張東蓀 (1886–1973).
[115] See Chapter 1, note 41.
[116] As related by Joshua A. Fogel, "On the 'Rediscovery' of the Chinese Past: Cui Shu and Related Cases," in *Between China and Japan: The Writings of Joshua Fogel* (Brill, 2015), p. 633: "A native of eastern Zhejiang and *landsmann* of Zhang Xuecheng, Zhang Ertian was the author of *Shiwei* [The Little Things in History], published in 1911, in which he actively attempted to revive the historiographic approach of his fellow native."

The myriad transformations and myriad changes, myriad things, and myriad affairs, mutually oppose and mutually complete. Extremely complex, extremely strange, what is

[p. 143]

manifested can be seen, but what is concealed is difficult to know. Those who analyze the parts are ignorant of the whole; those who investigate the small, overlook the large. (Equally, the error of pursuing the large but failing to discern it in the small and pursing the whole but failing to investigate it in the parts, cannot be remedied either.) Can we speak of philosophy if there is a not some inquiry into dialectics? This treatise posits the tenet of the non-duality of Reality and function. Origin (本原) and phenomena cannot be separated into two. (*Benyuan* 本原 refers to intrinsic Reality.) What is real and what changes cannot be separated into two. (For the Buddhists, dharmas that arise and cease are changing, whereas dharmas that neither arise nor cease are what is real [真實].[117] Western philosophy takes phenomena to be changing and noumena to be what is real. Their error is equal to that of the Buddhists.) The absolute and the relative cannot be separated into two, mind and matter cannot be separated into two (Mind and matter are simply two aspects, not different entities.), matter and energy cannot be separated into two, and Heaven and humans cannot be separated into two. All kinds of principles are endowed with the *Book of Changes*' dialectics.

[Early] in my life I was orphaned. In the Qing dynasty I took part in revolution and did not attend school.[118] When I was approaching the age of no longer having doubts I began to study assiduously (*Analects* [2.4]: "At forty I no longer had doubts.") but it was then that I was assailed by illness. Lacking a foundation in science, I had no means to draw on [scientific] materials to include in my writings. Nevertheless, I am confident that this treatise's fundamental teaching that Reality and function are non-dual is not false. This treatise has been preserved for the interim, awaiting talented persons in the future [to elaborate further on its fundamental teaching].

Above I have already provided a general account of how matter came to be formed. Next, I should continue to elucidate the subtleties of mind.

Chapter 5, "Explaining Mind" (To be continued.)

---

[117] The term 真實 was used to translate Sanskrit terms such as *bhūta, tathatva, tattva*.
[118] Both of Xiong's parents died in his early teenage years; his revolutionary activities began in 1905.

5

Explaining Mind (Forthcoming)

This chapter title appears in the original table of contents. It was never published as a chapter in the *Treatise*. For details, see the Translator's Introduction.

Works Cited

Amelung, Iwo. "Naming Physics: The Strife to Delineate a Field of Modern Science in Late Imperial China." In Michael Lackner and Natascha Vittinghoff, eds., *Mapping Meanings: The Field of New Learning in Late Qing China*. Leiden: Brill, 2004.

An Shigao 安世高 (fl. 148–170), trans. (?). *Ahan koujie shier yinyuan jing* 阿含口解十二因緣經 (Sutra on the Oral Explanation of the Twelve [Links of] Causal Conditions in the Agamas), T1508.

Apidamo da piposha lun 阿毘達磨大毘婆沙論 (*Abhidharma-mahā-vibhāṣā-śāstra*; Treatise of the Great Commentary on the Abhidharma), trans. Xuanzang 玄奘 (602–664), T1545.

Asaṅga (無著; 4th cent. CE). *Dasheng zhuangyan jing lun* 大乘莊嚴經論 (*Mahāyāna-sūtrālaṃkāra*; Treatise on the Scripture for Adorning the Great Vehicle), T1604.

Asaṅga (無著; 4th cent. CE). *She dasheng lun ben* 攝大乘論本 (*Mahāyāna-saṃgraha-śāstra*; Compendium of the Great Vehicle), trans. Xuanzang 玄奘 (602–664), T1594.

Ban Gu 班固 (32–92). *Hanshu* 漢書 (History of the Former Han Dynasty). Beijing: Zhonghua shuju, 1983.

Baoxing lun 寶性論 (*Ratnagotravibhāga*; Jewel Nature Treatise), trans. Ratnamati (勒那摩提; fl. 511), T1611.

Bhāviveka (清辨 c. 490–570). *Dasheng zhangzhen lun* 大乘掌珍論 (**Mahāyāna-hastaratna-śāstra*), trans. Xuanzang 玄奘 (602–664), T1578.

Bore boluomiduo xin jing 般若波羅蜜多心經 **Mahā-prajñāpāramitā-hṛdaya-sūtra*; (Heart Sutra), trans. Prajñā 般若 and Liyan 利言 (8th cent.), T253.

Cai Yuanpei 蔡元培 (1868–1940). "Xin jiaoyu yijian" 新教育意見 (My Views on New Education). In Wen Di 聞笛 and Shui Ru 水如 eds., *Cai Yuanpei meixue wenxuan* 蔡元培美學文選 (Selections from Cai Yuanpei's Writings on Aesthetics). Taipei: Shuxing chubanshe, 1989.

Chen Lai 陳來. *Renxue bentilun* 仁學本體論 (Ontology of Humaneness-Centered Learning). Beijing: Sanlian shudian, 2014.

Chengguan 澄觀 (738–839). *Da Huayan jing lüece* 大華嚴經略策 (Outline of [Chengguan's] [Commentary on] the *Flower Garland Sutra* [*Dafangguang fo Huayan jing shu* 大方廣佛華嚴經疏]), T1737.

Chuanshan quanshu 船山全書 (Complete Writings of Wang Fuzhi), *Chuanshan quanshu* bianji weiyuanhui 船山全書編輯委員會 ed. Changsha: Yuelu shushe, 1988.

Cook, Francis H. *Three Texts on Consciousness-Only*. Berkeley, CA: Numata Center for Buddhist Translation and Research, 1999.

Cox, Collett. "From Category to Ontology: The Changing Role of Dharma in Sarvāstivāda Abhidharma." *Journal of Indian Philosophy* 32, no. 5/6 (December 2004): 543–597.

Da baoji jing 大寶積經 (*Mahāratnakūṭa-sūtra*; Great Treasures Collection Sutra), trans. Bodhiruci (菩提留支; d. c. 535), T310.

Da bore boluomiduo jing 大般若波羅蜜多經 (*Mahāprajñāpāramitā-sūtra*; Perfection of Wisdom Sutra), trans. Xuanzang 玄奘 (602–664), T220.

240   WORK CITED

Da sazhe Niganzi suo shuo jing 大薩遮尼乾子所説經 (*Mahāsatya-nirgrantha-sūtra*; The Sutra Explained by the Mahāsattva Nirgrantha), trans. Bodhiruci (菩提留支; d. c. 535), T272.

Daban niepan jing 大般涅槃經 (*Mahāparinirvāṇa-sūtra*; Great Nirvana Sutra), T7. Traditionally, the translation has been attributed to Faxian 法顯 (d. c. 420).

Daoxuan 道宣 (596–667). *Sifen lü shanfan buque xingshi chao* 四分律刪繁補闕行事鈔 (Summary of the Procedures of the Four-Part Vinaya, Abridged with Supplements), T1804.

Daoxuan 道宣 (596–667), comp. *Xu Gaoseng zhuan* 續高僧傳 (Biographies of Eminent Monks, Continued), T2060.

Daoyuan 道原 (fl. 1004), comp. *Jingde chuandeng lu* 景德傳燈錄 (Record of the Transmission of the Lamp Published in the Jingde Reign Period), T2076.

Dasheng ru lengqie jing 大乘入楞伽經 (*Laṅkāvatāra-sūtra*; Sutra on the Buddha's Entering the Country of Lanka), trans. Śikṣānanda (實叉難陀; fl. 700), T672.

Dignāga (陳那; 6th century). *Guan suoyuan yuan lun* 觀所緣緣論 (*Ālambana-parīkṣā*; Treatise Investigating the Conditions for the Causal Support of Consciousness), trans. Xuanzang 玄奘 (602–664), T1624.

Dignāga (陳那; 6th century). *Wuxiang sichen lun* 無相思塵論 (*Ālambana-parīkṣā*; Treatise on Considerations [of the Fact That] Objects of Thought Have No Characteristics), trans. Paramārtha (眞諦; 499–569), T1619.

Ding Yun 丁耘. "Zhexue yu ti yong: Ping Chen Lai jiaoshou *Renxue bentilun*" 哲學與體用：評陳來教授《仁學本體論》(Philosophy and *Ti-Yong*: A Review of Professor Chen Lai's *Ontology of Humaneness-Centered Learning*). *Zhexuemen* 31 (2015): 279–294.

Dong Zhongshu 董仲舒 (179–104 BCE). *Chun qiu fan lu* 春秋繁露 (Luxuriant Dew of the Spring and Autumn Annals), *Sibu beiyao* 四部備要. Shanghai: Zhonghua shuju, 1936.

Dullyun 遁倫 (ca. 650–730). *Yuqie lun ji* (*Yuga rongi*) 瑜伽論記 (Commentaries on the *Yogācārabhūmi*), T1828.

Er ya zhu zi suo yin 爾雅逐字索引 (Concordance to *Erya*), D. C. Lau (Liu Dianjue 劉殿爵) et al. eds. Hong Kong: Shangwu yinshuguan, 1995.

Ess, Hans van, trans. Sima Qian 司馬遷, "Taishi gong zixu" 太史公自序 (Sequence of his Honor, the Grand Scribe's Own [History]). In William Nienhauser Jr., ed., *The Grand Scribe's Records, Volume XI: The Memoirs of Han China, Part IV*. Bloomington and Nanjing: Indiana University Press and Nanjing University Press, 2019.

Fazang 法藏 (643–712). *Xiu Huayan ao zhi wang jin huanyuan guan* 修華嚴奧旨妄盡還源觀 (Practicing the Discernment of Exhausting Delusion and Returning to the Source through the Profound Purport of Huayan), T1867.

Fo shuo hua shou jing 佛說華手經 (*Kuśalamūlasamparigraha*), trans. Kumārajīva (鳩摩羅什; 344–413), T657.

Fo yijiao jing lunshu jieyao 佛遺教經論疏節要 (Exegesis with Summary of the *Sūtra on the Buddha's Deathbed Injunction*), with exegesis by Jingyuan 淨源 (1011–1088) and supplementary notes by Zhuhong 袾宏 (1535–1615), T1820.

Fogel, Joshua A. "On the 'Rediscovery' of the Chinese Past: Cui Shu and Related Cases." In *Between China and Japan: The Writings of Joshua Fogel*. Leiden: Brill, 2015.

Guanzi 管子, *Sibu congkan chubian* (q.v.).

Guo Qiyong 郭齊勇. *Tiandi jian yige dushuren: Xiong Shili zhuan* 天地間一個讀書人：熊十力傳 (A Scholar Poised between Heaven and Earth: A Biography of Xiong Shili). Taipei: Yeqiang chubanshe, 1994.

Guo Qiyong 郭齊勇. *Xiong Shili zhexue yanjiu* 熊十力哲學研究 (A Study of Xiong Shili's Philosophy). Beijing: Renmin daxue chubanshe, 2011 (originally published 1993).

Han Fei 韓非 (d. 233 BCE). *Han Feizi* 韓非子 (Master Han Fei), 7.2a, *Sibu congkan chubian* (q.v.).

Harbsmeier, Christoph. *Language and Logic in Traditional China*, in *Science and Civilisation in China*, vol. 7, pt. 1. Cambridge: Cambridge University Press, 1998.

Hidenori Sakuma. "On Doctrinal Similarities between Sthiramati and Xuanzang," *Journal of the International Association of Buddhist Studies* 29, no. 2 (2006 [2008]): 357–382.

Hongzhi Chanshi guanglu 宏智禪師廣錄 (Extensive Record of the Chan Master Hongzhi), compiled by disciples of Hongzhi Zhengjue 宏智正覺 (1091–1157), T2001.

Hu Xu 胡煦 (1655–1736). *Gou deng yue zhi* 篝燈約旨 (Burning the Midnight Lamp [to Illuminate] the General Purport [of the *Book of Change*]), in his *Zhou Yi han shu, bieji* 周易函書別集 (Writings on the *Zhou Book of Change*, Author's Collected Works), *juan* 8, *Qinding Siku quanshu* (q.v.).

Hu Yong 胡勇. "Jindai foxue gegu yu ti yong quanshi de chuangxin 近代佛學革故與體用詮釋的創新 (A Revolution in Modern Buddhism and Innovations in Interpreting *Ti* and *Yong*). In Cheng Gongran 程恭讓 and Miaofan 妙凡 eds., *2016 Xingyun dashi renjian fojiao lilun shijian yanjiu* 2016 星雲大師人間佛教理論實踐研究 (Studies from 2016 on Putting Venerable Master Xingyun's Humanistic Buddhism into Practice). Gaoxiong: Foguang wenhua, 2017.

Hui Dong 惠棟 (1697–1758). *Zhou yi shu* 周易述 (Comments on the *Book of Change*), *Qinding Siku quanshu* (q.v.).

Huiyuan 慧遠 (523–592). *Dasheng niepan jing yiji* 大般涅槃經義記 (Commentary on the *Great Nirvana Sutra*), T1764.

Jia, Jinhua. *The Hongzhou School of Chan Buddhism in Eighth- Through Tenth-Century China*. New York: SUNY, 2006.

Jiao Xun 焦循 (1763–1820). *Yi guang ji* 易廣記 (Extended Notes on the *Book of Change*), Qing edition held in Beijing University Library. https://ctext.org/library.pl?if=gb&file=94449&page=77

Jie shenmi jing 解深密經 (*Saṃdhinirmocana-sūtra*; Sutra Explaining the Profound and Esoteric), trans. Xuanzang 玄奘 (602–664), T676.

Jin'gang bore boluomi jing 金剛般若波羅蜜經 (*Vajracchedikā-prajñāpāramitā-sūtra*; Diamond Sutra), trans. Kumārajīva (鳩摩羅什; 344–413), T235.

Jinshu 晉書 (Book of Jin), Fang Xuanling 房玄齡 et al., comps. Beijing: Zhonghua shuju, 1974.

Jizang 吉藏 (549–623). *Fahua yishu* 法華義疏 (Elucidation of the Meaning of the *Lotus Sutra*), T1721.

Jizang 吉藏 (549–623). *Zhongguan lun shu* 中觀論疏 (Subcommentary on the *Treatise on the Middle Way*), T1824.

Jorgensen, John. "Setting the Scene: The Different Perspectives of Yang Wenhui and Ouyang Jingwu on the *Treatise on Awakening Mahāyāna Faith* as an Authoritative Statement of Mahāyāna Doctrine." In John Makeham, ed., *The Awakening of Faith and New Confucian Philosophy* (q.v.).

Jorgensen, John, Dan Lusthaus, John Makeham, Mark Strange, trans. *Treatise on Awakening Mahāyāna Faith*. New York: Oxford University Press, 2019.

Kern, Martin. "Language and the Ideology of Kingship in the 'Canon of Yao.'" In Martin Kern and Dirk Meyer, eds., *Origins of Chinese Political Philosophy: Studies in the Composition and Thought of the Shangshu* (Classic of Documents). Leiden: Brill, 2017.

Kexue chubanshe 科學出版社 (China Science Publishing) editors, letter of reply to Xiong Shili, January 21, 1958. https://auction.artron.net/paimai-art00573311604/

Kirkova, Zornica. *Roaming into the Beyond: Representations of Xian Immortality in Early Medieval Chinese Verse*. Leiden: Brill, 2016.

Kuiji 窺基 (632–682). *Bian zhong bian lun shuji* 辯中邊論述記 (Commentary on the *Treatise Distinguishing the Middle from the Extremes*), T1835.

Kuiji 窺基 (632–682). *Bore boluomiduo xin jing you zan* 般若波羅蜜多心經幽贊 (Profound Explanation of the *Prajñāpāramitā Heart Sutra*), T1710.

Kuiji 窺基 (632–682). *Cheng weishi lun shuji* 成唯識論述記 (Commentary on *Demonstration of Nothing but Consciousness*), T1830.

Kuiji 窺基 (632–682). *Weishi ershi lun shuji* 唯識二十論述記 (Commentary on *Twenty Verses on Nothing but Consciousness*), T1834.

Kuiji 窺基 (632–682). *Yinming ru zhengli shu* 因明入正理論疏 (Commentary on the *Introduction to the Science of Reasoning*), T1840.

Kurtz, Joachim. *The Discovery of Chinese Logic*. Boston: Brill, 2011.

Lang Shiyuan 郎士元 (c. 727–c. 780). "Huanzeng Qian Yuanwai 'Ye su Lingtai si' jianji" 還贈錢員外夜宿靈臺寺見寄 (Presented in Reply to the Poem "Spending a Night at Lingtai Temple" Sent to Me by Supernumerary Qian [Qi] [錢起 (c. 722–780)])." In *Jin Shengtan xuanpi Tang shi liubai shou* 金聖嘆選批唐詩六百首 (Jin Shengtan's Selection of Six Hundred Tang Poems with Notes). Beijing: Lianjing chuban gongsi, 2018.

Lau, D. C., trans. *The Analects*. Harmondsworth: Penguin, 1979.

Li Dingzuo 李鼎祚 (Tang dynasty). *Zhou yi jijie* 周易集解 (Collected Explanations of the *Book of Change*), *Qinding Siku quanshu* (q.v.).

Li Jingde 李靖德 (fl. 1263), comp. *Zhuzi yulei* 朱子語類 (Topically Arranged Conversations of Master Zhu), Beijing: Zhonghua shuju, 1986.

Li Shangyin 李商隱 (813–858). "Chong guo shengnü ci" 重過聖女祠 (Once More Passing the Shrine of a Goddess). In *Quan Tang shi* 全唐詩 (Complete Works of Tang Poetry). Beijing: Zhonghua shuju, 1979.

Li Tongxuan 李通玄 (635–730 or 646–740). *Xin Huayan jing lun* 新華嚴經論 (Treatise on the New Translation of the *Flower Ornament Sutra*), T1739.

Liang Qichao 梁啟超. *Qing dai xueshu gailun* 清代學術概論 (An Overview of Qing Dynasty Scholarship). Shanghai: Shanghai guji chubanshe, 1998/2000.

Liji 禮記 (Book of Rites), Kong Yingda 孔穎達 (574–648) et al., comps. *Liji zhushu* 禮記註疏 (*Liji* with Annotations and Sub-commentary), *Shisan jing zhushu* (q.v.).

Liu, JeeLoo. *Neo-Confucianism: Metaphysics, Mind, and Morality*. Hoboken: Wiley-Blackwell, 2017.

Liu zu dashi fabao tan jing 六祖大師法寶壇經 (The Sixth Patriarch, Great Master Huineng's Dharma Treasure Platform Sutra), traditionally attributed to Huineng 慧能 (638–713), T2008.

Lu Deming 陸德明 (556–627). *Jingdian shiwen* 經典釋文 (Explanations of the Texts of the Classics), *Chizao Tang Siku quanshu cuiyao* 摛藻堂四庫全書薈要 (Essentials of *The Complete Collection of the Four Treasuries* from the Chizao Hall). Taipei: Shijie shuju, 1986–1989.

Lusthaus, Dan. *Buddhist Phenomenology: A Philosophical Investigation of Yogacara Buddhism and the Ch'eng Wei-shih Lun*, Curzon Critical Studies in Buddhism Series. London: Routledge, 2002.

Lynn, Richard John, trans. *The Classic of Changes: A New Translation of the I Ching as Interpreted by Wang Pi*. New York: Columbia University Press, 2004.

Makeham, John, ed. *The Awakening of Faith and New Confucian Philosophy*. Boston: Brill, 2021.

Makeham, John. "Monism and the Problem of the Ignorance and Badness in Chinese Buddhism and Zhu Xi's Neo-Confucianism." In John Makeham, ed., *The Buddhist Roots of Zhu Xi's Philosophical Thought*. New York: Oxford University Press, 2018.

Makeham, John, trans. *New Treatise on the Uniqueness of Consciousness*. New Haven: Yale University Press, 2015.

Makeham, John. "The Significance of Xiong Shili's Interpretation of Dignāga's *Ālambana-parīkṣā* (Investigation of the Object)." *Journal of Chinese Philosophy* 40:S (2013): 205–225.

Makeham, John. *Transmitters and Creators: Chinese Commentators and Commentaries on the Analects*. Cambridge, MA: Harvard University Asia Center, 2008.

Maybee, Julie E. "Hegel's Dialectics." *Stanford Encyclopedia of Philosophy* (2016). https://plato.stanford.edu/entries/hegel-dialectics/

Miaofa lianhua jing 妙法蓮華經 (*Saddharmapuṇḍarīka-sūtra*; Lotus Sutra), trans. Kumārajīva (鳩摩羅什; 344–413), T262.

Mohe bore boluomi jing 摩訶般若波羅蜜經 (*Pañca-viṃśati-sāhasrikā-prajñā-pāramitā*; The Perfection of Wisdom Sutra in 25,000 Verses), trans. Kumārajīva (鳩摩羅什; 344–413), T223.

Mohe bore boluomiduo xin jing 摩訶般若波羅蜜多心經 (Heart Sutra), trans. Xuanzang 玄奘 (602–664), T251.

Mou Zongsan 牟宗三. *Mou Zongsan quanji* 牟宗三全集 (The Complete Works of Mou Zongsan). Taipei: Lianjing, 2003.

Mou Zongsan 牟宗三. *Xinti yu xingti* 心體與性體 (Intrinsic Reality of the Mind and Intrinsic Reality of the Nature, vol. 1; 1968). In *Mou Zongsan quanji*, vol. 5 (q.v.).

Mou Zongsan 牟宗三. *Yuan shan lun* 圓善論 (On the *Summum Bonum*; 1985). In *Mou Zongsan quanji*, vol. 22 (q.v.).

Mou Zongsan 牟宗三. *Zhuangzi "Qi wu lun" jiangyan lu* (5) 莊子〈齊物論〉講演錄（五）(Lectures on *Zhuangzi*, "Discourse on Making All Things Equal" [5]), *Ehu yuekan* 鵝湖月刊 323, no. 5 (2002): 1–11.

Muller, A. Charles, ed. *Digital Dictionary of Buddhism* (July 31, 2022). http://buddhism-dict.net/ddb

Muller, A. Charles, trans. *The Diamond Sutra* (November 15, 2020). http://www.acmuller.net/bud-canon/diamond_sutra.html

Nāgārjuna (龍樹; ca. 150–250 CE) (attrib.). *Dazhidu lun* 大智度論 (*Mahāprajñāpāramitā-śāstra*; Treatise on the Great Perfection of Wisdom), trans. Kumārajīva (鳩摩羅什; 344–413), T1509.

Nāgārjuna (龍樹; ca. 150–250 CE). *Zhong lun* 中論 (*Mūla-madhyamaka-kārikā*; Treatise on the Middle Way), trans. Kumārajīva (鳩摩羅什; 344–413) with comments by Piṅgala (青目; 4th cent.), T1564.

Ouyang Jingwu 歐陽竟無 (1871–1943). "Kong Fo" 孔佛 (Confucians and Buddhists) (1936). In his *Kongxue zazhu* 孔學雜著 (Assorted Writings on Confucianism), in *Ouyang Jingwu xiansheng neiwai xue* 歐陽竟無先生內外學 (Mr Ouyang Jingwu's Buddhist and Non-Buddhist Learning), vol. 14. http://www.guoxue123.com/new/0002/bfehyx/043.htm.

Pines, Yuri, trans. *The Book of Lord Shang: Apologetics of State Power in Early China*. New York: Columbia University Press, 2017.

Powers, John, "Yogācāra: Indian Buddhist Origins," in John Makeham, ed., *Transforming Consciousness: Yogācāra Thought in Modern China*. New York: Oxford University Press, 2014.

Puguang 普光 (d. c. 664 CE). *Dasheng baifa ming men lun shu* 大乘百法明門論疏 (Commentary on the *Mahāyāna śatadharma-prakāśamukha-śāstra* [Lucid Introduction to the One Hundred Dharmas]), T1837.

Putai 普泰 (early 16th century). *Ba shi guiju buzhu* 八識規矩補註 (Supplementary Notes on the *[Verses on the] Structure of the Eight Consciousnesses*), T1865.

Qinding Siku quanshu 欽定四庫全書 (Imperially Ratified Complete Collection of the Four Treasuries), copy of edition held in Zhejiang University Library, https://ctext.org/library.pl?if=gb&collection=4.

Queen, Sarah A., and John S. Major, eds. and trans. *Luxuriant Gems of the Spring and Autumn*. New York: Columbia University Press, 2016.

Radich, Michael. "Was the *Mahāparinirvāṇa-sūtra* 大般涅槃經T7 Translated by 'Faxian'?: An Exercise in the Computer-Assisted Assessment of Attributions in the Chinese Buddhist Canon." *Hualin International Journal of Buddhist Studies*, 2 no. 1 (2019): 229–279.

Sang, Yu [桑雨]. *Xiong Shili's Understanding of Reality and Function, 1920–1937*. Boston: Brill, 2020.

Shang Yang 商鞅 (d. 338 BCE), attrib. *Shangzi* 商子 (also known as *Shang Jun shu* 商君書 [Book of Lord Shang]), *Sibu congkan chubian* (q.v.).

Shangshu 尚書 (Book of Documents), *Shisan jing zhushu* (q.v.).

Shi jing 詩經 (Book of Odes), *Shisan jing zhushu* (q.v.).

Shiba kong lun 十八空論 (Treatise on Eighteen Aspects of Emptiness), trans. Paramārtha (眞諦; 499–569), T1616.

Shimao, Eikoh. "Some Aspects of Japanese Science, 1868–1945." *Annals of Science* 46, no. 1 (1989): 69–91.

Shisan jing zhushu 十三經注疏 (The Thirteen Classics with Annotations and Sub-Commentaries), Ruan Yuan 阮元 (1764–1849) comp. Taipei: Yiwen yinshuguan, 1985.

Shou lengyan jing 首楞嚴經 (*Śūraṃgama-sūtra*; Sutra on Heroic Progress), T945.

Sibu congkan chubian 四部叢刊初編 (Collectanea of the Four Categories, First Series) Shanghai: Shangwu yinshuguan, 1919–1922.

Sima Qian 司馬遷 (born c. 145 BCE). *Shiji* 史記 (Records of the Grand Scribe). Beijing: Zhonghua shuju, 1983.

Slingerland, Edward. *Effortless Action: Wu-wei as Conceptual Metaphor and Spiritual Ideal in Early China*. New York: Oxford University Press, 2003.

Song Xijun 宋錫鈞 and Li Xiaofeng 李小峰, comps. *Luosu ji Bolake jiangyan ji* 羅素及勃拉克講演集 (Collected Talks of Russell and Black). Beijing: Weiyiri baoshe, 1922.

Tang Hezheng 唐鶴征 (1538–1619). *Taoxi zhaji* 桃溪劄記 (Reading Notes from Taoxi), in Huang Zongxi 黃宗羲 (1610–1695), comp. *Ming ru xue an* 明儒學案 (Case Studies of Ming Confucians), *Qinding Siku quanshu* (q.v.).

Tao Yuanming 陶淵明 (c. 365–427). "Gui yuan tian ju" 歸園田居 (Returning to Live in the Countryside). In Wang Yao, ed., *Tao Yuanming wenji* (q.v.).

Tao Yuanming 陶淵明 (c. 365–427). "Ni gu, qi qi" 擬古, 其七 (In Imitation of Old Poems, #7). In Wang Yao, ed., *Tao Yuanming wenji* (q.v.).

Ullaṅgha (欝楞迦; d.u.). *Yuan sheng lun* 緣生論 (*Pratītyasamutpāda-śāstra*; Treatise on Conditioned Arising), trans. Dharmagupta (達摩笈多; d. 619), T1652.

Vasubandhu (世親; 4th century). *She Dasheng lun shi* 攝大乘論釋 (Commentary to *Mahāyāna-saṃgraha* [Compendium of the Great Vehicle], T1597.
Vasubandhu (世親; 4th century). *Weishi sanshi lun song* 唯識三十論頌 (*Trimśika*; Thirty Verses on Nothing but Consciousness), trans. Xuanzang 玄奘 (602–664), T1586.
Wagner, Rudolph. "A Building Block of Argumentation: Initial Fu 夫 as a Phrase Status Marker." In Joachim Gentz and Dirk Meyer, eds., *Literary Forms of Argument in Early China*. Leiden, Brill, 2015.
Wan Shuchen 萬澍辰 (fl. 1873). *Zhou Yi bian tong jie* 周易變通解 (Explaining the Principle of Succeeding by Adjusting to Changing Circumstances in the *Zhou Book of Change*), in *Zhonghua congshu* 中華叢書 (China Book Series). Taipei: Zhonghua congshu bianshen weiyuanhui, 1960.
Wang Bi 王弼 (226–249). *Laozi Dao de jing zhu* 老子道德經注 (Laozi's *Classic of the Way and Its Power* Annotated). In Lou Yulie 樓宇烈, ed., *Wang Bi ji jiaoshi* 王弼集校釋 (Wang Bi's Collected Writings Collated and Annotated). Beijing: Zhonghua shuju, 1980.
Wang Fu 王符 (78–163). "Ming an" 明闇 (Clear-sightedness and Blindness), *Qian fu lun* 潛夫論 (Discourses of a Recluse), *Sibu congkan chubian* (q.v.).
Wang Fuzhi 王夫之 (1619–1692). "He Guishan 'Ci ri bu zai de shi tong xue'" 和龜山 "此日不再得示同學" (In Response to [Yang] Guishan's [Poem] "Now I Am No Longer Able to [Do the Following]. . . As an Instruction to My Students"), *Jiangzhai shi ji* 薑齋詩集 (Collection of Wang Fuzhi's Poetry), in *Jiangzhai xiansheng shiwenji* 薑齋詩文集 Collection of Wang Fuzhi's Poetry and Writings), *Sibu congkan chubian* (q.v.).
Wang Fuzhi 王夫之 (1619–1692). *Huang shu* 黃書 (Yellow Book), in Zeng Guofan 曾國藩 (1811–1872) and Zeng Guoquan 曾國荃 (1824–1890), comps., *Chuanshan yishu* 船山遺書 (Surviving Writings of Wang Fuzhi). Jinling: 1865.
Wang Fuzhi 王夫之 (1619–1692). *Si wen lu* 思問錄 (Records of Thinking and Questioning), in *Chuanshan quanshu*, vol. 12 (q.v.).
Wang Fuzhi 王夫之 (1619–1692). *Zhou yi da xiang jie* 周易大象解 (Explanation of the Great Images in the *Book of Change*) in *Chuanshan quanshu*, vol. 1 (q.v.).
Wang Yangming 王陽明 (1442–1529). *Chuan xi lu* 傳習錄 (Record of Practicing What Has Been Transmitted), *Wang Yangming quanji* 王陽明全集 (Complete Works of Wang Yangming), 2 vols. Shanghai: Shanghai guji chubanshe, 1992.
Wang Yao 王瑤, ed. *Tao Yuanming ji* 陶淵明集 (Tao Yuanming's Collected Writings). Beijing: Zuojia chubanshe, 1956.
Wang Yinglin 王應麟 (1223–1296), comp. *Zhou yi Zheng Kangcheng zhu* 周易鄭康成注 (Zheng Xuan's Commentary on the *Book of Change*). In Zhang Yuanji 張元濟 (1867–1959) comp. *Sibu congkan, sanbian* 四部叢刊三編 (Collectanea of the Four Categories, Third Series). Shanghai: Shangwu yinshuguan, 1935–1936.
Watson, Burton, trans. *The Complete Works of Chuang-tzu*. New York: Columbia University Press, 1968.
Wei Zheng 魏徵 (580–643) et al., comps. *Sui shu* 隋書 (Book of Sui). Beijing: Zhonghua shuju, 1973.
Woncheuk 圓測 (613–696). *Hae simmil gyeong so* 解深密經疏 (Commentary on the *Saṃdhinirmocana-sūtra*), *Dai Nihon zokuzōkyō* 大日本續藏經 (Kyoto Supplement to the Canon), CBETA Chinese Electronic Tripiṭaka Collection ebook edition, Taipei, www.cbeta.org, X21.369.

Wong, Dorothy C. *Buddhist Pilgrim-Monks as Agents of Cultural and Artistic Transmission: The International Buddhist Art Style in East Asia, ca. 645–770*. Singapore: NUS Press, 2018.

Xianyang shengjiao lun 顯揚聖教論 (Acclamation of the Holy Teaching Treatise), trans., Xuanzang 玄奘 (602–664), T1602.

Xiao Tong 蕭統 (501–531) et al., comps., Li Shan 李善 (630–689), annot. *Liu chen zhu wenxuan* 六臣註文選 (Selections of Refined Literature Annotated by Six Scholar-Officials), *Sibu congkan chubian* (q.v.).

Xiong Shili 熊十力. *Cui huo xian zong ji* 摧惑顯宗記 (Record to Destroy Confusion and Make My Tenets Explicit) (1950), *Xiong Shili quanji*, vol. 5 (q.v.).

Xiong Shili 熊十力. *Cun zhai suibi* 存齋隨筆 (Notes from the Studio of Preserving [the Source]) (1963), *Xiong Shili quanji*, vol. 7 (q.v.).

Xiong Shili 熊十力. "Da Ren Shuyong xiansheng" 答任叔永先生 (Reply to Mr Ren Shuyong), appended to *Ming xin pian* (q.v.).

Xiong Shili 熊十力. "Du Zhi lun chao" 讀智論鈔 (Reading notes on the *Treatise on the Great Perfection of Wisdom Sutra*), *Xiong Shili quanji*, vol. 4 (q.v.).

Xiong Shili 熊十力. *Dujing shiyao* 讀經示要 (Revealing the Main Points in Reading the Classics), *Xiong Shili quanji*, vol. 3 (q.v.).

Xiong Shili 熊十力. *Han Feizi pinglun* 韓非子評論 (Evaluation of Han Feizi), *Xiong Shili quanji*, vol. 5 (q.v.).

Xiong Shili 熊十力. Letter to editors at Kexue chubanshe 科學出版社 (China Science Publishing), January 7, 1958. https://auction.artron.net/paimai-art00573311604/.

Xiong Shili 熊十力. Letter to editors at Kexue chubanshe 科學出版社 (China Science Publishing), February 9, 1958 https://auction.artron.net/paimai-art0062720286/.

Xiong Shili 熊十力. *Ming xin pian* 明心篇 (Explaining Mind), *Xiong Shili quanji*, vol. 7 (q.v.).

Xiong Shili 熊十力. "Po 'Po Xin weishi lun'" 破《破新唯識論》(A Rebuttal of "A Rebuttal of *New Treatise on the Uniqueness of Consciousness*"), *Xiong Shili quanji*, vol. 2 (q.v.).

Xiong Shili 熊十力. *Shili congshu* 十力叢書 (Collection of Xiong Shili's Writings), 14 vols. Shanghai: Shanghai guji chubanshe, 2018, 2019.

Xiong Shili 熊十力. *Ti yong lun* 體用論 (Treatise on Reality and Function). Beijing: Longmen lianhe shuju 龍門聯合書局, 1958.

Xiong Shili 熊十力. *Ti yong lun* 體用論 (Treatise on Reality and Function), *Ti yong lun: wai yi zhong* 體用論:外一種 (Treatise on Reality and Function; Supplementary Correspondence and Additional Notes), *Shili congshu* (q.v.).

Xiong Shili 熊十力. *Ti yong lun* 體用論 (Treatise on Reality and Function), *Xiong Shili quanji*, vol. 7 (q.v.).

Xiong Shili 熊十力. *Weishixue gailun* 唯識學概論 (A General Account of Yogācāra Learning) (1923), *Xiong Shili quanji*, vol. 1 (q.v.).

Xiong Shili 熊十力. *Weishixue gailun* 唯識學概論 (A General Account of Yogācāra Learning) (1926), *Xiong Shili quanji*, vol. 1 (q.v.).

Xiong Shili 熊十力. *Xin weishi lun* 新唯識論 (New Treatise on the Uniqueness of Consciousness) (literary edition), *Xiong Shili quanji*, vol. 2 (q.v.).

Xiong Shili 熊十力. *Xin weishi lun* 新唯識論 (New Treatise on the Uniqueness of Consciousness) (vernacular edition), *Xiong Shili quanji*, vol. 3 (q.v.).

Xiong Shili 熊十力. *Xin weishi lun (shanding ben)* 新唯識論(刪定本) (New Treatise on the Uniqueness of Consciousness; Abridged Edition), *Xiong Shili quanji*, vol. 6 (q.v.).

Xiong Shili 熊十力. *Xiong Shili quanji* 熊十力全集 (The Complete Writings of Xiong Shili), 10 vols. Wuhan: Hubei jiaoyu chubanshe, 2001.

Xiong Shili 熊十力.*Yinming dashu shan zhu* 因明大疏刪注 (Abridged Edition of *Large Commentary on Introduction to Science of Reasoning* with Notes), *Xiong Shili quanji*, vol. 1 (q.v.).

Xiong Shili 熊十力. *Yuan Ru* 原儒 (To the Origin of the Ru), *Xiong Shili quanji*, vol. 6 (q.v.).

Xiong Shili 熊十力. *Zun wen lu* 尊聞錄 (Record of What Has Been Respectfully Heard), *Xiong Shili quanji*, vol. 1 (q.v.).

Xuanzang 玄奘 (602–664). *Cheng weishi lun* 成唯識論 (Demonstration of Nothing but Consciousness), T1585.

Xuanzang 玄奘 (602–664). "Xie Taizong Wen Huangdi zhi 'Sanzang Shengjiao xu' biao" 謝太宗文皇帝製三藏聖教序表 (Memorial to Thank Emperor Taizong for Writing the "Preface to the Sacred Teachings [Translated by] the Tripiṭaka [Master Xuanzang of the Great Tang"]. In *Shi shamen Xuanzang shang biao ji* 寺沙門玄奘上表記 (Memorials and Records Submitted by Monk Xuanzang), T2119.

Xun Yue 荀悅 (148–209 CE). *Shenjian* 申鑒 (Extended Reflections), Huang Xingzeng 黃省曾 (1496–1546) annot. *Shenjian zhu* 申鑒注 (Annotated *Extended Reflections*), *Sibu congkan chubian* (q.v.).

Yan Fu 嚴復 (1854–1921), trans. *Mule mingxue* 穆勒名學 (A System of Logic). Beijing: Sanlian, 1959.

Yan Ying 晏嬰 (6th cent. BCE), attrib. *Yanzi chunqiu* 晏子春秋 (The Spring and Autumn Annals of Master Yan), 13b, *Sibu congkan chubian*.

Yang Guorong 楊國榮. "Xingershangxue yu zhexue de neizai shiyu" 形而上學與哲學的內在視域 (Metaphysics and the Inner Horizon of Philosophy), *Xueshu yuekan* 12 (2004): 19–26.

Yang Lihua 楊立華. "Wei Zhongguo zhexue xin shidai dianji: Chen Lai xiansheng rentilun shulun" 為中國哲學新時代奠基：陳來先生仁體論述論 (Laying the Foundations for a New Era of Chinese Philosophy: A Discussion of Mr Chen Lai's Theory of Humaneness as Reality), *Zhongguo zhexueshi* 2 (2022): 5–10.

Yao Peizhong 姚配中 (1792–1844). *Zhou yi Yao shi xue* 周易姚氏學 (Mr Yao's Studies on the *Book of Change*). Hubei [n.p.]: Chongwen shuju, 1877.

Yao Zhihua 姚治華. "*Taiyi sheng shui* yu Taiyi Jiugong zhan 《太乙生水》與太乙九宮占 (*The Great Unity Generates Water* and the Divination [Method] of "The [Circulation of the] Great Unity in the Nine Palaces"). In Pang Pu 龐樸 ed., *Gumu xinzhi* 古墓新知 (New Knowledge from Ancient Tombs). Taipei: Taiwan guji chubanshe, 2002.

Yi wei: Qian zuodu 易緯：乾鑿度 (Apocryphon to the *Book of Change*: Opening the Laws of the Hexagram Qian), *Qinding Siku quanshu* (q.v.).

Yinshun 印順. "Ping Xiong Shili de *Xin weishi lun*" 評熊十力的新唯識論 (Review of Xiong Shili's *New Treatise on the Uniqueness of Consciousness*), reproduced in *Xiong Shili quanji*, supplementary volume A (q.v.).

Yuanqi jing 緣起經 (*Pratītya-samutpādādivibhaṅga-nirdeśa-sūtra*; Sutra on Conditioned Origination), trans. Xuanzang 玄奘 (602–664), T124.

Yuqie shidi lun 瑜伽師地論 (*Yogācārabhūmi-śāstra*; Discourse on Stages of Concentration Practice), trans. Xuanzang 玄奘 (602–664), T1579.

Zhang Taiyan 章太炎 (1869–1936). "Jianli zongjiao lun" 建立宗教論 (On Establishing a Religion), *Bielu, juan san* 別錄卷三 (Separate Category, *juan* 3). In *Taiyan wenlu chubian* 太炎文錄初編 (First Collection of Zhang Taiyan's Writings), *Zhang shi congshu* 章氏叢書 (Collectanea of Mr Zhang's Works), vol. 11. Hangzhou: Zhejiang tushuguan, 1919.

Zhang Zai 張載 (1020–1077). *Zhengmeng* 正蒙 (Correcting Youthful Ignorance). In Lin Lechang 林樂昌 comp. *Zhengmeng hejiao jishi, shang* 正蒙合校集釋, 上 (*Correcting Youthful Ignorance* with Combined Collations and Collected Interpretations, Part A). Beijing: Zhonghua shuju, 2012.

Zhanguo ce 戰國策 (Stratagems of the Warring States), *Sibu congkan* (q.v.).

Zhiyi 智顗 (538–597). *Miaofa lianhua jing xuanyi* 妙法蓮華經玄義 (The Profound Doctrine of the *Lotus Sutra*), T1716.

Zhong Ahan jing 中阿含經 (*Madhyamāgama*; Middle Length Āgama Sutras), T26.

Zhong bian fenbie lun 中邊分別論 (*Madhyānta-vibhāga*; Treatise Distinguishing the Middle from the Extremes), trans., Paramārtha (真諦; 499–569), T1599.

Zhou li zhuzi suoyin 周禮逐字索引 (Concordance to the *Zhou li*), D. C. Lau (Liu Dianjue 劉殿爵) et al. eds. Hong Kong: Shangwu yinshuguan, 1993.

Zhou yi 周易 (Book of Change), Kong Yingda 孔穎達 (574–648) et al., comps., *Zhou yi zhengyi* 周易正義 (Correct Interpretation of the *Book of Change*), *Shisan jing zhushu* (q.v.).

Zhu Xi 朱熹 (1130–1200). *Zhongyong zhangju* 中庸章句 (Section and Sentence Comments on *Balance as the Norm*). In *Sishu zhangju jizhu* 四書章句集注 (Section and Sentence Comments and Collected Annotations on the Four Books). Beijing: Zhonghua shuju, 1983.

Zhuangzi 莊子 (fl. 4th cent. BCE). *Zhuangzi* 莊子, Guo Qingfan 郭慶藩 (1844–1896), comp. *Zhuangzi jishi* 莊子集釋 (Collected Commentaries on *Zhuangzi*). Taipei: Muduo chubanshe, 1982.

Ziporyn, Brook. *Evil and/or/as The Good: Omnicentrism, Intersubjectivity, and Value Paradox in Tiantai Buddhist Thought*. Cambridge, MA: Harvard University Asia Center, 2000.

Index

For the benefit of digital users, indexed terms that span two pages (e.g., 52–53) may, on occasion, appear on only one of those pages

ālayavijñāna (*see* store consciousness)
apophatic and kataphatic exegesis, 65–66
Asaṅga, 58, 100, 102–3, 104–5
    and seeds, 110–12, 120–21
    atoms (極微; 細分; 元子), 61–62, 127–28, 178–79, 202–3
    and atomism, 202–3
    and *linxu* 鄰虛, 62–63, 126–28

Bhāviveka, 81–82, 101–2
    three-part inference of, 108–10
Book of Change (*see Yi jing*)
Bore xin jing 般若心經 (Heart Sutra), 59
    and the five aggregates, 59–61
    purport of, 61–67

causes
    direct and supporting, 217–19
    inductive, 39–40
chana 剎那 (*kṣaṇa*), 35–36
Chen Lai 陳來, xxi
    and the legacy of Xiong's onto-cosmology, xxxvii–xxxix
conditioned arising (緣生), xiii, 61–62, 93, 108, 130–31, 133–35, 136–37
    and the doctrine of emptiness, xiii, 148–49, 154–55, 156–57
    and Śākyamuni, 167–68
    see also conditioned origination (緣起)
conditioned origination (緣起), 62n.13, 104–13
    and Asaṅga and Vasubandhu, 175–76
    see also conditioned arising (緣生)
Confucius, 76–77, 82–83, 129, 222–23, 230–31
    and the *Yi jing* 易經 (*Book of Change*), 128
contraction (翕) and expansion (闢), 23–35, 182–87
    and function (用), xxviii, 55, 167, 202–3

    and mutually opposing and mutually completing, xxviii–xxxi
conventional truth, 46–47, 58
cosmology, xvi, 212–13, 221–22, 230, 234–35
    and Reality and function (體用), xix–xx, 55–56

Da bore boluomiduo jing 大般若波羅蜜多經 (*Mahāprajñāpāramitā-sūtra*; Perfection of Wisdom Sutra), 99–98, 203
    and Asaṅga and Vasubandhu, 101–2
    and doctrine of emptiness, 10
    and the Emptiness school, 66
    and Kuiji 窺基, 59
    and Nāgārjuna, 141–44
    and Xuanzang 玄奘, 101–2
dharma body (法身), 143–45
dharma nature (法性) and dharma characteristics (法相), 1–2, 56–58, 67, 72–73, 146, 149–50, 159
Dharma seal (法印), 65–66, 77–78
    and Nāgārjuna, 100–1
Dharmapāla, 82
    on innate and newly perfumed seeds, 118–19
dharmas
    cessation of in an instant, 38–50
    conditioned, xxxiv, 69–70, 100–1
    mental and material, 57–58, 61, 63–64, 73, 93, 96–97 99–100, 106–112 passim, 114–16, 120–21, 126–27, 136–37, 154–55, 157
    unconditioned, xxxiv, 69–70, 100–1
Dignāga, 109–10

eight consciousnesses, 60–61, 110–11
   and manifest activity (現行), 118–20
   object part (相分) and perceiving part (見分) of, 117
Emptiness school, xxxi
   criticisms of, xxxiii–xxxiv, 67–92, 124–25
   and *Da bore boluomiduo jing* 大般若波羅蜜多經 (*Mahāprajñāpāramitā-sūtra*; Perfection of Wisdom Sutra), 66
   doctrine of observing emptiness (觀空), 9–10, 89–90, 96, 174–75
   doctrine of refuting characteristics to reveal the nature (破相顯性), 58, 66–67
   doctrines of, 59–92
   and Existence school compared, 99
   and Prajñā school, 65–66, 131–35
   three proofs for the doctrine of emptiness, 126–31
   views on existence evaluated, 167–70
energy, 7–8
   and matter, xxviii, 7–8, 180–82, 187–96, 197–204 passim, 207–10, 215, 223–24, 228–32 passim
Existence school, xxxi, 104–5
   doctrinal deficiencies, xxxiv–xxxvii, 113–26
   doctrine of nothing but consciousness (唯識論), 9–10, 54, 102–3
   doctrine of seeds, xxxiv–xxxvi, 99–100, 107–8, 110–12, 117–21, 175–76
   doctrines of, 92–103
   and Emptiness school compared, 99
   and Xuanzang 玄奘, 175–76

five aggregates (五蘊), xxiii, 59–61
four conditions (四緣), 105–7, 110, 130–31, 136–37
Fu Xi 伏羲
   and *Yi jing* 易經 (Book of Change), 23, 221–22
function (用; 功用)
   and contraction (翕) and expansion (闢), 55, 167, 202–3, 210, 215
   and dharma characteristics, 57–58
   explanation of, 3, 5
   two aspects of, 161–63, 202–3, 215, 232

generative vitality (生命), 156–57, 184
   as expansion (闢), 31–33
   and Laozi and Zhuangzi, 235
Grand Primordium (泰初; 太初), 29, 118–19, 132n.64, 188–89, 199–203 passim, 215, 216–17, 221–22, 223–24, 226–28
Guo Xiang 郭象, 2–3, 48–49, 210

Hegel, G.W.F., xxix–xxx
Hīnayāna, 35–36, 72, 77–78, 88–89, 91, 99, 100–1, 105, 106–8, 113
   accounts of existents, 134–35, 143–44
   "holism"/"Reality qua whole thesis" (全體論), 179–82
Hui Shi 惠施
   and the pure and spirit-like, 182–83
   on "the smallest ones," 23–24, 195–203 passim
   writings of, 7, 199–200
   Zhuangzi's criticism of, 159–61

intrinsic Reality (本體), 83–84
   characteristics of, xvi–xviii, 21
   and "the origin of Qian" (乾元), 31–33
   three fallacies in cosmological accounts of, 210–15
   see also Reality; Reality and function (體用); function (用; 功用); ocean and waves analogy

Kuiji 窺基, 35–36, 64, 82
   and *Da bore boluomiduo jing* 大般若波羅蜜多經 (*Mahāprajñāpāramitā-sūtra*; Perfection of Wisdom Sutra), 109–10
   on Bhāviveka, 101–2, 109–10
Kumārajīva, 69–70, 107–8, 175–76
Kun 坤
   hexagram, 179–82, 185–86, 191–93
   as matter and energy, 188–89
   and Qian 乾, 8–9, 185–86, 234–35

Laozi and Zhuangzi
   and *Yi jing*, 49
   criticisms of, 6–7, 50
   and generative vitality (生命), 235

Madhyamaka (*see* Emptiness school)
Maheśvara, 111–16 passim, 136–37
matter, 28–29, 179–85 passim

and energy, xxviii, 7–8, 180–82, 187–96,
    197–204 passim, 207–10, 215,
    223–24, 228–32 passim
  and the pure-and-spirit like, 7–8, 55–56
mental associates (心所; caitta), 60
Mill, John Stuart
  and Yan Fu 嚴復, 127n.55
monism
  idealistic and material, 185–86, 197–98,
    211–15 passim, 230–31
Mou Zongsan 牟宗三, xx–xxi,
    xxi–xxiin.33, 17n.4
mutually opposing and mutually completing
    (相反相成), xxviii–xxxi, 22–23, 25–26
    C1P76–C1P78
  and function, 55
  and matter and energy, 190–91
  and the pure and spirit-like and the
    material, 34–35, 167, 184–85

Nāgārjuna, xxxiii–xxxiv, 54, 58, 67, 110
  and conditioned arising, 154–55
  and *Da bore boluomiduo jing*
    大般若波羅蜜多經
    (*Mahāprajñāpāramitā-sūtra*;
    Perfection of Wisdom Sutra), 141–44
  and the doctrine of emptiness, 169
  and the foundation of Mahāyāna, 168–69
  and Śākyamuni, 154
  see also Zhong lun 中論 (*Mūla-
    madhyamaka-kārikā*; Treatise on
    the Middle Way)

ocean and waves analogy
  and non-duality of Reality and function, 7–
    8, 22, 68–69, 85, 146, 161–63, 222–23
onto-cosmology
  and *bentilun* 本體論, xvi–xxiii
Ouyang Jingwu 歐陽竟無, 54, 86–87

Piṅgala, 135n.70, 137n.76, 139
Prajñā school (*see* Emptiness school)
primal *qi* (元氣), 43, 188–90, 199–200
  as name for matter and energy, xlii, 201
pure and spirit-like (精神)
  and expansion (闢), 184–85
  and matter/energy, xxviii, 7–8, 55–56,
    182–84, 215
  and Qian 乾, 184–85
  two unique features of, 219–22

Qian 乾
  defining characteristics of, 31, 50
  and expansion, xxviii, 31
  hexagram, 184–86, 191, 221–23
  and Kun 坤, 8–9, 185–86, 234–35
  and the pure and spirit-like, 184–85

Reality (實體; 本體)
  of the cosmos, 222–24, 228–30
  two opposing incipient tendencies of, 2
  see also intrinsic Reality; Reality and
    function; ocean and waves analogy
Reality and function (體用), 55–56
  and cosmology, xix–xx, 55–56
  and dharma nature and dharma
    characteristics, 57–58, 67
  non-duality of, xiii, 5, 7–8, 56, 68–69,
    72, 84–85, 87–88, 159–67, 176–77,
    211, 222–23
  and Three Truths, xxv–xxvii
  Wang Yangming on, 11–12
  and the-whole-that-is-Reality
    and its great function
    (全體大用), 11
  and *Yi jing*, 5, 9–10, 159–61, 176–77
  see also function (用; 功用); intrinsic
    Reality (本體); ocean and waves
    analogy
Russell, Bertand, 156–57

Śākyamuni, 37, 48, 72, 105, 151, 154
  and doctrine of conditioned arising,
    167–68
  three periods in the teachings of, 92–94,
    99
  and the Prajñā masters, 176–77
Sāṃkhya, 111–12
Six Classics
  as corrupted, 9–10, 132n.63, 166n.147
  four precepts in, 205
  "smallest ones," 23–24, 196–209
spirit-cum-*ātman* (神我), 111–12
store consciousness (阿賴耶識;
    ālayavijñāna)
  as constantly turning over, xviii–xix
  and seeds, xxxiv–xxxv, 110–16 passim,
    118–19
  as spirit-cum-*ātman*, 114–16
  Xuanzang on, xix, 113–14
  Zhang Taiyan on, 116

Tao Yuanming 陶淵明, 10, 80–81, 172–73
Three Natures, 120
Three Truths
    and Reality and function, xxv–xxvii
    transformation, 55–56, 73–74, 78–79, 84–89, 124, 132–33, 161–66 passim, 185–87, 190–91, 208, 209
        and contraction and expansion, 23–35
        dragon as metaphor for, 228
        five characteristics of, 50–54
        as function, 212
        and hexagram lines, 199
        principle of, 16–23
        and *Yi jing* 易經 (Book of Change), 208, 232–36 passim

ultimate truth, 46–47, 58

Vasubandhu, 58, 100, 101–3, 119
    and Xuanzang, 120

Wang Fuzhi 王夫之, 5, 78–79, 121–23, 226–27
Wang Yangming 王陽明, 232
    on creative transformation, 223–24
    on Reality and function (體用), 11–12, 85

Xin weishi lun 新唯識論 (New Treatise on the Uniqueness of Consciousness), xiii, 8–9
Xuanzang 玄奘, 58, 64, 69–70, 86–87, 89–90, 104–5, 107–8, 145
    and *Da bore boluomiduo jing* 大般若波羅蜜多經 (*Mahāprajñāpāramitā-sūtra*; Perfection of Wisdom Sutra), 176
    and the Existence school, 175–76
    on the store consciousness, xix, 113–14
    and Vasubandhu, 120
Xunzi 荀子, 72–73

Yan Fu 嚴復
    and John Stuart Mill, 127n.55
Yao Peizhong 姚配中, 48

Yi jing 易經 (Book of Change), 233–36
    as *Bian jing* 變經 (Book of Transformation), 1–2, 5, 9–10, 167–68
    and Confucius, 128
    as *Da yi* 大易 (Great Change), 5, 159–61
    Da you 大有 hexagram, 10, 50–51, 156–57
    dialectics of, 237
    hexagrams of, 198–99
    and the doctrine of arising and ceasing in an instant, 132–33
    fundamental purport of, 221–22
    and the "holism"/"Reality qua whole thesis," 179–80
    and non-duality of Reality and function, 5, 9–10, 159–61
    and observation of existence, 10
    and the "smallest ones," 201
    and transformation, 208, 232–36 passim
    and Zhuangzi, 48–49, 206
    see also Qian (乾); Kun (坤)
yinming 因明 (*hetu-vidyā*), 81–82, 161–63
    and Dignāga, 109–10
Yogācāra (*see* Existence school)

Zhang Zai 張載, 18–19, 72–73
Zhong lun 中論 (*Mūla-madhyamaka-kārikā*; Treatise on the Middle Way), 66, 69, 80, 106–7, 145
    doctrine of emptiness, 148–54
    and Nāgārjuna, xxxiii, 100–1, 110, 137, 141–44
    and verse 18, 135–48
    and the views of eternalism (常見) and nihilism (斷見), 151–53
    and the views of existence (有見) and emptiness (空見), 138–39
    and the views of existence (有見) and non-existence (無見), 151–52
Zhongyong 中庸 (Balance as the Norm), 23–24, 47, 53–54, 82–83, 127–28, 131–32, 176–77
Zhu Xi 朱熹, 44
Zhuangzi (*see* Laozi and Zhuangzi)